MORAL
RELATIVISM

D1527110

MORAL RELATIVISM

A Reader

Edited by

PAUL K. MOSER
Loyola University of Chicago

THOMAS L. CARSON
Loyola University of Chicago

New York   Oxford
OXFORD UNIVERSITY PRESS
2001

Oxford University Press

Oxford New York
Athens Auckland Bangkok Bogotá Buenos Aires Calcutta
Cape Town Chennai Dar es Salaam Delhi Florence Hong Kong Istanbul
Karachi Kuala Lumpur Madrid Melbourne Mexico City Mumbai
Nairobi Paris São Paulo Singapore Taipei Tokyo Toronto Warsaw

and associated companies in
Berlin Ibadan

Published by Oxford University Press, Inc.,
198 Madison Avenue, New York, New York, 10016
http://www.oup-usa.org

Oxford is a registered trademark of Oxford University Press

Library of Congress Cataloging-in-Publication Data

Moral relativism : a reader / [edited by] Paul K. Moser and Thomas L. Carson.
  p. cm.
  Includes bibliographical references and index.
  ISBN 0-19-513129-0 (hardcover : alk. paper) — ISBN 0-19-513130-4 (pbk. : alk. paper)
  1. Ethical relativism. I. Moser, Paul K., 1957– II. Carson, Thomas L., 1950–
  BJ37.M8185 2000
  171′.7—dc21   99-055853

Printing (last digit): 9 8 7 6 5 4 3 2

Printed in the United States of America
on acid-free paper

In memory of Mark Overvold and Richard Thorsen

CONTENTS

Preface

This book includes twenty contemporary selections on moral relativism. The selections are nontechnical and thus accessible to a wide range of readers, including college undergraduates from various disciplines. The book's selections fall under six main headings: (1) General Issues; (2) Relativism and Moral Diversity; (3) On the Coherence of Moral Relativism; (4) Defense and Criticism; (5) Relativism, Realism, and Rationality; and (6) Case Study on Relativism. Given the philosophical prominence and importance of its subject matter, this book can serve as a central text for a wide range of undergraduate and graduate university courses on ethics and ethical theory. The book includes a substantial general introduction (which presents summaries of the selections) and a topical bibliography on moral relativism. These items should enhance the book's pedagogical and research value.

Many people have aided our work on the book. We thank Robert Miller, executive editor at Oxford University Press, for help and encouragement in various ways, and several anonymous referees for Oxford. We also thank Marcia Baron, Betsy Postow, Julie Ward, and especially Tom Wren for helpful suggestions. We have benefited from the help of several philosophy graduate students at Loyola University of Chicago: Jason Beyer, Patrick Stone, and especially Peter Bergeron and Chris Meyers. We thank them for their fine help. Loyola University of Chicago has provided an excellent environment for work on the book.

P.K.M.
T.L.C.
Chicago

Introduction

THOMAS L. CARSON
PAUL K. MOSER

I. MORAL RELATIVISM: SPECIES, RATIONALES, AND PROBLEMS

Many different versions and notions of moral relativism populate contemporary moral reflection. So we do well to distinguish at least some prominent versions of moral relativism. Many people find, on examination, that they accept some versions of relativism and reject others. In addition, it is at least arguable that some versions of moral relativism are true and others false.

Moral relativism, characterized broadly, is relativism about any of the following: (a) the moral beliefs and standards accepted by individuals or societies, (b) the moral requirements binding on individuals or groups of individuals, and (c) the truth or correctness of moral judgments or moral standards. We may distinguish, correspondingly, three main types of relativism: descriptive relativism, moral-requirement relativism, and metaethical relativism.

Descriptive relativism (sometimes called "cultural relativism" or "descriptive cultural relativism") states that *beliefs* or *standards* about moral issues are relative to different individuals and different societies: that is, different individuals and different societies accept different moral beliefs or standards and thus disagree about the answers to moral questions. The fact that two people disagree about the answer to a particular moral question does not imply that they disagree in their basic moral standards. Sometimes people disagree about the answers to moral questions because they disagree about the answers to certain factual questions: for example, does capital punishment deter murder? We can distinguish between this kind of disagreement and *fundamental disagreement,* that is, disagreement that would persist even if the parties agreed about the factual properties of all the things in question. Richard Brandt, we shall see, has used the term *descriptive relativism* more narrowly to refer to the view that there are fundamental disagreements between the moral beliefs or moral standards of different individuals or different societies.

Moral-requirement relativism (a view akin to what is often called "normative relativism") states that different basic moral requirements apply to (at least some) different moral agents, or groups of agents, owing to different intentions, desires, or beliefs among such agents or groups. Moral-requirement relativism states that the moral requirements binding on a person depend on, or are "relative to," her intentions, desires, or beliefs (or the intentions, desires, or beliefs of people in her society). Moral-requirement relativism takes a number of forms in its contemporary garb. Two common forms are noteworthy. *Individual* moral-requirement relativism states that an action is morally obligatory for a person if and only if that action is prescribed by the basic moral principles accepted by that individual person. *Social* moral-requirement relativism states that an action is morally obligatory for a person if and only if that action is prescribed by the basic moral principles accepted by that person's society. The latter view is one of the most popular forms of moral relativism.

Moral-requirement relativism makes a claim about "basic" moral requirements, specifically that at least some different moral agents are subject to different basic moral requirements. A basic moral requirement for a person applies to that person independently of any other moral requirement. Suppose that I am subject to the moral requirement that I ought to help you move to your new apartment because I promised to help you move. My sister, however, is not subject to this requirement, because she did not make any such promise to you. Even so, my sister and I could still be subject to the same basic moral requirement that we moral agents should keep our promises. If I am morally obligated to help you move just because I promised to help you move, then it is a basic moral requirement for me that I ought to keep my promises. If, in contrast, the requirement that I ought to keep my promises depends on other moral requirements, then that requirement would not be basic for me (although it could still be binding on me as a nonbasic moral requirement).

Metaethical relativism states that moral judgments are not objectively true or false and thus that different individuals or societies can hold conflicting moral judgments without any of them being mistaken. Metaethical relativists sometimes say that the truth of moral judgments is relative, that is, that what is true for one person (or society) might not be true for another person (or society). For example, it might be true for me that slavery is wrong, but true for Jefferson Davis that slavery is right. As Richard Brandt notes in the first selection of this book, this terminology is misleading. Metaethical relativism denies that moral judgments are true at all in any ordinary sense of the word *true*. In the ordinary sense of the word *true*, to say that a statement is true is to say that it is true *for everyone*. For example, it is objectively true (true for everyone) that Lincoln was the sixteenth president of the United States. Anyone who denies this is just mistaken (and in need of a review of U.S. political history).

Metaethical relativism is compatible with many different accounts of "relative truth." Some metaethical relativists hold that *whatever* moral judgments a person accepts or believes are true for that person. Other accounts of relative truth are also compatible with metaethical relativism; so metaethical relativism does not necessarily commit one to that kind of "anything goes" version of relativism, according to which whatever moral judgments one accepts are true for one. A metaethical relativist can consistently endorse the following alternative account of what it is for a moral judgment to be "true for someone": a moral judgment is true for a particular person provided that she *would accept it* were she fully rational, that is, if she knew all the relevant facts about the issue in question and committed no errors of logic or reasoning in her thinking about that issue. Metaethical relativists favoring this account of relative truth need not hold that whatever I believe is true for me. They can say that a person's moral judgments *could be* mistaken. The moral judgments or standards that *I actually accept* might be very different from those *I would accept were I fully rational*.

We should distinguish between the following:

Extreme metaethical relativism: the view that *no* moral judgments or standards (about any moral questions) are objectively true (or, correct) or false (or, incorrect).

Moderate metaethical relativism: the view that (a) *some* moral judgments are objectively true or false (and thus there is an objectively true or correct answer to certain moral questions), and (b) some moral judgments are not objectively true or false (and thus there are some moral questions to which there is no objectively true or correct answer).

A number of this book's selections (for example, those by Richard Brandt and Philippa Foot) seem to accept moderate metaethical relativism.

Metaethical relativism differs from moral skepticism. Moral skeptics deny that people (can) *know* or *justifiedly believe* the answers to moral questions. For example, a moral skeptic might say that we cannot, or at least do not, know whether it would be right for somebody to have an abortion. Such a skeptic can still say that there is an objectively correct answer to this and other moral questions and thus that it is objectively true or false that it would be permissible for somebody to have an abortion. Skeptics deny only that anyone could or at least does ever know or justifiedly believe whether it would be right for somebody to have an abortion. Metaethical relativism is ontologically bolder than moral skepticism. Metaethical relativists hold not only that we cannot, or at least do not, know or justifiedly believe whether things are good or bad or right or wrong; they deny, in addition, that there are any moral *truths* (any objectively correct answers to moral questions) for us to know or to justifiedly believe.

Metaethical relativism presupposes the falsity of *moral realism*, the view that there are "moral facts" (for example, that torturing animals for "fun" is wrong) and that moral judgments or standards are objectively true independently of the beliefs and attitudes of human beings (even ideally rational human beings) about those judgments or standards. If moral realism is true and there are objectively true answers to (at least some) moral questions, then metaethical relativism is false. Contemporary moral philosophers debate whether moral nonrealism commits one to metaethical relativism. Some moral nonrealists, such as Roderick Firth and R. M. Hare, defend objectivism about moral truths. Another nonrealist, Richard Brandt, seems to endorse moderate metaethical relativism. This book's selection by Thomas Carson and Paul Moser argues that moral nonrealists have great difficulty avoiding (metaethical) relativism.

Questions about the truth of *descriptive* relativism are ultimately empirical questions. Most discussions of moral relativism take the truth of descriptive relativism for granted. Michelle Moody-Adams, in her selection below, dissents from this, arguing that the case for descriptive relativism is far from clear. Philosophers have offered many different arguments for metaethical relativism and normative relativism. Three arguments are noteworthy.

1. ARGUMENT FROM DISAGREEMENT

Some philosophers hold that the pervasive phenomenon of disagreement (both between individuals and societies) about moral questions supports metaethical relativism. This approach apparently presupposes the falsity of moral realism. If there are independent moral facts or truths, then the fact that people often disagree about the answers to moral questions does not show that there are no objectively true answers to those questions. The fact of such disagreement indicates only that at least some of the parties to the disagreement are mistaken.

The argument in question suggests that because people or societies disagree in fundamental ways about moral issues, moral judgments are not objectively true. Many anthropologists accept roughly this argument. Such an argument is, however, fallacious. The mere fact that we disagree about the answer to a question does not establish that there is no objectively correct answer to that question (see, for example, the selection by James Rachels on this). Suppose that two people disagree about the answer to a clearly defined math problem. There might still be an objectively correct answer to that problem. Metaethical relativists might counter that moral disagreements are relevantly different from other kinds of disagreements, including mathematical disagreements. Moral disagreements, they propose, are rationally undecidable because objective truth is lacking. Given moral nonrealism, the argument at hand merits serious consideration, but in the absence of a case for moral nonrealism, the argument fails to convince.

2. ARGUMENT FROM TOLERANCE

A second argument for metaethical relativism appeals to the ideal of tolerance. We should respect and tolerate diverse moral views and allow them to be freely expressed. Moral objectivism (the view that some moral judgments or standards are objectively true), however, suggests that some people's moral views are mistaken that thus not worthy of respect and toleration. This kind of argument motivates many people to endorse metaethical relativism. Even so, the argument is unconvincing. Moral objectivism is perfectly compatible with tolerance and a strong endorsement of tolerance. Moral objectivists claim that there are objective moral truths (although they need not claim to *know* all or many moral truths). This claim does not entail that moral objectivists think that those who disagree with them are bad or that they should be treated with disrespect or intolerance. In contrast, metaethical relativists (at least extreme metaethical relativists) cannot consistently endorse strong principles of tolerance. Metaethical relativists cannot consistently claim that such a principle as "one ought to be tolerant and respectful of the views of others" is objectively true, or "true for" everyone.

Some people endorse moral-requirement relativism (or normative relativism) out of a concern for the value of tolerance. They claim that it is unfair and mistaken to judge the actions of other people by one's own standards or the standards of one's own society. It is wrong, they claim, to condemn others for following their own consciences or the moral codes of their own societies. Such reasoning in favor of relativism is misguided. Suppose that you judge that other people sometimes do wrong on account of their violating moral requirements they (or their societies) do not accept. This would be perfectly consistent with your respecting and tolerating other people. In contrast, metaethical relativism and normative relativism give us no reason to think that everyone ought to be tolerant and respectful of (the views of) others. Other people or other societies may not accept moral principles requiring them to be tolerant of others.

3. ARGUMENT FROM MOTIVATION

A common argument for moral-requirement relativism assumes that a moral requirement applies to a person only if that person implicitly or explicitly accepts the requirement as reasonable for that person. Moral requirements, on this view, are agent-sensitive in a way that legal requirements, for example, are not. This view aims to sustain a connection between what is morally required of a person and what that person *approves of,* at least implicitly, and *has a convincing reason to do.* Legal requirements, of course, can apply to a citizen even if the citizen disapproves of them and has no convincing reasoning to follow them. Many relativists hold that the moral requirements binding on one are determined by what is rationally convincing for one. More generally, many relativists hold that a person's moral reasons (and thus what it is morally reasonable and morally required for a person to do) have their basis in that person's own psychological attitudes, such as that person's desires, intentions, or beliefs. In keeping with such a position, Gilbert Harman, for instance, proposes that " . . . for Hitler there might have been no [moral] reasons at all not to order the extermination of the Jews."[1] The underlying relativist position is Humean in claiming that the principles of morality are inadequate as a source of moral reasons and that certain psychological attitudes (e.g., intentions) of an agent are crucial to any source of moral reasons for that agent. The opposing Kantian view implies that moral principles themselves can yield compelling moral reasons and requirements.

Who is right? The Humean or the Kantian? Without pretending to decide the matter conclusively here, we can put the key issue as follows: is a moral agent subject to a moral requirement only if that agent has a psychological attitude, such as an intention, that recommends, implicitly or explicitly, the satisfaction of that requirement? We can distinguish two ways of "being subject" to a moral requirement: on the one hand, as a *motivating* principle, and, on the other hand, as a *rightness-determining* principle. A moral requirement is a motivating principle for you if and only if you have, owing to your psychological attitudes, an inclination to satisfy that principle. In contrast, a moral requirement is a rightness-determining principle for you if and only if that principle determines whether an action you might perform is morally right. Some moral requirements are, of course, both motivating and rightness-determining for a person, but we do well to avoid conceptual confusion of the two ways of being subject to a moral requirement. The first concerns *motivation for an agent;* the second concerns *moral rightness of an action for an agent.*

Psychological attitudes can, of course, vary among people in a way that leaves me, for instance, inclined to do things that you are not at all inclined to do. As a result, given my peculiar inclinations and resulting actions, I may be morally guilty for having done certain things that you have no motivation whatever to do. This underlies a kind of *motivational* moral-requirement relativism: the basic moral requirements that actually motivate a person can vary, at least to some extent, among moral agents. This is relativism about the *motivational efficacy* of certain moral requirements, not about the rightness-determining relevance of moral requirements. The rightness-determining relevance is untouched, because a person's motivating psychological attitudes are not automatically morally obligatory or even morally permissible for one. Even though certain of Hitler's psychological attitudes motivated him to slaughter millions of innocent people, Hitler morally should have renounced those attitudes, owing to their obviously resulting in unjust barbarous harm to others.

Evidently, a person's lack of motivation to follow a certain alleged moral requirement does not entail that the requirement in question fails to apply to that person. Moral-requirement relativists might counter by appealing to the familiar principle that "ought implies can." I can only be obligated to follow those requirements I am *able* to follow. Such reasoning is unconvincing, because we have considerable indirect control over our own beliefs and attitudes. The fact that I am not motivated to follow a certain moral requirement does not entail that I am incapable of being motivated to follow it. Indeed, my lack of motivation in such a case may be a moral defect subject to critical moral assessment.

We have no reason to bar controllable psychological attitudes from moral assessment. This holds for deontological (Kantian) as well as consequentialist (Millian) approaches to moral assessment. For instance, some intentions are (at least indirectly) controllable causes of morally relevant actions; they contribute, in a controllable manner, to actions responsible for the occurrence of pleasure, pain, desire-satisfaction, and duty-satisfaction. If we therefore acknowledge such psychological attitudes as intentions to be subject to moral assessment, we can challenge a familiar form of moral-requirement relativism that grounds moral requirements in one's actual intentions. A person's intending not to act in agreement with a certain moral principle may be just a case where that person's intending is morally improper and where the moral principle in question is, in contrast, impeccable. A person's simply failing to intend invites a similar point, as failing to intend is not morally relevantly different from one's intending, so long as the psychological situation is at least indirectly voluntary. It is doubtful, then, that the relevance of a moral principle to moral rightness for an agent's actions is determined by the agent's actual psychological attitudes such as controllable intentions. Intentions are dispositional states and not episodic actions, but if intentions are morally defective, then the actions in service of those intentions may very well be morally defective too.

If the moral rightness of an action for an agent is not determined by an agent's actual intentions, what then does determine such rightness? A plausible nonrelativist view is: the moral rightness of an action is determined by the action's consistency with what is prescribed by the set of correct moral principles. Beyond actions, if a moral principle is a member of the aforementioned set, then that principle determines moral rightness for actions. We cannot blithely specify the exact conditions for a moral principle's belonging to the set in question; that task requires much honest toil, in keeping with most philosophical tasks. Fortunately, however, we need not finish that demanding task to recognize that a rightness-determining moral principle for an agent does not depend on that agent's intending, implicitly or explicitly, to satisfy that principle. A moral principle can be rightness-determining for you even if you intend not to act in accordance with it. Morality, as ordinarily understood, is evidently intention-independent at least in this respect. Some relativists may reply that there is no such thing as a "correct" moral principle in the sense assumed. In that case, these relativists will need to identify the defect in the view that moral principles are correct in the sense assumed. This task will raise complex issues about the relation between relativism and nonrealism about moral truth. We cannot digress now to these difficult issues, but some relevant consequences of moral nonrealism may be found in this book's selections in Part 5.

The general point is that rightness-determining moral principles for an agent need not be actually motivating reasons for that agent, particularly if the agent's psychological attitudes are defective in a certain manner. Some relativists will balk, as suggested, on the ground that moral requirements must be principles of rationality for an agent. The latter ground is inconclusive, however, owing to indeterminateness in its notion of rationality. If the relevant kind of rationality is motivational rationality, whereby an agent must be actually motivated by all binding moral requirements, the claim is dubious given our previous distinction between two ways of being subject to a moral requirement. We have no reason to hold that an agent's violating a rightness-determining moral requirement entails that this agent is motivationally irrational, that is, irrational on the basis of the agent's being in conflict with his or her motivational psychological attitudes such as intentions and desires. The moral wrongness of an agent's action should not be confused with an agent's being motivationally irrational. This kind of confusion underlies some cases for moral relativism. Treatment of the question "Why should I be moral?" must avoid such confusion. If "should" means "morally should" rather than "motivationally should," the question does not reduce to an issue of what features of one's psychological attitudes motivate one to be moral.

Motivational moral relativism, we have noted, implies that the basic moral requirements that actually motivate a person can vary, at least to some extent, among moral agents. We have no basis to gainsay such relativism, but this is no problem at all. Motivational moral relativism lacks the sharp bite of moral-requirement relativism, because the former commits us simply to a view about variability of motivation among agents. This view does not entail that rightness-determining moral principles vary in the way moral-requirement relativism suggests. The view that the motivations of moral agents vary does not justify the view that basic rightness-determining moral principles vary among moral agents.

Perhaps relativists will deny that one's having an intention to act, or at least one's failing to have such an intention, is ever subject to moral assessment. This would be a desperate move of last resort. One's having an intention to act can sometimes be indirectly controlled by one, and it can bring about a range of morally significant phenomena: for example, intentional actions, pleasure, and pain. So relativists should look elsewhere for a way out of the predicament at hand. Suppose, then, that relativists acknowledge that it can be morally improper for agents to have certain intentions or to fail to have certain intentions. In that case, relativists will be hard put to substantiate that the rightness-determining principles bearing on an agent are necessarily grounded in the actual intentions of that agent. The problem is that the agent in question may very well have morally improper intentions, and when the grounding intentions are morally improper, the moral principles grounded thereby may very well be morally defective too. In other words, we have no reason to suppose that the rightness-determining principles for agents must be grounded in morally defective intentions of those agents. A relativist might reply that some morally relevant intentions are controllable for certain people but not for others, and that this allows for variability in basic moral requirements, even if "ought" implies "can." This kind of reply may or may not save relativism. It raises, at any rate, the complex issue of the role of freedom in moral agency. Inasmuch as we cannot settle that big issue here, we do not offer the present antirelativist argument as decisive against all species of moral-requirement relativism. The scope of our argument, for now, is more modest.

The problem at hand for relativists explains why relativists typically avoid the matter of the moral assessment of an agent's having an intention or failing to have an intention. Even so, it is theoretically implausible to avoid this ethically important matter. Intentions often play the kind of role in ethically relevant action that makes intentions themselves subject to moral assessment. So relativists claiming otherwise are open to the charge of an ad hoc move to salvage their relativism.

Perhaps moral-requirement relativism gains credibility from its apparent moral tolerance, that is, its permitting abundant diversity in binding moral requirements among moral agents. The key issue, however, is what kind of diversity in moral requirements is actually morally defensible. If one maps the relevant diversity in moral requirements onto merely motivating reasons, as many relativists do, then we have to face the problem presented above: namely, the problem of confusing (a) moral principles that are *motivating,* relative to an agent's psychological attitudes, and (b) moral principles that are *rightness-determining* for an agent. For the reasons just indicated, we should steer clear of any such confusion. In the end, *if* moral requirement relativism depends on this kind of confusion, we do well to dispense with moral requirement relativism altogether. Whether relativism can ultimately avoid this kind of confusion should be decided in light of this book's selections, which represent a wide range of perspectives on moral relativism. The following section offers summaries of the book's selections.

II. SUMMARIES OF THE SELECTIONS

1. General Issues

In "Ethical Relativism," Richard Brandt presents a widely employed taxonomy of different forms of ethical relativism. He distinguishes three versions of ethical relativism. (1) "Descriptive relativism" (sometimes called "cultural relativism") states that the values or ethical views of some people or cultures conflict in a "fundamental way" with the values or ethical views of other people or cultures. To say that an ethical disagreement is *fundamental* is to say that it would persist even if the parties agreed about the factual properties of all the things in question. (2) "Metaethical relativism" denies that there is always only one correct (or, true) appraisal or judgment about any given ethical question. For example, my judgment that a given act is morally wrong and your judgment that the same act is morally right could both be true or correct. Sometimes, relativists claim that ethical truth is relative: for example, it might be "true for me" that slavery is wrong and "true for Jefferson Davis" that slavery is not wrong. Brandt claims that this way of speaking is seriously misleading. Metaethical relativism seems to deny that ethical judgments can be true at all, in any ordinary sense of the word *true.* Ordinarily, we say that two conflicting statements cannot both be true. (3) "Normative relativism" states that the rightness or wrongness of a given person's actions depends on her moral beliefs or the moral principles of her society. Brandt presents two versions of normative relativism. The first says that "if someone thinks that it is right (wrong) to do. *A,* then it *is* right (wrong) for him to do *A.*" The second says that "if the moral principles recognized in the society of which *X* is a member imply that it is wrong to do *A* in certain circumstances *C,* then it *is* wrong for *X* to do *A* in *C.*" Brandt argues that the truth of descriptive relativism does not entail the truth of metaethical relativism. He also claims that neither descriptive relativism nor metaethical relativism commits one to normative relativism.

In "Facts, Standards, and Truth," Karl Popper views relativism as a kind of irrationalism that makes the choice between competing views arbitrary. Popper defines relativism (in a very generic sense not confined to moral relativism) as follows: "the theory that the choice between competing theories is arbitrary; since either, there is no such thing as objective truth; or, if there is, no such thing as a theory which is true or at any rate (though perhaps not true) nearer to the truth than another theory; or, if there are two or more theories, no ways or means of deciding whether one of them is better than another." Popper defends a correspondence theory of truth; he says that a statement or "belief, is true if, and only if, it corresponds to the facts." He distinguishes sharply between having a *concept* of truth and having a *criterion* of truth and claims that we can have a clear concept of truth about some matter even if we do not have an adequate criterion of truth about that matter. Similarly, a person can have a clear concept of what tuberculosis is even if she is not able to determine who does and does not have tuberculosis. Popper claims that there is no general criterion of truth (no criterion of truth for all statements). This, he says, commits us to *fallibilism,* the view that it is always possible that we are mistaken about something we think we know. This is not, however, a ground to question the objectivity of truth: "the idea of error implies that of truth as a standard of which we may fall short." He rejects the relativist's view that conflicting judgments can be equally correct or true. Popper says that standards cannot correspond to the facts in the way that statements can. Thus, moral and other sorts of standards cannot be true in the same way that factual statements can be true. Standards can, however, still be criticized and we can give reasons for preferring certain standards to others. Popper holds that something analogous to verisimilitude or nearness to the truth holds for standards. Some (moral) standards are improvements on other moral standards. Popper claims that the view that we should do "unto others, whenever possible, as *they* want to be done by" is an improvement on alternative versions of the Golden Rule implying that we should do unto others as *we* would like them to do unto *us*.

In "The Challenge of Cultural Relativism," James Rachels recounts some striking differences between the moral views of different societies. For example, our society strongly disapproves of infanticide, but Eskimo society condones infanticide and practices it on a large scale (female infants are much more likely to be killed than male infants). Rachels lists six distinct claims commonly made by cultural relativists. Among these are the following:

1. Different societies have different moral codes.

2. There is no objective standard to judge one societal code better than another.

3. The moral code of a society determines what is right in that society.

Rachels uses the term *cultural relativism* in a much broader sense than Brandt. The six views he lists include what Brandt calls "descriptive relativism," "metaethical relativism," and "normative relativism." According to Rachels, many cultural relativists argue that, since different cultures have different moral codes, moral judgments cannot be objectively true. This argument, he contends, is clearly invalid; the conclusion does not follow. The fact that people disagree about something (for example, whether the earth is flat) does not, by itself, show that there are no objective truths about that matter. Rachels argues that cultural relativism has several implications that, on examination, are difficult to accept. Cultural relativism implies that we can *never* be justified in criticizing the customs of another society and that reformers who challenge or reject the ideals of their own societies are mistaken, by definition.

Rachels gives reasons for thinking that, on examination, the differences between the moral views of different societies are often less dramatic than they appear to be. (For example, when understood in light of the very harsh circumstances of Eskimo life, their views about infanticide seem less at odds with our own.) He argues that there are limits to the extent to which moral codes can vary. The moral code of any viable society must contain rules that provide for the care of infants and rules that prohibit murder and lying. A society that lacked such rules could not long endure. Rachels suggests a standard whereby the moral rules of different societies can be evaluated: "We may ask *whether the practice promotes or hinders the welfare of the people whose lives are affected by it.*"

2. RELATIVISM AND MORAL DIVERSITY

A number of leading anthropologists have argued that the great diversity of moral beliefs and standards among humans is evidence in favor of moral relativism. The five selections in this section discuss the implications of cultural diversity for morality.

In "Folkways," W. G. Sumner claims that the different circumstances of different societies produce different customs or folkways. Folkways are adaptations of groups of people to their particular circumstances in life. Moral beliefs and principles, according to Sumner, are all the products of folkways and customs. Folkways are not conscious creations of individuals; they evolve over a long periods of time and change in light of changing circumstances. Sumner claims that folkways tend to be maximally adaptive. He defends a version of normative relativism by appeal to the meaning of moral concepts. He writes: "`immoral' never means anything but contrary to the mores of the time and place." All moral judgments are relative to the mores of a given culture. Sumner holds that we are always mistaken if we criticize the mores or practices of another culture, even such things as the institutions of slavery: "Everything in the mores of a time and place must be regarded as justified with regard to that time and place," according to Sumner. This commitment to normative relativism not withstanding, Sumner holds that there are grounds for thinking that some folkways are preferable to others. Some folkways are more successful in satisfying people's needs than others. In addition, Sumner acknowledges that some folkways can be harmful (for example, customs calling for the destruction of a person's goods upon his death).

In "Anthropology and the Abnormal," Ruth Benedict notes some striking of examples of behavior and traits of character that would be strongly disapproved of and considered signs of paranoia in Western societies but that are condoned and even regarded as "normal" in other societies. She argues that "normality is culturally defined." To say that an action is "normal" simply means that it "is one that falls well within the limits of expected behavior for a particular society." There are, she says, no objective or neutral grounds for saying that some standards of normality are preferable to others. Benedict writes: "Mankind has always preferred to say, "It is morally good," rather than "It is habitual," and the fact of this preference is matter enough for a critical science of ethics. But historically the two phrases are synonymous. The concept of the normal is properly a variant of the concept of the good. It is that which society has approved. A normal action is one which falls within the limits of expected behavior for a particular society." Benedict thus defends a version of normative relativism by appeal to the meaning of moral terms.

In "The Meaning of Right," W. D. Ross argues that the account of the meaning of moral terms defended by Sumner and Benedict is mistaken. "Action X is morally right" cannot, according to Ross, simply *mean* "X is in accordance with the present mores or moral standards of my society." Such a view would make it *impossible* for anyone to dissent from the moral code of her own time and place without being inconsistent. According to the theory in question, it is *self-contradictory* to say that an action or policy generally approved of by one's society is morally wrong. Throughout history, however, many people have criticized the moral standards and practices of their own time and place. Such dissent is intelligible and has had a significant social impact. It is not self-contradictory to say that a certain practice is wrong even though the norms of one's own society permit or require it. For example, those individuals who criticized the moral standards of their own time and place by calling for the abolition of slavery were not guilty of self-contradiction. On the contrary, they exemplified moral wisdom.

Michelle Moody-Adams defines "descriptive cultural relativism" as the claim that "differences in the moral practices of diverse social groups generate 'ultimate' or 'fundamental' moral disputes, disputes that are neither reducible to nonmoral disagreement nor susceptible of rational resolution—disputes that are in principle irresolvable."[2] In "The Empirical Underdetermination of Descriptive Cultural Relativism" (taken from the aforementioned book), Moody-Adams observes that most parties to debates about relativism and anthropology assume that descriptive relativism is true. They disagree about whether the truth of descriptive relativism constitutes evidence for moral relativism (metaethical relativism). She thinks that the case for descriptive cultural relativism is far less clear than is generally assumed. There are, she claims, serious methodological flaws with the best empirical data alleged to support descriptive relativism.

Moody-Adams pays special attention to philosophers Richard Brandt and John Ladd, who did extensive empirical research into cultural differences between different societies. Brandt studied the moral beliefs of the Hopi Indians, and Ladd studied the Navaho Indians. She faults Ladd (and Brandt) for uncritical selections of native "authorities" to give descriptions of the society's moral beliefs. Ladd and various anthropologists overlook the level of dissent and disagreement within "traditional" societies. Brandt says that the most salient disagreement between Hopi moral beliefs and those of the larger American society is that the Hopi see little, if any, moral presumption against causing suffering to animals. Moody-Adams suggests that Brandt is somewhat cavalier in his characterization of the views of Americans about the treatment of animals, and that he ignores that many Americans are indifferent to the suffering of animals in factory farms.[3]

Moody-Adams rehearses Karl Duncker's arguments against descriptive relativism. According to Duncker, differences in moral beliefs always depend on disagreements about factual matters. The same factual situations are never evaluated differently. Moody-Adams stops short of endorsing Duncker's position. She stresses (a) the difficulty of determining whether the empirical evidence counts as evidence for irresolvable disagreement and (b) the failure of descriptive relativists to disprove Duncker's view.

In "The Ethical Implications of Cultural Relativity," Carl Wellman gives an argument similar to Ross's against the view that "right" means "is in accordance with the mores of society." He claims that this view is untenable because it implies that all social reformers who criticize the customs and practices of their societies are guilty of self-contradiction. Wellman grants that the rightness of certain acts can be relative to social contexts. This, he says, is so because the social contexts of actions largely determine their consequences. The killing of an aged parent has consequences in a very poor society different from its consequences in an affluent society. Wellman writes: "In our society disposing of old and useless parents merely allows one to live in greater luxury; to an Eskimo this act may mean the difference between barely adequate subsistence and malnutrition for himself and his family." Even so, Wellman sees no reason to suppose that one and the same act can be right in one society but not in another unless it has different consequences in the two societies. He also says that the fact that different societies have different moral standards or different standards for moral reasoning does not preclude that certain moral standards or standards of moral reasoning are objectively true or correct. According to Wellman, the fact that different societies have different normative concepts entails that the moral beliefs of one society may not be fully stateable or intelligible in terms of the concepts of the other: "to some extent at least the ethics of different cultures are incommensurate."

3. On the Coherence of Moral Relativism

Some versions of relativism are incoherent or self-refuting. A very simple version of this problem is the following: the statement that everything is relative is, if true, itself relative. The statement that everything is relative (or that no statement is objectively true) seems to undercut itself; it calls its own status into question. It is possible to avoid this kind of self-refutation or self-undermining by distinguishing between first-order statements and meta-statements. Defenders of metaethical relativism typically say that first-order moral judgments (for example, that your lying to me about the price of the car was morally wrong) are not objectively true or false but only true or false *relative to* certain standards, societies, or individuals. Metaethical relativists can consistently hold, however, that metaethical relativism is itself objectively true. Metaethical relativism is not itself a first-order moral theory, but is rather a theory about the status of first-order moral judgments.

The main question addressed by this section's selections is whether moral relativism is tantamount to moral nihilism or, alternatively, whether accepting moral relativism is consistent with making first-order moral judgments and taking them seriously. Most moral relativists are not moral nihilists; they make first-order moral judgments. Betsy Postow and David Lyons both argue that certain forms of moral relativism are inconsistent or lead to incoherence if their proponents make first-order moral judgements. T. M. Scanlon tries to sketch a version of relativism that is consistent with making first-order moral judgments. (The selections from Part 4 by Foot, Graham, and Nagel also bear on the issue of the coherence of relativism.)

Betsy Postow's "Dishonest Relativism" considers the relativist position that normative views that conflict with one's own well grounded normative views can be well grounded or acceptable themselves. (This view is similar to what Brandt calls "metaethical relativism.") She claims that proponents of this view are guilty of a kind of dishonesty if they make any first-order judgments to the effect that people morally ought to do certain things. According to Postow, a minimal condition of one's accepting a prescriptive principle, *P*, is that one be willing to recommend that others follow *P*. Suppose that I accept a moral theory that includes *P* and you accept a conflicting moral theory that I claim is just as well grounded as my own. Your moral theory does not include *P*, but it includes *P1*. *P1* permits *X*. Suppose that I claim that *X* is wrong, because it is forbidden by *P*. If I am a relativist and grant that your moral theory is as well grounded as my own theory, then I must grant that you have no reason to refrain from doing *X*. However, to advise or to exhort you to do something that, in my opinion, you have no reason to do is dishonest. Thus, it is dishonest for a relativist to hold that any act is morally obligatory. To hold that *X* is morally obligatory is to be willing to recommended that others do *X* and exhort them to do *X*. Being a relativist, however, I must grant that others accept moral principles that are as well grounded as my own that do not require them to do *X* and even imply that they should not do *X*.

In "Ethical Relativism and the Problem of Incoherence," David Lyons argues that certain versions of ethical relativism are incoherent in that they commit us to the view that certain acts are both wrong and not wrong. He distinguishes between what he calls "agent's group relativism" and "appraiser's group relativism." Agent's group relativism holds "that an act is right, if and only if, it accords with the norms of the agent's group." Appraiser's group relativism holds "that a moral judgment is valid if, and only if, it accords with the norms of the appraiser's social group." Lyons holds that agent's group relativism is coherent, that it does not commit us to the view that certain acts are both wrong and not wrong. It "seems to imply that any single item of conduct can correctly be judged in one and only one way." Appraiser's group relativism seems to validate conflicting ethical judgments. One and the same act can be judged right according to the norms of one social group and wrong according to the norms of another group. Lyons considers an alternative version of appraiser relativism according to which "one's moral judgment is valid if, and only if, one would accept it under certain hypothetical circumstances (such as knowing all of the relevant facts) that are conceived of as ideal for deciding upon one's moral principles." This theory does not avoid the problem of incoherence, "because there is no guarantee that different individuals will subscribe to the same principles, even under 'ideal' conditions."

Lyons considers the version of appraiser's group relativism stating that when I make a moral judgment that some act is right (or wrong), I simply *mean* that the norms of my group permit (or do not permit) the act. He takes this to be highly implausible because it denies that many ostensible cases of agreement or disagreement about moral questions really constitute cases of agreement or disagreement. For example, suppose that you say that it was wrong for a person, S, to do action A, and I say that it was not wrong for S to do A. It seems that we disagree. On the present view, however, we are not really disagreeing. You are saying that A is inconsistent with the norms of your group and I am saying that A is consistent with the norms of my group. (Ross and Wellman also criticize the view in question.)

Thomas Scanlon's "Fear of Relativism" examines the widespread view that the acceptance of moral relativism somehow undermines claims about the authority or importance of morality. Scanlon focuses on metaethical relativism, the view that conflicting moral judgments can be equally true (or equally correct or justified). Scanlon argues that there are benign versions of relativism that one could accept without denying the importance or significance of one's own moral views. According to Scanlon, the most serious difficulty for someone seeking a benign version of relativism is to be able to say that other people have equally good reasons for accepting alternative standards without undermining one's commitment to one's own standards. In order for relativism to be benign, the relativist must be able to regard both her own standards and those of others as worthy of respect and adherence, but still hold that she has reasons to adhere to her own standards. According to Scanlon, this could be the case in the following way: a person could see herself as having reasons to adhere to her own moral tradition even if she views others as having equally good reasons to adhere to their (different) moral traditions. This possibility is real if the person in question holds that both moral traditions are worthy of respect and adherence.

Scanlon takes issue with Gilbert Harman's aforementioned relativist position implying that we cannot say that it was wrong of Hitler to murder the Jews. A defect of relativism, according to Scanlon, is its depriving us in such a case of the legitimacy of our condemning certain actions. We deem some moral judgments to be clearly true, according to Scanlon, and relativism "is a threat in so far as it would force us to withdraw those judgments, or would undermine their claim to importance."

4. DEFENSE AND CRITICISM OF RELATIVISM

The selections in this section focus on metaethical relativism, the view that moral judgments are not objectively true or false.

In "Is There a Single True Morality?" Gilbert Harman claims that morality arises from conventions or understandings between people. Since different people arrive at different understandings, "there are no basic moral demands that apply to everyone." He holds that "our ordinary factual beliefs provide us with evidence that there is an independent world of objects because our having those beliefs cannot be plausibly explained without assuming we interact with an independent world of objects external to ourselves." Harman argues that there are no comparable reasons to suppose that there is an independent (nonrelative) realm of values and obligations. Our having the moral beliefs we have can be entirely explained in terms of our upbringing and psychology; we do not need to posit objective values in order to explain them.

To say that there are absolute or nonrelative values is to say that there are things that everyone has reason to do or hope for. Absolute nonrelative moral values (if they exist) create moral demands that everyone has sufficient reasons to follow. Harman argues that such values do not exist. Absolutists would claim that everyone has reasons to observe the prohibition against harming others, but Harman claims that this is not the case. His argument for this rests on two assumptions. (1) If someone has adequate reasons to do something, there must be warranted reasoning that would lead the person to decide to do the thing in question. If the person fails to do the thing in question it must be due to "inattention, lack of time, failure to consider or appreciate certain arguments, ignorance of relevant evidence, an error of reasoning, irrationality, unreasonableness, or weakness of will." (2) Some people who do not observe the prohibition against harming others do not fail to do so for any of the above reasons. Harman distinguishes relativistic naturalism in ethics from an absolutist position of autonomous ethics (where the relevant autonomy is with regard to a scientific account of the world). He finds no conclusive argument in favor of either position.

Philippa Foot, in "Moral Relativism," holds that standards of beauty are relative to different societies. Terms such as *elegant* and *handsome* require shared standards and shared reactions within a community of judgment. Different societies have different standards of beauty. We recognize this and continue to employ our own "local" standards of beauty without claiming that our own standards are true (or better than other standards). Judgments to the effect that someone is or is not handsome are relative in that they can only be said to be true or false relative to one or another set of possible standards and no one standard can be said to be true or better than all other standards. Foot asks whether the truth of moral judgments is relative in the same way. She claims that there are *some* objective moral facts, that some moral judgments are objectively true: "It is clearly an objective moral fact that the Nazi treatment of the Jews was morally indefensible." She questions, however, whether there are comparable objective truths about *all* moral issues. She expresses sympathy for a kind of mixed view according to which moral judgments about some (but not all) moral questions are objectively true or false. (This seems to be a moderate version of metaethical relativism.)

Foot notes common features of the human condition: common needs and interests that might be said to argue for objective moral standards. (Nussbaum develops this idea at considerable length in her contribution.) Foot considers the view that relativists who deny that any one moral assertion is any truer than any others cannot consistently make any moral judgments of their own. (Postow holds something similar to this.) Foot rejects this view by appealing to the analogy with standards of beauty. We can call people handsome or beautiful, by appealing to our own local standards of beauty, even though we do not claim that those standards are better than alternative standards of beauty. Foot also discusses the version of normative relativism according to which a person should always follow her own conscience. She rejects the view that following one's conscience guarantees that one's act is right, but argues that a person who acts against her own conscience "always acts badly."

In "Non-Relative Virtues," Martha Nussbaum argues that virtue ethics can avoid relativism if it is properly based on an account of human nature, or human flourishing, that is transcultural. According to Nussbaum, Aristotle attempted to ground an objective theory of the virtues in an account of human nature. One important piece of evidence for the claim that Aristotle wanted his specification of the virtues to be independent of local traditions is that he uses them to criticize some common Greek conceptions of the virtues. Aristotle tried to defend an objectivist theory of the virtues by identifying spheres of human experience common to all human beings: for example, (a) our fear of harm, especially death, (b) our possessing bodily appetites with corresponding pleasures, and (c) our need to distribute scarce resources. There are virtues corresponding to each of these spheres of experience. For each sphere, Aristotle offers his specific theory of the corresponding virtue, where virtues are stable dispositions to act appropriately in a given sphere of conduct. This leaves open what counts as virtue in any given area.

How does one defend particular conceptions of virtue and the standards for appropriate and inappropriate behavior they embody? Nussbaum is rather guarded in what she says about this, and she makes large concessions to the relativist position. She thinks it very likely that there is a plurality of different plausible conceptions of virtue for any given sphere of common human action. There might be more than one plausible conception of the virtue of justice and no single conception of justice that is more plausible then any other. Nussbaum continues: "The process of comparative and critical debate will, I imagine, eliminate numerous contenders—for example, the view of justice that prevailed in Cyme. But what remains might be called a plurality of acceptable accounts. Success in the eliminative task will still be no trivial accomplishment." This is not a full-blown objectivism according to which there is one and only one correct or true answer to a moral question (or only one acceptable understanding of a given virtue), but, Nussbaum insists, this is not an "anything goes" view implying that all moral judgments (or all accounts of a given virtue) are equally valid. Nor does her view commit her to saying that "the whole idea of searching for the truth is an old fashioned error." Nussbaum adds that "certain ways in which people see the world can still be criticized exactly as Aristotle criticized them: as stupid, pernicious and false." She considers Karl Marx's objection that some virtues (for example, justice and generosity) "presuppose conditions and structures that are not ideal and that will be eliminated when communism is achieved." Marx's objection is plausible, according to Nussbaum, in the case of generosity, because generosity seems to presuppose the existence of private property. Even so, she does not concede Marx's claim that humans would have no need of the virtues of justice and courage in an ideal society.

Gordon Graham's "Tolerance, Pluralism, and Relativism" discusses the relationship between tolerance, pluralism, and moral relativism. The following three positions are widely endorsed: (1) pluralism (the phenomenon of moral disagreement or the plurality of views about moral questions) commits us to moral relativism, (2) moral relativism provides support for toleration, and (3) moral objectivism is incompatible with the view that we should tolerate moral views we judge to be mistaken. Graham rejects all three positions and argues that a belief in objectivism "sits best with a belief in toleration." Graham distinguishes between subjectivism, relativism, realism, and objectivism. He argues that defenders of epistemological moral objectivism (those who claim "that for any evaluative question there is in principle the possibility of a right answer") need not be Platonists or realists who posit metaphysically suspect entities. He argues that objectivism is an "inescapable" postulate or presupposition of practical deliberation. Unless we accept the idea that there are better and worse answers to the practical questions we raise about what we should do, "we cannot sensibly deliberate about them." Our practice of practical deliberation gives us reason to accept an objectivist moral epistemology. Graham concludes by examining some arguments for and against tolerance; he takes all of these arguments to be consistent with moral objectivism.

In "Ethics," Thomas Nagel aims to defend the objectivity of moral reasoning without appealing to moral realism. He rejects attempts to argue against the objectivity of moral reasoning on the ground that moral beliefs are just the product of historical and culturally conditioned desires. He also rejects criticisms of the objectivity of moral judgments by appeal to a Humean theory of practical reasoning. According to Nagel, moral questions are fundamentally questions about whether we should have certain desires or, given that we have certain desires, whether we should act on them. Desires are open to rational assessment. As free reflective agents, we can choose whether to follow our desires on the basis of an assessment of their reasonableness. Nagel argues that the perspective of first-order practical reasoning involves implicit commitment to the existence of objective reasons for action. Rejection of this is inconsistent with ordinary ways of thinking and is bought at a high price. We cannot deliberate about what we should do if we just take ourselves to be acting on desires that we have no reason to have. Even in light of information about the causes of our beliefs and desires, we can ask ourselves "What should I do in light of this?" Many defenses of moral relativism and subjectivism proceed in disregard of the features of practical reasoning that presuppose the existence of objective reasons for action.

5. RELATIVISM, REALISM, AND RATIONALITY

Moral realism states that there are objective, nonrelative moral facts independent of what we believe or desire (and independent of what we would believe or desire if we were rational). It implies that objective values or moral facts are "part of the fabric of the universe." Moral realism is clearly incompatible with (metaethical) relativism. To be a metaethical relativist one must be a nonrealist, but moral nonrealism per se does not commit one to metaethical relativism. Many or most nonrealist moral theories rejecting relativism are based on theories of rationality. These theories state that there are objective facts about what is good or bad or right or wrong and that these facts are somehow determined by what things rational people would desire or by what moral principles rational people would endorse. To avoid metaethical relativism, such theories need to assume that rational people would all agree in their relevant beliefs or attitudes.

In "The Subjectivity of Values," J. L. Mackie argues that there are no objective values. He takes this to be an ontological or metaphysical claim, rather than a first-order ethical judgment or a claim about the meanings of moral terms. Mackie says that objective values, if they existed, would constitute grounds for categorical imperatives of the sort that Kant describes. Objective values would give people unconditional reasons for action that are not contingent on any desires they have. In denying that there are objective values, Mackie denies the objective validity of categorical imperatives. According to Mackie, the objectivity of values is presupposed in traditional ethical theory and in ordinary, commonsense moral judgments. Mackie holds that the common claim to objectivity in moral discourse is, nonetheless, false. Thus, he holds an "error theory" of morality entailing that all moral judgments are false or mistaken in that they purport to be objectively true but actually are not. Mackie claims that the phenomenon of moral disagreement and the variability of moral standards that people endorse is evidence against the existence of objective values. He also argues against the existence of objective values on the grounds that if they existed "they would be entities or qualities or relations of a very strange sort, utterly different from anything else in the universe." Mackie attributes the belief in objective values to a kind of objectification or projection of our attitudes onto things in the world. According to Mackie, moral realists (mistakenly) project their attitudes onto the world in the same way that a person who is disgusted by a fungus reads his feelings onto their objects if he ascribes "to the fungus itself a non-natural quality of foulness." Mackie concedes, in conclusion, that if there were a God who authored moral imperatives, moral values could be considered objective. He does not, however, deem theism defensible.

Richard Brandt's "Relativism Refuted?" considers the view that when the fundamental moral principles of different individuals or groups conflict there is "no way to show that one view is better justified even in the presence of ideally complete factual information; in that sense the principles are equally justified or 'valid.'" Brandt holds that moral codes or fundamental moral principles are justified to the extent that all fully informed and rational persons would support the same moral code (or the same fundamental principles) for a given society. Whether this version of relativism is true depends on whether all fully informed rational persons would support the same moral system for a given society. Brandt expresses preference for a kind of moderate (metaethical) relativism. He suggests that all rational people would prefer that their societies be governed by some sort of moral code and that all rational people would agree in desiring certain "core" features for that code. He appeals to Foot's claims about common human needs and interests. Brandt thinks it unlikely, however, that every rational person would support or desire exactly the same moral code for any given society.

Carson's and Moser's "Relativism and Normative Nonrealism: Basing Morality on Rationality" focuses on nonrealist normative theories that are based on theories of rationality. Many important nonrealist moral theories, including the theories of Rawls, Firth, Gauthier, Brandt, and Hare, are based squarely on theories of rationality. These nonrealist theories take facts about what is rational or irrational to be logically prior to what is moral; they assume that things are right or good because it is rational to choose them or at least to have a certain attitude of approval toward them. Such theories presuppose that the theory of rationality endorsed by the theory is the correct account of rationality. Otherwise, we may reasonably prefer an alternative moral theory based on a different account of rationality. The authors argue that theories of rationality (such as that underlying familiar versions of normative nonrealism) cannot be defended, in a nonquestion-begging manner, on *semantic* grounds, by appeal to "the meaning" of "rational." First, it is highly doubtful that the word *rational* has a single, univocal meaning in either ordinary language or philosophical discourse. Second, even if there were a single, univocal meaning of *rational,* one might sensibly ask, "Why should I care about being rational in that sense?" The authors consider pragmatic arguments for adopting a full-information theory of rationality. They contend that these arguments appeal to contingent features of humans that are not shared by every human. Given the difficulty of defending any particular theory of rationality as "the" correct account of rationality, it seems likely that nonrealists who base normative theories on theories of rationality are committed to endorsing moral relativism (metaethical relativism).

6. CASE STUDY ON RELATIVISM

The book concludes with Loretta Kopelman's case study entitled "Female Circumcision/Genital Mutilation and Ethical Relativism." Kopelman gives a detailed account of female circumcision involving the removal of all or part of the clitoris and labia minora. She details its consequences, including possible loss of ability to experience sexual pleasure, infections, incontinence, painful intercourse, infertility, and death. Kopelman regards female circumcision/genital mutilation as a test case for certain versions of ethical relativism because the practice is generally approved of within the societies that practice it and generally disapproved of in other societies. She surveys some of the justifications commonly given for the practice and argues that some of these rest on false beliefs. She argues that "these rituals of female genital mutilation are wrong. . . . They are wrong because the usual forms of the surgery deny women orgasms and because they cause medical complications and even death." She also argues that this and other examples show that "ethical relativism—the view that to say something is right means it has cultural approval and to say it is wrong means it has cultural disapproval—is implausible."

NOTES

1. Gilbert Harman, "Moral Relativism Defended," *The Philosophical Review* 84 (1975): 9.

2. Michelle Moody-Adams, *Fieldwork in Familiar Places* (Cambridge: Harvard University Press, 1997), p. 15.

3. There do seem to be fundamental disagreements between *individuals* regarding the treatment of animals. Many individuals see little or no reason to avoid hurting animals, whereas others take this to be prima facie very wrong. Often such disagreements are not based on factual disagreements; whether these disagreements are "rationally undecidable" is a different matter altogether.

PART ONE

GENERAL ISSUES

Ethical Relativism

RICHARD BRANDT

The term "ethical relativism" is always used to designate some ethical principle or some theory about ethical principles, but within this limitation different authors use it quite differently. Contemporary philosophers generally apply the term to some position they disagree with or consider absurd, seldom to their own views; social scientists, however, often classify themselves as relativists. Writers who call themselves relativists always accept the first and second and sometimes accept the third of the theses described as descriptive relativism, metaethical relativism, and normative relativism, respectively.

DESCRIPTIVE RELATIVISM

The first thesis, without which the others would lose interest, is that the values, or ethical principles, of individuals conflict in a fundamental way ("fundamental" is explained below). A special form of this thesis, called "cultural relativism," is that such ethical disagreements often follow cultural lines. The cultural relativist emphasizes the cultural tradition as a prime source of the individual's views and thinks that most disagreements in ethics among individuals stem from enculturation in different ethical traditions, although he need not deny that some ethical disagreements among individuals arise from differences of innate constitution or personal history between the individuals.

Fundamental Disagreement

The most important and controversial part of the first thesis is the claim that diversities in values (and ethics) are fundamental. To say that a disagreement is "fundamental" means that it would not be removed even if there were perfect agreement about the properties of the thing being evaluated. (If disagreement is nonfundamental then it may be expected that all ethical diversity can be removed, in principle, by the advance of science, leading to

Reprinted, by permission of the publisher and copyright holder, from Richard Brandt, "Ethical Relativism," in Paul Edwards, ed., *The Encyclopedia of Philosophy*, Vol. 3, pp. 75–78. New York: Macmillan, 1967.

agreement about the properties of things being appraised.) Thus it is not necessarily a case of fundamental disagreement in values if one group approves of children's executing their parents at a certain age or stage of feebleness whereas another group disapproves of this very strongly. It may be that in the first group the act is thought necessary for the welfare of the parent in the afterlife, whereas in the second group it is thought not to be. The disagreement might well be removed by agreement about the facts, and indeed both parties might subscribe, now, to the principle "It is right for a child to treat a parent in whatever way is required for the parent's long-run welfare." The disagreement might be simply about the implications of this common principle, in the light of differing conceptions of the facts. There is fundamental ethical disagreement only if ethical appraisals or valuations are incompatible, even when there is mutual agreement between the relevant parties concerning the nature of the act that is being appraised.

METAETHICAL RELATIVISM

A person might accept descriptive relativism but still suppose that there is always only one correct moral appraisal of a given issue. Such a position has been widely held by nonnaturalists and by some naturalists (see, for example, the interest theory of R. B. Perry). The metaethical relativist, however, rejects this thesis and denies that there is always one correct moral evaluation. The metaethical relativist thesis is tenable only if certain views about the meaning of ethical (value) statements are rejected. For instance, if "*A* is right" *means* "Doing *A* will contribute at least as much to the happiness of sentient creatures as anything else one might do," it is obvious that one and only one of the two opinions "*A* is right" and "*A* is not right" is correct. Thus, the metaethical relativist is restricted to a certain range of theories about the meaning of ethical statements. He might, for instance, subscribe to some form of emotive theory, such as the view that ethical statements are not true or false at all but express the attitudes of the speaker. Or he might adopt the naturalist view that "is wrong" means "belongs to the class of actions toward which I tend to take up an impartial attitude of angry resentment" (held by the relativist E. A. Westermarck) or the view (suggested by the anthropologist Ruth Benedict) that the phrase "is morally good" means "is customary."

ETHICAL REASONING

At the present time metaethical relativists do not wish to rest their case solely on an appeal to what ethical statements mean; nor would their critics. The point of active debate is rather whether there is some method of ethical reasoning whose acceptance can be justified to thoughtful people with force comparable to the force with which acceptance of inductive logic can be justified. Is there any such method of ethical reasoning that can be expected in principle to show, when there is a conflict of values or ethical principles, that one and only one solution is correct in some important and relevant sense of "correct"? Metaethical relativists deny that there is any such method, and their denial may take either of two forms: They may deny that there is any method of ethical reasoning that can be justified with force comparable to that with which scientific method (inductive logic) can be justified. Or they may agree that there is such a method but say that its application is quite limited, and in particular that the fullest use of it could not show, in every case of a conflict of ethical convictions or of values, that one and only one position is correct in any important sense of "correct."

USE OF THE TERM "RELATIVISM"

Many writers, both in philosophy and in the social sciences, accept a combination of descriptive relativism and metaethical relativism. Philosophers who hold this view, however, seldom label themselves "relativists," apparently because they think the term confusing in this context. There is seldom objection to "cultural relativism" as a descriptive phrase, for it can be taken to mean that a person's values are "relative" to his culture in the sense of being a function of or causally dependent on it. But if "ethical relativism" is construed in a similar way, to mean that ethical *truth* is relative to, in the sense of being dependent on or a function of, something (for example, a person's cultural tradition), then this term is thought to be confusing since it is being used to name a theory that essentially denies that there is such a thing as ethical "truth."

One frequent confusion about what implies ethical relativism should be avoided. Suppose metaethical relativism is mistaken, and there is a single "correct" set of general ethical principles or value statements. It may still be true, and consistent with acceptance of this "correct" set of principles, that an act that is right in some circumstances will be wrong in other circumstances. Take, for instance, the possible "correct" principle "It is always right to do what will make all affected at least as happy as they could be made by any other possible action." It follows from this principle that in some situations it will be right to lie (for instance, to tell a man that he is not mortally ill when one knows he is, if he cannot bear the truth) and that in other situations it will be wrong to lie. Thus, even if metaethical relativism is false there is a sense in which the rightness of an act is relative to the circumstances or situation. The fact that the rightness of an act is relative to the circumstances in this way does not, of course, imply the truth of metaethical relativism.

NORMATIVE RELATIVISM

Neither descriptive nor metaethical relativism commits one logically to any ethical statement. The former is simply an assertion about the diversity of moral principles or values actually espoused by different persons; the latter is only a general statement about whether ethical principles are ever "correct." Nothing in particular about what ought to be, or about what someone ought to do, follows from them. Of particular interest is the fact that it does not follow that persons, depending on their cultural attachments, ought to do different things. In contrast, a person who holds to some form of what I shall call "normative relativism" asserts that something is wrong or blameworthy if some person or group—variously defined—thinks it is wrong or blameworthy. Anyone who espoused either of the following propositions would therefore be a normative relativist:

(*a*) "If someone thinks it is right (wrong) to do *A*, then it *is* right (wrong) for him to do *A*." This thesis has a rather wide popular acceptance today but is considered absurd by philosophers if it is taken to assert that what someone thinks right really is right for him. It is held to be absurd because taken in this way, it implies that there is no point in debating with a person what is right for him to do unless he is in doubt himself; the thesis says that if he *believes* that *A* is right, then it *is* right, at least for him. The thesis may be taken in another sense, however, with the result that it is no longer controversial, and no longer relativist. The thesis might mean: "If someone thinks it is right for him to do *A*, then he cannot properly be condemned for doing *A*." This statement merely formulates the view, widespread in the Western world, that a person cannot be condemned morally for doing what he sincerely believes to be right. (In order to receive universal approval, some additions must doubtless be added to the thesis, such as that the person's thoughts about what is right must have been the product of a reasonable amount of careful reflection, not influenced by personal preferences, and so on.) The thesis is not relativist, since it is not asserted that any person's or group's belief that something is blameworthy is either a necessary or a sufficient condition of its being blameworthy.

(*b*) "If the moral principles recognized in the society of which *X* is a member imply that it is wrong to do *A* in certain circumstances *C*, then it *is* wrong for *X* to do *A* in *C*." This principle says, in effect, that a person ought to act in conformity with the moral standards of his group. Like the preceding principle, this one has a good deal of popular acceptance today, is espoused by some anthropologists, and has some plausibility; it will be discussed below.

DIFFICULTIES IN THE RELATIVIST POSITIONS

The following appear to be the most important questions about the various relativist theses: (*a*) Is descriptive relativism supported by the scientific evidence? There are methodological obstacles in the way of answering the question whether there *is* fundamental diversity of ethical views. Such diversity would be established by producing two individuals, or cultures, who attribute identical properties to an act but nevertheless appraise it differently. But it is not easy to be sure when one has produced two such individuals or cultures. First, it is difficult to demonstrate that an act is believed to have identical properties by individuals or groups who appraise it differently. Is theft the same thing in societies where conceptions or systems of property differ? Is incest the same thing in societies with different kinship terminologies, different ways of counting lineage, and different beliefs about the effects of incest? It is possible to question members of different cultural traditions in an abstract way so that such differences in conception are ruled out, but then it is likely that the informant will not grasp the question and that his answer will be unreliable. The second difficulty is that there is no simple test for showing that groups or individuals really conflict in their appraisals. We may know that we think it morally wrong to do so-and-so, but it is not clear how to determine whether a Navaho agrees with us. Perhaps we have first to determine whether the Navaho language contains an expression synonymous with "is morally wrong." Or can we show that a Navaho does not think it morally wrong to do *A* by the fact that he feels no guilt about doing *A*? Or perhaps a mere conflict of *preferences* is sufficient to establish a disagreement in personal values. These questions deserve more discussion among anthropologists than they have received.

The evidence for descriptive relativism consists mostly of reports from observers about what is praised, condemned, or prohibited in various societies, usually with only scanty information on the group's typical conception of what is praised or blamed. In some instances projective methods and dream analysis have been utilized, and discussions with informants have elicited fragments of the conceptual background behind the appraisals. On the basis of such material most social scientists believe there is some fundamental diversity of values and ethical principles. A few years ago some investigators (among them W. G. Sumner and Ruth Benedict) supposed that the extent of diversity was practically unlimited, but today it is believed that there is also considerable uniformity (for example, universal disapproval of homicide and cruelty). One reason for believing there is considerable uniformity is that it appears that it would be difficult for a social group even to survive without the presence of certain features in its value system. (A social system must provide methods for rearing and educating the young, for mating, for division of labor, for avoiding serious personal insecurity, and so on.) Uniformity of evaluation is the rule in areas that pertain to survival or to conditions for tolerable social relationships; in other areas there are apt to be fundamental differences. Psychology adds some support to this construction of the empirical data. It offers a theory of enculturation that explains how fundamentally different values can be learned, and it also suggests how some universal human goals can set limitations to diversity among value systems.

(*b*) Does descriptive relativism support metaethical relativism? It is evident that from descriptive relativism nothing follows about what ethical statements mean or could fruitfully be used to mean. It is also evident that nothing follows about whether there is some method of ethical reasoning that can correctly adjudicate between conflicting ethical commitments, at least in some cases. Descriptive relativism may very well have bearing, however, on whether a justifiable method of reasoning in ethics (assuming there is one) could succeed in adjudicating between all clashes of ethical opinion. To be sure about this we would need to have an account of the reasonable method of ethical reflection before us. But let us take an example. Suppose we think that the only reasonable way to correct a person's ethical appraisal is to show him that it does not coincide with the appraisal he would make if he were vividly informed about all the relevant facts and were impartial in his judgment. Then suppose the descriptive relativist tells us that some people are simply left cold by the ideal of equality of welfare and that others view it as a basic human right, when both groups have exactly the same beliefs about what equality of welfare is and what its consequences would be. In this case we might be convinced that both parties were already impartial (if the views were not just typical of different social or economic classes) and that further information probably would not change their views. Doubtless much more analysis of the situation is necessary, but it is clear that given the described assumption about actual ideals and the assumption about the limitation of ethical argument, one might be led to a cautious acceptance of the view that not all ethical disputes can be resolved by this justifiable method of ethical reasoning.

(c) Are cultural and metaethical relativism necessarily committed to any form of normative relativism? Neither the cultural relativist nor the metaethical relativist is committed logically to any form of normative relativism. It is consistent to assert either of these positions and also to affirm any value judgment or ethical proposition one pleases. However, the second proposition cited under normative relativism (that a person ought to act in conformity with the moral standards of his group) at least presupposes the acceptance of cultural relativism. There would be no point in asserting this normative principle if cultural relativism were not accepted.

How strong are the arguments that can be advanced in favor of this form of normative relativism? Suppose that in X's society it is a recognized moral obligation for a person to care for his father, but not for his father's siblings (at least to anything like the same degree), in illness or old age. Suppose also that in Y's society it is recognized that one has no such obligation toward one's father or his siblings but does have it toward one's mother and her siblings. In such a situation it is hard to deny that X seems to have some obligation to care for his father and that Y seems not to have, at least to the same degree. (Some philosophers hold that there is no obligation on anyone, unless one's society recognizes such an obligation for the relevant situation.) So far, the principle seems intuitively acceptable. In general, however, it appears less defensible, for the fact that X's society regards it as wrong to play tennis on Sunday, to marry one's deceased wife's sister, and to disbelieve in God does not, we should intuitively say, make it wrong for X to do these things. Thus, our principle seems valid for some types of cases but not for others. The solution of this paradox probably is that for those cases (like an obligation to one's father) where the principle seems acceptable, the reasons for which it seems acceptable are extremely complex and are not based simply on the fact that society has asserted that an obligation exists. When society recognizes a moral obligation, there are many repercussions that basically affect the types of responsibility the individual may have toward other members of his society. For instance, one result of a society's recognizing a son's moral obligation to care for his father is that no one else will take care of the father if the son does not. Another is that a kind of equitable insurance system is set up in which one pays premiums in the form of taking responsibility for one's own father and from which one gets protection in one's old age. So it is at least an open question whether it can seriously be claimed that the moral convictions of a society have, in themselves, any implication for what a member of the society is morally bound to do, in the way our suggested principle affirms that they do.

BIBLIOGRAPHY

Aberle, D. F., et al., "The Functional Prerequisites of a Society." *Ethics,* Vol. 60 (1950), 100–111.

Asch, S. E., *Social Psychology,* Chs. 12, 13. Englewood Cliffs, N.J., 1952. An excellent critique of the evidential basis for descriptive relativism.

Benedict, Ruth, "Anthropology and the Abnormal." *Journal of General Psychology,* Vol. 10 (1934), 59–82. A graphic account of some ethnological data in support of a rather extreme type of relativism.

Brandt, R. B., *Hopi Ethics.* Chicago, 1954. An analysis of the values of the Hopi Indians with special reference to relativism. Methodologically oriented.

Brandt, R. B., *Ethical Theory,* Chs. 5, 6, 11. Englewood Cliffs, N.J., 1959. A cautious review and assessment of the evidence.

Firth, R., *Elements of Social Organization,* Ch. 6. London, 1951. A learned survey of anthropological material by an anthropologist with leanings toward relativism.

Ginsberg, Morris, *Essays in Sociology and Social Philosophy,* Vol. I. New York, 1957. A learned survey of the evidence by a sociologist.

Herskovits, M., *Man and His Works,* Ch. 5. New York, 1948. One of the most vigorous contemporary defenses of relativism by an anthropologist.

Kluckhohn, C., "Ethical Relativity." *Journal of Philosophy,* Vol. 52 (1955), 663–677. A cautious assessment of the evidence by an anthropologist who stresses the uniformities of value systems.

Ladd, J., *Structure of a Moral Code.* Cambridge, Mass., 1956. A fine study of the Navaho, emphasizing methodological problems.

Linton, R., "Universal Ethical Principles: An Anthropological View," in R. N. Anshen, ed., *Moral Principles of Action.* New York, 1952. An excellent statement, by an anthropologist of the middle-of-the-road position, emphasizing both uniformities and diversity.

Westermarck, E. A., *The Origin and Development of the Moral Ideas,* Vol. I, Chs. 1–5. New York, 1906. One of the most influential statements of the relativist position, with encyclopedic documentation; however, it is methodologically somewhat unsophisticated.

Westermarck, E. A., *Ethical Relativity,* Ch. 5. New York, 1932. A shorter defense of the relativist position, intended primarily for persons interested in philosophy.

Facts, Standards, and Truth: A Further Criticism of Relativism

KARL POPPER

The main philosophical malady of our time is an intellectual and moral relativism, the latter being at least in part based upon the former. By relativism—or, if you like, scepticism—I mean here, briefly, the theory that the choice between competing theories is arbitrary; since either, there is no such thing as objective truth; or, if there is, no such thing as a theory which is true or at any rate (though perhaps not true) nearer to the truth than another theory; or, if there are two or more theories, no ways or means of deciding whether one of them is better than another.

In this *addendum*[1] I shall first suggest that a dose of Tarski's theory of truth, stiffened perhaps by my own theory of getting nearer to the truth, may go a long way towards curing this malady, though I admit that some other remedies might also be required, such as the non-authoritarian theory of knowledge which I have developed elsewhere.[2] I shall also try to show (in sections 12 ff. below) that the situation in the realm of standards—especially in the moral and political field—is somewhat analogous to that obtaining in the realm of facts.

1. TRUTH

Certain arguments in support of relativism arise from the question, asked in the tone of the assured sceptic who knows for certain that there is no answer: *"What is truth?"* But Pilate's question can be answered in a simple and reasonable way—though hardly in a way that would have satisfied him—as follows: an assertion, proposition, statement, or belief, is true if, and only if, it corresponds to the facts.

Yet what do we mean by saying that a statement corresponds to the facts?

Though to our sceptic or relativist this second question may seem just as unanswerable as the first, it actually can be equally readily answered. The answer is not difficult—as one might expect if one reflects upon the fact that every judge assumes that the witness knows what truth (in the sense of correspondence with the facts) means. Indeed, the answer turns out to be almost trivial.

In a way it *is* trivial—that is, once we have learnt from Tarski that the problem is one in which we *refer to or speak about* statements and facts and some relationship of correspondence holding between statement and facts; and that, therefore, the solution must also be one that *refers to or speaks about* statements and facts, and some relation between them. Consider the following:

The statement "Smith entered the pawnshop shortly after 10:15" corresponds to the facts if, and only if, Smith entered the pawnshop shortly after 10:15.

When we read this italicized paragraph, what is likely to strike us first is its triviality. But never mind its triviality: if we look at it again, and more carefully, we see (1) that it refers to a statement; and (2) to some facts; and (3) that it can therefore state the very obvious conditions which we should expect to hold whenever we wish to say that the statement referred to corresponds to the facts referred to.

Those who think that this italicized paragraph is too trivial or too simple to contain anything interesting should be reminded of the fact, already referred to, that since everybody knows what truth, or correspondence with the facts, means (as long as he does not allow himself to speculate about it) this must be, in a sense, a trivial matter.

That the idea formulated in the italicized paragraph is correct, may be brought out by the following second italicized paragraph.

The assertion made by the witness, "Smith entered the pawnshop shortly after 10:15" is true if and only if Smith entered the pawnshop shortly after 10:15.

It is clear that this second italicized paragraph is again very trivial. Nevertheless, it states in full the conditions for applying the predicate "is true" to any statement made by a witness.

Some people might think that a better way to formulate the paragraph would be the following:

The assertion made by the witness "I saw that Smith entered the pawnshop shortly after 10:15" is true if and only if the witness saw that Smith entered the pawnshop shortly after 10:15.

Comparing this third italicized paragraph with the second we see that while the second gives the conditions for the truth of a statement about Smith and what he did, the third gives the conditions for the truth of a statement about the witness and what he did (or saw). But this is the only difference between the two paragraphs: both state the full conditions for the truth of the two different statements which are quoted in them.

It is a rule of *giving evidence* that eye-witnesses should confine themselves to stating what they *actually saw*. Compliance with this rule may sometimes make it easier for the judge to *distinguish* between true evidence and false evidence. Thus the third italicized paragraph may perhaps be said to have some advantages over the second, if regarded from the point of view of truth-*seeking* and truth-*finding*.

But it is essential for our present purpose not to mix up questions of actual truth-seeking or truth-finding (i.e. epistemological or methodological questions) with the question of what we mean, or what we intend to say, when we speak of truth, or of correspondence with the facts (the logical or ontological question of truth). Now from the latter point of view, the third italicized paragraph has no advantage whatever over the second. Each of them states to the full the conditions for the truth of the statement to which it refers.

Each, therefore, answers the question—"What is truth?" in precisely the same way; though each does it only indirectly, by giving *the conditions for the truth for a certain statement*—and each for a different statement.

2. CRITERIA

It is decisive to realize that knowing what truth means, or under what conditions a statement is called true, is not the same as, and must be clearly distinguished from, possessing a means of deciding—a *criterion* for deciding— whether a given statement is true or false.

The distinction I am referring to is a very general one, and it is of considerable importance for an assessment of relativism, as we shall see.

We may know, for example, what we mean by "good meat" and by "meat gone bad"; but we may not know how to tell the one from the other, at least in some cases: it is this we have in mind when we say that we have no *criterion* of the "goodness" of good meat. Similarly, every doctor knows, more or less, what he means by "tuberculosis"; but he may not always recognize it. And even though there may be (by now) batteries of tests which amount almost to a decision method—that is to say, to a *criterion*—sixty years ago there certainly were no such batteries of tests at the disposal of doctors, and no criterion. But doctors knew then very well what they meant—a lung infection due to a certain kind of microbe.

Admittedly, a criterion—a definite method of decision—if we could obtain one, might make everything clearer and more definite and more precise. It is therefore understandable that some people, hankering after precision, demand criteria. And if we can get them, the demand may be reasonable.

But it would be a mistake to believe that, before we have a criterion for deciding whether or not a man is suffering from tuberculosis, the phrase "X is suffering from tuberculosis" is meaningless; or that, before we have a criterion of the goodness or badness of meat, there is no point in considering whether or not a piece of meat has gone bad; or that, before we have a reliable lie-detector, we do not know what we mean when we say that X is deliberately lying, and should therefore not even consider this "possibility," since it is no possibility at all, but meaningless; or that, before we have a criterion of truth, we do not know what we mean when we say of a statement that it is true.

Thus those who insist that, without a criterion—a reliable test—for tuberculosis, or lying, or truth, we cannot mean anything by the words "tuberculosis" or "lying" or "true," are certainly mistaken. In fact, construction of a battery of tests for tuberculosis, or for lying, comes *after* we have established—perhaps only roughly—what we mean by "tuberculosis" or by "lying."

It is clear that in the course of developing tests for tuberculosis, we may learn a lot more about this illness; so much, perhaps, that we may say that the very meaning of the term "tuberculosis" has changed under the influence of our new knowledge, and that after the establishment of the criterion the meaning of the term is no longer the same as before. Some, perhaps, may even say that "tuberculosis" can now be defined in terms of the criterion. But this does not alter the fact that we meant something before—though we may, of course, have known less about the thing. Nor does it alter the fact that there are few diseases (if any) for which we have either a criterion or a clear definition, and that few criteria (if any) are reliable. (But if they are not reliable, we had better not call them "criteria.")

There may be no criterion which helps us to establish whether a pound note is, or is not, genuine. But should we find two pound notes with the same serial number, we should have good reasons to assert, even in the absence of a criterion, that one of them at least is a forgery; and this assertion would clearly not be made meaningless by the absence of a criterion of genuineness.

To sum up, the theory that in order to determine what a word means we must establish a criterion for its correct use, or for its correct application, is mistaken: we practically never have such a criterion.

3. CRITERION PHILOSOPHIES

The view just rejected—the view that we must have criteria in order to know what we are talking about, whether it is tuberculosis, lying, or existence, or meaning, or truth—is the overt or implicit basis of many philosophies. A philosophy of this kind may be called a *"criterion philosophy."*

Since the basic demand of a criterion philosophy cannot as a rule be met, it is clear that the adoption of a criterion-philosophy will, in many cases, lead to disappointment, and to relativism or scepticism.

I believe that it is the demand for a *criterion of truth* which has made so many people feel that the question "What is truth?" is unanswerable. *But the absence of a criterion of truth does not render the notion of truth non-significant any more than the absence of a criterion of health renders the notion of health non-significant. A sick man may seek health even though he has no criterion for it. An erring man may seek truth even though he has no criterion for it.*

And both may simply seek health, or truth, without much bothering about the meanings of these terms which they (and others) understand well enough for their purposes.

One immediate result of Tarski's work on truth is the following theorem of logic: *there can be no general criterion of truth* (except with respect to certain artificial language systems of a somewhat impoverished kind).

This result can be exactly established; and its establishment makes use of the notion of truth as correspondence with the facts.

We have here an interesting and philosophically very important result (important especially in connection with the problem of an authoritarian theory of knowledge).[3] But this result has been established with the help of a notion—in this case the notion of truth—for which we have no criterion. The unreasonable demand of the criterion-philosophies that we should not take a notion seriously before a criterion has been established would therefore, if adhered to in this case, have for ever prevented us from attaining a logical result of great philosophical interest.

Incidentally, the result that there can be no general criterion of truth is a direct consequence of the still more important result (which Tarski obtained by combining Gödel's undecidability theorem with his own theory of truth) that there can be no general criterion of truth even for the comparatively narrow field of number theory, or for any science which makes full use of arithmetic. It applies *a fortiori* to truth in any extra-mathematical field in which unrestricted use is made of arithmetic.

4. FALLIBILISM

All this shows not only that some still fashionable forms of scepticism and relativism are mistaken, but also that they are obsolete; that they are based on a logical confusion—between the meaning of a term and the criterion of its proper application—although the means for clearing up this confusion have been readily available for some thirty years.

It must be admitted, however, that there is a kernel of truth in both scepticism and relativism. The kernel of truth is just that there exists no general criterion of truth. But this does not warrant the conclusion that the choice between competing theories is arbitrary. It merely means, quite simply, that we can always err in our choice—that we can always miss the truth, or fall short of the truth; that certainty is not for us (nor even knowledge that is highly probable, as I have shown in various places, for example in chapter 10 of *Conjectures and Refutations*); that we are fallible.

This, for all we know, is no more than the plain truth. There are few fields of human endeavour, if any, which seem to be exempt from human fallibility. What we once thought to be well-established, or even certain, may later turn out to be not quite correct (but this means false), and in need of correction.

A particularly impressive example of this is the discovery of heavy water, and of heavy hydrogen (*deuterium*, first separated by Harold C. Urey in 1931). Prior to this discovery, nothing more certain and more settled could be imagined in the field of chemistry than our knowledge of water (H_2O) and of the chemical elements of which it is composed. Water was even used for the "operational" definition of the gramme, the unit standard of mass of the "absolute" metric system; it thus formed one of the basic units of experimental physical measurements. This illustrates the fact that our knowledge of water was believed to be so well established that it could be used as the firm basis of all other physical measurements. But after the discovery of heavy water, it was realized that what had been believed to be a chemically pure compound was actually a mixture of chemically indistinguishable but physically very different compounds, with very different densities, boiling points, and freezing points—though for the definitions of all these points, "water" had been used as a standard base.

This historical incident is typical; and we may learn from it that we cannot foresee which parts of our scientific knowledge may come to grief one day. Thus the belief in scientific certainty and in the authority of science is just wishful thinking: *science is fallible, because science is human.*

But the fallibility of our knowledge—or the thesis that all knowledge is guesswork, though some consists of guesses which have been most severely tested—must not be cited in support of scepticism or relativism. From the fact that we can err, and that a criterion of truth which might save us from error does not exist, it does not follow that the choice between theories is arbitrary, or non-rational: that we cannot learn, or get nearer to the truth: that our knowledge cannot grow.

5. FALLIBILISM AND THE GROWTH OF KNOWLEDGE

By "fallibilism" I mean here the view, or the acceptance of the fact, that we may err, and that the quest for certainty (or even the quest for high probability) is a mistaken quest. But this does not imply that the quest for truth is mistaken. On the contrary, the idea of error implies that of truth as the standard of which we may fall short. It implies that, though we may seek for truth, and though we may even find truth (as I believe we do in very many cases), we can never be quite certain that we have found it. There is always a possibility of error; though in the case of some logical and mathematical proofs, this possibility may be considered slight.

But fallibilism need in no way give rise to any sceptical or relativist conclusions. This will become clear if we consider that all the *known* historical examples of human fallibility—including all the *known* examples of miscarriage of justice—are *examples of the advance of our knowledge.* Every discovery of a mistake constitutes a real advance in our knowledge. As Roger Martin du Gard says in *Fean Barois,* "it is something if we know where truth is not to be found."

For example, although the discovery of heavy water showed that we were badly mistaken, this was not only an advance in our knowledge, but it was in its turn connected with other advances, and it produced many further advances. *Thus we can learn from our mistakes.*

This fundamental insight is, indeed, the basis of all epistemology and methodology; for it gives us a hint how to learn more systematically, how to advance more quickly (not necessarily in the interests of technology; for each individual seeker after truth, the problem of how to hasten one's advance is most urgent). This hint, very simply, is that *we must search for our mistakes*—or in other words, that *we must try to criticize our theories.*

Criticism, it seems, is the only way we have of detecting our mistakes, and of learning from them in a systematic way.

6. GETTING NEARER TO THE TRUTH

In all this, the idea of the growth of knowledge—of getting nearer to the truth—is decisive. Intuitively, this idea is as clear as the idea of truth itself. A statement is true if it corresponds to the facts. It is nearer to the truth than another statement if it corresponds to the facts more closely than the other statement.

But though this idea is intuitively clear enough, and its legitimacy is hardly questioned by ordinary people or by scientists, it has, like the idea of truth, been attacked as illegitimate by some philosophers (for example quite recently by W. V. Quine).[4] It may therefore be mentioned here that, combining two analyses of Tarski, I have recently been able to give a "definition" of the idea of approaching to truth in the purely logical terms of Tarski's theory. (I simply combined the ideas of truth and of content, obtaining the idea of the truth-content of a statement *a*, i.e. the class of all true statements following from *a*, and its falsity content, which can be defined, roughly, as its content minus its truth content. We can then say that a statement *a* gets nearer to the truth than a statement *b* if and only if its truth content has increased without an increase in its falsity content; see chapter 10 of my *Conjectures and Refutations*.) There is therefore no reason whatever to be sceptical about the notion of getting nearer to the truth, or of the advancement of knowledge. And though we may always err, we have in many cases (especially in cases of crucial tests deciding between two theories) a fair idea of whether or not we have in fact got nearer to the truth.

It should be very clearly understood that the idea of one statement *a* getting nearer to the truth than another statement *b* in no way interferes with the idea that every statement is either true or false, and that there is no third possibility. It only takes account of the fact that there may be a lot of truth in a false statement. If I say "It is half past three—too late to catch the 3:35" then my statement might be false because it was not too late for the 3:35 (since the 3:35 happened to be four minutes late). But there was still a lot of truth—of true information—in my statement; and though I might have added "unless indeed the 3:35 is late (which it rarely is)," and thereby added to its truth-content, this additional remark might well have been taken as understood. (My statement might also have been false because it was only 3:28 not 3:30, when I made it. But even then there was a lot of truth in it.)

A theory like Kepler's which describes the track of the planets with remarkable accuracy may be said to contain a lot of true information, even though it is a false theory because deviations from Kepler's ellipses do occur.

And Newton's theory (even though we may assume here that it is false) contains, for all we know, a staggering amount of true information—much more than Kepler's theory. Thus Newton's theory is a better approximation than Kepler's—it gets nearer to the truth. But this does not make it true: it can be nearer to the truth and it can, at the same time, be a false theory.

7. ABSOLUTISM

The idea of a philosophical absolutism is rightly repugnant to many people since it is, as a rule, combined with a dogmatic and authoritarian claim to possess the truth, or a criterion of truth.

But there is another form of absolutism—a fallibilistic absolutism—which indeed rejects all this: it merely asserts that our mistakes, at least, are absolute mistakes, in the sense that if a theory deviates from the truth, it is simply false, even if the mistake made was less glaring than that in another theory. Thus the notions of truth, and of falling short of the truth, can represent absolute standards for the fallibilist. This kind of absolutism is completely free from any taint of authoritarianism. And it is a great help in serious critical discussions. Of course, it can be criticized in its turn, in accordance with the principle that *nothing is exempt from criticism.* But at least at the moment it seems to me unlikely that criticism of the (logical) theory of truth and the theory of getting nearer to the truth will succeed.

8. SOURCES OF KNOWLEDGE

The principle that *everything is open to criticism* (from which this principle itself is not exempt) leads to a simple solution of the problem of the sources of knowledge, as I have tried to show elsewhere (see the Introduction to my *Conjectures and Refutations*). It is this: every "source"—tradition, reason, imagination, observation, or what not—is admissible and may be used, *but none has any authority.*

This denial of authority to the sources of knowledge attributes to them a role very different from that which they were supposed to play in past and present epistemologies. But it is part of our critical and fallibilist approach: every source is welcome, but no statement is immune from criticism, whatever its "source" may be. Tradition, more especially, which both the intellectualists (Descartes) and the empiricists (Bacon) tended to reject, can be admitted by us as one of the most important "sources," since almost all that we learn (from our elders, in school, from books) stems from it. I therefore hold that anti-traditionalism must be rejected as futile. Yet traditionalism—which stresses the authority of traditions—must be rejected too; not as futile, but as mistaken—just as mistaken as any other epistemology which accepts some source of knowledge (intellectual intuition, say, or sense intuition) as an authority, or a guarantee, or a criterion, of truth.

9. IS A CRITICAL METHOD POSSIBLE?

But if we really reject any claim to authority, of any particular source of knowledge, how can we then criticize any theory? Does not all criticism proceed from some assumptions? *Does not the validity of any criticism, therefore, depend upon the truth of these assumptions?* And what is the good of criticizing a theory if the criticism should turn out to be invalid? Yet in order to show that it is valid, must we not establish, or justify, its assumptions? And is not the establishment or the justification of any assumption just the thing which everybody attempts (though often in vain) and which I here declare to be impossible? But if it is impossible, is not then (valid) criticism impossible too?

I believe that it is this series of questions or objections which has largely barred the way to a (tentative) acceptance of the point of view here advocated: as these questions show, one may easily be led to believe that the critical method is, logically considered, in the same boat with all other methods: since it cannot work without making assumptions, it would have to establish or justify those assumptions; yet the whole point of our argument was that we cannot establish or justify anything as certain, or even as probable, but have to content ourselves with theories which withstand criticism.

Obviously, these objections are very serious. They bring out the importance of our principle that nothing is exempt from criticism, or should be held to be exempt from criticism—not even this principle of the critical method itself.

Thus these objections constitute an interesting and important criticism of my position. But this criticism can in its turn be criticized; and it can be refuted.

First of all, even if we were to admit that all criticism starts from certain assumptions, this would not necessarily mean that, for it to be valid criticism, these assumptions must be established and justified. For the assumptions may, for example, be part of the theory against which the criticism is directed. (In this case we speak of "immanent criticism.") Or they may be assumptions which would be generally found acceptable, even though they do not form part of the theory criticized. In this case the criticism would amount to pointing out that the theory criticized contradicts (unknown to its defenders) some generally accepted views. This kind of criticism may be very valuable even when it is unsuccessful; for it may lead the defenders of the criticized theory to question those generally accepted views, and this may lead to important discoveries. (An interesting example is the history of Dirac's theory of anti-particles.)

Or they may be assumptions which are of the nature of a competing theory (in which case the criticism may be called "transcendent criticism," in contradistinction to "immanent criticism"): the assumptions may be, for example, hypotheses, or guesses, which can be independently criticized and tested. In this case the criticism offered would amount to a challenge to carry out certain crucial tests in order to decide between two competing theories.

These examples show that the important objections raised here against my theory of criticism are based upon the untenable dogma that criticism, in order to be "valid," must proceed from assumptions which are established or justified.

Moreover, criticism may be important, enlightening, and even fruitful, without being valid: the arguments used in order to reject some invalid criticism may throw a lot of new light upon a theory, and can be used as a (tentative) argument in its favour; and of a theory which can thus defend itself against criticism we may well say that it is supported by critical arguments.

Quite generally, we may say that valid criticism of a theory consists in pointing out that a theory does not succeed in solving the *problems* which it was supposed to solve; and if we look at criticism in this light then it certainly need not be dependent on any particular set of assumptions (that is, it can be "immanent"), even though it may well be that some assumptions which were foreign to the theory under discussion (that is, some "transcendent" assumptions) inspired it to start with.

10. DECISIONS

From the point of view here developed, theories are not, in general, capable of being established or justified; and although they may be supported by critical arguments, this support is never conclusive. Accordingly, we shall frequently have to make up our minds whether or not these critical arguments are strong enough to justify the *tentative* acceptance of the theory—or in other words, whether the theory seems preferable, in the light of the critical discussion, to the competing theories.

In this sense, *decisions* enter into the critical method. But it is always a tentative decision, and a decision subject to criticism.

As such it should be contrasted with what has been called "decision" or "leap in the dark" by some irrationalist or anti-rationalist or existentialist philosophers. These philosophers, probably under the impact of the argument (rejected in the preceding section) of the impossibility of criticism without presuppositions, developed the theory that all our tenets must be based on some fundamental decision—on some leap in the dark. It must be a decision, a leap, which we take with closed eyes, as it were; for as we cannot "know" without assumptions, without already having taken up a fundamental position, this fundamental position cannot be taken up on the basis of knowledge. It is, rather, a choice—but a kind of fateful and almost irrevocable choice, one which we take blindly, or by instinct, or by chance, or by the grace of God.

Our rejection of the objections presented in the preceding section shows that the irrationalist view of decisions is an exaggeration as well as an overdramatization. Admittedly, we must decide. But unless we decide against listening to argument and reason, against learning from our mistakes, and against listening to others who may have objections to our views, our decisions need not be final; not even the decision to consider criticism. (It is only in its decision *not* to take an irrevocable leap into the darkness of irrationality that rationalism may be said not to be self-contained.)

I believe that the critical theory of knowledge here sketched throws some light upon the great problems of all theories of knowledge: how it is that we know so much and so little; and how it is that we can lift ourselves slowly out of the swamp of ignorance—by our own bootstraps, as it were. We do so by working with guesses, and by improving upon our guesses, through criticism.

11. SOCIAL AND POLITICAL PROBLEMS

The theory of knowledge sketched in the preceding sections of this *addendum* seems to me to have important consequences for the evaluation of the social situation of our time, a situation influenced to a large extent by the decline of authoritarian religion. This decline has led to a widespread relativism and nihilism: to the decline of all beliefs, even the belief in human reason, and thus in ourselves.

But the argument here developed shows that there are no grounds whatever for drawing such desperate conclusions. The relativistic and the nihilistic (and even the "existentialistic.") arguments are all based on faulty reasoning. In this they show, incidentally, that these philosophies actually do accept reason, but are unable to use it properly; in their own terminology we might say that they fail to understand "the human situation," and especially man's ability to grow, intellectually and morally.

As a striking illustration of this misunderstanding—of desperate consequences drawn from an insufficient understanding of the epistemological situation—I will quote a passage from one of Nietzsche's *Tracts Against the Times* (from section 3 of his essay on Schopenhauer).

> This was the first danger in whose shadow Schopenhauer grew up: isolation. The second was: despair of finding the truth. This latter danger is the constant companion of every thinker who sets out from Kant's philosophy; that is if he is a real man, a living human being, able to suffer and yearn, and not a mere rattling automation, a mere thinking and calculating machine . . . Though I am reading everywhere that [owing to Kant] . . . a revolution has started in all fields of thought, I cannot believe that this is so as yet . . . But should Kant one day begin to exert a more general influence, then we shall find that this will take the form of a creeping and destructive scepticism and relativism; and only the most active and the most noble of minds . . . will instead experience that deep emotional shock, and that despair of truth, which was felt for example by Heinrich von Kleist . . . "Recently," he wrote, in his moving way, "I have become acquainted with the philosophy of Kant; and I must tell you of a thought of which I need not be afraid that it will shake you as deeply and as painfully as it shook me:—It is impossible for us to decide whether that to which we appeal as truth is in truth the truth, or whether it merely seems to us so. If it is the latter, then all that truth to which we may attain here will be as nothing after our death, and all our efforts to

produce and acquire something that might survive us must be in vain.—If the sharp point of this thought does not pierce your heart, do not smile at one who feels wounded by it in the holiest depth of his soul. My highest, my only aim has fallen to the ground, and I have none left."

I agree with Nietzsche that Kleist's words are moving; and I agree that Kleist's reading of Kant's doctrine that it is impossible to attain any knowledge of things in themselves is straightforward enough, even though it conflicts with Kant's own intentions; for Kant believed in the possibility of science, and of finding the truth. (It was only the need to explain the paradox of the existence of an a priori science of nature which led him to adopt that subjectivism which Kleist rightly found shocking.) Moreover, Kleist's despair is at least partly the result of disappointment—of seeing the downfall of an over-optimistic belief in a simple criterion of truth (such as self-evidence). Yet whatever may be the history of this philosophic despair, it is not called for. Though truth is not self-revealing (as Cartesians and Baconians thought), though certainty may be unattainable, the human situation with respect to knowledge is far from desperate. On the contrary, it is exhilarating: here we are, with the immensely difficult task before us of getting to know the beautiful world we live in, and ourselves; and fallible though we are we nevertheless find that our powers of understanding, surprisingly, are almost adequate for the task—more so than we ever dreamt in our wildest dreams. We really do learn from our mistakes, by trial and error. And at the same time we learn how little we know—as when, in climbing a mountain, every step upwards opens some new vista into the unknown, and new worlds unfold themselves of whose existence we knew nothing when we began our climb.

Thus we can *learn,* we can *grow* in knowledge, even if we can never *know*—that is, know for certain. Since we can learn, there is no reason for despair of reason; and since we can never know, there are no grounds here for smugness, or for conceit over the growth of our knowledge.

It may be said that this new way of knowing is too abstract and too sophisticated to replace the loss of authoritarian religion. This may be true. But we must not underrate the power of the intellect and the intellectuals. It was the intellectuals—the "second-hand dealers in ideas," as F. A. Hayek calls them—who spread relativism, nihilism, and intellectual despair. There is no reason why some intellectuals—some more enlightened intellectuals—should not eventually succeed in spreading the good news that the nihilist ado was indeed about nothing.

12. DUALISM OF FACTS AND STANDARDS

In the body of this book I spoke about the *dualism of facts and decisions,* and I pointed out, following L. J. Russell, that this dualism may be described as one of propositions and proposals. The latter terminology has the advantage of reminding us that both propositions, which state facts, and proposals, which propose policies, including principles or standards of policy, are open to rational discussion. Moreover, a decision—one, say, concerning the adoption of a principle of conduct—reached after the discussion of a proposal, may well be tentative, and it may be in many respects very similar to a decision to adopt (also tentatively), as the best available hypothesis, a proposition which states a fact.

There is, however, an important difference here. For the proposal to adopt a policy or a standard, its discussion, and the decision to adopt it, may be said to *create* this policy or this standard. On the other hand, the proposal of a hypothesis, its discussion, and the decision to adopt it—or to accept a proposition—does not, in the same sense, create a fact. This, I suppose, was the reason why I thought that the term "decision" would be able to express the contrast between the acceptance of policies or standards, and the acceptance of facts. Yet there is no doubt that it would have been clearer had I spoken of a *dualism of facts and policies,* or of a *dualism of facts and standards,* rather than of a dualism of facts and decisions.

Terminology apart, the important thing is the irreducible dualism itself: whatever the facts may be, and whatever the standards may be (for example, the principles of our policies), the first thing is to distinguish the two, and to see clearly why standards cannot be reduced to facts.

13. PROPOSALS AND PROPOSITIONS

There is, then, a decisive asymmetry between standards and facts: through the decision to accept a proposal (at least tentatively) we create the corresponding standard (at least tentatively); yet through the decision to accept a proposition we do *not* create the corresponding fact.

Another asymmetry is that standards always *pertain to* facts, and that facts are *evaluated by* standards; these are relations which cannot be simply turned round.

Whenever we are faced with a fact—and more especially, with a fact which we may be able to change—we can ask whether or not it complies with certain standards. It is important to realize that this is very far from being the same as asking whether we like it; for although we may often adopt standards which correspond to our likes or dislikes, and although our likes and dislikes may play an important role in inducing us to adopt or reject some proposed standard, there will as a rule be many other possible standards which we have not adopted; and it will be possible to judge, or evaluate, the facts by any of them. This shows that the relationship of evaluation (of some questionable fact by some adopted or rejected standard) is, logically considered, totally different from a person's psychological relation (which is not a standard but a fact), of like or dislike, to the fact in question, or to the standard in question. Moreover, our likes and dislikes are facts which can be evaluated like any other facts.

Similarly, the fact that a certain standard has been adopted or rejected by some person or by some society must, as a fact, be distinguished from *any* standard, including the adopted or rejected standard. And since it is a fact (and an alterable fact) it may be judged or evaluated by some (other) standards.

These are a few reasons why standards and facts, and therefore proposals and propositions, should be clearly and decisively distinguished. Yet once they have been distinguished, we may look not only at the dissimilarities of facts and standards but also at their similarities.

First, both proposals and propositions are alike in that we can discuss them, criticize them, and come to some decision about them. Secondly, there is some kind of regulative idea about both. In the realm of facts it is the idea of correspondence between a statement or a proposition and a fact; that is to say, the idea of truth. In the realm of standards, or of proposals, the regulative idea may be described in many ways, and called by many terms, for example, by the terms "right" or "good." We may say of a proposal that it is right (or wrong) or perhaps good (or bad); and by this we may mean, perhaps, that it corresponds (or does not correspond) to certain standards which we have decided to adopt. But we may also say of a standard that it is right or wrong, or good or bad, or valid or invalid, or high or low; and by this we may mean, perhaps, that the corresponding proposal should or should not be accepted. It must therefore be admitted that the logical situation of the regulative ideas, of "right," say, or "good," is far less clear than that of the idea of correspondence to the facts.

This difficulty is a logical one and cannot be got over by the introduction of a religious system of standards. The fact that God, or any other authority, commands me to do a certain thing is no guarantee that the command is right. It is I who must decide whether to accept the standards of any authority as (morally) good or bad. God is good only if His commandments are good; it would be a grave mistake—in fact an immoral adoption of authoritarianism—to say that His commandments are good simply because they are His, unless we have first decided (at our own risk) that He can only demand good or right things of us.

This is Kant's idea of autonomy, as opposed to heteronomy.

Thus no appeal to authority, not even to religious authority, can get us out of the difficulty that the regulative idea of absolute "rightness" or "goodness" differs in its logical status from that of absolute truth; and we have to admit the difference. This difference is responsible for the fact, alluded to above, that in a sense we *create* our standards by proposing, discussing, and adopting them.

All this must be admitted; nevertheless we may take the idea of absolute truth—of correspondence to the facts—as a kind of model for the realm of standards, in order to make it clear to ourselves that, just as we may *seek* for absolutely true propositions in the realm of facts or at least for propositions which come nearer to the truth, so we may *seek* for absolutely right or valid proposals in the realm of standards—or at least for better, or more valid, proposals.

However, it would be a mistake, in my opinion, to extend this attitude beyond the *seeking* to the *finding*. For though we should seek for absolutely right or valid proposals, we should never persuade ourselves that we have definitely found them; for clearly, there cannot be a *criterion of absolute right-ness*—even less than a criterion of absolute truth. The maximization of happiness *may* have been intended as a criterion. On the other hand I certainly never recommended that we adopt the minimization of misery as a criterion, though I think that it is an improvement on some of the ideas of utilitarianism. I also suggested that the reduction of avoidable misery belongs to the agenda of public policy (which does not mean that any question of public policy is to be decided by a calculus of minimizing misery) while the maximization of one's happiness should be left to one's private endeavour. (I quite agree with those critics of mine who have shown that if used as a *criterion*, the minimum misery principle would have absurd consequences; and I expect that the same may be said about any other moral criterion.)

But although we have no criterion of absolute rightness, we certainly can make progress in this realm. As in the realm of facts, we can make discoveries. That cruelty is always "bad"; that it should always be avoided where possible; that the golden rule is a good standard which can perhaps even be improved by doing unto others, wherever possible, as *they* want to be done by: these are elementary and extremely important examples of discoveries in the realm of standards.

These discoveries create standards, we might say, out of nothing: as in the field of factual discovery, we have to lift ourselves by our own bootstraps. This is the incredible fact: that we can learn; by our mistakes, and by criticism; and that we can learn in the realm of standards just as well as in the realm of facts.

14. TWO WRONGS DO NOT MAKE TWO RIGHTS

Once we have accepted the absolute theory of truth it is possible to answer an old and serious yet deceptive argument in favour of relativism, of both the intellectual and the evaluative kind, by making use of the analogy between true facts and valid standards. The deceptive argument I have in mind appeals to the discovery that other people have ideas and beliefs which differ widely from ours. Who are we to insist that ours are the right ones? Already Xenophanes sang, 2500 years ago (Diels-Kranz, B, 16, 15):

> The Ethiops say that their gods are flat-nosed and black,
> While the Thracians say that theirs have blue eyes and red hair.
> Yet if cattle or horses or lions had hands and could draw,
> And could sculpture like men, then the horses would draw their gods
> Like horses, and cattle like cattle; and each they would shape
> Bodies of gods in the likeness, each kind, of their own.

So each of us sees his gods, and his world, from his own point of view, according to his tradition and his upbringing; and none of us is exempt from this subjective bias.

This argument has been developed in various ways; and it has been argued that our race, or our nationality, or our historical background, or our historical period, or our class interest, or our social habitat, or our language, or our personal background knowledge, is an insurmountable, or an almost insurmountable, barrier to objectivity.

The facts on which this argument is based must be admitted; and indeed, we can never rid ourselves of bias. There is, however, no need to accept the argument itself, or its relativistic conclusions. For first of all, we can, in stages, get rid of some of this bias, by means of critical thinking and especially of listening to criticism. For example, Xenophanes doubtless was helped, by his own discovery, to see things in a less biased way. Secondly, it is a fact that people with the most divergent cultural backgrounds can enter into fruitful discussion, provided they are interested in getting nearer to the truth, and are ready to listen to each other, and to learn from each other. This shows that, though there are cultural and linguistic barriers, they are not insurmountable.

Thus it is of the utmost importance to profit from Xenophanes' discovery in every field; to give up cocksureness, and become open to criticism. Yet it is also of the greatest importance not to mistake this discovery, this step towards criticism, for a step towards relativism. If two parties disagree, this may mean that one is wrong, or the other, or both: this is the view of the criticist. It does not mean, as the relativist will have it, that both may be equally right. They may be equally wrong, no doubt, though they need not be. But anybody who says that to be equally wrong means to be equally right is merely playing with words, or with metaphors.

It is a great step forward to learn to be self-critical; to learn to think that the other fellow may be right—more right than we ourselves. But there is a great danger involved in this: we may think that both, the other fellow and we ourselves, may be right. But this attitude, modest and self-critical as it may appear to us, is neither as modest nor as self-critical as we may be inclined to think; for it is more likely that both, we ourselves and the other fellow, are wrong. Thus self-criticism should not be an excuse for laziness and for the adoption of relativism. And as two wrongs do not make a right, two wrong parties to a dispute do not make two right parties.

15. "EXPERIENCE" AND "INTUITION" AS SOURCES OF KNOWLEDGE

The fact that we can learn from our mistakes, and through criticism, in the realm of standards as well as in the realm of facts, is of fundamental importance. But is the appeal to criticism sufficient? Do we not have to appeal to the authority of experience or (especially in the realm of standards) of intuition?

In the realm of facts, we do not merely criticize our theories, we criticize them by an appeal to experimental and observational *experience*. It is a serious mistake, however, to believe that we can appeal to anything like an *authority* of experience, though philosophers, particularly empiricist philosophers, have depicted sense perception, and especially sight, as a source of knowledge which furnishes us with definite "data" out of which our experience is composed. I believe that this picture is totally mistaken. For even our experimental and observational experience does not consist of "data." Rather, it consists of a web of guesses—of conjectures, expectations, hypotheses, with which there are interwoven accepted, traditional, scientific, and unscientific, lore and prejudice. There simply is no such thing as *pure* experimental and observational experience—experience untainted by expectation and theory. There are no pure "data," no empirically given "sources of knowledge" to which we can appeal, in our criticism. "Experience," whether ordinary or scientific experience, is much more like what Oscar Wilde had in mind in *Lady Windermere's Fan*, Act iii:

> DUMBY: Experience is the name everyone gives to their mistakes.
>
> CECIL GRAHAM: One shouldn't commit any.
>
> DUMBY: Life would be very dull without them.

Learning from our mistakes—without which life would indeed be dull—is also the meaning of "experience" which is implied in Dr. Johnson's famous joke about "the triumph of hope over experience"; or in C. C. King's remark (in his *Story of the British Army*, 1897, p. 112): "But the British leaders were to learn . . . in the 'only school fools learn in, that of experience.'"

It seems, then, that at least some of the ordinary uses of "experience" agree much more closely with what I believe to be the character of both "scientific experience" and "ordinary empirical knowledge" than with the traditional analyses of the philosophers of the empiricist schools. And all this seems to agree also with the original meaning of "*empeiria*" (from "*peiraō*"—to try, to test, to examine) and thus of "*experientia*" and "*experimentum*." Yet it must not be held to constitute an argument; neither one from ordinary usage nor one from origin. It is intended only to illustrate my logical analysis of the structure of experience. According to this analysis, experience, and more especially scientific experience, is the result of usually mistaken guesses, of testing them, and of learning from our mistakes. Experience (in this sense) is not a "source of knowledge"; nor does it carry any authority.

Thus criticism which appeals to experience is not of an authoritative character. It does not consist in contrasting dubious results with established ones, or with "the evidence of our senses" (or with "the given"). It consists, rather, in comparing some dubious results with others, often equally dubious, which may, however, be taken as unproblematic for the moment, although they may at any time be challenged as new doubts arise, or else because of some inkling or conjecture; an inkling or a conjecture, for example, that a certain experiment may lead to a new discovery.

Now the situation in acquiring knowledge about standards seems to me altogether analogous.

Here, too, philosophers have looked for the authoritative *sources* of this knowledge, and they found, in the main, two: feelings of pleasure and pain, or a moral sense or a moral intuition for what is right or wrong (analogous to perception in the epistemology of factual knowledge), or, alternatively, a source called "practical reason" (analogous to "pure reason," or to a faculty of "intellectual intuition," in the epistemology of factual knowledge). And quarrels continually raged over the question whether all, or only some, of these authoritative sources of moral knowledge existed.

I think that this problem is a pseudo-problem. The main point is not the question of the "existence" of any of these faculties—a very vague and dubious psychological question—but whether these may be authoritative "sources of knowledge" providing us with "data" or other definite starting-points for our constructions or, at least, with a definite frame of reference for our criticism. I deny that we have any authoritative sources of this kind, either in the epistemology of factual knowledge or in the epistemology of the knowledge of standards. And I deny that we need any such definite frame of reference for our criticism.

How do we learn about standards? How, in this realm, do we learn from our mistakes? First we learn to imitate others (incidentally, we do so by trial and error), and so learn to look upon standards of behaviour as if they consisted of fixed, "given" rules. Later we find (also by trial and error) that we are making mistakes—for example, that we may hurt people. We may thus learn the golden rule; but soon we find that we may misjudge a man's attitude, his background knowledge, his aims, his standards; and we may learn from our mistakes to take care even beyond the golden rule.

Admittedly, such things as sympathy and imagination may play an important role in this development; but they are not authoritative sources of knowledge—no more than any of our sources in the realm of the knowledge of facts. And though something like an intuition of what is right and what is wrong may also play an important role in this development, it is, again, not an authoritative source of knowledge. For we may see today very clearly that we are right, and yet learn tomorrow that we made a mistake.

"Intuitionism" is the name of a philosophical school which teaches that we have some faculty or capacity of intellectual intuition allowing us to "see" the truth; so that what we have seen to be true must indeed be true. It is thus a theory of some authoritative source of knowledge. Anti-intuitionists have usually denied the existence of this source of knowledge while asserting, as a rule, the existence of some other source such as sense-perception. My view is that both parties are mistaken, for two reasons. First, I assert that there exists something like an intellectual intuition which makes us feel, most convincingly, that we see the truth (a point denied by the opponents of intuitionism). Secondly, I assert that this intellectual intuition, though in a way indispensable, often leads us astray in the most dangerous manner. Thus we do not, in general, see the truth when we are most convinced that we see it; and we have to learn, through mistakes, to distrust these intuitions.

What, then, are we to trust? What are we to accept? The answer is: whatever we accept we should trust only tentatively, always remembering that we are in possession, at best, of partial truth (or rightness), and that we are bound to make at least some mistake or misjudgment somewhere—not only with respect to facts but also with respect to the adopted standards; secondly, we should trust (even tentatively) our intuition only if it has been arrived at as the result of many attempts to use our imagination; of many mistakes, of many tests, of many doubts, and of searching criticism.

It will be seen that this form of anti-intuitionism (or some may say, perhaps, of intuitionism) is radically different from the older forms of anti-intuitionism. And it will be seen that there is one essential ingredient in this theory: the idea that we may fall short—perhaps always—of some standard of absolute truth, or of absolute rightness, in our opinions as well as in our actions.

It may be objected to all this that, whether or not my views on the nature of ethical knowledge and ethical experience are acceptable, they are still "relativist" or "subjectivist." For they do not *establish* any absolute moral standards: at best they show that the idea of an absolute standard is a regulative idea, of use to those who are already converted—who are already eager to learn about, and search for, true or valid or good moral standards. My reply is that even the "establishment"—say, by means of pure logic—of an absolute standard, or a system of ethical norms, would make no difference in this respect. For assuming we have succeeded in logically proving the validity of an absolute standard, or a system of ethical norms, so that we could logically prove to somebody how he ought to act: even then he might take no notice; or else he might reply: "I am not in the least interested in your 'ought,' or in your moral rules—no more so than in your logical proofs, or, say, in your higher mathematics." Thus even a logical proof cannot alter the fundamental situation that only he who is prepared to take these things seriously and to learn about them will be impressed by ethical (or any other) arguments. You cannot force anybody by arguments to take arguments seriously, or to respect his own reason.

16. THE DUALISM OF FACTS AND STANDARDS AND THE IDEA OF LIBERALISM

The dualism of facts and standards is, I contend, one of the bases of the liberal tradition. For an essential part of this tradition is the recognition of the injustice that does exist in this world, and the resolve to try to help those who are its victims. This means that there is, or that there may be, a conflict, or at least a gap, between facts and standards: facts may fall short of right (or valid or true) standards—especially those social or political facts which consist in the actual acceptance and enforcement of some code of justice.

To put it in another way, liberalism is based upon the dualism of facts and standards in the sense that it believes in searching for ever better standards, especially in the field of politics and of legislation.

But this dualism of facts and standards has been rejected by some relativists who have opposed it with arguments like the following:

1. The acceptance of a proposal—and thus of a standard—is a social or political or historical fact.
2. If an accepted standard is judged by another, not yet accepted standard, and found wanting, then this judgment (whoever may have made it) is also a social or political or historical fact.
3. If a judgment of this kind becomes the basis of a social or political movement, then this is also a historical fact.
4. If this movement is successful, and if in consequence the old standards are reformed or replaced by new standards, then this is also a historical fact.
5. Thus—so argues the relativist or moral positivist—we never have to transcend the realm of facts, if only we include in it social or political or historical facts: there is no dualism of facts and standards.

I consider this conclusion (5) to be mistaken. It does not follow from the premises (1) to (4) whose truth I admit. The reason for rejecting (5) is very simple: we can always ask whether a development as here described—a social movement based upon the acceptance of a programme for the reform of certain standards—was "good" or "bad." In raising this question, we reopen the gulf between standards and facts which the monistic argument (1) to (5) attempts to close.

From what I have just said, it may be rightly inferred that the monistic position—*the philosophy of the identity of facts and standards*—is dangerous; for even where it does not identify standards with existing facts—even where it does not identify present might and right—it leads necessarily to the identification of future might and right. Since the question whether a certain movement for reform is right or wrong (or good or bad) cannot be raised, according to the monist, except in terms of another movement with opposite tendencies, nothing can be asked except the question which of these opposite movements succeeded, in the end, in establishing its standards as a matter of social or political or historical fact.

In other words, the philosophy here described—the attempt to "transcend" the dualism of facts and standards and to erect a monistic system, a world of facts only—leads to *the identification of standards either with established might or with future might:* it leads to a moral positivism, or to a moral historicism.

NOTES

1. I am deeply indebted to Dr. William W. Bartley's incisive criticism which induced me to make important changes in the present *addendum*.

2. See for example "On the Sources of Knowledge and of Ignorance," now the Introduction to my *Conjectures and Refutations* and, more especially, Chapter 10 of that book; also, of course, my *The Logic of Scientific Discovery*.

3. For a description and criticism of authoritarian (or non-fallibilist) theories of knowledge see especially sections v, vi, and x, ff., of the Introduction to my *Conjectures and Refutations*.

4. See W. V. Quine, *Word and Object*, 1959, p. 23.

3

The Challenge of
Cultural Relativism

JAMES RACHELS

> Morality differs in every society, and is a convenient term for socially
> approved habits.
>
> RUTH BENEDICT, PATTERNS OF CULTURE (1934)

HOW DIFFERENT CULTURES HAVE
DIFFERENT MORAL CODES

Darius, a king of ancient Persia, was intrigued by the variety of cultures he
encountered in his travels. He had found, for example, that the Callatians (a
tribe of Indians) customarily ate the bodies of their dead fathers. The Greeks,
of course, did not do that—the Greeks practiced cremation and regarded the
funeral pyre as the natural and fitting way to dispose of the dead. Darius
thought that a sophisticated understanding of the world must include an
appreciation of such differences between cultures. One day, to teach this lesson, he summoned some Greeks who happened to be present at his court and
asked them what they would take to eat the bodies of their dead fathers. They
were shocked, as Darius knew they would be, and replied that no amount of
money could persuade them to do such a thing. Then Darius called in some
Callatians, and while the Greeks listened asked them what they would take
to burn their dead fathers' bodies. The Callatians were horrified and told
Darius not even to mention such a dreadful thing.

This story, recounted by Herodotus in his *History,* illustrates a recurring
theme in the literature of social science: Different cultures have different
moral codes. What is thought right within one group may be utterly abhorrent to the members of another group, and vice versa. Should we eat the
bodies of the dead or burn them? If you were a Greek, one answer would

seem obviously correct; but if you were a Callatian, the opposite would seem equally certain.

It is easy to give additional examples of the same kind. Consider the Eskimos. They are a remote and inaccessible people. Numbering only about 25,000, they live in small, isolated settlements scattered mostly along the northern fringes of North America and Greenland. Until the beginning of the 20th century, the outside world knew little about them. Then explorers began to bring back strange tales.

Eskimo customs turned out to be very different from our own. The men often had more than one wife, and they would share their wives with guests, lending them for the night as a sign of hospitality. Moreover, within a community, a dominant male might demand and get regular sexual access to other men's wives. The women, however, were free to break these arrangements simply by leaving their husbands and taking up with new partners— free, that is, so long as their former husbands chose not to make trouble. All in all, the Eskimo practice was a volatile scheme that bore little resemblance to what we call marriage.

But it was not only their marriage and sexual practices that were different. The Eskimos also seemed to have less regard for human life. Infanticide, for example, was common. Knud Rasmussen, one of the most famous early explorers, reported that he met one woman who had borne 20 children but had killed 10 of them at birth. Female babies, he found, were especially liable to be destroyed, and this was permitted simply at the parents' discretion, with no social stigma attached to it. Old people also, when they became too feeble to contribute to the family, were left out in the snow to die. So there seemed to be, in this society, remarkably little respect for life.

To the general public, these were disturbing revelations. Our own way of living seems so natural and right that for many of us it is hard to conceive of others living so differently. And when we do hear of such things, we tend immediately to categorize those other peoples as "backward" or "primitive." But to anthropologists and sociologists, there was nothing particularly surprising about the Eskimos. Since the time of Herodotus, enlightened observers have been accustomed to the idea that conceptions of right and wrong differ from culture to culture. If we assume that our ideas of right and wrong will be shared by all peoples at all times, we are merely naive.

CULTURAL RELATIVISM

To many thinkers, this observation—"Different cultures have different moral codes"—has seemed to be the key to understanding morality. The idea of universal truth in ethics, they say, is a myth. The customs of different societies are all that exist. These customs cannot be said to be "correct" or "incorrect," for that implies we have an independent standard of right and wrong by which they may be judged. But there is no such independent standard; every standard is culture-bound. The great pioneering sociologist William Graham Sumner, writing in 1906, put the point like this:

The "right" way is the way which the ancestors used and which has been handed down. The tradition is its own warrant. It is not held subject to verification by experience. The notion of right is in the folkways. It is not outside of them, of independent origin, and brought to test them. In the folkways, whatever is, is right. This is because they are traditional, and therefore contain in themselves the authority of the ancestral ghosts. When we come to the folkways we are at the end of our analysis.

This line of thought has probably persuaded more people to be skeptical about ethics than any other single thing. Cultural Relativism, as it has been called, challenges our ordinary belief in the objectivity and universality of moral truth. It says, in effect, that there is no such thing as universal truth in ethics; there are only the various cultural codes, and nothing more. Moreover, our own code has no special status; it is merely one among many.

As we shall see, this basic idea is really a compound of several different thoughts. It is important to separate the various elements of the theory because, on analysis, some parts turn out to be correct, while others seem to be mistaken. As a beginning, we may distinguish the following claims, all of which have been made by cultural relativists:

1. Different societies have different moral codes.
2. There is no objective standard that can be used to judge one societal code better than another.
3. The moral code of our own society has no special status; it is merely one among many.
4. There is no "universal truth" in ethics; that is, there are no moral truths that hold for all peoples at all times.
5. The moral code of a society determines what is right within that society; that is, if the moral code of a society says that a certain action is right, then that action *is* right, at least within that society.
6. It is mere arrogance for us to try to judge the conduct of other peoples. We should adopt an attitude of tolerance toward the practices of other cultures.

Although it may seem that these six propositions go naturally together, they are independent of one another, in the sense that some of them might be false even if others are true. In what follows, we will try to identify what is correct in Cultural Relativism, but we will also be concerned to expose what is mistaken about it.

THE CULTURAL DIFFERENCES ARGUMENT

Cultural Relativism is a theory about the nature of morality. At first blush it seems quite plausible. However, like all such theories, it may be evaluated by subjecting it to rational analysis; and when we analyze Cultural Relativism we find that it is not so plausible as it first appears to be.

The first thing we need to notice is that at the heart of Cultural Relativism there is a certain *form of argument.* The strategy used by cultural relativists is to argue from facts about the differences between cultural outlooks to a conclusion about the status of morality. Thus we are invited to accept this reasoning:

1. The Greeks believed it was wrong to eat the dead, whereas the Callatians believed it was right to eat the dead.
2. Therefore, eating the dead is neither objectively right nor objectively wrong. It is merely a matter of opinion, which varies from culture to culture.

Or, alternatively:

1. The Eskimos see nothing wrong with infanticide, whereas Americans believe infanticide is immoral.
2. Therefore, infanticide is neither objectively right nor objectively wrong. It is merely a matter of opinion, which varies from culture to culture.

Clearly, these arguments are variations of one fundamental idea. They are both special cases of a more general argument, which says:

1. Different cultures have different moral codes.
2. Therefore, there is no objective "truth" in morality. Right and wrong are only matters of opinion, and opinions vary from culture to culture.

We may call this the Cultural Differences Argument. To many people, it is persuasive. But from a logical point of view, is it sound?

It is not sound. The trouble is that the conclusion does not follow from the premise—that is, even if the premise is true, the conclusion still might be false. The premise concerns what people *believe.* In some societies, people believe one thing; in other societies, people believe differently. The conclusion, however, concerns *what really is the case.* The trouble is that this sort of conclusion does not follow logically from this sort of premise.

Consider again the example of the Greeks and Callatians. The Greeks believed it was wrong to eat the dead; the Callatians believed it was right. Does it follow, *from the mere fact that they disagreed,* that there is no objective truth in the matter? No, it does not follow; for it could be that the practice was objectively right (or wrong) and that one or the other of them was simply mistaken.

To make the point clearer, consider a different matter. In some societies, people believe the earth is flat. In other societies, such as our own, people believe the earth is (roughly) spherical. Does it follow, *from the mere fact that people disagree,* that there is no "objective truth" in geography? Of course not;

we would never draw such a conclusion because we realize that, in their beliefs about the world, the members of some societies might simply be wrong. There is no reason to think that if the world is round everyone must know it. Similarly, there is no reason to think that if there is moral truth everyone must know it. The fundamental mistake in the Cultural Differences Argument is that it attempts to derive a substantive conclusion about a subject from the mere fact that people disagree about it.

This is a simple point of logic, and it is important not to misunderstand it. We are not saying (not yet, anyway) that the conclusion of the argument is false. It is still an open question whether the conclusion is true or false. The logical point is just that the conclusion does not *follow from* the premise. This is important, because in order to determine whether the conclusion is true, we need arguments in its support. Cultural Relativism proposes this argument, but unfortunately the argument turns out to be fallacious. So it proves nothing.

THE CONSEQUENCES OF TAKING CULTURAL RELATIVISM SERIOUSLY

Even if the Cultural Differences Argument is invalid, Cultural Relativism might still be true. What would it be like if it were true?

In the passage quoted above, William Graham Sumner summarizes the essence of Cultural Relativism. He says that there is no measure of right and wrong other than the standards of one's society: "The notion of right is in the folkways. It is not outside of them, of independent origin, and brought to test them. In the folkways, whatever is, is right."

Suppose we took this seriously. What would be some of the consequences?

1. *We could no longer say that the customs of other societies are morally inferior to our own.* This, of course, is one of the main points stressed by Cultural Relativism. We would have to stop condemning other societies merely because they are "different." So long as we concentrate on certain examples, such as the funerary practices of the Greeks and Callatians, this may seem to be a sophisticated, enlightened attitude.

However, we would also be stopped from criticizing other, less benign practices. Suppose a society waged war on its neighbors for the purpose of taking slaves. Or suppose a society was violently anti-Semitic and its leaders set out to destroy the Jews. Cultural Relativism would preclude us from saying that either of these practices was wrong. We would not even be able to say that a society tolerant of Jews is *better* than the anti-Semitic society, for that would imply some sort of transcultural standard of comparison. The failure to condemn *these* practices does not seem enlightened; on the contrary, slavery and anti-Semitism seem wrong wherever they occur. Nevertheless, if we took Cultural Relativism seriously, we would have to regard these social practices as also immune from criticism.

2. *We could decide whether actions are right or wrong just by consulting the standards of our society.* Cultural Relativism suggests a simple test for determining what is right and what is wrong: All one need do is ask whether the action is in accordance with the code of one's society. Suppose in 1975 a resident of South Africa was wondering whether his country's policy of *apartheid*—a rigidly racist system—was morally correct. All he has to do is ask whether this policy conformed to his society's moral code. If it did, there would have been nothing to worry about, at least from a moral point of view.

This implication of Cultural Relativism is disturbing because few of us think that our society's code is perfect; we can think of ways it might be improved. Yet Cultural Relativism would not only forbid us from criticizing the codes of other societies; it would stop us from criticizing our own. After all, if right and wrong are relative to culture, this must be true for our own culture just as much as for other cultures.

3. *The idea of moral progress is called into doubt.* Usually, we think that at least some social changes are for the better. (Although, of course, other changes may be for the worse.) Throughout most of Western history the place of women in society was narrowly circumscribed. They could not own property; they could not vote or hold political office; and generally they were under the almost absolute control of their husbands. Recently much of this has changed, and most people think of it as progress.

If Cultural Relativism is correct, can we legitimately think of this as progress? Progress means replacing a way of doing things with a better way. But by what standard do we judge the new ways as better? If the old ways were in accordance with the social standards of their time, then Cultural Relativism would say it is a mistake to judge them by the standards of a different time. Eighteenth-century society was, in effect, a different society from the one we have now. To say that we have made progress implies a judgment that present-day society is better, and that is just the sort of transcultural judgment that, according to Cultural Relativism, is impermissible.

Our idea of social *reform* will also have to be reconsidered. Reformers such as Martin Luther King, Jr., have sought to change their societies for the better. Within the constraints imposed by Cultural Relativism, there is one way this might be done. If a society is not living up to its own ideals, the reformer may be regarded as acting for the best: The ideals of the society are the standard by which we judge his or her proposals as worthwhile. But the "reformer" may not challenge the ideals themselves, for those ideals are by definition correct. According to Cultural Relativism, then, the idea of social reform makes sense only in this limited way.

These three consequences of Cultural Relativism have led many thinkers to reject it as implausible on its face. It does make sense, they say, to condemn some practices, such as slavery and anti-Semitism, wherever they occur. It makes sense to think that our own society has made some moral progress, while admitting that it is still imperfect and in need of reform. Because Cultural Relativism says that these judgments make no sense, the argument goes, it cannot be right.

WHY THERE IS LESS DISAGREEMENT THAN IT SEEMS

The original impetus for Cultural Relativism comes from the observation that cultures differ dramatically in their views of right and wrong. But just how much do they differ? It is true that there are differences. However, it is easy to overestimate the extent of those differences. Often, when we examine what seems to be a dramatic difference, we find that the cultures do not differ nearly as much as it appears.

Consider a culture in which people believe it is wrong to eat cows. This may even be a poor culture, in which there is not enough food; still, the cows are not to be touched. Such a society would appear to have values very different from our own. But does it? We have not yet asked why these people will not eat cows. Suppose it is because they believe that after death the souls of humans inhabit the bodies of animals, especially cows, so that a cow may be someone's grandmother. Now do we want to say that their values are different from ours? No; the difference lies elsewhere. The difference is in our belief systems, not in our values. We agree that we shouldn't eat Grandma; we simply disagree about whether the cow is (or could be) Grandma.

The point is that many factors work together to produce the customs of a society. The society's values are only one of them. Other matters, such as the religious and factual beliefs held by its members, and the physical circumstances in which they must live, are also important. We cannot conclude, then, merely because customs differ, that there is a disagreement about *values*. The difference in customs may be attributable to some other aspect of social life. Thus there may be less disagreement about values than there appears to be.

Consider again the Eskimos, who often kill perfectly normal infants, especially girls. We do not approve of such things; a parent who killed a baby in our society would be locked up. Thus there appears to be a great difference in the values of our two cultures. But suppose we ask why the Eskimos do this. The explanation is not that they have less affection for their children or less respect for human life. An Eskimo family will always protect its babies if conditions permit. But they live in a harsh environment, where food is in short supply. A fundamental postulate of Eskimo thought is: "Life is hard, and the margin of safety small." A family may want to nourish its babies but be unable to do so.

As in many "primitive" societies, Eskimo mothers will nurse their infants over a much longer period of time than mothers in our culture. The child will take nourishment from its mother's breast for four years, perhaps even longer. So even in the best of times there are limits to the number of infants that one mother can sustain. Moreover, the Eskimos are a nomadic people—unable to farm, they must move about in search of food. Infants must be carried, and a mother can carry only one baby in her parka as she travels and goes about her outdoor work. Other family members help whenever they can.

Infant girls are more readily disposed of because, first, in this society the males are the primary food providers—they are the hunters, according to the traditional division of labor—and it is obviously important to maintain a sufficient number of food providers. But there is an important second reason as well. Because the hunters suffer a high casualty rate, the adult men who die prematurely far outnumber the women who die early. Thus if male and female infants survived in equal numbers, the female adult population would greatly outnumber the male adult population. Examining the available statistics, one writer concluded that "were it not for female infanticide . . . there would be approximately one-and-a-half times as many females in the average Eskimo local group as there are food-producing males."

So among the Eskimos, infanticide does not signal a fundamentally different attitude toward children. Instead, it is a recognition that drastic measures are sometimes needed to ensure the family's survival. Even then, however, killing the baby is not the first option considered. Adoption is common; childless couples are especially happy to take a more fertile couple's "surplus." Killing is only the last resort. I emphasize this in order to show that the raw data of the anthropologists can be misleading; it can make the differences in values between cultures appear greater than they are. The Eskimos' values are not all that different from our values. It is only that life forces upon them choices that we do not have to make.

HOW ALL CULTURES HAVE SOME VALUES IN COMMON

It should not be surprising that, despite appearances, the Eskimos are protective of their children. How could it be otherwise? How could a group survive that did *not* value its young? It is easy to see that, in fact, all cultural groups must protect their infants:

1. Human infants are helpless and cannot survive if they are not given extensive care for a period of years.

2. Therefore, if a group did not care for its young, the young would not survive, and the older members of the group would not be replaced. After a while the group would die out.

3. Therefore, any cultural group that continues to exist must care for its young. Infants that are not cared for must be the exception rather than the rule.

Similar reasoning shows that other values must be more or less universal. Imagine what it would be like for a society to place no value at all on truth telling. When one person spoke to another, there would be no presumption at all that he was telling the truth for he could just as easily be speaking falsely. Within that society, there would be no reason to pay attention to what anyone says. (I ask you what time it is, and you say "Four o'clock." But there is no presumption that you are speaking truly; you could just as easily have said the first thing that came into your head. So I have no reason to pay attention to your answer; in fact, there was no point in my asking you in the first place.) Communication would then be extremely difficult, if not impossible. And because complex societies cannot exist without communication among their members, society would become impossible. It follows that in any complex society there must be a presumption in favor of truthfulness. There may of course be exceptions to this rule: There may be situations in which it is thought to be permissible to lie. Nevertheless, these will be exceptions to a rule that *is* in force in the society.

Here is one further example of the same type. Could a society exist in which there was no prohibition on murder? What would this be like? Suppose people were free to kill other people at will, and no one thought there was anything wrong with it. In such a "society," no one could feel secure. Everyone would have to be constantly on guard. People who wanted to survive would have to avoid other people as much as possible. This would inevitably result in individuals trying to become as self-sufficient as possible—after all, associating with others would be dangerous. Society on any large scale would collapse. Of course, people might band together in smaller groups with others that they *could* trust not to harm them. But notice what this means: They would be forming smaller societies that did acknowledge a rule against murder. The prohibition of murder, then, is a necessary feature of all societies.

There is a general theoretical point here, namely, that *there are some moral rules that all societies will have in common, because those rules are necessary for society to exist.* The rules against lying and murder are two examples. And in fact, we do find these rules in force in all viable cultures. Cultures may differ in what they regard as legitimate exceptions to the rules, but this disagreement exists against a background of agreement on the larger issues. Therefore, it is a mistake to overestimate the amount of difference between cultures. Not every moral rule can vary from society to society.

JUDGING A CULTURAL PRACTICE TO BE UNDESIRABLE

In 1996, a 17-year-old girl named Fauziya Kassindja arrived at Newark International Airport and asked for asylum. She had fled her native country of Togo, a small west African nation, to escape what people there call "excision."

Excision is a permanently disfiguring procedure that is sometimes called "female circumcision," although it bears little resemblance to the Jewish ritual. More commonly, at least in Western newspapers, it is referred to as "genital mutilation." According to the World Health Organization, the practice is widespread in 26 African nations, and two million girls each year are "excised." In some instances, excision is part of an elaborate tribal ritual, performed in small traditional villages, and girls look forward to it because it signals their acceptance into the adult world. In other instances, the practice is carried out by families living in cities on young women who desperately resist.

Fauziya Kassindja was the youngest of five daughters in a devoutly Muslim family. Her father, who owned a successful trucking business, was opposed to excision, and he was able to defy the tradition because of his wealth. His first four daughters were married without being mutilated. But when Fauziya was 16, he suddenly died. Fauziya then came under the authority of his father, who arranged a marriage for her and prepared to have her excised. Fauziya was terrified, and her mother and oldest sister helped her to escape. Her mother, left without resources, eventually had to formally apologize and submit to the authority of the patriarch she had offended.

Meanwhile, in America, Fauziya was imprisoned for two years while the authorities decided what to do with her. She was finally granted asylum, but not before she became the center of a controversy about how foreigners should regard the cultural practices of other peoples. A series of articles in the *New York Times* encouraged the idea that excision is a barbaric practice that should be condemned. Other observers were reluctant to be so judgmental—live and let live, they said; after all, our practices probably seem just as strange to them.

Suppose we are inclined to say that excision is bad. Would we merely be applying the standards of our own culture? If Cultural Relativism is correct, that is all we can do, for there is no culture-neutral moral standard to which we may appeal. Is that true?

IS THERE A CULTURE-NEUTRAL STANDARD OF RIGHT AND WRONG?

There is, of course, a lot that can be said against the practice of excision. Excision is painful and it results in the permanent loss of sexual pleasure. Its short-term effects include hemorrhage, tetanus, and septicemia. Sometimes the woman dies. Long-term effects include chronic infection, scars that hinder walking, and continuing pain.

Why, then, has it become a widespread social practice? It is not easy to say. Excision has no obvious social benefits. Unlike Eskimo infanticide, it is not necessary for the group's survival. Nor is it a matter of religion. Excision is practiced by groups with various religions, including Islam and Christianity, neither of which commend it.

Nevertheless, a number of reasons are given in its defense. Women who are incapable of sexual pleasure are said to be less likely to be promiscuous; thus there will be fewer unwanted pregnancies in unmarried women. Moreover, wives for whom sex is only a duty are less likely to be unfaithful to their husbands; and because they will not be thinking about sex, they will be more attentive to the needs of their husbands and children. Husbands, for their part, are said to enjoy sex more with wives who have been excised. (The women's own lack of enjoyment is said to be unimportant.) Men will not want unexcised women, as they are unclean and immature. And above all, it has been done since antiquity, and we may not change the ancient ways.

It would be easy, and perhaps a bit arrogant, to ridicule these arguments. But we may notice an important feature of this whole line of reasoning: it attempts to justify excision by showing that excision is beneficial—men, women, and their families are all said to be better off when women are excised. Thus we might approach this reasoning, and excision itself, by asking which is true: Is excision, on the whole, helpful or harmful?

Here, then, is the standard that might most reasonably be used in thinking about excision: We may ask *whether the practice promotes or hinders the welfare of the people whose lives are affected by it.* And, as a corollary, we may ask if there is an alternative set of social arrangements that would do a better job of promoting their welfare. If so, we may conclude that the existing practice is deficient.

But this looks like just the sort of independent moral standard that Cultural Relativism says cannot exist. It is a single standard that may be brought to bear in judging the practices of any culture, at any time, including our own. Of course, people will not usually see this principle as being "brought in from the outside" to judge them, because, like the rules against lying and homicide, the welfare of its members is a value internal to all viable cultures.

WHY THOUGHTFUL PEOPLE MAY NEVERTHELESS BE RELUCTANT TO CRITICIZE OTHER CULTURES

Although they are personally horrified by excision, many thoughtful people are reluctant to say it is wrong, for at least three reasons.

First, there is an understandable nervousness about "interfering in the social customs of other peoples." Europeans and their cultural descendents in America have a shabby history of destroying native cultures in the name of Christianity and Enlightenment, not to mention self-interest. Recoiling from this record, some people refuse to make any negative judgments about other cultures, especially cultures that resemble those that have been wronged in the past. We should notice, however, that there is a difference between (a) judging a cultural practice to be morally deficient and (b) thinking that we should announce the fact, conduct a campaign, apply diplomatic pressure, or send in the army to do something about it. The first is just a matter of trying to see the world clearly, from a moral point of view. The second is another matter altogether. Sometimes it may be right to "do something about it," but often it will not be.

People also feel, rightly enough, that they should be tolerant of other cultures. Tolerance is, no doubt, a virtue—a tolerant person is willing to live in peaceful cooperation with those who see things differently. But there is nothing in the nature of tolerance that requires you to say that all beliefs, all religions, and all social practices are equally admirable. On the contrary, if you did not think that some were better than others, there would be nothing for you to tolerate.

Finally, people may be reluctant to judge because they do not want to express contempt for the society being criticized. But again, this is misguided: To condemn a particular practice is not to say that the culture is on the whole contemptible or that it is generally inferior to any other culture, including one's own. It could have many admirable features. In fact, we should expect this to be true of most human societies—they are mixes of good and bad practices. Excision happens to be one of the bad ones.

WHAT CAN BE LEARNED FROM
CULTURAL RELATIVISM

At the outset, I said that we were going to identify both what is right and what is wrong in Cultural Relativism. Thus far I have mentioned only its mistakes: I have said that it rests on an invalid argument, that it has consequences that make it implausible on its face, and that the extent of moral disagreement is far less than it implies. This all adds up to a pretty thorough repudiation of the theory. Nevertheless, it is still a very appealing idea, and the reader may have the feeling that all this is a little unfair. The theory must have something going for it, or else why has it been so influential? In fact, I think there is something right about Cultural Relativism, and now I want to say what that is. There are two lessons we should learn from the theory, even if we ultimately reject it.

1. Cultural Relativism warns us, quite rightly, about the danger of assuming that all our preferences are based on some absolute rational standard. They are not. Many (but not all) of our practices are merely peculiar to our society, and it is easy to lose sight of that fact. In reminding us of it, the theory does a service.

Funerary practices are one example. The Callatians, according to Herodotus, were "men who eat their fathers"—a shocking idea, to us at least. But eating the flesh of the dead could be understood as a sign of respect. It could be taken as a symbolic act that says: We wish this person's spirit to dwell within us. Perhaps this was the understanding of the Callatians. On such a way of thinking, burying the dead could be seen as an act of rejection, and burning the corpse as positively scornful. If this is hard to imagine, then we may need to have our imaginations stretched. Of course we may feel a visceral repugnance at the idea of eating human flesh in any circumstances. But what of it? This repugnance may be, as the relativists say, only a matter of what is customary in our particular society.

There are many other matters that we tend to think of in terms of objective right and wrong that are really nothing more than social conventions. Should women cover their breasts? A publicly exposed breast is scandalous in our society, whereas in other cultures it is unremarkable. Objectively speaking, it is neither right nor wrong—there is no objective reason why either custom is better. Cultural Relativism begins with the valuable insight that many of our practices are like this; they are only cultural products. Then it goes wrong by inferring that, because some practices are like this, all must be.

2. The second lesson has to do with keeping an open mind. In the course of growing up, each of us has acquired some strong feelings: We have learned to think of some types of conduct as acceptable, and others we have learned to reject. Occasionally, we may find those feelings challenged. We may encounter someone who claims that our feelings are mistaken. For example, we may have been taught that homosexuality is immoral, and we may feel quite uncomfortable around gay people and see them as alien and "different." Now someone suggests that this may be a mere prejudice; that there is nothing evil about homosexuality; that gay people are just people, like anyone else, who happen, through no choice of their own, to be attracted to others of the same sex. But because we feel so strongly about the matter, we may find it hard to take this seriously. Even after we listen to the arguments, we may still have the unshakable feeling that homosexuals must, somehow, be an unsavory lot.

Cultural Relativism, by stressing that our moral views can reflect the prejudices of our society, provides an antidote for this kind of dogmatism. When he tells the story of the Greeks and Callatians, Herodotus adds:

> For if anyone, no matter who, were given the opportunity of choosing from amongst all the nations of the world the set of beliefs which he thought best, he would inevitably, after careful consideration of their relative merits, choose that of his own country. Everyone without exception believes his own native customs, and the religion he was brought up in, to be the best.

Realizing this can result in our having more open minds. We can come to understand that our feelings are not necessarily perceptions of the truth— they may be nothing more than the result of cultural conditioning. Thus when we hear it suggested that some element of our social code is *not* really the best, and we find ourselves instinctively resisting the suggestion, we might stop and remember this. Then we may be more open to discovering the truth, whatever that might be.

We can understand the appeal of Cultural Relativism, then, even though the theory has serious shortcomings. It is an attractive theory because it is based on a genuine insight that many of the practices and attitudes we think so natural are really only cultural products. Moreover, keeping this insight firmly in view is important if we want to avoid arrogance and have open minds. These are important points, not to be taken lightly. But we can accept these points without going on to accept the whole theory.

PART TWO

RELATIVISM AND MORAL DIVERSITY

4 *Folkways*

WILLIAM GRAHAM SUMNER

1. DEFINITION AND MODE OF ORIGIN OF THE FOLKWAYS

If we put together all that we have learned from anthropology and ethnography about primitive men and primitive society, we perceive that the first task of life is to live. Men begin with acts, not with thoughts. Every moment brings necessities which must be satisfied at once. Need was the first experience, and it was followed at once by a blundering effort to satisfy it. It is generally taken for granted that men inherited some guiding instincts from their beast ancestry, and it may be true, although it has never been proved. If there were such inheritances, they controlled and aided the first efforts to satisfy needs. Analogy makes it easy to assume that the ways of beasts had produced channels of habit and predisposition along which dexterities and other psychophysical activities would run easily. Experiments with newborn animals show that in the absence of any experience of the relation of means to ends, efforts to satisfy needs are clumsy and blundering. The method is that of trial and failure, which produces repeated pain, loss, and disappointments. Nevertheless, it is a method of rude experiment and selection. The earliest efforts of men were of this kind. Need was the impelling force. Pleasure and pain, on the one side and the other, were the rude constraints which defined the line on which efforts must proceed. The ability to distinguish between pleasure and pain is the only psychical power which is to be assumed. Thus ways of doing things were selected, which were expedient. They answered the purpose better than other ways, or with less toil and pain. Along the course on which efforts were compelled to go, habit, routine, and skill were developed. The struggle to maintain existence was carried on, not individually, but in groups. Each profited by the other's experience; hence there was concurrence towards that which proved to be most expedient. All at last adopted the same way for the same purpose; hence the ways turned into customs and became mass phenomena. Instincts were developed in connection with them. In this way folkways arise. The young learn them by tradition, imitation, and authority. The folkways, at a time, provide for all the needs of life then and there. They are uniform, universal in the group, imperative, and invariable. As time goes on, the folkways become more and more arbitrary, positive, and imperative. If asked why they act in a certain way in certain cases, primitive people always answer that it is because they and their ancestors always have done so. A sanction also arises from ghost fear. The ghosts of ancestors would be angry if the living should change the ancient folkways.

2. THE FOLKWAYS ARE A SOCIETAL FORCE

The operation by which folkways are produced consists in the frequent repetition of petty acts, often by great numbers acting in concert or, at least, acting in the same way when face to face with the same need. The immediate motive is interest. It produces habit in the individual and custom in the group. It is, therefore, in the highest degree original and primitive. By habit and custom it exerts a strain on every individual within its range; therefore it rises to a societal force to which great classes of societal phenomena are due. Its earliest stages, its course, and laws may be studied; also its influence on individuals and their reaction on it. It is our present purpose so to study it. We have to recognize it as one of the chief forces by which a society is made to be what it is. Out of the unconscious experiment which every repetition of the ways includes, there issues pleasure or pain, and then, so far as the men are capable of reflection, convictions that the ways are conducive to societal welfare. These two experiences are not the same. The most uncivilized men, both in the food quest and in war, do things which are painful, but which have been found to be expedient. Perhaps these cases teach the sense of social welfare better than those which are pleasurable and favorable to welfare. The former cases call for some intelligent reflection on experience. When this conviction as to the relation to welfare is added to the folkways they are converted into mores, and, by virtue of the philosophical and ethical element added to them, they win utility and importance and become the source of the science and the art of living.

3. FOLKWAYS ARE MADE UNCONSCIOUSLY

It is of the first importance to notice that, from the first acts by which men try to satisfy needs, each act stands by itself, and looks no further than the immediate satisfaction. From recurrent needs arise habits for the individual and customs for the group, but these results are consequences which were never conscious, and never foreseen or intended. They are not noticed until they have long existed, and it is still longer before they are appreciated. Another long time must pass, and a higher stage of mental development must be reached, before they can be used as a basis from which to deduce rules for meeting, in the future, problems whose pressure can be foreseen. The folkways, therefore, are not creations of human purpose and wit. They are like products of natural forces which men unconsciously set in operation, or they are like the instinctive ways of animals, which are developed out of experience, which reach a final form of maximum adaptation to an interest, which are handed down by tradition and admit of no exception or variation, yet change to meet new conditions, still within the same limited methods, and without rational reflection or purpose. From this it results that all the life of human beings, in all ages and stages of culture, is primarily controlled by a vast mass of folkways handed down from the earliest existence of the race, having the nature of the ways of other animals, only the topmost layers of which are subject to change and control, and have been somewhat modified by human philosophy, ethics, and religion, or by other acts of intelligent reflection. We are told of savages that "It is difficult to exhaust the customs and small ceremonial usages of a savage people. Custom regulates the whole of a man's actions,—his bathing, washing, cutting his hair, eating, drinking, and fasting. From his cradle to his grave he is the slave of ancient usage. In his life there is nothing free, nothing original, nothing spontaneous, no progress towards a higher and better life, and no attempt to improve his condition, mentally, morally, or spiritually."[1] All men act in this way with only a little wider margin of voluntary variation. . . .

5. THE STRAIN OF IMPROVEMENT AND CONSISTENCY

The folkways, being ways of satisfying needs, have succeeded more or less well, and therefore have produced more or less pleasure or pain. Their quality always consisted in their adaptation to the purpose. If they were imperfectly adapted and unsuccessful, they produced pain, which drove men on to learn better. The folkways are, therefore, (1) subject to a strain of improvement towards better adaptation of means to ends, as long as the adaptation is so imperfect that pain is produced. They are also (2) subject to a strain of consistency with each other, because they all answer their several purposes with less friction and antagonism when they cooperate and support each other. The forms of industry, the forms of the family, the notions of property, the constructions of rights, and the types of religion show the strain of consistency with each other through the whole history of civilization. The two great cultural divisions of the human race are the oriental and the occidental. Each is consistent throughout; each has its own philosophy and spirit; they are separated from top to bottom by different mores, different standpoints, different ways, and different notions of what societal arrangements are advantageous. In their contrast they keep before our minds the possible range of divergence in the solution of the great problems of human life, and in the views of earthly existence by which life policy may be controlled. If two planets were joined in one, their inhabitants could not differ more widely as to what things are best worth seeking, or what ways are most expedient for well living. . . .

15. ETHNOCENTRISM

Ethnocentrism is the technical name for this view of things in which one's own group is the center of everything, and all others are scaled and rated with reference to it. Folkways correspond to it to cover both the inner and the outer relation. Each group nourishes its own pride and vanity, boasts itself superior, exalts its own divinities, and looks with contempt on outsiders. Each group thinks its own folkways the only right ones, and if it observes that other groups have other folkways, these excite its scorn. Opprobrious epithets are derived from these differences. "Pig-eater," "cow-eater," "uncircumcised," "jabberers," are epithets of contempt and abomination. The Tupis called the Portuguese by a derisive epithet descriptive of birds which have feathers around their feet, on account of trousers.[2] For our present purpose the most important fact is that ethnocentrism leads a people to exaggerate and intensify everything in their own folkways which is peculiar and which differentiates them from others. It therefore strengthens the folkways. . . .

28. FOLKWAYS DUE TO FALSE INFERENCE

Furthermore, folkways have been formed by accident, that is, by irrational and incongruous action, based on pseudo-knowledge. In Molembo a pestilence broke out soon after a Portuguese had died there. After that the natives took all possible measures not to allow any white man to die in their country.[3] On the Nicobar islands some natives who had just begun to make pottery died. The art was given up and never again attempted.[4] White men gave to one Bushman in a kraal a stick ornamented with buttons as a symbol of authority. The recipient died leaving the stick to his son. The son soon died. Then the Bushmen brought back the stick lest all should die.[5] Until recently no building of incombustible materials could be built in any big town of the central province of Madagascar, on account of some ancient prejudice.[6] A party of Eskimos met with no game. One of them returned to their sledges and got the ham of a dog to eat. As he returned with the ham bone in his hand he met and killed a seal. Ever afterwards he carried a ham bone in his hand when hunting.[7] The Belenda women (peninsula of Malacca) stay as near to the house as possible during the [menstrual] period. Many keep the door closed. They know no reason for this custom. "It must be due to some now forgotten superstition."[8] Soon after the Yakuts saw a camel for the first time smallpox broke out amongst them. They thought the camel to be the agent of the disease.[9] A woman amongst the same people contracted an endogamous marriage. She soon afterwards became blind. This was thought to be on account of the violation of ancient customs.[10] A very great number of such cases could be collected. In fact they represent the current mode of reasoning of nature people. It is their custom to reason that, if one thing follows another, it is due to it. A great number of customs are traceable to the notion of the evil eye, many more to ritual notions of uncleanness.[11] No scientific investigation could discover the origin of the folkways mentioned, if the origin had not chanced to become known to civilized men. We must believe that the known cases illustrate the irrational and incongruous origin of many folkways. In civilized history also we know that customs have owed their origin to "historical accident,"—the vanity of a princess, the deformity of a king, the whim of a democracy, the love intrigue of a statesman or prelate. By the institutions of another age it may be provided that no one of these things can affect decisions, acts, or interests, but then the power to decide the ways may have passed to clubs, trades unions, trusts, commercial rivals, wire-pullers, politicians, and political fanatics. In these cases also the causes and origins may escape investigation.

29. HARMFUL FOLKWAYS

There are folkways which are positively harmful. Very often these are just the ones for which a definite reason can be given. The destruction of a man's goods at his death is a direct deduction from other-worldliness; the dead man is supposed to want in the other world just what he wanted here. The destruction of a man's goods at his death was a great waste of capital, and it must have had a disastrous effect on the interests of the living, and must have very seriously hindered the development of civilization. With this custom we must class all the expenditure of labor and capital on graves, temples, pyramids, rites, sacrifices, and support of priests, so far as these were supposed to benefit the dead. The faith in goblinism produced other-worldly interests which overruled ordinary worldly interests. Foods have often been forbidden which were plentiful, the prohibition of which injuriously lessened the food supply. There is a tribe of Bushmen who will eat no goat's flesh, although goats are the most numerous domestic animals in the district.[12] Where totemism exists it is regularly accompanied by a taboo on eating the totem animal. Whatever may be the real principle in totemism, it overrules the interest in an abundant food supply. "The origin of the sacred regard paid to the cow must be sought in the primitive nomadic life of the Indo-European race," because it is common to Iranians and Indians of Hindostan.[13] The Libyans ate oxen but not cows.[14] The same was true of the Phonicians and Egyptians.[15] In some cases the sense of a food taboo is not to be learned. It may have been entirely capricious. Mohammed would not eat lizards, because he thought them the offspring of a metamorphosed clan of Israelites.[16] On the other hand, the protective taboo which forbade killing crocodiles, pythons, cobras, and other animals enemies of man was harmful to his interests, whatever the motive. "It seems to be a fixed article of belief throughout southern India, that all who have willfully or accidentally killed a snake, especially a cobra, will certainly be punished, either in this life or the next, in one of three ways: either by childlessness, or by leprosy, or by ophthalmia."[17] Where this faith exists man has a greater interest to spare a cobra than to kill it. India furnishes a great number of cases of harmful mores. "In India every tendency of humanity seems intensified and exaggerated. No country in the world is so conservative in its traditions, yet no country has undergone so many religious changes and vicissitudes."[18] "Every year thousands perish of disease that might recover if they would take proper nourishment, and drink the medicine that science prescribes, but which they imagine that their religion forbids them to touch." "Men who can scarcely count beyond twenty, and know not the letters of the alphabet, would rather die than eat food which had been prepared by men of lower caste, unless it had been sanctified by being offered to an idol; and would kill their daughters rather than endure the disgrace of having unmarried girls at home beyond twelve or thirteen years of age."[19] In the last case the rule of obligation and duty is set by the mores. The interest comes under vanity. The sanction of the caste rules is in a boycott by all members of the caste. The rules are often very harmful. "The authority of caste rests partly on written laws, partly on legendary fables or narratives, partly on the injunctions of instructors and priests, partly on custom and usage, and partly on the caprice and convenience of its votaries."[20] The harm of caste rules is so great that of late they have been broken in some cases, especially in regard to travel over sea, which is a great advantage to Hindoos.[21] The Hindoo folkways in regard to widows and child marriages must also be recognized as socially harmful. . . .

31. THE FOLKWAYS ARE "RIGHT." RIGHTS. MORALS

The folkways are the "right" ways to satisfy all interests, because they are traditional, and exist in fact. They extend over the whole of life. There is a right way to catch game, to win a wife, to make one's self appear, to cure disease, to honor ghosts, to treat comrades or strangers, to behave when a child is born, on the warpath, in council, and so on in all cases which can arise. The ways are defined on the negative side, that is, by taboos. The "right" way is the way which the ancestors used and which has been handed down. The tradition is its own warrant. It is not held subject to verification by experience. The notion of right is in the folkways. It is not outside of them, of independent origin, and brought to them to test them. In the folkways, whatever is, is right. This is because they are traditional, and therefore contain in themselves the authority of the ancestral ghosts. When we come to the folkways we are at the end of our analysis. The notion of right and ought is the same in regard to all the folkways, but the degree of it varies with the importance of the interest at stake. The obligation of conformable and coöperative action is far greater under ghost fear and war than in other matters, and the social sanctions are severer, because group interests are supposed to be at stake. Some usages contain only a slight element of right and ought. It may well be believed that notions of right and duty, and of social welfare, were first developed in connection with ghost fear and other-worldliness, and therefore that, in that field also, folkways were first raised to mores. "Rights" are the rules of mutual give and take in the competition of life which are imposed on comrades in the in-group, in order that the peace may prevail there which is essential to the group strength. Therefore rights can never be "natural" or "God-given," or absolute in any sense. The morality of a group at a time is the sum of the taboos and prescriptions in the folkways by which right conduct is defined. Therefore morals can never be intuitive. They are historical, institutional, and empirical.

World philosophy, life policy, right, rights, and morality are all products of the folkways. They are reflections on, and generalizations from, the experience of pleasure and pain which is won in efforts to carry on the struggle for existence under actual life conditions. The generalizations are very crude and vague in their germinal forms. They are all embodied in folklore, and all our philosophy and science have been developed out of them. . . .

34. DEFINITION OF THE MORES

When the elements of truth and right are developed into doctrines of welfare, the folkways are raised to another plane. They then become capable of producing inferences, developing into new forms, and extending their constructive influence over men and society. Then we call them the mores. The mores are the folkways, including the philosophical and ethical generalizations as to societal welfare which are suggested by them, and inherent in them, as they grow. . . .

65. WHAT IS GOODNESS OR BADNESS OF THE MORES

It is most important to notice that, for the people of a time and place, their own mores are always good, or rather that for them there can be no question of the goodness or badness of their mores. The reason is because the standards of good and right are in the mores. If the life conditions change, the traditional folkways may produce pain and loss, or fail to produce the same good as formerly. Then the loss of comfort and ease brings doubt into the judgment of welfare (causing doubt of the pleasure of the gods, or of war power, or of health), and thus disturbs the unconscious philosophy of the mores. Then a later time will pass judgment on the mores. Another society may also pass judgment on the mores. In our literary and historical study of the mores we want to get from them their educational value, which consists in the stimulus or warning as to what is, in its effects, societally good or bad. This may lead us to reject or neglect a phenomenon like infanticide, slavery, or witchcraft, as an old "abuse" and "evil," or to pass by the crusades as a folly which cannot recur. Such a course would be a great error. Everything in the mores of a time and place must be regarded as justified with regard to that time and place. "Good" mores are those which are well adapted to the situation. "Bad" mores are those which are not so adapted. The mores are not so stereotyped and changeless as might appear, because they are forever moving towards more complete adaptation to conditions and interests, and also towards more complete adjustment to each other. People in mass have never made or kept up a custom in order to hurt their own interests. They have made innumerable errors as to what their interests were and how to satisfy them, but they have always aimed to serve their interests as well as they could. This gives the standpoint for the student of the mores. All things in them come before him on the same plane. They all bring instruction and warning. They all have the same relation to power and welfare. The mistakes in them are component parts of them. We do not study them in order to approve some of them and condemn others. They are all equally worthy of attention from the fact that they existed and were used. The chief object of study in them is their adjustment to interests, their relation to welfare, and their coordination in a harmonious system of life policy. For the men of the time there are no "bad" mores. What is traditional and current is the standard of what ought to be. The masses never raise any question about such things. If a few raise doubts and questions, this proves that the folkways have already begun to lose firmness and the regulative element in the mores has begun to lose authority. This indicates that the folkways are on their way to a new adjustment. The extreme of folly, wickedness, and absurdity in the mores is witch persecutions, but the best men of the seventeenth century had no doubt that witches existed, and that they ought to be burned. The religion, statecraft, jurisprudence, philosophy, and social system of that age all contributed to maintain that belief. It was rather a culmination than a contradiction of the current faiths and convictions, just as the dogma that all men are equal and that one ought to have as much political power in the state as another was the culmination of the political dogmatism and social philosophy of the nineteenth century. Hence our judgments of the good or evil consequences of folkways are to be kept separate from our study of the historical phenomena of them, and of their strength and the reasons for it. The judgments have their place in plans and doctrines for the future, not in a retrospect. . . .

439. MEANING OF "IMMORAL"

When, therefore, the ethnographers apply condemnatory or depreciatory adjectives to the people whom they study, they beg the most important question which we want to investigate; that is, What are standards, codes, and ideas of chastity, decency, propriety, modesty, etc., and whence do they arise? The ethnographical facts contain the answer to this question, but in order to reach it we want a colorless report of the facts. We shall find proof that "immoral" never means anything but contrary to the mores of the time and place. Therefore the mores and the morality may move together, and there is no permanent or universal standard by which right and truth in regard to these matters can be established and different folkways compared and criticised. Only experience produces judgments of the expediency of some usages. For instance, ancient peoples thought pederasty was harmless and trivial. It has been well proved to be corrupting both to individual and social vigor, and harmful to interests, both individual and collective. Cannibalism, polygamy, incest, harlotry, and other primitive customs have been discarded by a very wide and, in the case of some of them, unanimous judgment that they are harmful. On the other hand, in the *Avesta* spermatorrhea is a crime punished by stripes.[22] The most civilized peoples also maintain, by virtue of their superior position in the arts of life, that they have attained to higher and better judgments and that they may judge the customs of others from their own standpoint. For three or four centuries they have called their own customs "Christian," and have thus claimed for them a religious authority and sanction which they do not possess by any connection with the principles of Christianity. Now, however, the adjective seems to be losing its force. The Japanese regard nudity with indifference, but they use dress to conceal the contour of the human form while we use it to enhance, in many ways, the attraction. "Christian" mores have been enforced by the best breechloaders and ironclads, but the Japanese now seem ready to bring superiority in those matters to support their mores. It is now a known and recognized fact that our missionaries have unintentionally and unwittingly done great harm to nature people by inducing them to wear clothes as one of the first details of civilized influence. In the usages of nature peoples there is no correlation at all between dress and sentiments of chastity, modesty, decency, and propriety.[23] . . .

503. THE GREAT VARIETY IN THE CODES

All the topics which have been treated in this chapter are branches or outreachings of the social code. They show how deep is the interest of human beings in the sex taboo, and in the self-perpetuation of society. Men have always tried, and are trying still, to solve the problem of well living in this respect. The men, the women, the children, and the society have joint and several interests, and the complication is great. At the present time population, race, marriage, childbirth, and the education of children present us our greatest problems and most unfathomable mysteries. All the contradictory usages of chastity, decency, propriety, etc., have their sense in some assumed relation to the welfare of society. To some extent they have come out of caprice, but chiefly they have issued from experience of good and ill, and are due to efforts to live well. Thus we may discern in them policies and philosophies, but they never proceed to form any such generalities as do rationally adopted motives. There is logic in the folkways, but never rationality. Given the premises, in a notion of kin, for instance, and the deductions are made directly and generally correctly, but the premises could never be verified, and they were oftener false than true. Each group took its own way, making its own assumptions, and following its own logic. So there was great variety and discord in their policies and philosophies, but within the area of a custom, during its dominion, its authority is absolute; and hence, although the usages are infinitely various, directly contradictory, and mutually abominable, they are, within their area of dominion, of equal value and force, and they are the standards of what is true and right. The groups have often tried to convert each other by argument and reason. They have never succeeded. Each one's reasons are the tradition which it has received from its ancestors. That does not admit of argument. Each tries to convince the other by going outside of the tradition to some philosophic standard of truth. Then the tradition is left in full force. Shocking as it must be to any group to be told that there is no rational ground for any one of them to convert another group to its mores (because this seems to imply, although it does not, that their folkways are not better than those of other groups), yet this must be said, for it is true. By experience and science the nations which by name are Christian have reached ways which are better fitted, on the whole, for well living than those of the Mohammedan nations, although this superiority is not by any means so complete and sweeping as current opinion in Christian countries believes. If Christians and Mohammedans come together and argue, they never make the slightest impression on each other. During the crusades, in Andalusia, and in cities of the near East where they live side by side, they have come to peace, mutual respect, and mutual influence. Syncretism begins. There is giving and taking. In Egypt at present the Moslems see the power of the English to carry on industry, commerce, and government, and this observation produces effect on the folkways. That is the chief way in which folkways are modified or borrowed. It was by this process that Greeks and Romans influenced the folkways of barbarians, and that white men have influenced those of negroes, Indians, Polynesians, Japanese, etc.

NOTES

1. JAI, XX, 140.
2. Martius, *Ethnog. Brasil.*, 51.
3. Bastian, *San Salvador*, 104.
4. Ratzel, *Anthropogeog.*, II, 699.
5. Lichtenstein, *South Africa*, II, 61.
6. Sibree, *Great African Island*, 301.
7. *Bur. Eth.*, XVIII (Part I), 325.
8. *Ztsft. f. Eth.*, XXVIII, 170.
9. Wilken, *Volkenkunde*, 546.
10. Sieroshevski, *Yakuty*, 558.
11. See Chapter XIV.
12. Ratzel, *Hist. Mankind*, II, 276.
13. W. R. Smith, *Religion of the Semites*, 299.

14. Herodotus, IV, 186.

15. Porphyry, *De Abstin.,* II, ɪɪ; Herodotus, II, 41.

16. W. R. Smith, *Religion of the Semites,* 88.

17. Monier-Williams, *Brahmanism and Hinduism,* 324.

18. Ibid., 101.

19. Wilkins, *Hinduism,* 299.

20. Ibid., 125.

21. JASB, IV, 353.

22. Darmstetter, *Zend-Avesta,* I, 100.

23. Marsden, *Sumatra,* 52.

5   *Anthropology and the Abnormal*

RUTH BENEDICT

Modern social anthropology has become more and more a study of the varieties and common elements of cultural environment and the consequences of these in human behavior. For such a study of diverse social orders primitive peoples fortunately provide a laboratory not yet entirely vitiated by the spread of a standardized world-wide civilization. Dyaks and Hopis, Fijians and Yakuts are significant for psychological and sociological study because only among these simpler peoples has there been sufficient isolation to give opportunity for the development of localized social forms. In the higher cultures the standardization of custom and belief over a couple of continents has given a false sense of the inevitability of the particular forms that have gained currency, and we need to turn to a wider survey in order to check the conclusions we hastily base upon this near-universality of familiar customs. Most of the simpler cultures did not gain the wide currency of the one which, out of our experience, we identify with human nature, but this was for various historical reasons, and certainly not for any that gives us as its carriers a monopoly of social good or of social sanity. Modern civilization, from this point of view, becomes not a necessary pinnacle of human achievement but one entry in a long series of possible adjustments.

These adjustments, whether they are in mannerisms like the ways of showing anger, or joy, or grief in any society, or in major human drives like those of sex, prove to be far more variable than experience in any one culture would suggest. In certain fields, such as that of religion or of formal marriage arrangements, these wide limits of variability are well known and can be fairly described. In others it is not yet possible to give a generalized account, but that does not absolve us of the task of indicating the significance of the work that has been done and of the problems that have arisen.

One of these problems relates to the customary modern normal-abnormal categories and our conclusions regarding them. In how far are such categories culturally determined, or in how far can we with assurance regard

Reprinted, by permission of the publisher and copyright holder, from Ruth Benedict, "Anthropology and the Abnormal" (excerpts), in *The Journal of General Psychology* 10 (1934): 59–60, 65–75, 79.

them as absolute? In how far can we regard inability to function socially as diagnostic of abnormality, or in how far is it necessary to regard this as a function of the culture?

As a matter of fact, one of the most striking facts that emerge from a study of widely varying cultures is the ease with which our abnormals function in other cultures. It does not matter what kind of "abnormality" we choose for illustration, those which indicate extreme instability, or those which are more in the nature of character traits like sadism or delusions of grandeur or of persecution, there are well-described cultures in which these abnormals function at ease and with honor, and apparently without danger or difficulty to the society.

The most notorious of these is trance and catalepsy. Even a very mild mystic is aberrant in our culture. But most peoples have regarded even extreme psychic manifestations not only as normal and desirable, but even as characteristic of highly valued and gifted individuals. This was true even in our own cultural background in that period when Catholicism made the ecstatic experience the mark of sainthood. It is hard for us, born and brought up in a culture that makes no use of the experience, to realize how important a rôle it may play and how many individuals are capable of it, once it has been given an honorable place in any society. . . .

The most spectacular illustrations of the extent to which normality may be culturally defined are those cultures where an abnormality of our culture is the cornerstone of their social structure. It is not possible to do justice to these possibilities in a short discussion. A recent study of an island of northwest Melanesia by Fortune describes a society built upon traits which we regard as beyond the border of paranoia. In this tribe the exogamic groups look upon each other as prime manipulators of black magic, so that one marries always into an enemy group which remains for life one's deadly and unappeasable foes. They look upon a good garden crop as a confession of theft, for everyone is engaged in making magic to induce into his garden the productiveness of his neighbors'; therefore no secrecy in the island is so rigidly insisted upon as the secrecy of a man's harvesting of his yams. Their polite phrase at the acceptance of a gift is, "And if you now poison me, how shall I repay you this present?" Their preoccupation with poisoning is constant; no woman ever leaves her cooking pot for a moment untended. Even the great affinal economic exchanges that are characteristic of this Melanesian culture area are quite altered in Dobu since they are incompatible with this fear and distrust that pervades the culture. They go farther and people the whole world outside their own quarters with such malignant spirits that all-night feasts and ceremonials simply do not occur here. They have even rigorous religiously enforced customs that forbid the sharing of seed even in one family group. Anyone else's food is deadly poison to you, so that communality of stores is out of the question. For some months before harvest the whole society is on the verge of starvation, but if one falls to the temptation and eats up one's seed yams, one is an outcast and a beachcomber for life. There is no coming back. It involves, as a matter of course, divorce and the breaking of all social ties.

Now in this society where no one may work with another and no one may share with another, Fortune describes the individual who was regarded by all his fellows as crazy. He was not one of those who periodically ran amok and, beside himself and frothing at the mouth, fell with a knife upon anyone he could reach. Such behavior they did not regard as putting anyone outside the pale. They did not even put the individuals who were known to be liable to these attacks under any kind of control. They merely fled when they saw the attack coming on and kept out of the way. "He would be all right tomorrow." But there was one man of sunny, kindly disposition who liked work and liked to be helpful. The compulsion was too strong for him to repress it in favor of the opposite tendencies of his culture. Men and women never spoke of him without laughing; he was silly and simple and definitely crazy. Nevertheless, to the ethnologist used to a culture that has, in Christianity, made his type the model of all virtue, he seemed a pleasant fellow.

An even more extreme example, because it is of a culture that has built itself upon a more complex abnormality, is that of the North Pacific Coast of North America. The civilization of the Kwakiutl, at the time when it was first recorded in the last decades of the nineteenth century, was one of the most vigorous in North America. It was built up on an ample economic supply of goods, the fish which furnished their food staple being practically inexhaustible and obtainable with comparatively small labor, and the wood which furnished the material for their houses, their furnishings, and their arts being, with however much labor, always procurable. They lived in coastal villages that compared favorably in size with those of any other American Indians and they kept up constant communication by means of sea-going dug-out canoes.

It was one of the most vigorous and zestful of the aboriginal cultures of North America, with complex crafts and ceremonials, and elaborate and striking arts. It certainly had none of the earmarks of a sick civilization. The tribes of the Northwest Coast had wealth, and exactly in our terms. That is, they had not only a surplus of economic goods, but they made a game of the manipulation of wealth. It was by no means a mere direct transcription of economic needs and the filling of those needs. It involved the idea of capital, of interest, and of conspicuous waste. It was a game with all the binding rules of a game, and a person entered it as a child. His father distributed wealth for him, according to his ability, at a small feast or potlatch, and each gift the receiver was obliged to accept and to return after a short interval with interest that ran to about 100 percent a year. By the time the child was grown, therefore, he was well launched, a larger potlatch had been given for him on various occasions of exploit or initiation, and he had wealth either out at usury or in his own possession. Nothing in the civilization could be enjoyed without validating it by the distribution of this wealth. Everything that was valued, names and songs as well as material objects, were passed down in family lines, but they were always publicly assumed with accompanying sufficient distributions of property. It was the game of validating and exercising all the privileges one could accumulate from one's various forbears, or by gift, or by marriage, that made the chief interest of the culture. Everyone in his degree took part in it, but many, of course, mainly as spectators. In its highest form it was played out between rival chiefs representing not only themselves and their family lines but their communities, and the object of the contest was to glorify oneself and to humiliate one's opponent. On this level of greatness the property involved was no longer represented by blankets, so many thousand of them to a potlatch, but by higher units of value. These higher units were like our bank notes. They were incised copper tablets, each of them named, and having a value that depended upon their illustrious history. This was as high as ten thousand blankets, and to possess one of them, still more to enhance its value at a great potlatch, was one of the greatest glories within the compass of the chiefs of the Northwest Coast.

The details of this manipulation of wealth are in many ways a parody on our own economic arrangements, but it is with the motivations that were recognized in this contest that we are concerned in this discussion. The drives were those which in our own culture we should call megalomaniac. There was an uncensored self-glorification and ridicule of the opponent that it is hard to equal in other cultures outside of the monologues of the abnormal. Any of the songs and speeches of their chiefs at a potlatch illustrate the usual tenor:

. . . .
Wa, out of the way, Wa, out of the way. Turn your faces
that I may give way to my anger by striking my fellow chiefs.

Wa, great potlatch, greatest potlatch.[1] The little ones[2] only
pretend, the little stubborn ones, they only sell one copper again
and again and give it away to the little chiefs of the tribe.
Ah, do not ask in vain for mercy. Ah, do not ask in vain for
mercy and raise your hands, you with lolling tongues! I shall
break,[3] I shall let disappear the great copper that has the name
Kentsegum, the property of the great foolish one, the great
extravagant one, the great surpassing one, the one farthest
ahead, the great Cannibal dancer among the chiefs.[4]

I am the great chief who makes people ashamed.
I am the great chief who makes people ashamed.
Our chief brings shame to the faces.
Our chief brings jealousy to the faces.
Our chief makes people cover their faces by what he is continually
doing in this world, from the beginning to the end of
the year,
Giving again and again oil feasts to the tribes.

I am the great chief who vanquishes.
I am the great chief who vanquishes.
Only at those who continue running round and round in this
world, working hard, losing their tails,[5] I sneer, at the chiefs
below the true chief.[6]

Have mercy on them![7] Put oil on their dry heads with brittle
hair, those who do not comb their hair!

I sneer at the chiefs below the true, real chief. I am the great
chief who makes people ashamed.

. . . .

I am the only great tree, I the chief.
I am the only great tree, I the chief.
You are my subordinates, tribes.
You sit in the middle of the rear of the house, tribes.
Bring me your counter of property, tribes, that he may in vain
try to count what is going to be given away by the great
copper-maker, the chief.
Oh, I laugh at them, I sneer at them who empty boxes[8] in their
houses, their potlatch houses, their inviting houses that are
full only of hunger. They follow along after me like young
sawbill ducks. I am the only great tree, I the chief.

. . . .

I have quoted a number of these hymns of self-glorification because by
an association which psychiatrists will recognize as fundamental these delusions of grandeur were essential in the paranoid view of life which was so
strikingly developed in this culture. All of existence was seen in terms of
insult.[9] Not only derogatory acts performed by a neighbor or an enemy, but
all untoward events, like a cut when one's axe slipped, or a ducking when
one's canoe overturned, were insults. All alike threatened first and foremost
one's ego security, and the first thought one was allowed was how to get
even, how to wipe out the insult. Grief was little institutionalized, but sulk-
ing took its place. Until he had resolved upon a course of action by which to
save his face after any misfortune, whether it was the slipping of a wedge in
felling a tree, or the death of a favorite child, an Indian of the Northwest
Coast retired to his pallet with his face to the wall and neither ate nor spoke.
He rose from it to follow out some course which according to the traditional
rules should reinstate him in his own eyes and those of the community: to
distribute property enough to wipe out the stain, or to go head-hunting in
order that somebody else should be made to mourn. His activities in neither
case were specific responses to the bereavement he had just passed through,
but were elaborately directed toward getting even. If he had not the money to
distribute and did not succeed in killing someone to humiliate another, he
might take his own life. He had staked everything, in his view of life, upon a
certain picture of the self, and, when the bubble of his self-esteem was
pricked, he had no interest, no occupation to fall back on, and the collapse of
his inflated ego left him prostrate.

Every contingency of life was dealt with in these two traditional ways. To
them the two were equivalent. Whether one fought with weapons or "fought
with property," as they say, the same idea was at the bottom of both. In the
olden times, they say, they fought with spears, but now they fight with prop-

erty. One overcomes one's opponents in equivalent fashion in both, matching forces and seeing that one comes out ahead, and one can thumb one's nose at the vanquished rather more satisfactorily at a potlatch than on a battle field. Every occasion in life was noticed, not in its own terms, as a stage in the sex life of the individual or as a climax of joy or of grief, but as furthering this drama of consolidating one's own prestige and bringing shame to one's guests. Whether it was the occasion of the birth of a child, or a daughter's adolescence, or of the marriage of one's son, they were all equivalent raw material for the culture to use for this one traditionally selected end. They were all to raise one's own personal status and to entrench oneself by the humiliation of one's fellows. A girl's adolescence among the Nootka was an event for which her father gathered property from the time she was first able to run about. When she was adolescent he would demonstrate his greatness by an unheard of distribution of these goods, and put down all his rivals. It was not as a fact of the girl's sex life that it figured in their culture, but as the occasion for a major move in the great game of vindicating one's own greatness and humiliating one's associates.

In their behavior at great bereavements this set of the culture comes out most strongly. Among the Kwakiutl it did not matter whether a relative had died in bed of disease, or by the hand of an enemy, in either case death was an affront to be wiped out by the death of another person. The fact that one had been caused to mourn was proof that one had been put upon. A chief's sister and her daughter had gone up to Victoria, and either because they drank bad whiskey or because their boat capsized they never came back. The chief called together his warriors. "Now I ask you, tribes, who shall wail? Shall I do it or shall another?" The spokesman answered, of course, "Not you, Chief. Let some other of the tribes." Immediately they set up the war pole to announce their intention of wiping out the injury, and gathered a war party. They set out, and found seven men and two children asleep and killed them. "Then they felt good when they arrived at Sebaa in the evening."

The point which is of interest to us is that in our society those who on that occasion would feel good when they arrived at Sebaa that evening would be the definitely abnormal. There would be some, even in our society, but it is not a recognized and approved mood under the circumstances. On the Northwest Coast those are favored and fortunate to whom that mood under those circumstances is congenial, and those to whom it is repugnant are unlucky. This latter minority can register in their own culture only by doing violence to their congenial responses and acquiring others that are difficult for them. The person, for instance, who, like a Plains Indian whose wife has been taken from him, is too proud to fight, can deal with the Northwest Coast civilization only by ignoring its strongest bents. If he cannot achieve it, he is the deviant in that culture, their instance of abnormality.

This head-hunting that takes place on the Northwest Coast after a death is no matter of blood revenge or of organized vengeance. There is no effort to tie up the subsequent killing with any responsibility on the part of the victim for the death of the person who is being mourned. A chief whose son has died goes visiting wherever his fancy dictates, and he says to his host, "My prince has died today, and you go with him." Then he kills him. In this, according to their interpretation, he acts nobly because he has not been downed. He has thrust back in return. The whole procedure is meaningless without the fundamental paranoid reading of bereavement. Death, like all the other untoward accidents of existence, confounds man's pride and can only be handled in the category of insults.

Behavior honored upon the Northwest Coast is one which is recognized as abnormal in our civilization, and yet it is sufficiently close to the attitudes of our own culture to be intelligible to us and to have a definite vocabulary with which we may discuss it. The megalomaniac paranoid trend is a definite danger in our society. It is encouraged by some of our major preoccupations, and it confronts us with a choice of two possible attitudes. One is to brand it as abnormal and reprehensible, and is the attitude we have chosen in our civilization. The other is to make it an essential attribute of ideal man, and this is the solution in the culture of the Northwest Coast.

These illustrations, which it has been possible to indicate only in the briefest manner, force upon us the fact that normality is culturally defined. An adult shaped to the drives and standards of either of these cultures, if he were transported into our civilization, would fall into our categories of abnormality. He would be faced with the psychic dilemmas of the socially unavailable. In his own culture, however, he is the pillar of society, the end result of socially inculcated mores, and the problem of personal instability in his case simply does not arise.

No one civilization can possibly utilize in its mores the whole potential range of human behavior. Just as there are great numbers of possible phonetic articulations, and the possibility of language depends on a selection and standardization of a few of these in order that speech communication may be possible at all, so the possibility of organized behavior of every sort, from the fashions of local dress and houses to the dicta of a people's ethics and religion, depends upon a similar selection among the possible behavior traits. In the field of recognized economic obligations or sex tabus this selection is as nonrational and subconscious a process as it is in the field of phonetics. It is a process which goes on in the group for long periods of time and is historically conditioned by innumerable accidents of isolation or of contact of peoples. In any comprehensive study of psychology, the selection that different cultures have made in the course of history within the great circumference of potential behavior is of great significance.

Every society,[10] beginning with some slight inclination in one direction or another, carries its preference farther and farther, integrating itself more and more completely upon its chosen basis, and discarding those types of behavior that are uncongenial. Most of those organizations of personality that seem to us most incontrovertibly abnormal have been used by different civilizations in the very foundations of their institutional life. Conversely the most valued traits of our normal individuals have been looked on in differently organized cultures as aberrant. Normality, in short, within a very wide range, is culturally defined. It is primarily a term for the socially elaborated segment of human behavior in any culture; and abnormality, a term for the segment that that particular civilization does not use. The very eyes with which we see the problem are conditioned by the long traditional habits of our own society.

It is a point that has been made more often in relation to ethics than in relation to psychiatry. We do not any longer make the mistake of deriving the morality of our own locality and decade directly from the inevitable constitution of human nature. We do not elevate it to the dignity of a first principle. We recognize that morality differs in every society, and is a convenient term for socially approved habits. Mankind has always preferred to say, "It is a morally good," rather than "It is habitual," and the fact of this preference is matter enough for a critical science of ethics. But historically the two phrases are synonymous.

The concept of the normal is properly a variant of the concept of the good. It is that which society has approved. A normal action is one which falls well within the limits of expected behavior for a particular society. Its variability among different peoples is essentially a function of the variability of the behavior patterns that different societies have created for themselves, and can never be wholly divorced from a consideration of culturally institutionalized types of behavior.

Each culture is a more or less elaborate working-out of the potentialities of the segment it has chosen. In so far as a civilization is well integrated and consistent within itself, it will tend to carry farther and farther, according to its nature, its initial impulse toward a particular type of action, and from the point of view of any other culture those elaborations will include more and more extreme and aberrant traits.

Each of these traits, in proportion as it reinforces the chosen behavior patterns of that culture, is for that culture normal. Those individuals to whom it is congenial either congenitally, or as the result of childhood sets, are accorded prestige in that culture, and are not visited with the social contempt or disapproval which their traits would call down upon them in a society that was differently organized. On the other hand, those individuals whose characteristics are not congenial to the selected type of human behavior in that community are the deviants, no matter how valued their personality traits may be in a contrasted civilization.

The Dobuan who is not easily susceptible to fear of treachery, who enjoys work and likes to be helpful, is their neurotic and regarded as silly. On the Northwest Coast the person who finds it difficult to read life in terms of an insult contest will be the person upon whom fall all the difficulties of the culturally unprovided for. The person who does not find it easy to humiliate a neighbor, nor to see humiliation in his own experience, who is genial and loving, may, of course, find some unstandardized way of achieving satisfactions in his society, but not in the major patterned responses that his culture requires of him. If he is born to play an important role in a family with many hereditary privileges, he can succeed only by doing violence to his whole personality. If he does not succeed, he has betrayed his culture; that is, he is abnormal.

I have spoken of individuals as having sets toward certain types of behavior, and of these sets as running sometimes counter to the types of behavior which are institutionalized in the culture to which they belong. From all that we know of contrasting cultures it seems clear that differences of temperament occur in every society. The matter has never been made the subject of investigation, but from the available material it would appear that these temperament types are very likely of universal recurrence. That is, there is an ascertainable range of human behavior that is found wherever a sufficiently large series of individuals is observed. But the proportion in which behavior types stand to one another in different societies is not universal. The vast majority of the individuals in any group are shaped to the fashion of that culture. In other words, most individuals are plastic to the moulding force of the society into which they are born. In a society that values trance, as in India, they will have supernormal experience. In a society that institutionalizes homosexuality, they will be homosexual. In a society that sets the gathering of possessions as the chief human objective, they will amass property. The deviants, whatever the type of behavior the culture has institutionalized, will remain few in number, and there seems no more difficulty in moulding the vast malleable majority to the "normality" of what we consider an aberrant trait, such as delusions of reference, than to the normality of such accepted behavior patterns as acquisitiveness. The small proportion of the number of the deviants in any culture is not a function of the sure instinct with which that society has built itself upon the fundamental sanities, but of the universal fact that, happily, the majority of mankind quite readily take any shape that is presented to them.

The relativity of normality is not an academic issue. In the first place, it suggests that the apparent weakness of the aberrant is most often and in great measure illusory. It springs not from the fact that he is lacking in necessary vigor, but that he is an individual upon whom that culture has put more than the usual strain. His inability to adapt himself to society is a reflection of the fact that that adaptation involves a conflict in him that it does not in the so-called normal.

Therapeutically, it suggests that the inculcation of tolerance and appreciation in any society toward its less usual types is fundamentally important in successful mental hygiene. The complement of this tolerance, on the patients' side, is an education in self-reliance and honesty with himself. If he can be brought to realize that what has thrust him into his misery is despair at his lack of social backing he may be able to achieve a more independent and less tortured attitude and lay the foundation for an adequately functioning mode of existence. . . .

The problem of understanding abnormal human behavior in any absolute sense independent of cultural factors is still far in the future. The categories of borderline behavior which we derive from the study of the neuroses and psychoses of our civilization are categories of prevailing local types of instability. They give much information about the stresses and strains of Western civilization, but no final picture of inevitable human behavior. Any conclusions about such behavior must await the collection by trained observers of psychiatric data from other cultures. Since no adequate work of the kind has been done at the present time, it is impossible to say what core of definition of abnormality may be found valid from the comparative material. It is as it is in ethics: all our local conventions of moral behavior and of immoral are without absolute validity, and yet it is quite possible that a modicum of what is considered right and what wrong could be disentangled that is shared by the whole human race. When data are available in psychiatry, this minimum definition of abnormal human tendencies will be probably quite unlike our culturally conditioned, highly elaborated psychoses such as those that are described, for instance, under the terms of schizophrenia and manic-depressive.

NOTES

1. The feast he is now engaged in giving.

2. His opponents.

3. To break a copper, showing in this way how far one rose above even the most superlatively valuable things, was the final mark of greatness.

4. Himself.

5. As salmon do.

6. Himself.

7. Irony, of course.

8. Of treasure.

9. Insult is used here in reference to the intense susceptibility to shame that is conspicuous in this culture. All possible contingencies were interpreted as rivalry situations, and the gamut of emotions swung between triumph and shame.

10. This phrasing of the process is deliberately animistic. It is used with no reference to a group mind or a superorganic, but in the same sense in which it is customary to say, "Every art has its own canons."

6   *The Meaning of Right*

W. D. ROSS

Any one who is satisfied that neither the subjective theories of the meaning of "right," nor what is far the most attractive of the attempts to reduce it to simpler objective elements, is correct, will probably be prepared to agree that "right" is an irreducible notion.

Nor is this result impugned by inquiries into the historical development of our present moral notions from an earlier state of things in which "what is right" was hardly disentangled from "what the tribe ordains." The point is that we can now see clearly that "right" does not mean "ordained by any given society." And it may be doubted whether even primitive men thought that it did. Their thoughts about what in particular was right were to a large extent limited by the customs and sanctions of their race and age. But this is not the same as to say that they thought that "right" just meant "what my race and age ordains." Moral progress has been possible just because there have been men in all ages who have seen the difference and have practised, or at least preached, a morality in some respects higher than that of their race and age. And even the supporters of the lower morality held, we may suspect, that their laws and customs were in accordance with a "right" other than themselves. "It is the custom" has been accompanied by "the custom is right," or "the custom is ordained by some one who has the right to command." And if human consciousness is continuous, by descent, with a lower consciousness which had no notion of right at all, that need not make us doubt that the notion is an ultimate and irreducible one, or that the rightness (prima facie) of certain types of act is self-evident; for the nature of the self-evident is not to be evident to every mind however undeveloped, but to be apprehended directly by minds which have reached a certain degree of maturity, and for minds to reach the necessary degree of maturity the development that takes place from generation to generation is as much needed as that which takes place from infancy to adult life.

In this connexion it may be well to refer briefly to a theory which has enjoyed much popularity, particularly in France—the theory of the sociological school of Durkheim and Lévy-Bruhl, which seeks to replace moral philos-

Reprinted, by permission of the publisher and copyright holder, from W. D. Ross, "The Meaning of Right," in Ross, *The Right and the Good*, pp. 12–15. Oxford: Clarendon Press, 1930.

ophy by the "science des moeurs," the historical and comparative study of the moral beliefs and practices of mankind. It would be foolish to deny the value of such a study, or the interest of many of the facts it has brought to light with regard to the historical origin of many such beliefs and practices. It has shown with success that many of the most strongly felt repulsions towards certain types of conduct are relics of a bygone system of totems and fetishes, their connexion with which is little suspected by those who feel them. What must be denied is the capacity of any such inquiry to take the place of moral philosophy. The attitude of the sociological school towards the systems of moral belief that they find current in various ages and races is a curiously inconsistent one. On the one hand we are urged to accept an existing code as something analogous to an existing law of nature, something not to be questioned or criticized but to be accepted and conformed to as part of the given scheme of things; and on this side the school is able sincerely to proclaim itself conservative of moral values, and is indeed conservative to the point of advocating the acceptance in full of conventional morality. On the other hand, by showing that any given code is the product partly of bygone superstitions and partly of out-of-date utilities, it is bound to create in the mind of any one who accepts its teaching (as it presupposes in the mind of the teacher) a sceptical attitude towards any and every given code. In fact the analogy which it draws between a moral code and a natural system like the human body (a favourite comparison) is an entirely fallacious one. By analysing the constituents of the human body you do nothing to diminish the reality of the human body as a given fact, and you learn much which will enable you to deal effectively with its diseases. But beliefs have the characteristics which bodies have not, of being true or false, of resting on knowledge or of being the product of wishes, hopes, and fears; and in so far as you can exhibit them as being the product of purely psychological and nonlogical causes of this sort, while you leave intact the fact that many people hold such opinions you remove their authority and their claim to be carried out in practice.

It is often said, in criticism of views such as those of the sociological school, that the question of the validity of a moral code is quite independent of the question of its origin. This does not seem to me to be true. An inquiry into the origin of a judgement may have the effect of establishing its validity. Take, for instance, the judgment that the angles of a triangle are equal to two right angles. We find that the historical origin of this judgment lies in certain pre-existing judgments which are its premises, plus the exercise of a certain activity of inferring. Now if we find that these pre-existing judgements were really instances of knowing, and that the inferring was also really knowing—was the apprehension of a necessary connexion—our inquiry into the origin of the judgement in question will have established its validity. On the other hand, if any one can show that A holds actions of type B to be wrong simply because (for instance) he knows such actions to be forbidden by the society he lives in, he shows that A has no real reason for believing that such actions have the specific quality of wrongness, since between being forbidden by the community and being wrong there is no necessary connexion. He does not, indeed, show the belief to be untrue, but he shows that *A* has no sufficient reason for holding it true; and in this sense he undermines its validity.

This is, in principle, what the sociological school attempts to do. According to this school, or rather according to its principles if consistently carried out, no one moral code is any truer, any nearer to the apprehension of an objective moral truth, than any other; each is simply the code that is necessitated by the conditions of its time and place, and is that which most completely conduces to the preservation of the society that accepts it. But the human mind will not rest content with such a view. It is not in the least bound to say that there has been constant progress in morality, or in moral belief. But it is competent to see that the moral code of one race or age is in certain respects inferior to that of another. It has in fact an a priori insight into certain broad principles of morality, and it can distinguish between a more and a less adequate recognition of these principles. There are not merely so many moral codes which can be described and whose vagaries can be traced to historical causes; there is a system of moral truth, as objective as all truth must be, which, and whose implications, we are interested in discovering; and from the point of view of this, the genuinely ethical problem, the sociological inquiry is simply beside the mark. It does not touch the questions to which we most desire answers.[1]

NOTE

1. For a lucid and up to a point appreciative account of the sociological school, and a penetrating criticism of its deficiencies, see ch. 2 of M. D. Parodi's *Le Problème Moral et la Pensée Contemporaine.*

7

The Empirical Underdetermination of Descriptive Cultural Relativism*

MICHELE MOODY-ADAMS

Many theorists in philosophy and anthropology, as well as many thoughtful people in everyday life, find some version of meta-ethical relativism compelling because they take it to involve a series of virtually irresistible inferences from experience—a series of inferences that allegedly support the claims of descriptive cultural relativism. Herskovits claimed, for instance, that a simple understanding of a few basic facts about cultural diversity in moral practices would eventually issue in a potent relativism about justification and about the nature of morality. He insisted that relativism is simply "a scientific, inductive attack on an age-old philosophical problem, using fresh, cross-cultural data, hitherto not available to scholars, gained from the study of the underlying value-systems of societies having the most diverse customs" (Herskovits 1972, 14). Borrowing liberally from the terminology of William James, Herskovits characterizes his relativism as simply a "tough-minded"—that is, truly empirical—approach to understanding the "nature and role of values in culture." This "tough-minded" anthropology, as I have noted, leads to the claim that moral evaluations are "always relative to the cultural background out of which they arise" (Herskovits 1972, 37–38; 14; cf. 1964, 61–78). But what does this claim really come to?

Descriptive cultural relativism is anything *but* a "neutral" account of the facts of cultural diversity. To be sure, all empirical hypotheses are underdetermined by available data; the acceptance of empirical hypotheses involves

*Editors' note: Moody-Adams defines "descriptive cultural relativism" as follows: "Descriptive cultural relativism is the claim that differences in the moral practices of diverse social groups generate 'ultimate' or 'fundamental' moral disputes, disputes that are neither reducible to non-moral disagreement nor susceptible of rational resolution—disputes that are in principle irresolvable" (*Fieldwork in Familiar Places* [Cambridge: Harvard University Press, 1997], p. 15).

Reprinted, by permission of the publisher and copyright holder, from Michele Moody-Adams, "The Empirical Underdetermination of Descriptive Cultural Relativism," in Moody-Adams, *Fieldwork in Familiar Places*, pp. 28–43. Cambridge: Harvard University Press, 1997.

implicit commitments to explanatory and predictive virtues that function—
in Quine's phrase—as "guides to the framing of hypotheses" (Quine and
Ullian 1978, 64–82). Considerations such as the simplicity of a new hypothesis, or the extent to which a hypothesis might maximize the conservation of
current beliefs or offer generality of explanation, figure as important non-
empirical constraints on the choice of empirical theories. Moreover, while the
epistemological values presupposed by reliance on these virtues differ in
kind from those values presupposed by the acceptance of particular *moral*
virtues, descriptive cultural relativism clearly cannot be evaluatively neutral.
Yet descriptive relativism is in need of special scrutiny since empirical generalizations about moral practices are quite special instances of the general phenomenon of underdetermination. Of course, any such generalization will
embody complex judgments that draw comparisons, and especially con-
trasts, between the moral practices of different human groups. But these contrastive and comparative judgments imply—and rely on—descriptive claims
about moral practices that are also underdetermined by available data.

To understand the importance of this underdetermination, consider that
the effort to construct empirical hypotheses about the data of moral experience, even in observing a familiar group, is thoroughly structured by an elaborate set of non-empirical assumptions even about what is to count as data.
Familiar debates in contemporary moral philosophy between Kantians and
non-Kantians who disagree about the moral status of emotions provide an
important example of the sorts of questions at issue. Matters become even
more complex when hypotheses concern the moral practices of unfamiliar
groups. Ironically, moral relativists seldom hesitate to assume that the natural languages of the groups they encounter contain a concept of morality—or,
more precisely, some concept that plays a role very much like that which the
concept of morality plays in the language of the typical anthropologist—
observer. But this assumption (however plausible) presupposes a sophisticated judgment about a concept—the concept of morality—so complex that
its content is "essentially contested," in W. B. Gallie's phrase, even by speakers of the same language.[1]

Decisions about how to determine precisely *which* phenomena constitute
the moral data of a particular way of life create special difficulties. John
Ladd's account of his efforts to describe Navajo ethics, detailed in *The Structure of a Moral Code* (1957), provides useful (if unwitting) testimony to the
extent of these difficulties. Ladd criticizes methods relied on by R. B. Brandt,
in his *Hopi Ethics* (1954), which also offered a descriptive account of the
morality of a Native American community. Ladd contends, for instance, that
Brandt's methods were insufficiently attentive to the Hopi perspective, and
that they could really yield only a study of the extent to which the Hopi
accept "principles like our own" (Ladd 1957, 316). Yet Ladd's own account
shows that determining what constitutes *sufficient* attention to a group's perspective on their own morality is a vexing problem. Thus, for example (in
what Ladd himself recognizes is a problematic feature of his account), he
relies principally on interviews (through interpreters) with only two Navajo

informants (Ladd 1957, 335–425). Of course, his decision to use such a small number of informants probably rested on a judgment from someone familiar with the Navajo, or perhaps even a member of the Navajo, that certain people would be more likely than others to provide an "authoritative" version of Navajo values and practices. Yet it is no easy matter to justify this kind of confidence in authoritative versions.

Any such confidence embodies a complex evaluative stance that will sometimes prove neither methodologically nor morally benign. Very often such confidence overlooks the possibility of internal conflict, as when a community practice has been subjected to criticism from within. Imagine, for example, that in some community a certain common practice has been the subject of intense criticism from a small but forceful group within that community. An outside observer who undertakes to describe this community's moral practices may well be told that the internal critics are not authoritative voices but mere aberrations. But a failure to record the substance of the internal criticism will issue in a description that is false to the internal complexity of the community's way of life. What is more, this very complexity may itself be of supreme *moral* importance for the culture, for sometimes a critic is a vehicle for the kind of self-scrutiny that reveals an accepted practice to be incompatible with some deep commitment of the group. This is, after all, the Socratic view of moral reasoning which gave such force to the stance of nonviolent civil disobedience in the American South.[2] For an ethnographer to participate— knowingly or unknowingly—in potentially silencing such reflection is to give legitimacy to an evaluatively nonneutral version of the moral practices of the group. Indeed, perhaps no attempt to describe a group's moral practices and beliefs can be a morally neutral act, especially given the artificiality of the anthropologist's "ethnographic present," which fails to suggest the inherent potential for ongoing evolution of complex moral practices. But the constant danger that any description may fail at neutrality is ignored by claims such as those of Brandt, for example, who at one point argues that the beliefs of "the average member" of a group are central to an adequate empirical study of that group's ethics (Brandt 1959, 89). Even if it were possible to identify a clear referent of the term "average member," there will always be important moral questions on which the perspective of the person who is *not* average, or even the person who is in some way "marginal," is equally important—if not more so—to a sufficiently informative account of the moral principles of a culture (Scheper-Hughes 1984, 90). What would it mean, for example, to try to describe the moral import of homelessness in America by interviewing only the "average American," who is unlikely to be homeless?

The non-empirical and evaluative commitments of any attempt to describe a people's moral practices are thus quite numerous, and quite obviously in need of close scrutiny. Likewise, descriptive cultural relativism, which makes an empirical generalization about the actual moral practices *of all human beings,* is in need of even greater scrutiny. Yet little philosophical attention has been devoted to this task. Many philosophers would simply defend the non-empirical commitments embodied in descriptive cultural relativism without further ado, because for them the doctrine is just an influential confirmation of the view that fundamental conflicts are an essential feature of morality itself. Thus, for instance, Stuart Hampshire has claimed that there "must" always be moral conflicts which "cannot" be resolved "by any constant and generally acknowledged method of reasoning." Indeed, according to Hampshire, morality "has its sources in conflicts"—conflicts "in the divided soul and between contrary claims" (Hampshire 1983, 152). David Wong makes a similar claim: if one takes moral disagreement seriously, one simply recognizes that there will always be "irresolvable" moral disagreements. Wong also takes the inevitability of such disagreements to support a "limited" meta-ethical relativism on which "there is no single true morality" (Wong 1986, 95; cf. 1984).[3] Hampshire vehemently denies that he is arguing, in Herskovits's apt phrase, for the relativism of "ethical indifference" (Hampshire 1983, 154). Yet he never considers the possibility that his view of the "sources" of morality—which is remarkably similar to Wong's view that the principal "point" of morality is to regulate conflicts—might implicitly commit him to a weak meta-ethical relativism.[4] Instead, he simply urges that his principal concern is to warn of the "harm" that moral philosophy can do if it implies that "there ought to be, and that there can be, fundamental agreement on, or convergence in, moral ideals." His avowed purpose is to chide the moral theorist who would look for "an underlying harmony and unity behind the facts of moral experience" (Hampshire 1983, 155; 151).

The view that fundamental conflict is intrinsic to morality has become so widespread that it appears in the most unexpected quarters. It has been claimed, for example, that even a robust moral realism—on which there are moral facts and real moral properties whose existence and nature are independent of "our beliefs" about right and wrong—must allow for the inevitability of fundamental moral disagreement (Brink 1989, 7–8; 202). Thus, David Brink argues for a realism about moral facts and properties that also accepts the persistence of disputes involving "incommensurable" (but, in his view, equally "objectively valuable") considerations, as well as "moral ties"—disputes, that is, all of which have "no uniquely correct answers" (Brink 1989, 202). Of course, even Brink acknowledges that there "are limits" (though he does not define them) to how often one can construe moral disputes as fundamental—as "not resolvable even in principle"—and yet also defend the independent existence of moral facts and properties (Brink 1989, 202). Brink is somewhat too sanguine about how easy it might be to establish these limits. But my point is simply that even robust moral realists have come to expect that they must accommodate belief in the inevitability of fundamental moral conflicts. This is a particularly striking example of how profoundly philosophy's supposed insensitivity to moral disagreement has influenced contemporary philosophical thinking about morality.

But what element of human experience could encourage the belief that fundamental moral conflict is an ineliminable feature of the social world? For many—both in philosophy as well as outside it—the data of cultural diversity provide the best evidence of moral conflicts which allegedly cannot be reduced to non-moral disagreement and cannot be resolved by reasoning and argument. One society defends polygamy while another rejects such arrangements as morally unacceptable; one group practices female circumcision and infibulation while another rejects it and the assumptions that seem to underlie it; one culture appears to approve ritual headhunting while members of other cultures would condemn the practice: such disputes are often cited as paradigmatic cases of fundamental moral conflict. Yet though these differences are real, and though the conflicts they sometimes generate are quite serious, it is not clear why it *must* be assumed that such conflicts cannot be reduced to non-moral disagreement and—in Hampshire's phrase—are not susceptible of resolution "by any constant and generally recognized method of reasoning" (Hampshire 1983, 152). Comparative anthropology provides obvious evidence of cultural variability in moral practices, but why should it be assumed that the moral disagreements sometimes occasioned by that variability are also *fundamental*—rationally irresolvable— moral conflicts?

In the first part of the twentieth century, a number of Gestalt psychologists who were dissatisfied with relativism—thinkers such as Karl Duncker, Max Wertheimer, and later Solomon Asch, among others—posed the very same question. These theorists then went on to challenge the empirical basis of descriptive relativism, effectively denying the reasonableness of the move from the fact of cultural variability to the doctrine of descriptive cultural relativism.[5] A central positive aim of these views was to argue that all purportedly fundamental moral disagreements might be shown ultimately to reduce to disagreements in beliefs about the non-moral properties of the actions or practices under consideration. Moreover, many Gestalt theorists (especially Duncker) made still stronger claims, attempting to demonstrate the existence of "invariant" laws of ethical valuation. The challenge that the Gestalt critique might pose to descriptive cultural relativism is seldom given sufficient attention, but as psychologists such as Asch maintained—and as philosophers such as Brandt and Frankena ultimately recognized—its challenge to the evidential basis for descriptive ethical relativism can be detached from the controversial aspects of the Gestalt theorist's positive commitments.[6] Moreover, that challenge is of great value. First, it helps reveal the precise ways in which descriptive ethical relativism is not a neutral description of the data of cultural diversity, and how, as Asch once remarked, it presupposes an ultimately insupportable conception of the radical "alienness" of diverse cultural traditions (Asch 1952, 381–383). Second, and equally important, the Gestalt theorist's challenge helps show how descriptive cultural relativism actually hinders a serious understanding of the conditions under which *real*—not simply apparent—moral disagreement is possible at all.

In an important article in *Mind*, entitled "Ethical Relativity? (An Inquiry into the Psychology of Ethics)" (1939), Karl Duncker discussed the philosophical relevance of Gestalt psychology's criticisms of relativism. Duncker began by identifying important features of the "psychological situation" with reference to which participants in any social practice actually behave: the "situational meanings" of the practice. The situational meaning of any practice, as he and other Gestalt theorists understood that notion, would typically include a complex set of non-moral beliefs about both the "objective" (especially causal) properties and the "subjective" features (or affective associations) of the action (Duncker 1939, 43–44). Duncker then claimed that moral judgments "on the whole" are based on socially developed patterns of situational meaning that vary widely from one culture to another, and that anthropological reports are insufficiently attentive to important variations in the situational meanings of the practices they purport to describe. One of his most important examples concerned possible variations in the situational meaning of the practice of killing superannuated parents. Disputes about the implications of this practice (famously described, for instance, in early accounts of the pursuit of the Northwest Passage) had historically played an important role in philosophical exchanges about the nature of morality.

Duncker's contribution to the debate was really quite simple. He argued, first, that where killing one's aged parents is understood, for example, as a means of sparing them the misery of a lingering death, or of increasing their chances of getting into a promised heaven, the situational meaning of the practice could be expected to give it "a quality of benevolence" (Duncker 1939, 42). He then contrasted such cases with those in which it would be denied that the killing of aged parents has any such properties. Here, he contended, the practice would quite expectedly be the object of extreme disapproval. Now, descriptive cultural relativism claims that different cultures connect "different and even opposed evaluations" to the *same* action (Asch 1952, 376). But, on Duncker's view, killing one's aged parents where that practice has the socially sanctioned meaning of sparing them a lingering death simply *is not* the same action as killing aged parents where this would be viewed as causing the early and unnecessary death of innocent persons. Ethical valuation, he argued, "is not concerned with acts as abstract events in space-time. The ethical essence of an act depends upon its concrete pattern of situational meanings" (Duncker 1939, 43).

Duncker went on to claim—quite controversially—that "the same act, being the same" has never been observed to have different moral valuations, and then to attribute this presumed fact to the existence of invariant "inner laws" of ethical valuation (Duncker 1939, 50–51). There are indeed serious obstacles in the way of proving the truth of these claims, but my aim is not to resuscitate the Gestalt theorist's positive account of morality. I simply want to show that recognizing the importance of situational meanings reveals serious methodological obstacles to proving the truth of descriptive relativism about morality. And these obstacles may be insuperable. As Brandt once observed, it is difficult (at best) to establish that one has indeed *found* a genuine instance of fundamental moral diversity (Brandt 1967, 76). In order to do so, it would be necessary to produce two people, or two cultures, who attribute identical non-moral properties to an action that they nonetheless appraise differently—and it is extremely difficult, Brandt argues, to accomplish this. Moreover, the nature and extent of the difficulty can even be discerned in familiar moral disputes. Debates about abortion, for instance, typically turn on quite complex relationships between situational meanings, on the one hand, and moral evaluations, on the other. Competing positions on abortion are often linked to patterns of situational meaning structured around disputed understandings of the properties of the fetus, and (implicitly) even of the pregnant woman. Such debates thus provide quite palpable evidence of the importance of Duncker's notion of situational meanings.

But the Gestalt theorist's insistence on the importance of socially determined differences between situational meanings might seem to concede too much to the relativist. For anthropologists such as Herskovits typically argue that relativism is just an inescapable consequence of giving due recognition to "the force of enculturative conditioning in shaping thought and behavior" in general (Herskovits 1972, 32). Enculturation, as Herskovits conceived of it, is the "all-pervasive," largely "unconscious" process of "conditioning" by which one learns a culture. Moreover, the force of that conditioning, he argued, would be felt as powerfully in the realm of factual beliefs (and hence in socially sanctioned patterns of situational meanings) as in the realm of moral evaluations themselves. Duncker vehemently asserts that the "ethical essence" of an act depends on "concrete" patterns of situational meanings. But an astute relativist would surely respond that variation in these concrete patterns must be recognized as an important methodological obstacle to establishing the existence—at least empirically—of the Gestalt theorist's invariant laws of moral valuation.[7]

Yet while the dependence of moral valuation on situational meanings may be an important obstacle to establishing empirically the positive claims of Gestalt theory, pointing out those obstacles simply produces a theoretical standoff—not a conclusive victory for descriptive relativism. Moreover, even if there is little hope for positive proof that there are invariant laws of ethical valuation, Duncker's criticisms pose a particularly serious challenge to a doctrine whose proponents appeal to its superior empirical credentials. Anthropologists such as Herskovits, Benedict, and Boas, as well as philosophers such as Ladd and Mackie, want to maintain that descriptive relativism is simply a plausible "inductive attack" on the problem of moral valuation. If that is the case, however, it should be possible to show how a careful descriptive relativism might convincingly overcome its admitted methodological difficulties.

An illuminating and important attempt to show just this is contained in Brandt's discussions of relativism in *Ethical Theory* (1959). These are of particular interest, since his study of Hopi ethics seems to have provided numerous occasions for reflecting on the potential obstacles to describing adequately the moral practices and beliefs of an unfamiliar culture. Moreover, several contemporary discussions of relativism, in both philosophy and anthropology, continue to treat Brandt's claims about descriptive relativism as authoritative.[8] Brandt begins by acknowledging how difficult it is to determine whether there is ever fundamental—or "ultimate"—moral disagreement between different cultures; he then criticizes what he sees as the shortcomings of standard anthropological treatments of the issues. Relying on familiar features of the Gestalt theorist's critique, he argues that

> most of the comparative material assembled . . . tells us . . . simply whether various peoples approve or condemn lying, suicide, industry, cleanliness, adultery, homosexuality, cannibalism, and so on. But this is not enough. We need, for our purpose, to know how various people conceive of these things. Do they eat human flesh because they like its taste, and do they kill these slaves merely for the sake of a feast? Or do they eat flesh because they think this is necessary for tribal fertility, or because they think they will then participate in the manliness of the person eaten? (Brandt 1959, 101–102)

Brandt even posits, somewhat unexpectedly, that those who currently condemn cannibalism might relinquish their condemnation were the socially accepted situational meaning to undergo sufficient change. Thus, "perhaps those who condemn cannibalism would not do so if they thought that eating the flesh of an enemy is necessary for the survival of the group. If we are to estimate whether there is ultimate disagreement of ethical principle, we must have information about this, about the beliefs, more or less conscious, of various peoples about what they do" (Brandt 1959, 102–103). This concern with the "more or less conscious" beliefs about the situational meanings of a practice even leads Brandt to take a position on parricide that is remarkably like that of Duncker (Brandt 1959, 99–100).

Brandt thus eschews appeals to the sorts of practices typically claimed to embody attitudes and assumptions that are "noncomparable" or "incommensurable" with "our" attitudes and assumptions about the world—practices such as socially sanctioned parricide, cannibalism, and witchcraft. A more typical treatment of these issues appears in Harman's "soberly logical" defense of relativism (Harman 1975, 3). Harman constructs a hypothetical example of a group of cannibals attacking the lone survivor of a shipwreck, in an effort to illuminate "our" intuitive conviction that a social practice of cannibalism would be evidence of "a primitive morality" held by "savages" best assumed to be "beyond the motivational reach" of "our" moral judgments (Harman 1975, 8). Harman's claims for moral relativism, as one commentator has argued, thus appeal to figures imagined as entirely beyond the pale—as utterly alien and "other" (Matilal 1989, 345–346). Evans-Pritchard's ethnographic study *Witchcraft, Oracles, and Magic among the Azande* (1937) contains a similar emphasis. His account continues to generate philosophical debate about the extent to which—in Peter Winch's words—the Azande "hold beliefs that we cannot possibly share and engage in practices which it is peculiarly difficult for us to comprehend. They believe that certain of their numbers are witches, exercising a malignant occult influence on the lives of their fellows. They engage in rites to counteract witchcraft; they consult oracles and use magic medicines to protect themselves from harm" (Winch 1972, 78). It is a matter of some importance that Brandt avoids these fairly standard ways of attempting to establish fundamental ethical disagreement between "us" and "them." His resistance to these approaches draws on his conviction that comparative surveys have provided insufficient data about the non-moral beliefs associated with social practices. "We must concede," he asserts, that anthropology has not provided "an adequate account of a single case, clearly showing that there is ultimate disagreement in ethical principle" (Brandt 1959, 102).

Given this last concession, however, it is startling that just a few paragraphs later Brandt himself claims to have found one example capable of establishing that there is *in fact* ultimate disagreement between cultures. At one point he even contends (on the basis of that example) that the case for fundamental disagreement is "well-established," though he later retreats from this stance, asserting more hesitantly that "probably—we must admit the case is not definitively closed—there is at least one ultimate difference of ethical principle" (Brandt 1959, 102; 103). More surprising still is the substance of the example that he takes to establish the reality of fundamental moral disagreement. It is "notorious," Brandt begins, that "many peoples seem quite indifferent to the suffering of animals." He then describes the practices of certain groups in Latin America who, he contends, sometimes pluck chickens alive "so that they will be more succulent on the table," and, later, a Hopi Indian children's game in which "children often catch birds and make 'pets' of them. A string is tied to their legs, and they are then 'played' with. The birds seldom survive this 'play' for long: their legs are broken, their wings pulled off, and so on. One informant put it: 'Sometimes they get tired and die. Nobody objects to this.' Another informant said: 'My boy sometimes brings in birds, but there is nothing to feed them and they die'" (Brandt 1959, 102–103).[9] At this point, however, the discussion takes a remarkable turn. For Brandt's argument to establish the existence of an ultimate ethical difference between *cultures* comes down to a series of open-ended rhetorical challenges to "the reader": "The reader is invited to ask himself whether he would consider it justified to pluck a chicken alive for this purpose"; "Would the reader approve of this [Hopi game], or permit his children to do this sort of thing?"; and so on (Brandt 1959, 102; 103). That such rhetorical appeals might be thought to lend empirical support to the doctrine of descriptive relativism seems to *this* reader to rest on a number of curious and ultimately implausible assumptions.[10] That they have not been criticized as such may suggest how axiomatic descriptive relativism has come to seem. Curious as they are, these assumptions are worth examining in detail because they commonly underwrite attempts to generalize about the nature and extent of cross-cultural moral disagreement, and they are usually implicit in influential attempts—both relativist and ethnocentrist—to challenge the objectivity of morality. I intend to show that these assumptions cannot be defended, and ultimately that they obstruct attention to any plausible defense of the objectivity of morality and moral inquiry.

Brandt's discussion presumes, to begin with, not only that "the reader" will in fact disapprove of the described practices, but also that this disapproval should be taken to manifest a general *cultural* sensitivity to the suffering of animals. But why should it be assumed that there will be some *one* kind of response from all imaginable readers of Brandt's *Ethical Theory,* and that such a response could legitimately be taken to represent a monolithic moral concern for animals in those readers' culture(s)? To be sure, many people reading the relevant passage might well disapprove of the described practices; they might even recoil in horror at the idea of plucking a chicken alive or carelessly breaking the wings of a small bird. Brandt goes on to report his "decided impression" that Hopi disapproval of causing pain to animals was "milder than he would suppose typical in suburban Philadelphia—certainly much milder than he would feel himself" (Brandt 1959, 102). Nevertheless, even if one concedes Brandt special insight into the culture of "suburban Philadelphia," such responses could not prove the existence of a general concern for animal suffering in his readers' culture(s)—unless of course, all his readers were assumed to inhabit suburban Philadelphia. Indeed, a substantial subset of Brandt's readers would be markedly indifferent to forms of animal suffering that are regularly sanctioned by their own culture(s). Thus, for example, the suburban American parents who unthinkingly give animals as "presents" to children who are unprepared to care for them are not so different from the Hopi parents in Brandt's example, as the continued existence of societies for the prevention of cruelty to animals reminds us. Even further, anyone teaching a course in contemporary moral problems to a large group of American undergraduates may encounter a surprising number of students who report difficulty in sharing concern about the suffering of animals in slaughterhouses and factory farms. Given all these considerations, just how great an ethical difference could there really be between the attitude toward animal suffering in the culture of "the reader," on the one hand, and that attitude in the Hopi and Latin American cultures described, on the other?

Brandt returns to the disputed example in a later chapter, and the resulting discussion reveals his own dissatisfaction with his initial argument. But his attempts to strengthen the case are even more problematic than his earlier appeals to the evaluative responses of "the reader." He contends that "on the whole, primitive groups show little feeling that it is wrong to cause pain to animals, whereas the columns of the *New York Times* are testimony to the fact that many persons in the U.S.A. take a vigorous interest in what goes on in slaughterhouses ... There is at least some question whether [primitive groups] have a vivid imagination of what the suffering of an animal is like, comparable to that of the authors of letters to the *Times*" (Brandt 1959, 284–285). Why should the imaginative powers allegedly displayed by a subset of authors of letters to the *New York Times* be taken to reveal an entire culture's moral convictions? Moreover, why does Brandt consider it unimportant that—even according to his own example—not everyone in the United States objects to the existence of slaughterhouses? The internal complexity of American attitudes about animal suffering cannot be irrelevant to understanding "the morality" of American culture, nor can it be irrelevant to any defensible attempt to contrast that morality with the indifference to animal suffering suggested by Brandt's examples. More generally, if descriptive cultural relativism is just a "tough-minded" account of the facts, it ought to be possible to say how the descriptive relativist knows what those facts really are.

The problem is that it is profoundly difficult to construct a reliable description of the moral practices of an entire *culture*—a description of the sort that could license judgments contrasting one culture's basic moral beliefs with those of other cultures. To be sure, some of the difficulties in formulating the contrastive judgments needed to defend descriptive relativism reflect methodological obstacles that plague the construction of *any* reliable descriptive morality and not simply a description of the moral practices of a given culture. Well-known controversies generated by the claims of empirical psychologists attempting to describe patterns of moral reasoning—such as the controversy surrounding the debate between Carol Gilligan and Lawrence Kohlberg—point to some of the central difficulties.[11] Thus, for instance, a psychologist typically relies on verbal reports that are subject to self-deception, or even to intentional attempts to deceive a researcher. Further, the design of any study intended to elicit the verbal data to be interpreted may itself be subject to markedly non-neutral assumptions about what is appropriately construed as a moral conviction. Finally, even if neutrality in the design of an empirical study of moral reasoning is a realizable goal, there is still the question of how to produce a neutral *interpretation* of the data obtained in such a study.

Special concerns arise when, as in the case of ethnography, the study of verbal responses is combined with the observation of nonverbal behavior, whose interpretation is fraught with peculiar difficulties. Some of these difficulties are a function of the complex relation between judgment and action. If, for instance, weakness of the will is a genuine feature of human behavior—if, that is, human beings sometimes fail to conform their conduct to moral convictions that they truly accept—this fact will surely complicate the interpretation of behavior. But even where there is no reason to presume weakness of the will, it is remarkably difficult to read off correctly unstated moral beliefs and attitudes (or even non-moral beliefs about situational meanings) from behavior. At one point Brandt implicitly concedes this when he assures the reader that he tried to discover some belief "in the Hopi subconscious" that might make it possible to say that Hopi practices did not reveal some ultimate difference in ethical principle between the Hopi and "the reader" (Brandt 1959, 103).[12] Yet the notion that there might be some psychological monolith called "the Hopi subconscious," which is capable of revealing hidden truths about Hopi practices when their "more or less conscious beliefs" would not, is just as problematic as Brandt's accompanying readiness to overlook the existence of socially sanctioned indifference to animal suffering in the larger American culture.

The most serious obstacles to formulating contrastive judgments about the moral practices of particular human groups, and to establishing the truth of descriptive relativism, reflect a difficulty peculiar to the study of cultures: that of deciding who—if anyone—has the "authority" to represent the defining principles, especially the basic moral principles, of a given culture. Should the undergraduate who is unwilling seriously to contemplate arguments about animal rights or interests, for example, be treated as representative of the American moral stance toward animals? Or is the moral fervor of the animal rights activist who periodically fires off a letter to the *New York Times* perhaps more representative? Of course, neither stance adequately represents the moral convictions of American culture as a whole. But if it is reasonable to expect in the culture of a large industrialized nation-state moral complexity of the sort that might frustrate the attempt to formulate meaningful generalizations about moral beliefs, would it then be reasonable to expect the same kind of complexity in the culture of small, preindustrial, and often "preliterate" communities? If not, why not? The answers to such questions have important implications for deciding whether descriptive cultural relativism yields a plausible picture of the social world. I will argue that a careful accounting of the facts of cultural complexity, and the associated difficulty in establishing moral authority, makes it difficult (if not impossible) for descriptive cultural relativism—and the various skepticisms about moral objectivity often alleged to follow from it—ever to get off the ground.

NOTES

1. On the notion of "essentially contested concepts," see Gallie (1964).

2. I discuss this stance in greater detail in Chapter 3 and, especially, Chapter 5 of *Fieldwork in Familiar Places*.

3. Wong also claims—like Hampshire—that morality has its source in conflict: "the point of morality" is "to regulate internal and interpersonal conflicts" (Wong 1986, 101–102).

4. Judith DeCew (1990) discusses the complexities of Hampshire's denial of relativism.

5. See Duncker (1939) and Wertheimer (1935). See also Solomon Asch, "The Fact of Culture and the Problem of Relativism" (1952, 364–384). It is worth noting that in discussing the Gestalt view in his 1959 *Ethical Theory*, Brandt rejects Duncker's claim. Yet in his 1967 *Encyclopedia of Philosophy* article "Ethical Relativism," Brandt is more sympathetic to the Gestalt attack on relativism; indeed, in the bibliography to that article, he describes Asch's version of the Gestalt argument as an "excellent critique of the evidential basis for descriptive relativism" (Brandt 1967, 78).

6. See Asch (1952, 381). After extended discussion of Duncker's and Wertheimer's objections to the evidential basis for descriptive relativism (Asch 1952, 376–384) Asch concludes that these objections cannot "settle the extent to which values are invariant, but rather . . . suggest a way of thinking about their identities and differences" that amounts to an "alternative to the positions of absolutism and diversity" p. 376–384; (Asch 1952, 383).

7. For a vehement, if occasionally confused, attempt to defend Herskovits's view on similar grounds, see Renteln (1988, 60–61).

8. See Renteln (1988) for a criticism of Brandt's views from within anthropology. See also DeCew (1990), who—from within philosophy—simply accepts the truth of Brandt's claims without argument.

9. See also Brandt, *Hopi Ethics* ([1954] 1974, 231–215; 245–246; 373).

10. In an early review of *Hopi Ethics.* Hubert Alexander (1955) also notes the problems with Brandt's reliance on such appeals.

11. For discussion of some of the problematic features of the debate between Gilligan and Kohlberg, see Moody-Adams (1991).

12. Brandt suggests here that a belief that animals are unconscious automata—or even that animals would be rewarded in an afterlife for suffering in this life—would have served the purpose.

REFERENCES

Alexander, Hubert G. 1955. "Brandt on Hopi Ethics." *Review of Metaphysics* 9:106–111.

Asch, Solomon. 1952. *Social Psychology.* New York: Prentice-Hall.

Brandt, Richard. 1959. *Ethical Theory.* Englewood Cliffs, N.J.: Prentice-Hall.

———. 1967. "Ethical Relativism." In *Encyclopedia of Philosophy.* Vol. 3. Edited by Paul Edwards. New York: Macmillan and Free Press.

———. [1954] 1974. *Hopi Ethics: A Theoretical Analysis.* Chicago: University of Chicago Press.

Brink, David O. 1986. "Externalist Moral Realism." *Southern Journal of Philosophy* Supp. 24:23–41.

———. 1989. *Moral Realism and the Foundation of Ethics.* Cambridge: Cambridge University Press.

DeCew, Judith W. 1990. "Moral Conflicts and Ethical Relativism." *Ethics* 101:27–41.

Duncker, Karl. 1939. "Ethical Relativity? (An Inquiry into the Psychology of Ethics)." *Mind* 48:39–57.

Evans-Pritchard, E. E. 1937. *Witchcraft, Oracles, and Magic among the Azande.* Oxford: Oxford University Press.

Gallie, W. B. 1964. *Philosophy and the Historical Understanding.* New York: Schocken Books.

Gilligan, Carol. 1982. *In a Different Voice.* Cambridge, Mass.: Harvard University Press.

Hampshire, Stuart. 1983. *Morality and Conflict.* Cambridge, Mass.: Harvard University Press.

Harman, Gilbert. 1975. "Moral Relativism Defended." *Philosophical Review* 84:3–22.

Herskovits, Melville. 1964. *Man and His Works: The Science of Cultural Anthropology.* New York: Alfred A. Knopf.

———. 1972. *Cultural Relativism: Perspectives in Cultural Pluralism.* Edited by Frances Herskovits. New York: Random House.

Ladd, John. 1957. *The Structure of a Moral Code.* Cambridge, Mass.: Harvard University Press.

Matilal, Bimal Krishna. 1989. "Ethical Relativism and Confrontation of Cultures." In *Relativism: Interpretation and Confrontation.* Edited by Michael E. Krausz. Notre Dame: University of Notre Dame Press.

Moody-Adams, Michele M. 1991. "Gender and the Complexity of Moral Voices." In *Feminist Ethics.* Edited by Claudia Card. Lawrence: University of Kansas Press.

Quine, W. V. O., and Ullian, J. S. 1978. *The Web of Belief.* 2d ed. New York: Random House.

Renteln, Alison D. 1988. "Relativism and the Search for Human Rights." *American Anthropologist* 90:56–72.

Scheper-Hughes, Nancy. 1984. "The Margaret Mead Controversy: Culture, Biology, and Anthropological Inquiry." *Human Organization* 43:85–93.

Wertheimer, Max. 1935. "Some Problems in the Theory of Ethics." *Social Research* 2:353–367.

Winch, Peter. 1972. "Understanding a Primitive Society." In *Ethics and Action*. London: Routledge and Kegan Paul.

Wong, David. 1986. "On Moral Realism without Foundations." *Southern Journal of Philosophy* 24 (Supp.): 95–113.

8

The Ethical Implications of
Cultural Relativity

CARL WELLMAN

I

It is often thought that the discoveries of anthropology have revolutionary
implications for ethics. Readers of Sumner, Benedict, and Herskovits are apt
to come away with the impression that the only moral obligation is to conform to one's society, that polygamy is as good as monogamy, or that no ethical judgment can be rationally justified. While these anthropologists might
complain that they are being misinterpreted, they would not deny that their
real intent is to challenge the traditional view of morals. Even the anthropologist whose scientific training has made him skeptical of sweeping generalities and wary of philosophical entanglements is inclined to believe that the
scientific study of cultures has undermined the belief in ethical absolutes of
any kind.

Just what has been discovered that forces us to revise our ethics? Science
has shown that certain things that were once thought to be absolute are actually relative to culture. Something is relative to culture when it varies with
and is causally determined by culture. Clearly, nothing can be both relative to
culture and absolute, for to be absolute is to be fixed and invariable, independent of man and the same for all men.

Exactly which things are relative and in what degree is a question—
still—being debated by cultural anthropologists. Important as this question
is, I do not propose to discuss it. It is the empirical scientist who must tell us
which things vary from culture to culture and to what extent each is causally
determined by its culture. It is not for me to question the findings of the
anthropologists in this area. Instead, let me turn to the philosophical problem
of the implications of cultural relativity. Assuming for the moment that cultural relativity is a fact, what follows for ethics?

What follows depends in part upon just what turns out to be relative.
Anthropologists are apt to use the word "values" to refer indiscriminately to

Reprinted, by permission of the publisher and copyright holder, from Carl Wellman, "The Ethical Implications of Cultural Relativity," in *The Journal of Philosophy* 55 (1963): 169–184.

the things which have value, the characteristics which give these things their value, the attitudes of the persons who value these things, and the judgments of those people that these things have value. Similarly, one finds it hard to be sure whether "morals" refers to the mores of a people, the set of principles an observer might formulate after observing their conduct, the practical beliefs the people themselves entertain, or the way they feel about certain kinds of conduct. Until such ambiguities are cleared up, one hardly knows what is being asserted when it is claimed that "values" or "morals" are relative.

It seems to me there are at least ten quite different things of interest to the ethicist that the anthropologist might discover to be relative to culture: mores, social institutions, human nature, acts, goals, value experiences, moral emotions, moral concepts, moral judgments, and moral reasoning. Since I can hardly discuss all the ethical conclusions that various writers have tried to draw from these different facts of cultural relativity, what I propose to do is to examine critically the reasoning by which one ethical conclusion might be derived from each of them.

II

It has long been recognized that mores are relative to culture. Mores are those customs which are enforced by social pressure. They are established patterns of action to which the individual is expected to conform and from which he deviates only at the risk of disapproval and punishment. It seems clear that mores vary from society to society and that the mores of any given society depend upon its culture. What does this imply for ethics?

The conclusion most frequently drawn is that what is right in one society may be wrong in another. For example, although it would be wrong for one of us to kill his aged parents, this very act is right for an Eskimo.[1] This is because our mores are different from those of Eskimo society, and it is the mores that make an act right or wrong.[2]

Let us grant, for the sake of discussion, that different societies do have different mores. Why should we grant that the mores make an act right or wrong? It has been claimed that this is true by definition.[3] "Right" simply means according to the mores, and "wrong" means in violation of the mores. There is something to be said for this analysis of our concepts of right and wrong.

It seems to explain both the imperativeness and the impersonality of obligation. The "ought" seems to tell one what to do and yet to be more than the command of any individual; perhaps its bindingness lies in the demands of society. Attractive as this interpretation appears at first glance, I cannot accept it. It can be shown that no naturalistic analysis of the meaning of ethical words is adequate.[4] In addition, this particular analysis is objectionable in that it makes it self-contradictory to say that any customary way of acting is wrong. No doubt social reformers are often confused, but they are not always inconsistent.

If the view that the mores make an act right or wrong is not true by definition, it amounts to the moral principle that one ought always to conform to the mores of his society. None of the ways in which this principle is usually supported is adequate. (*a*) Any society unconsciously develops those mores which are conducive to survival and well-being under its special circumstances.[5] Each individual ought to obey the mores of his society because this is the best way to promote the good life for the members of that society. I admit that there is a tendency for any society to develop those mores which fit its special circumstances, but I doubt that this is more than a tendency. There is room for reform in most societies, and this is particularly true when conditions are changing for one reason or another. (*b*) One ought to obey the mores of his society because disobedience would tend to destroy those mores. Without mores any society would lapse into a state of anarchy that would be intolerable for its members.[6] It seems to me that this argument deserves to be taken seriously, but it does not prove that one ought always to obey the mores of his society. What it does show is that one ought generally to obey the mores of his society and that whenever he considers disobedience he should give due weight to the effects of his example upon social stability. (*c*) One ought to obey the mores of his society because disobedience tends to undermine their existence. It is important to preserve the mores, not simply to avoid anarchy, but because it is their mores which give shape and meaning to the life of any people.[7] I grant that the individual does tend to think of his life in terms of the mores of his group and that anything which disrupts those mores tends to rob his life of significance. But once again, all this shows is that one should conform to the mores of his society on the whole. Although there is some obligation to conformity, this is not the only nor the most important obligation on the member of any society.

Therefore, it does not seem to me that one can properly say that the mores make an act right or wrong. One cannot define the meaning of these ethical words in terms of the mores, nor can one maintain the ethical principle that one ought always to obey the mores of his society. If the mores do not make acts right or wrong, the fact that different societies have different mores does not imply that the same kind of act can be right in one society and wrong in another.

III

Cultural relativity seems to apply to institutions as well as to mores. A social institution is a type of organization; it involves a pattern of activity in which two or more people play recognized roles. The family, the church, the government, the liberal arts college, the bridge club are all social institutions. Institutions can be classified more or less specifically. Thus monogamy, polygamy, and polyandry are specific institutions which fall under the generic institution of the family. Since the specific form an institution takes seems to vary from society to society depending upon the culture of that society, let us grant that social institutions are relative to culture. What does this imply for ethics?

A conclusion that is sometimes drawn is that we should never try to adopt an institution from another society or seek to impose one of our institutions upon another people. The main argument for this view is that each institution is an expression of the total culture of which it is a part.[8] To try to take an institution out of its cultural environment is sure to maim or even kill it; to try to bring an institution into an alien culture is likely to disorganize and even destroy that cultural pattern. Thus the attempt to transport an institution from one society to another will fail to achieve its intended result and will produce many unintended and socially undesirable effects.

No doubt the attempt to import or export a social institution is often a dismal failure. The transported institution becomes a mere caricature of its former self, and the society into which it is introduced becomes demoralized or even destroyed. Extreme caution is certainly necessary. But is it not incautious to conclude that the attempt will always fail? The most glaring examples of cultural demoralization and destruction, such as the intervention of the white man in Africa, have involved much more than the imposition of one or two institutions. Moreover, some institutions may be less alien to a given culture than others. If so, there might be some institutions that the society could adopt with only minor modifications. In fact, societies seem to have been borrowing from one another for centuries. While the effects of this borrowing have often been bad, they have not always been totally destructive or even grossly demoralizing. Occasionally they may have been beneficial. It seems unnecessary to conclude that we should never import or export an institution from the fact that social institutions are culturally relative.

Another thing which may be relative to culture is human nature. As soon as one ponders the differences between the Chinese aristocrat and the Australian bushman, the American tycoon and the Indian yogi, one finds it hard to believe that there is anything basic to human nature which is shared by all men. And reflection upon the profound effects of enculturation easily leads one to the conclusion that what a man is depends upon the society in which he has been brought up. Therefore, let us assume that human nature is culturally relative and see what this implies.

This seems to imply that no kind of action, moral character, or social institution is made inevitable by human nature. This conclusion is important because it cuts the ground out from under one popular type of justification in ethics. For example, capitalism is sometimes defended as an ideal on the grounds that this is the only economic system that is possible in the light of man's greedy and competitive nature. Or it might be claimed that adultery is permissible because the ideal of marital fidelity runs counter to man's innate drives or instincts. If there is no fixed human nature, such arguments are left without any basis.

One may wonder, however, whether the only alternatives are an entirely fixed and an entirely plastic human nature. It might be that enculturation could mold a human being but only within certain limits. These limits might exist either because certain parts of human nature are not at all plastic or because all parts are only moderately plastic. For example, it might turn out that the need for food and the tendency to grow in a certain way cannot be modified at all by enculturation, or it might turn out that every element in human nature can be modified in some ways but not in others. In either case, what a man becomes would depend partly upon enculturation and partly upon the nature of the organism being enculturated.

Thus cultural relativity may be a matter of degree. Before we can decide just what follows from the fact that human nature is relative to culture we must know how far and in what ways it is relative. If there are certain limits to the plasticity of human nature, these do rule out some kinds of action, character, or institution. But anthropology indicates that within any such limits a great many alternatives remain. Human nature may make eating inevitable, but what we eat and when we eat and how we eat is up to us. At least we can say that to the degree that human nature is relative to culture no kind of action, moral character, or social institution is made impossible by human nature.

IV

It has been claimed that acts are also relative to culture. This is to say that the same general type of action may take on specific differences when performed in different societies because those societies have different cultures. For example, it is one thing for one of us to kill his aged parent; it is quite a different thing for an Eskimo to do such an act. One difference lies in the consequences of these two acts. In our society disposing of old and useless parents merely allows one to live in greater luxury; to an Eskimo this act may mean the difference between barely adequate subsistence and malnutrition for himself and his family. What are we to make of this fact that the nature of an act is culturally relative?

One possible conclusion is that the same kind of act may be right in one society and wrong in another. This presupposes that the rightness of an act depends upon its consequences and that its consequences may vary from society to society. Since I accept these presuppositions, I agree that the rightness or wrongness of an act is relative to its social context.

It is important, however, to distinguish this conclusion from two others with which it is often confused. To say that the rightness of an act is relative to the society in which it is performed is not to say that exactly the same sort of act can be both right and wrong. It is because the social context makes the acts different in kind that one can be right while the other is wrong. Compare an act of infanticide in our society with an act of infanticide in some South Seas society.[9] Are these two acts the same or different? They are of the same kind inasmuch as both are acts of killing an infant. On the other hand, they are different in that such an act may be necessary to preserve the balance between family size and food resources in the South Seas while this is not the case in our society. These two acts are generically similar but specifically different; that is, they belong to different species of the same genus. Therefore, the conclusion that the same kind of act may be right in one society and wrong in another does not amount to saying that two acts which are precisely the same in every respect may differ in rightness or wrongness.

Neither is this conclusion to be confused with the view that acts are made right or wrong by the mores of society. No doubt our society disapproves of infanticide and some South Seas societies approve of it, but it is not *this* which makes infanticide wrong for us and right for them. If infanticide is wrong for us and right for them, it is because acts of infanticide have very different consequences in our society and in theirs, not because the practice is discouraged here and customary there.

V

The goals that individuals or groups aim for also seem relative to culture. What objects people select as goals varies from society to society depending upon the cultures of those societies. One group may strive for social prestige and the accumulation of great wealth, another may aim at easy comfort and the avoidance of any danger, a third may seek military glory and the conquest of other peoples. What follows from this fact of cultural relativity?

This fact is often taken as a basis for arguing that it is impossible to compare the value of acts, institutions, or total ways of life belonging to different societies. The argument rests on the assumptions that acts, institutions, and ways of life are means directed at certain ends, that means can be evaluated only in terms of their ends, and that ends are incommensurable with respect to value.[10]

Granted these assumptions, the argument seems a good one, but I doubt that ends are really incommensurable. It seems to me that we can recognize that certain ends are more worth while than others, for example that pleasure is intrinsically better than pain. I may be mistaken, but until this has been shown, the conclusion that it is impossible to compare the value of acts, institutions, or ways of life belonging to different societies has not been established.

VI

People from different societies apparently experience the same object or situation in quite different ways depending upon the cultural differences between their societies. The satisfying experience that a cultured Chinese might derive from eating bird's nest soup would be diametrically opposed to the experience I would undergo if I forced myself to gulp down my helping of that exotic dish out of politeness. Again, an experience which I would greatly value, sitting in the bleachers watching the Red Sox clinch the pennant, would be nothing but a boring observation of meaningless motions accompanied by the sensations of scorching sun, trickling sweat, and unyielding benches to a Hottentot visitor. In large measure the nature of any experience is determined by the process of enculturation that the experiencer has undergone. Thus, value experiences are also relative to culture.

It might seem to follow that the same experience could be good to one person and bad to another, but this is just what does *not* follow. The difference in value stems from the fact that, although confronted with similar objects or situations, the two people have very different experiences. The nature of a person's experience depends upon the kind of person he has become through the process of enculturation as much as upon the external stimulus. It would be a mistake to conclude that qualitatively identical experiences are good to me and bad to the Hottentot. Although he and I are in the same ballpark watching the same game, we are having very different experiences.

What one should conclude is that the same kind of object or situation can have different values to people from different societies. This follows from the fact that the nature of a person's experience depends in large measure upon the way in which he has been enculturated, together with the assumption that the value of any object or situation depends upon its effects on experience. Since my ethical view is that the value of objects and situations is derived from their impact upon experience, I accept the conclusion that the same kind of object or situation can have very different values to people who come from different cultures.

VII

It appears that moral emotions are also relative to culture. What a person desires, approves, or feels guilty about seems to vary from society to society depending upon the cultural differences between those societies. What does the fact that moral emotions are culturally relative imply for ethics?

One possible conclusion would be that the same kind of act or person can be morally good in one society and morally bad in another. This is supposed to follow from the fact that the same kind of act or person can be approved in one society and disapproved in another together with the view that to be morally good or bad is simply to be approved or disapproved.

That infanticide is approved in certain South Seas societies and disapproved in ours need not be doubted.[11] That infanticide constitutes exactly the same kind of act in the two societies is, as we have seen, more dubious. But even if it did, I would not accept the conclusion in question; for I would not admit that the moral value of any act or person depends upon whether it is approved or disapproved. That the grounds for moral evaluation lie outside the moral emotions can be seen by the fact that it always makes sense to ask someone *why* he approves or disapproves of something. If approving or disapproving made its object morally good or bad, there would be no need of such justification. Thus, the fact that moral emotions are culturally relative does not prove that identical acts or persons can be morally good in one society and morally bad in another.

VIII

Both linguistic and psychological studies have suggested that people living in different societies conceptualize their experience in different ways.[12] Probably moral concepts vary from society to society depending upon the cultural backgrounds from which they arise. The ancient Greek thought of virtue quite differently from the modern American; the Christian conception of obligation is probably absent from the mind of the African who has escaped the influence of any missionary. What are we to conclude from the fact that moral concepts are relative to culture?

The obvious implication appears to be that people of different cultural backgrounds are almost sure to disagree on any ethical question. Obvious as it may seem, this is not implied at all. In fact, people using different concepts could never disagree, for disagreement presupposes that both parties are thinking in the same terms. For one thing, on what question are they supposed to be disagreeing? If each person is using his own set of concepts, each person formulates his own question in his own terms. And if the two persons do not have any common set of ethical concepts, there is no way for formulating a single question that will be intelligible to both of them. Again, in what sense do their respective answers disagree? When an American says that Poland is undemocratic and a Russian insists that it is a fine example of democracy, it appears that they are disagreeing. No doubt they do disagree in many ways, but not in their utterances. Their statements are quite compatible, for they are using the words "democracy" in different senses. Similarly, people of different cultures would only seem to disagree, if they attached different concepts to their ethical words.

The proper conclusion to draw is that any comparison between the ethical views of the members of different cultures can be only partial. As long as each view is stated only in its own terms there can be no comparison between them; comparison becomes possible only when they are stated in the same set of concepts. But if the sets of concepts are not identical, any translation of one view into the language of the other or of both into some neutral language will be approximate at best. Even where something approaching adequate translation is possible, some of the meaning will be lost or something will be added that was not in the original concept. For this reason, any claim that the ethical views of people in different societies are either identical or contradictory is likely to tell only part of the story. To some extent, at least, the ethics of different cultures are incommensurate.

IX

The aspect of cultural relativity most often emphasized is that pertaining to moral judgments. Objects that the members of one society think to be good are considered bad by another group; acts considered wrong in one society are thought of as right in another. Moreover, these differences in judgments of value and obligation seem to reflect cultural differences between the respective societies. There is a great deal of evidence to suggest that ethical judgments are relative to culture.

To many anthropologists and philosophers it is a corollary of this fact that one of a set of contrary ethical judgments is no more valid than another, or, put positively, that all ethical judgments are equally valid. Unfortunately, there is a crucial ambiguity lurking in this epistemological thicket. Ethical judgments might have equal validity either because all are valid or because none are: similarly one ethical judgment might be no more valid than another either because both are equally valid or because both are equally lacking in validity. Since these two interpretations are quite different, let us consider them separately.

On the first interpretation, the conclusion to be drawn from the fact that ethical judgments are relative to culture is that every moral judgment is valid for the society in which it is made. Instead of denying the objective validity of ethical judgments, this view affirms it, but in a qualified form which will allow for the variations in ethical belief.

There seem to be three main ways of defending this position. (*a*) Ethical judgments have objective validity because it is possible to justify them rationally. However, this validity is limited to a given society because the premises used in such justification are those which are agreed upon in that society. Since there are no universally accepted premises, no universal validity is possible.[13] I would wish to deny that justification is real if it is limited in this way. If all our reasoning really does rest on certain premises which can be rejected by others without error, then we must give up the claim to objective validity. When I claim validity for ethical judgments, I intend to claim more than that it is possible to support them with logical arguments; I also claim that it is incorrect to deny the premises of such arguments. (*b*) Any ethical judgment is an expression of a total pattern of culture.[14] Hence it is possible to justify any single judgment in terms of its coherence with the total cultural configuration of the judger. But one cannot justify the culture as a whole, for it is not part of a more inclusive pattern. Therefore, ethical judgments have objective validity, but only in terms of a given cultural pattern. I would make the same objection to this view as to the preceding one. Since it allows justification to rest upon an arbitrary foundation, it is inadequate to support any significant claim to objective validity. (*c*) Any ethical judgment has objective validity because it is an expression of a moral code. The validity of a moral code rests on the fact that without conformity to a common code social cohesion breaks down, leading to disastrous results. Since any given moral code provides cohesion for one and only one society, each ethical judgment has validity for a single society.[15] There are at least two difficulties with this defence of objectivity. Surely one could deny some ethical judgments without destroying the entire moral code they reflect; not every judgment could be shown to be essential to social stability. Moreover, the argument seems to rest on the ethical judgment that one ought not to contribute to the breakdown of social stability. How is this judgment to be shown to be valid? One must either appeal to some other basis of validity or argue in a circle. None of these arguments to show that every moral judgment is valid for the society in which it is made is adequate.

On the second interpretation, the conclusion to be drawn from the fact that moral judgments are relative to culture is that moral judgments have no objective validity. This amounts to saying that the distinction between true and false, correct and incorrect, does not apply to such judgments. This conclusion obviously does not follow simply from the fact that people disagree about ethical questions. We do not deny the objective validity of scientific judgments either on the grounds that different scientists propose alternative theories or on the grounds that the members of some societies hold fast to many unscientific beliefs.

Why, then, does the fact that moral judgments are relative to culture imply that they have no objective validity? (*a*) Individuals make different ethical judgments because they judge in terms of different frames of reference, and they adopt these frames of reference uncritically from their cultures.[16] Since ethical judgments are the product of enculturation rather than reasoning, they cannot claim rational justification. I do not find this argument convincing, for it seems to confuse the origin of a judgment with its justification. The causes of a judgment are one thing; the reasons for or against it are another. It remains to be shown that any information about what causes us to judge as we do has any bearing on the question of whether or not our judgments are correct. (*b*) It is impossible to settle ethical questions by using the scientific method.[17] Therefore, there is no objective way to show that one ethical judgment is any more correct than another, and, in the absence of any method of establishing the claim to objective validity, it makes no sense to continue to make the claim. I will concede that, if there is no rational method of establishing ethical judgments, then we might as well give up the claim to objective validity. And if the scientific method is restricted to the testing of hypotheses by checking the predictions they imply against the results of observation and experiment, it does seem to be inapplicable to ethical questions. What I will not concede is the tacit assumption that the scientific method is the only method of establishing the truth. Observation and experimentation do not figure prominently in the method used by mathematicians. I even wonder whether the person who concludes that ethical judgments have no objective validity can establish *this* conclusion by using the scientific method. The fact that ethical judgments cannot be established scientifically does not by itself prove that they cannot be established by any method of reasoning. (*c*) There might be some method of settling ethical disputes, but it could not be a method of reasoning. Any possible reasoning would have to rest upon certain premises. Since the members of different societies start from different premises, there is no basis for argument that does not beg the question.[18] I suspect, however, that we have been looking for our premises in the wrong place. The model of deduction tempts us to search for very general premises from which all our more specific judgments can be deduced. Unfortunately, it is just in this area of universal moral principles that disagreement seems most frequent and irremedial. But suppose that these ethical general-izations are themselves inductions based upon particular moral judgments. Then we could argue for or against them in terms of relatively specific ethical judgments and the factual judgments that are in turn relevant to these. Until this possibility is explored further, we need not admit that there is no ade-quate basis for ethical reasoning. Thus it appears that none of these refuta-tions of the objective validity of ethical judgments is really conclusive.

The fact that ethical judgments are relative to culture is often taken to prove that no ethical judgment can claim to be any more valid than any of its contraries. I have tried to show that, on neither of the two possible interpre-tations of this conclusion, does the conclusion necessarily follow from the fact of cultural relativity.

X

Finally, moral reasoning might turn out to be relative to culture. When some ethical statement is denied or even questioned, the person who made the statement is apt to leap to its defense. He attempts to justify his statement by producing reasons to support it. But speakers from different societies tend to justify their statements in different ways.[19] The difference in their reasoning may be of two kinds. Either their reasoning may rest on different assump-tions or they may draw inferences in a different manner. That is, the argu-ments they advance may either start from different premises or obey differ-ent logics. We can ignore the former case here; for it boils down to a difference in their judgments, and we have discussed that at length in the preceding sec-tion. Instead let us assume that people who belong to different societies tend to draw their moral conclusions according to different logics depending upon their respective cultures. What difference would it make if moral rea-soning were thus culturally relative?

The most interesting conclusion that might be drawn from the fact that moral reasoning is relative to culture is that it has no objective validity. The claim to objective validity is empty where it cannot be substantiated. But how could one justify the claim that any given kind of moral reasoning is valid? To appeal to the same kind of reasoning would be circular. To appeal to some other kind of reasoning would not be sufficient to justify this kind; for each kind of reasoning involves principles of inference which go beyond, and therefore cannot be justified by appealing to, any other kind.

I find this line of argument inconclusive for several reasons. First, it is not clear that a given kind of reasoning cannot be justified by appealing to a dif-ferent kind of reasoning. In fact, this seems to be a fairly common practice in logic. Various forms of syllogistic argument can be shown to be valid by reducing them to arguments of the form Barbara. Again, a logician will some-times justify certain rules for natural deduction by an involved logical argu-ment which does not itself use these same rules. Second, in what sense is it impossible to show another person that my moral arguments are valid? I can show him that the various moral arguments I advance conform to the principles of my logic. If he does not accept these principles, he will remain unconvinced. This may show that I cannot persuade him that my arguments are valid, but does it show that I have not proved that they are? It is not obvious that persuading a person and proving a point are identical. Third, is the claim to objective validity always empty in the absence of any justification for it? Perhaps some reasoning is ultimate in that it requires no further justification. To assume the opposite seems to lead to an infinite regress. If every valid justification stands in need of further justification, no amount of justification would ever be sufficient.

I do not claim to have established the objective validity of moral reasoning. I am not even sure how that validity might be established or even whether it needs to be established. All I have been trying to do is to suggest that such validity is not ruled out by the fact, if it is a fact, that moral reasoning is relative to culture.

CONCLUSION

It is fashionable either to ignore the facts of cultural relativity or to draw startling conclusions from them. I have argued that it is unnecessary to accept any of the following conclusions: Qualitatively identical acts may be right or good in one society and wrong or bad in another. We should never try to adopt an institution from another society or to impose one of ours upon another people. No kind of action, moral character, or social institution is made impossible by human nature. It is impossible to compare the value of acts, institutions, or ways of life belonging to different societies. The same experience can be good to one person and bad to another. People from different cultures are bound to disagree on ethical questions. Ethical judgments have no objective validity. Every moral judgment is valid for the society in which it is made. Moral reasoning has no objective validity.

The various arguments by which these conclusions are usually derived from the facts of cultural relativity are, in my opinion, either invalid or inconclusive. On the other hand, there are some important ethical conclusions which can and should be drawn from these same facts. Among the genuine implications of cultural relativity I would include these: Our own institutions are far from inevitable. Generically similar objects or situations may have different values in different societies. Generically similar acts may be right or good in one society and wrong or bad in another. Any comparison between the ethical views of the members of different societies can be only partial.

No doubt the reader will wish to challenge my acceptance or rejection of this or that particular conclusion. Quite apart from such specific ethical questions, however, there are certain over-all logical conclusions which seem to me inevitable. (1) What conclusions one can legitimately draw from the facts of cultural relativity will depend upon *which* facts one starts from. It is worth distinguishing between the relativity of mores, social institutions, human nature, acts, goals, value experiences, moral emotions, moral concepts, moral judgments, and moral reasoning; for each of these has different implications for ethics. (2) By themselves the facts of cultural relativity do not imply anything for ethics. Any argument that is both interesting and valid requires additional premises. Thus it is only in conjunction with certain statements that go beyond anthropology that the findings of anthropology have any bearing at all on ethics. (3) What conclusions one should draw will obviously depend upon which of these additional premises one accepts. Therefore, one's ethical and epistemological theory will determine the significance one will attach to cultural relativity. (4) Before we can criticize or even understand the arguments by which ethical conclusions are derived from the facts of such relativity, we must make these additional premises explicit and see what can be said for or against them. My main purpose in this paper has been to make a start in this complicated yet crucial task.

NOTES

1. A. L. Kroeber, *Anthropology* (New York: Harcourt Brace, 1948), p. 265.

2. W. G. Sumner, *Folkways* (Boston: Ginn & Co., 1907), p. 521.

3. R. Benedict, "Anthropology and the Abnormal," *Journal of General Psychology,* 10 (January, 1934), p. 73.

4. C. Wellman, *The Language of Ethics* (Cambridge: Harvard University Press, 1961), ch. II.

5. A. T. Culwick, *Good Out of Africa* (Livingstone: Rhodes-Livingstone Institute, 1943), p. 6.

6. M. J. Herskovits, *Man and His Works* (New York: Knopf, 1948), p. 77.

7. Benedict, *Patterns of Culture* (Boston: Houghton Mifflin, 1934), p. 22.

8. Ibid., pp. 43–44.

9. R. Firth, *Elements of Social Organization* (London: Watts & Co., 1951), p. 202.

10. Benedict, *Patterns of Culture*, p. 223.

11. Firth, op. cit., p. 202.

12. M. Edel & A. Edel, *Anthropology and Ethics* (Springfield, Ill.: Charles Thomas, 1959), pp. 117–119.

13. Kroeber, op. cit., p. 266.

14. Benedict, *Patterns of Culture*, pp. 45–47.

15. Herskovits, op. cit., pp. 75–76.

16. Herskovits, op. cit., pp. 65–66.

17. R. Redfield, *The Primitive World and Its Transformations* (Ithaca: Cornell University Press, 1953), p. 144.

18. Herskovits, op. cit., p. 61.

19. Edel & Edel, op. cit., p. 162.

PART THREE

ON THE COHERENCE OF MORAL RELATIVISM

9 *Dishonest Relativism*

BETSY POSTOW

In this paper I shall argue that a sort of moral position which is fairly common among philosophers and other thoughtful people is in some sense dishonest. The sort of moral position with which I am concerned has two components: (1) some view according to which people sometimes morally ought to do certain things, and (2) some meta-ethical view according to which a normative view that conflicts with one's own well grounded normative view may itself be a well grounded or acceptable moral view. The first component is held by almost all people with moral convictions[1]; the second component is held by a smaller but still considerable number of people who, despite their moral convictions, are impressed with the seeming impossibility of finding an objective foundation for one correct moral view. Many philosophers concur in this; the grounds on which they take their own normative views to be rationally justified would justify conflicting normative views as well as their own. John Rawls, to take a well known example, considers a normative theory to be justified if it represents a reflective equilibrium between our moral intuitions and the demands of theory.[2] But, as Rawls himself points out, conflicting normative theories might represent reflective equilibrium for persons with differing moral intuitions. "Even should everyone attain wide reflective equilibrium, many contrary moral conceptions may still be held."[3] The fact that this situation would deprive him of any grounds for saying that a theory contrary to his own is mistaken does not disturb Rawls, for "the procedure of reflective equilibrium does not assume that there is one correct moral conception."[4]

The question which I would like to consider here is whether it is legitimate to continue to accept one's *own* normative view in such a situation. I am willing to grant that it is legitimate to continue to believe that one's own normative view is well grounded in such a situation, for a meta-ethical theory like Rawls' defines "well-groundedness" in such a way that conflicting normative views may in fact both be well grounded. But accepting a normative view involves more than believing that it is well grounded. (If it did not, one would have to accept conflicting views which one believed to be well

Reprinted, by permission of the publisher and copyright holder, from Betsy Postow, "Dishonest Relativism," in *Analysis* 39 (1979): 45–48.

grounded.) Accepting a moral view involves, in addition to the belief that the view is well grounded, some sort of practical commitment to the view. It is the legitimacy of this practical commitment which I wish to question in cases where one believes that a rival normative view is equally as well grounded as the view which one accepts.

It is notoriously difficult to characterize the practical commitment inherent in accepting a normative theory, but we can say enough to make the problem clear. Included in a whole-hearted acceptance of a normative view is at least some sort of minimal assent to certain prescriptions which I shall call the prescriptions that correspond directly to the view: If P is a normative view which is itself taken to be a prescription, then the prescription which "corresponds" directly to it will simply be P itself. If P is the judgment (or judgment analogue) that lying in certain circumstances is always wrong, the directly corresponding prescription would prohibit lying in these circumstances. If P is the judgment that Fred ought not to lie, the directly corresponding prescription forbids Fred to lie. Now what is involved in "minimal assent" to a prescription? It seems reasonable to say that A gives at least minimal assent to a prescription which commands something of B (who may or may not be identical with A) only if A would be willing to use the prescription or its equivalent to offer guidance to B in appropriate circumstances, assuming that A is not especially timid. By "appropriate circumstances" I mean circumstances in which, in A's opinion, it would be proper and prudent to offer sincere guidance to B. For example, if Alice assents to a prescription directing Bob to return the money which he has embezzled, then she should be willing in appropriate circumstances to advise Bob (or exhort him, or whatever) to return the money. If she is not willing to do this in appropriate circumstances, this indicates that she does not assent to the prescription. My thesis requires that the acceptance of a normative view involves at least this sort of minimal assent to the prescriptions which correspond directly to the view.

It may be thought that where P is a judgement about a particular person's obligations, someone who accepts P must assent not only to the directly corresponding prescription, but also to the universal prescription which corresponds indirectly to P. For if I think that a particular person ought to do a particular act in certain circumstances, then consistency requires that I also think that all people in circumstances which are defined as relevantly similar by my moral view ought to do acts which are defined as relevantly similar by my moral view. But although consistency may require this, it seems that I could be confused and inconsistent in not holding the generalized view, yet still be said to accept the particular judgment. In this case, I would assent to the prescription directly corresponding to P, but I would not assent to the prescriptions that are [quasi] implied by P. I would not object to the specification of a stronger sense of "accept" in which a person would be said to accept a set of judgement/prescriptions P only if that person also accepts all judgement/prescriptions that are [quasi] implied by the members of P, perhaps together with descriptions of nonmoral facts; but the problem with which I am concerned can be stated in terms of the weaker sense of "accept."

Let me illustrate why it seems illegitimate for a person to accept a normative theory while believing that a conflicting theory is equally well grounded. Suppose that Alice's moral theory implies that Bob (and other people in ordinary circumstances) ought to abstain from animal products. Because she assents to the corresponding prescription, Alice is willing in appropriate circumstances to use this prescription to advise or exhort Bob to abstain from animal products. But Alice believes that Bob's moral theory, which condones and even commands the use of animal products, is equally well grounded as her own. Therefore she believes that Bob has no moral reason to abstain from animal products. She may also believe that he has no nonmoral reason to abstain, in that abstinence would not serve any of his nonmoral goals. By hypothesis, Alice would be willing in such a case to advise or exhort Bob to do something which, in her opinion, he has no reason to do—and this seems in some sense unreasonable or dishonest.

Now Alice might not agree that Bob has no moral reason to abstain from animal products. She might point out that although *his* moral theory does not provide a reason for him or anyone to abstain, *her* moral theory provides a reason for everyone to abstain. And surely it would be correct to cite the fact that Bob has an obligation to do something as a reason for him to do it when one is advising or exhorting him to do it. Thus if Alice's moral theory is well grounded, Alice can cite Bob's obligation according to this theory as a reason for him to abstain from animal products.

There is an easy reply to Alice's objection in the case where Bob's moral theory implies an obligation to use animal products. For if his obligation according to Alice's well grounded theory to abstain from animal products constitutes a reason for him to abstain, then his obligation according to his own well grounded theory to use animal products constitutes an equally good reason for him not to abstain. These reasons cancel each other out. Thus Bob has no all-things-considered reason to abstain from animal products. Since Alice should realize this, she would be unreasonable or dishonest to exhort Bob to abstain in such a case.

Let us now consider the case where Bob is merely permitted rather than obligated to use animal products according to his own moral theory. It would by hypothesis be equally reasonable for him to accept his own view and reject Alice's, as it would be for him to accept Alice's and reject his own. Now I assume that it would not be even more reasonable to accept both his own view and Alice's conflicting view rather than to accept one and reject the other. Thus rejecting Alice's view would be an optimally reasonable position. And if he takes this position, he can reasonably refuse to accord any weight at all to moral reasons provided by Alice's view. But if it would be equally as reasonable for Bob to refuse to accord any weight at all to the only reason which Alice can cite for his abstaining from animal products as it would be for him to accord weight to this reason, it seems that the overall force of reasons cannot be said to favour Bob's abstaining from animal products over his using them. The guidance which Alice is prepared to offer, however, explicitly favours Bob's abstaining over his using animal products. So once again the guidance which she is prepared to offer is not supported by the overall force of reasons.

Of course Alice may never actually be in a situation in which she is willing to offer someone guidance which fails to be supported by the overall force of reasons; but she must be *prepared* to do so in appropriately specified hypothetical situations. And so must the holder of any normative view which ascribes obligations to agents, if she or he also holds that a contrary normative view may be equally well grounded (and if that fact would not make her or him give up the original normative view). Now in order to specify what the holder of any particular normative theory, such as Rawls', must be prepared in hypothetical situations to exhort people to do, it would be necessary to delve into the intricacies of the particular normative theory in question. But it seems enough reason to call a position dishonest, that a person who adopts it must be prepared in *some* hypothetical situation to advise or exhort someone to do *something* which, according to the position, there is no all-things-considered reason (including reasons furnished by morality) for that person to do.[5]

NOTES

1. It is possible to have moral convictions about what ought to be the case without having any moral convictions that anyone ought to do anything. See I. L. Humberstone, "Two Sorts of 'Ought's," *Analysis* 32.1 (1971–2), pp. 8–11.

2. *A Theory of Justice*, Cambridge, Mass: Harvard University Press, 1971, pp. 48–50.

3. "The Independence of Moral Theory," *Proceedings and Addresses of the American Philosophical Association*, 48 (1974–75), 9.

4. Ibid.

5. Thanks to Gilbert Harman, Thomas Nagel, and the editor of *Analysis* for their helpful comments and suggestions.

10   *Ethical Relativism and the Problem of Incoherence*

DAVID LYONS

It is natural to suppose that "ethical relativism" names a single type of theory that either makes good sense or none at all. Opponents of relativism may therefore be expected to argue that it is an incoherent doctrine. Some have done so, understanding it as the combination of blatantly inconsistent claims. Recently, Gilbert Harman has objected to such a strategy of "dissuasive definition" and has shown its inadequacies by developing a theory that is recognizably relativistic while lacking any obvious inconsistencies.[1] It may therefore seem as if ethical relativism is immune to such charges and can continue to demand our respect.

I agree with Harman that relativistic theories do not uniformly lapse into incoherence, but there nevertheless remain reasons for suspecting many relativistic theories of being untenable—reasons not of accidental formulation but rooted deeply in certain ways of thinking about morality. As a consequence, whole classes of relativistic theories may well prove to be incoherent.

In this paper I shall explore the nature and extent of one important threat of incoherence to ethical relativism. I shall sketch the source of that particular threat, I shall show how relativistic theories differ in their vulnerability to it, and I shall suggest that our fears for relativism may be tempered slightly. Then I shall consider two ways in which relativists might try to avoid (or might luckily succeed in avoiding) such incoherence—that is, by resorting to "relativistic" notions of justification in ethics and by construing moral judgments as having a hidden relativistic structure.

THE PROBLEM

Suppose that Alice and Barbara have been discussing Claudia's proposed abortion. They know Claudia well, and they agree about the circumstances and the likely consequences of the act. But they disagree in their evaluations, Alice maintaining that it would be wrong and Barbara that it would not be wrong for Claudia to have the abortion.

Reprinted, by permission of the publisher and copyright holder, from David Lyons, "Ethical Relativism and the Problem of Incoherence," in *Ethics* 86 (1976): 107–121.

Now, according to some theories about morality, both Alice and Barbara could be making perfectly valid moral judgments. Some anthropologists have suggested, for example, that one's judgment is valid if, and only if, it agrees with the norms or code of one's social group.[2] These writers evidently think it possible for Alice and Barbara to belong to different groups, their groups to have codes that differ about abortion, and their respective judgments to conform to their respective group codes. They are therefore committed to regarding both judgments as valid in some cases. Some philosophers have held that one's moral judgment is fully justified if it accords with the relevant facts and with principles to which one would freely subscribe on due reflection under ideal conditions.[3] Since it is admittedly possible for different persons to embrace differing principles even under ideal conditions, such theorists are committed to endorsing both judgments—that Claudia's act would be wrong and that Claudia's act would not be wrong—in some possible cases.

This clearly generates a problem which, while tacitly acknowledged in the philosophical literature, has not been discussed directly. The judgments made by Alice and Barbara appear to be logically incompatible. They might be straightforward contradictories—unless "wrong" and "not wrong" have restricted ranges of application, in which cases they would seem to be at least strict logical contraries. Appearances can be misleading, of course, but the relevant considerations are not negligible; they involve not merely surface grammar but also the conviction shared by laymen and philosophers that only one of these judgments could possibly be right and also our ways of discussing such cases, which include advancing reasons that are held to warrant drawing or refusing one judgment or the other.[4] Such theories seem to endorse (at least the possibility of) contradictions. Unless something further can be said, they are incoherent and may be committed to the philosophical scrap heaps.

For this reason, or some other, relativists often claim, in effect, that such judgments are not logically incompatible; so of course we cannot assume the opposite here. For convenience, however, I shall refer to such pairs of judgments as "conflicting," thus reflecting the presumption that they are logically incompatible while leaving open our final judgment on the nature of the conflict between them.

It should also be noted that I shall use the term "incoherence" generally rather than "inconsistency" and shall speak of validity rather than truth, because I wish to include within this survey certain ethical theories which deny that moral judgments are either true or false. Since these theories nevertheless regard moral judgments as subject to significant validation or justification, they too are affected by the same threat of incoherence.

TWO KINDS OF RELATIVISM

Not all relativistic ethical theories flirt with this sort of incoherence. We can see this when we try to disambiguate the anthropologists' suggestions. Generally speaking, the idea they embrace is that the existing norms of a social group are the only valid basis for moral appraisals. Beyond this, their suggestion is not entirely clear. Is it that the norms within each group must be used in judging conduct within that group? Or is it that such norms directly govern all the judgments made by members of the group? (There are other possibilities, but these are the most plausible and will serve our purposes.) It makes a great deal of difference which is meant.

Take the first possibility, the one most strongly suggested by the anthropologists, which I shall call agent's-group relativism. It may be understood as the notion that an act is right if, and only if, it accords with the norms of the agent's group. Now, such writers are anxious to impress on us that there are many different social groups, each group having its own norms which can be different from those of other groups. Against that background it seems reasonable to regard such a theory as relativistic, for it recognizes (or at least countenances) a number of different, independent bases for moral appraisals.[5] Nevertheless, such a theory seems not to validate conflicting moral judgments, because each group is regarded, so to speak, as a separate moral realm. If we wish to judge a given act, such as Claudia's proposed abortion, this theory tells us to apply the norms of her social group. It therefore seems to imply that any single item of conduct can correctly be judged in one and only one way.[6]

The second possible interpretation of the anthropologists' idea can be called appraiser's-group relativism because it says, in effect, that a moral judgment is valid if, and only if, it accords with the norms of the appraiser's social group. Such a theory does seem to validate conflicting moral judgments, for reasons we have already noted. Any single act can be judged by people in different social groups, and so judgments of Claudia's proposed abortion, for example, can be governed by different norms. Both Alice's and Barbara's conflicting judgments might well be validated by this theory.

These two theories give us differing instructions for judging conduct within other groups. Both theories tolerate more than one basis for moral appraisals, but the appraiser theory allows differing standards to have overlapping applications[7] while the agent theory apparently does not.

This contrast has, of course, nothing to do with the rampant conventionalism of such theories; it can be found in other families of relativistic theory too. Consider, for example, the individualistic philosophers' theory that was noted at the outset. This says, in effect, that one's moral judgment is valid if, and only if, one would accept it under certain hypothetical circumstances (such as knowing all the relevant facts) that are conceived of as ideal for deciding upon one's moral principles. Now, there is no guarantee that different individuals will subscribe to the same principles, even under "ideal" conditions, so such a theory is relativistic. This is also an appraiser theory and could well validate conflicting moral judgments. By now we can also see the possibility of a contrasting agent theory, which says that a person's conduct must be judged by the principles to which he himself would subscribe under such ideal conditions. This theory would not seem to validate conflicting moral judgments.[8] These two theories give us differing instructions for judging another person's conduct, and the appraiser version does, while the agent version apparently does not, flirt with incoherence.

What seems to make all these theories qualify as relativistic is their acceptance of more than one set of *basic* moral standards (social norms or personal principles, for example). But some allow these standards to have overlapping applications, while others do not, and this determines whether a theory will endorse conflicting moral judgments. The threat of incoherence that we are investigating, therefore, does not affect relativistic theories equally.

I have not said that it does not affect agent theories at all because such theories, despite their apparent intentions, can sometimes countenance conflicting judgments too. Consider agent's-group relativism. It may seem secure, so long as we forget that individuals can belong to more than one social group at any time. While suggesting their group-oriented theories, anthropologists have seemed strangely insensible of the fact that, even within the relatively small societies to which they typically refer, social classes, families, and other real social groups (of the sort social scientists are concerned to investigate) are maintained.[9] And social norms can be ascribed to many such groups. Most important, one can belong to groups that have differing values (as well as be disaffected from values that prevail within a group to which one continues to belong). Claudia, for example, might be in a church that condemns abortion and at the same time in a family, peer group, voluntary organization, social class, or political community that condones it. Now, the basic notion underlying agent's-group relativism seems to be that membership in a group makes its prevailing standards validly applicable to one's conduct. If so, the theory implies that Claudia's proposed abortion should be judged by the norms of all the groups to which she belongs. This would allow it to validate conflicting moral judgments—indeed, to both validate and invalidate a single judgment.

Such complications clearly can afflict other agent theories too. Any theory is vulnerable unless it guarantees that differing standards have no overlapping applications to specific cases. Of course, it is possible to secure this, if one is willing to pay the price of necessary revisions. But it is not always clear how to change a theory so as to avoid such embarrassments, while preserving its original point. Most important, it remains to be seen whether incoherence can be avoided in a truly nonarbitrary manner. If a theory has incoherent implications, it is, presumably, quite strictly untenable. But one that avoids incoherence arbitrarily, through ad hoc revisions lacking any independent rationale, cannot be much more tenable. I shall revert to this point later. Meanwhile, I shall restrict my attention to appraiser theories, since the relevant problem affects them primarily. Agent theorists must be wary, but their difficulties present us with no new problems to consider.

THE CHARGE OF INCOHERENCE QUALIFIED

We may need to temper slightly our ideas about the possible incoherence of relativistic theories. Even when a theory is in the worst straits, and seems to tell us that contradictory judgments are both true, there are reasons for hesitating to call that theory incoherent and hence untenable. Since the present point has more general significance than its bearing upon relativism, it may be best to explain it in relation to another sort of theory that is sometimes suspected of incoherence—ethical egoism.

It may be said that egoism is incoherent because it can be used to generate contradictory judgments about cases in which the interests of different individuals conflict. But consider an egoist who also believes in the natural harmony of human interests—that is, between the overall, long-term interests of differing persons. He denies, in effect, that there ever are any cases of the sort just mentioned, which are responsible for the alleged incoherence of his principle. From his overall position, which includes this belief in the natural harmony of human interests as well as ethical egoism, it seems impossible to derive the contradictory judgments in question. If so, his position cannot fairly be charged with incoherence on such grounds. And yet his position includes the egoistic principle. If that were incoherent—if it had literally inconsistent (or otherwise incoherent) implications—then presumably we could still generate contradictions from it, even when it is conjoined with some contingent claim. Since we cannot, it seems to follow that such judgments are not entailed by principles like egoism alone, and thus that the egoistic principle itself cannot fairly be charged with incoherence. The relevant implications derive from more complex positions, including beliefs about the relevant facts; and so it is these positions which may or may not be charged with incoherence.

Now, I do not mean to suggest that the implications of a principle are limited to actual cases. This cannot be right, since they are thought to cover possible cases too, such as Claudia's proposed abortion. But the foregoing argument does not restrict their implications to actual cases. My suggestion is that we must differentiate between what can strictly be ascribed to a principle alone and what can only be ascribed to a larger position. Nor do I mean to suggest that one must positively believe in the divergence of different persons' interests in order to be charged with incoherence for holding such a principle. Perhaps an egoist with an open mind about the relevant facts could fairly be charged with having an incoherent position (assuming the principle does in fact yield inconsistent judgments for such cases), because such a person would accept, in effect, the possibility of contradictions. But there seems to be a significant sense in which an egoist who believes in the natural harmony of human interests is not committed to such judgments. Clearly, I have only scratched the surface of a complex question on which more work is needed. For the sake of argument here, let us suppose my suggestion is correct.

If it is, it would seem to follow that a relativistic theory cannot be regarded as incoherent simply because it can be used to generate logically incompatible judgments in the ways we have considered (supposing for the moment that they are strictly incompatible or that a theory so construes them). For, someone might combine a relativistic theory with certain contingent beliefs which imply that the relevant cases never will occur, thus effectively blocking the offending judgments. For example, an appraiser's-group relativist might conceivably maintain that every social group inevitably shares the same set of basic values; someone endorsing the individualistic analogue of that theory might believe that identical basic values must be ascribed to all persons. Such beliefs would block the validation of conflicting moral judgments by such theories. If so, not only the overall positions but also the principles they contain cannot fairly be charged with incoherence. Strictly speaking, such principles would not be rationally untenable.

But even if we accept this line of reasoning, the resulting concession to relativism would seem minimal. A relativist could not deliberately exploit the point, for he could not save his real views from incoherence by merely mouthing certain saving beliefs. To profit from the point, he must sincerely hold those beliefs. (As I have suggested above, he cannot save himself by having an open mind on the matter, for that would still leave him tolerant of contradictions.) And we are unlikely to find such a relativist, because the required beliefs are not only implausible but would deprive his principle of what he is most likely to regard as part of its point—namely, the basis for recognizing several independent grounds for moral appraisals. Moreover, even if there were such a relativist, the possibility of his holding such a principle would not remove its stigma for anyone who lacked his sort of convictions about the relevant facts. For anyone without his special beliefs, such a principle would be rationally untenable. For these reasons, I shall hereafter ignore this qualification on the charge of incoherence.

RELATIVISTIC JUSTIFICATION

The threat of incoherence arises for the relativist because he seems to endorse logically incompatible judgments as simultaneously true. The possible lines of escape therefore seem obvious; he must either show that he is not endorsing them both as true or else deny that the judgments are truly incompatible. The second approach is the standard maneuver, the first being rarely entertained in such a context. The first deserves some special treatment, to which I now turn.

It might appear obvious that a relativist could avoid incoherence if he embraces a noncognitive conception of moral discourse. For, if moral judgments are neither true nor false, it might seem that they could not possibly contradict one another.

There are two reasons for rejecting this suggestion as it stands. In the first place, a relativist cannot simply deny that moral judgments have truth values. He must also regard them as subject to some significant sort of validation or justification and hold that there is more than one basis for such appraisals. It remains to be seen whether the conflicting judgments that he is then committed to endorsing are related in a coherent manner.

In the second place, I wish to separate the issues as far as possible, and so I do not wish to discuss right now (what will be discussed later) whether relativism can be saved if we suppose that apparently conflicting judgments are not really incompatible in the relevant, troublesome cases. Right now we wish to see what difference it might make for a relativist to deny that the relevant conflicting judgments are true, while he nevertheless regards them as logically incompatible. To put the point another way, we wish to see how relativism can fare when it accepts as far as possible the relevant logical appearances—for example, the apparent incompatibility of certain moral judgments that he may wish simultaneously to endorse.

To see what this possibility amounts to, we must shift our focus slightly. What becomes crucial here is not so much the lack of truth values as the character of the relativist's appraisal of moral judgments. Within a noncognitive moral theory, he refrains from endorsing them as true. Is there then a way of endorsing conflicting moral judgments which maintains the spirit of relativism and yet avoids incoherence? I shall argue to the contrary. I shall show, first, how a clearly coherent position that seems relativistic on the surface forsakes relativism entirely. I shall indicate what must be done to transform such a theory into a form of ethical relativism and suggest why that may be impossible. Finally, I shall show how a clearly relativistic theory developed within the present guidelines generates apparently unintelligible results. I will not show that a coherent form of relativism within the current guidelines is impossible, but I will give reasons for supposing that the prospects are not encouraging.

It would be difficult to imagine how to proceed if we did not have Hare's ethical theory to serve as the basis for discussion. At any rate, it seems at first to meet our requirements. Hare regards moral judgments as "prescriptions" for action[10] and so does not construe them as either true or false. Nevertheless, he takes the apparent logic of moral discourse quite seriously, and he offers an apparently relativistic theory of justification.

It seems fair to say that Hare's analysis of the logic of moral discourse is committed to preserving and explaining most of the logical phenomena, save what seems most intimately connected with the notions of truth and falsity. Hare would seem to regard Alice and Barbara's conflicting judgments about Claudia's proposed abortion as logically incompatible, because he believes that such relations are not restricted to the realm of "factual" assertions. Hare tries to account for these phenomena not despite, but rather by means of, his specific noncognitive theory. Thus, the essential meaning of a moral judgment is alleged to be (something like) its prescriptive force, such as the condemnation of Claudia's proposed abortion (by Alice) or the withholding of such condemnation (by Barbara). The relevant relations between such utterances are held to be substantially the same as the relations between an assertion and its denial. But the details (and of course the soundness) of Hare's theory are not at issue here. The main point is that he wishes to preserve the relevant logical phenomena—to treat such judgments as conflicting in the strictest logical sense.

Hare believes, furthermore, that moral judgments can be justified by subsuming them under general principles from which they can be derived when suitable assumptions are made about the facts. One's judgment can be faulted—shown to be unjustified—if such support is unavailable. But a defense is only as good as the support that is offered. Unless one can show not only that one's factual assumptions are reasonable but also that one's basic moral principles are not arbitrary, it would be implausible to speak of justifying moral judgments. It is therefore important that, on Hare's view, even one's basic principles are subject to a kind of rational criticism. It will suffice for our purposes to note here Hare's original suggestions about such criticism (for his later elaborations do not affect the relevant points).

One must consider the "consequences" of a (basic) principle and the "way of life" it represents and make a "decision of principle" whether to accept or reject it. If one accepts a principle under those conditions, one's decision is justified: it is neither "arbitrary" nor "unfounded," Hare says, because "it would be based upon a consideration of everything upon which it could possibly be founded."[11]

The upshot seems to be a form of appraiser relativism, for moral principles are supposed by Hare to have universal scope, and those emerging from decisions of principle can conceivably diverge. As Hare fully recognizes, whether or not a principle can pass the sort of test he describes is a psychological fact about a given person. The relevant dispositions of individuals can vary, so that two persons might make decisions of principle with differing results (for example, one condemning abortion, the other condoning it); their principles could then be applied most rigorously in conjunction with the same set of true factual beliefs about an action (Claudia's proposed abortion, for example) to obtain what in Hare's view would be fully justified moral judgments, which could not be faulted in any way, though they conflicted.

Does this show that an appraiser theory can endorse logically incompatible judgments without lapsing into incoherence? I believe not. If we interpret Hare's theory of justification in the most natural way, its limited claims hardly deserve to be called "relativistic" (they seem in fact to be perfectly innocuous), while a truly relativistic reinterpretation yields a theory that is difficult to understand, if it is at all intelligible.

Hare's theory of justification seems to concern the conditions under which a person can be justified in making or maintaining a moral judgment. It says nothing whatsoever about the judgment itself (its content). Thus, on Hare's theory, Alice can be justified in judging Claudia's proposed abortion to be wrong, and Barbara can simultaneously be justified in judging Claudia's proposed abortion not to be wrong; but Hare's theory speaks only of their judging, not of the contents of their judgments—that is, that Claudia's abortion would be wrong and that Claudia's abortion would not be wrong.

There is nothing especially "relativistic" about a theory which acknowledges the possibility that two individuals can be justified in making their respective judgments, even when the judgments themselves are (regarded as) logically incompatible. Consider a case outside ethics. Alice might be justified in predicting rain tonight while Barbara is justified in predicting none, because justification here is "relative" (in a perfectly innocuous sense) to such things as evidence and reasons, which two people do not necessarily share. Hare may be understood as claiming that justification in morals is similarly "relative" (so far, in this same perfectly innocuous sense) to individuals' "decisions of principle." But that alone is not ethical relativism, because it is compatible with all that an antirelativist might ever desire. Consider Alice's and Barbara's conflicting weather predictions once more. They may both be justified; but one is correct and the other incorrect, regardless of their justifications; that is to say, either it will or it will not rain tonight. The parallel supposition in ethics is perfectly compatible with Hare's theory of justification in morals as we have so far construed it. Hare's theory tells us nothing at all about the validity of the judgments themselves. For all we have said so far, it may be the case that Alice's judgment (that is, that Claudia's proposed abortion would be wrong) is correct and that Barbara's conflicting judgment is consequently incorrect.

Now, it may be observed that Hare seems also to believe that moral judgments cannot be, as it were, "objectively" appraised—that they cannot be correct or incorrect independently of the justification one may have for making them. Indeed, his reasons for this belief seem partly to underlie his theory of justification. Hare maintains that "factual" judgments cannot guide conduct, while moral judgments do. He also maintains that moral judgments therefore have (something like) an imperatival character or component, and he assumes that factual judgments must be expressed in the indicative mood. He then argues that "imperatives" cannot be deduced from "indicatives" alone, which he therefore takes as implying that moral judgments cannot be deduced from factual considerations. From this he infers that moral judgments are logically independent of the facts. One must take account of the facts when making moral judgments, but one must also appeal to (imperative-like) general principles. When one arrives at basic principles, arbitrariness is avoided by the sort of rational reflection that is involved in making decisions of principle. Thus, Hare seems to say, the most that we can possibly do by way of appraising moral principles is to subject them to such personal criticism. And this, he believes, is not negligible. It entitles us to talk quite seriously of "justification."

I wish to maintain, however, that we are not obliged to accept this more radical position, even if we endorse a noncognitive conception of moral discourse like Hare's. In the first place, Hare's line of reasoning to his more radical position is fallacious. Hare begs a crucial question by assuming that "factual" judgments must be understood in the indicative while moral judgments must be assimilated to the imperative. This bias seems based on Hare's unwarranted assumption that "factual" judgments, and generally judgments that are properly expressed in the indicative mood, cannot be guides to action. Most important, Hare fails to consider seriously the possibility of logically sound nondeductive arguments from factual premises to moral conclusions. So, Hare has not shown (or even given us any reason to believe) that moral judgments are independent of the facts and cannot be objectively appraised for that (or some other) reason. I have no idea how that might be shown.

In the second place, Hare's noncognitive conception of moral discourse does not seem to preclude the possibility that moral judgments are "objectively" correct or incorrect. It is clear that both Bentham and J. S. Mill, for example, regarded moral judgments as objectively correct or incorrect. And there are good reasons for ascribing to them a noncognitive theory of moral discourse roughly like Hare's.[12] The difference is that they believe what Hare appears to deny—namely, that basic principles are objectively correct or incorrect. The result is not obviously untenable. But perhaps an analogy might help to suggest the possibility of such a position. It is not implausible to regard prudential judgments as objectively correct or incorrect, and this idea would seem to have no bearing on the question of whether prudential judgments require a noncognitive analysis. But if that can be said for prudential judgments, why not for moral judgments too?

In the third place, the idea of combining Hare's innocuously "relativistic" theory of justification with the claim that moral judgments are not themselves objectively correct or incorrect is itself suspect. Consider what the resulting position would be like. One would be maintaining that Alice can be justified in judging that Claudia's proposed abortion would be wrong, but that the judgment itself—that Claudia's proposed abortion would be wrong—can be neither correct nor incorrect. The suggestion is dubious, partly because the very notion of "relative" justification has its home among items which can be appraised in objective terms (such as weather predictions). Indeed, we seem to get an understanding of what is meant by justifying one's judgments in that "relative" sense partly by contrasting it with objective appraisal of the judgment itself. It is unclear whether the idea of "relative" justification has any proper application, any reasonable interpretation, outside such a context.

The usual suggestions that it does are based on the notion that the best we can do always counts as justification. That idea is endorsed by Hare when he says that a "decision of principle" can be regarded as justified "because it would be based upon a consideration of everything upon which it could possibly be founded." This is much too indulgent, for it would oblige us to regard any totally unjustifiable assertion as completely justified! (This is especially embarrassing to Hare, since he recognizes no good, logically respectable arguments from factual premises to moral principles; thus he seems to encourage the endorsement of principles that are not only without foundation but also indistinguishable, on his own account of justification, from totally unjustifiable positions.)

To transform Hare's theory into a truly relativistic position, therefore, one needs a good argument for denying that moral judgments themselves are objectively correct or incorrect plus an account of how the notion of "relative" justification can nevertheless apply. I have never seen a plausible account of this matter, and I am uncertain, for the reasons indicated above, whether any such account is possible. Let us see if others can meet this challenge.

Meanwhile, I suggest that if we wish to see what a truly relativistic theory of justification would be like within the present guidelines, we must build upon Hare's theory quite differently. I shall use the materials provided by Hare, without suggesting that the results would meet with his approval.

Such a theory would concern the judgments themselves, not one's making or maintaining them. And here I am uncertain of what terms of appraisal to use. It seems misleading to adopt the term "justified," since it most naturally applies to the attitude rather than its object. And we cannot here, within the confines of noncognitivism, speak of truth. So I suggest that we use the term most favored by ethical relativists—"valid"—hoping it will have no misleading connotations.

The theory can be sketched as follows. More than one basis for moral appraisals is recognized, and these make it possible to validate conflicting moral judgments. For purposes of illustration, let us suppose that the bases are decisions of principle and that Alice and Barbara subscribe to differing principles, such that the judgment condemning Claudia's act is validated by Alice's principles while the withholding of such condemnation is validated by Barbara's principles. To avoid irrelevant complications, we assume further that Alice and Barbara each have internally consistent moral positions, in the sense that the principles attributable to one of them cannot be used to both validate and invalidate one of these judgments or to validate both of them.

Difficulties arise when we imagine the following sort of case. Suppose that Barbara's actual judgment, on this occasion, conflicts with the principles to which she would subscribe on due reflection. Her actual judgment is therefore held to be invalid. (This must be possible, or the theory would imply that all actual judgments are valid.) It is important now to see that, so far as such a theory is concerned, the actual judgments made by Alice and Barbara are identical in content; they have the same meaning. (On the particular theory we are using for purposes of illustration, they have the same meaning because they both condemn Claudia's abortion.) Now, the theory appraises judgments in respect to their contents and by reference to personal principles. But, since different persons' judgments can be identical in meaning, the standards that are invoked cannot, so to speak, tell the difference between one person's judgments and another's. So, whether the relativist likes it or not, Alice's principles can be used to appraise Barbara's judgments as well as her own, and vice versa. The upshot is that such a theory allows one and the same judgment (in respect of content) to be both valid and invalid. In the case we have just imagined, the judgment that Claudia's proposed abortion would be wrong is held valid because it accords with (or is derivable from) Alice's principles and invalid because it conflicts with Barbara's. But it is difficult to understand what this might mean—that such a judgment (the judgment itself, not someone's making it) is simultaneously both valid and invalid.[13]

One might expect the relativist here to try to relativize the notion of validity. But we are speaking of the contents of judgments, not someone's making them, so it is not clear how that might be done; the innocuously "relative" notion of justification seems out of place, for example. It remains to be seen whether any sensible interpretation can be given to this paradoxical appraisal.

The foregoing arguments do not conclusively show that a truly relativistic theory which accommodates most of the relevant logical phenomena is impossible, but it strongly suggests that conclusion. I therefore tentatively conclude that relativism must reject the apparent logic of moral discourse and resort to more desperate theoretical measures.

RELATIVISTIC ANALYSES

Relativistic theories that are threatened by incoherence might try to avoid it by claiming that the relevant conflicting moral judgments are not really incompatible. This has, in fact, been suggested by anthropologists when they claim that to say that an act is wrong simply means that the act conflicts with certain norms.[14] On this approach, appraiser's-group relativism would be modified so that it understands Alice's utterance, "Claudia's proposed abortion would be wrong," to mean that Claudia's contemplated act conflicts with the norms of Alice's group while construing Barbara's assertion, "Claudia's proposed abortion would not be wrong," to mean that Claudia's act would not conflict with the norms of Barbara's group. Now, Alice and Barbara either belong to the same group or they do not. If they do, then the theory regards their judgments as incompatible, which accords with the logical appearances. The troublesome sort of case arises when Alice and Barbara belong to different groups whose respective norms disagree about abortion. The present theory would allow both Alice's and Barbara's judgments to be true but denies that they are incompatible, since one judgment relates the act to one set of norms while the other judgment relates it to another set. In this way, such a theory can avoid endorsing inconsistencies.

Some of the consequences of such theories should not pass unnoticed. On the surface it appears that Alice and Barbara are disagreeing about Claudia's proposed abortion, saying incompatible things about it. But, according to this sort of theory, they are confused if they believe their judgments to be incompatible. In fact, the theory says, they are actually talking at cross purposes.

And consider what the theory says when Alice and Barbara seem to agree about Claudia's proposed abortion, both saying it would be wrong or both denying that. It implies that Alice and Barbara must be understood as meaning different things, appearances notwithstanding.

An attempt might be made to reconcile such theories with our own views about what goes on in moral discourse by accounting for the perceived agreements and disagreements in terms of shared or conflicting attitudes that are expressed by such judgments. When Alice and Barbara disagree in their judgments, their difference is not propositional but rather attitudinal. They have, and their judgments express, different attitudes toward the act in question, one condemning the act (let us say) and the other refusing to condemn it. When they agree about the act, it is not that they make the same assertion but rather that they share an attitude toward the act, both condemning or both refusing to condemn it.

I do not wish to deny that attitudes are expressed by such judgments. The trouble with the suggestion is that Alice's and Barbara's beliefs may be ignored. But their beliefs are essentially connected with the relevant attitudes, in that the condemnatory attitude expressed by the judgment that Claudia's act would be wrong either is, or is grounded upon, the belief that Claudia's act would be wrong. So we cannot account for agreement or disagreement in such cases without deciding how the relevant beliefs are to be analyzed. Such theories are then committed to analyzing the beliefs relativistically along the lines adopted in construing the corresponding utterances. This simply returns us to the original decision of such theories, to reject clear logical phenomena in favor of preserving relativism.

It seems reasonable to say that such a relativist has incurred a sizable debt of explanation and justification. He must give very good reasons why we should regard apparently conflicting judgments as compatible and apparently identical judgments as different, and he must presumably show that they require analysis in one particular relativistic way rather than another. But what reasons are actually given? So far as I can see, they are not clearly reasons for analyzing moral judgments in a certain way.

The anthropologists who suggest such relativistic analyses seem tacitly to reason as follows: When individuals in a given society judge conduct, they typically invoke prevailing standards. Therefore, what it means to call an act "wrong" is that the act conflicts with the group's norms. This reasoning is painfully fallacious.

Harman suggests a different sort of argument for his relativistic analysis. His theory is limited to what he calls "inner" moral judgments—the ones we make when we judge it right or wrong of a particular person to do something or that some particular person ought or ought not to do something. Harman allows that we might judge a certain type of act nonrelativistically, even when we relativistically judge such conduct as performed by a given person.

The relevant part of Harman's reasoning may be summarized as follows: He gives examples to show that, when we judge a person's conduct, we take into account that person's own attitudes. We do not invoke considerations which we believe would not count as reasons for him, would not move him or influence his decision. These considerations are closely connected, in Harman's view, with that person's own moral standards. Thus, we refrain from saying that it is wrong of someone to do a certain thing (or that he ought not to do it) if we believe that he would not be moved by the considerations that concern us, or that his action conforms to his own moral code, even when we are ready to condemn the sort of conduct he practices. Therefore (Harman seems to reason), judgments to the effect that it is wrong of someone to do something (or that he ought not to do it) make essential reference to—by their very meaning invoke—that person's own attitudes and moral standards.

This amounts, in effect, to an agent theory, so Harman does not seem (does not perhaps intend) to endorse conflicting moral judgments. Because it is a rare attempt to justify a relativistic analysis, however, it merits our attention.

What concerns me is that the data assumed by Harman could equally well be accounted for in other ways—for example, by reference to our substantive convictions about the pointlessness of advising a person when we think we cannot influence him and, more generally, the unfairness of judging a person for doing something (as opposed to judging the sort of act he performs viewed more abstractly) by standards other than his own. We have no clear reason for rejecting this alternative account in favor of Harman's theory about the meaning of the relevant class of judgments. So we have no good reason to reject the nonrelativistic logical phenomena as illusory.

I mention Harman's case because I believe it typical. Relativistic analyses are not supported in the way they need to be. Now, it may be asked what all this shows. Have I succeeded in suggesting any more than that such theories are unfounded and perhaps implausible? That would be far from showing them untenable because of their incoherence.

But the only clear reason that we seem to have for resorting to relativistic analyses of moral judgments is that this will save the vulnerable forms of relativism from the scrap heaps of incoherence. As I suggested earlier, a theory that avoids incoherence by arbitrary modifications, that lacks independent theoretical justification, cannot command our respect. My suggestion now is that similar considerations apply to theories that avoid incoherence through the same devices, not by deliberate design but, as it were, by luck or accident—for example, by fashionably formulating their claims as analyses of meaning, claims which, if formulated in other ways (which happen to be equally supported by the facts) would be untenable.

It looks as if relativism can be given a coherent gloss, even when it endorses conflicting moral judgments. But theories that avoid incoherence by such unjustified claims are, it seems, much worse than unfounded and implausible.

NOTES

I began working on this paper while a Fellow of the Society for the Humanities at Cornell University. I am grateful for that institution's most congenial support as well as for the many helpful comments I have received from many persons when reading drafts at Vassar College, the Creighton Club, and at Brown, Cornell, Michigan, and Utah Universities.

1. Gilbert Harman, "Moral Relativism Defended," *Philosophical Review* 84 (January 1975): 3–22.

2. See, for example, W. G. Sumner, *Folkways* (Boston: Ginn & Co., 1940); M. J. Herskovits, *Man and His Works* (New York: Alfred A. Knopf, 1948), chap. 5, and *Cultural Anthropology* (New York: Alfred A. Knopf, 1955), chap. 19.

3. See, for example, R. M. Hare, *The Language of Morals* (Oxford: Clarendon Press, 1952) and *Freedom and Reason* (Oxford: Clarendon Press, 1963).

4. For an emphatic presentation of such points in another connection, see Carl Wellman, "Emotivism and Ethical Objectivity," *American Philosophical Quarterly* 5 (April 1968): 90–92.

5. As Sumner makes clear and Herskovits implies, this does not mean that the norms themselves are beyond evaluation. Their approach to the norms is, in fact, broadly utilitarian and thus (in a significant sense) nonrelativistic. (Sumner seems to reason that the function of the norms is adaptation to the circumstances, that something is good insofar as it performs its function well, and thus that norms are good insofar as they are adapted to circumstances—in which case, he assumes, they serve societal welfare.) But the appraisal of conduct is treated as an independent matter, governed by existing norms. (Sumner seems to struggle with the tension here, tying "immorality" to conformity and yet praising enlightened dissent.)

6. I am here ignoring the possibility that some norms of a group may themselves conflict.

7. One could eliminate this feature of the theory, for example, by invalidating "cross-cultural" judgments. But for our purposes we can ignore this possibility.

8. Harman's theory, so far as it goes (it concerns only one type of judgment about conduct), has the basic features of an agent theory, since it allows no more than one set of values (to which one is a tacit subscriber) to govern one's conduct.

9. And the relations between social groups, such as economic exploitation, suggest how naive is the assumption that prevailing social norms serve "societal welfare."

10. As Hare seems to recognize (*The Language of Morals*, pp. 20–24), this characterization ignores half of our possible judgments of conduct, such as Barbara's judgment that Claudia's proposed abortion would not be wrong, which is by no means a "prescription" or imperatival. But Hare's general idea could be expanded into a more adequate theory, as Bentham, for example, was aware; see my *In the Interest of the Governed.* (Oxford: Clarendon Press, 1973), chap. 6.

11. Hare, *The Language of Morals,* p. 69.

12. For Bentham, see *In the Interest of the Governed,* chap. 6; for Mill, one must begin with his *System of Logic,* bk. 6, chap. xii. Neither writer will seem unambiguous to modern readers; there are textual grounds for the standard view of them as ethical "naturalists." I am only suggesting a possible interpretation that seems interestingly compatible with their antirelativism.

13. The foregoing argument does not, in fact, require that the two judgments have precisely the same meaning. It would suffice if they were so related that their respective negations were logical contraries. But to regard them as identical is to respect the logical appearances as fully as possible.

14. See, for example, Sumner (sec. 439) and Ruth Benedict ("Anthropology and the Abnormal," reprinted in *Value and Obligation,* ed. R. B. Brandt [New York: Harcourt, Brace & World, 1961], p. 457).

11   *Fear of Relativism*

T. M. SCANLON

1. INTRODUCTION

Relativism is a hot topic. By this I do not mean merely that it is now much discussed but, rather, that its discussion always arouses certain passions. From some, relativism provokes passionate denial, the passion and haste of these denials suggesting a kind of fear. Others are eager to affirm it, and often do so with a particular exhilaration and sense of satisfaction, perhaps even of superiority. The question that I will begin with here is, what gives the topic this heat? Since my own reaction to relativism has generally been one of opposition, I will approach the question mainly from that side, by asking why we should want our judgements of value in general, or our moral judgments in particular, to have some property that relativism would deny them. As will become clear, my thoughts about this topic have been in large part shaped by Philippa Foot's writings.

2. WHAT IS RELATIVISM?

Before addressing this question I want to say something about what I take relativism to be. Relativism is sometimes described as the view that conflicting judgements can be equally correct or equally justified.[1] How could this be so? As a first step, it would seem that part of what the relativist is claiming must be that there is no single standard of "correctness" or "justifiability" by which all judgments of the kind in question are to be judged, no matter who makes them or to whom they are applied. Accordingly, I will take it to be a *necessary* condition for an account of judgements of a certain kind to be relativistic that it must hold that the cardinal virtue for judgements of that kind (whether this is being true, being justified, or some other property) cannot be assigned absolutely, but only relative to certain conditions or parameters. These parameters can vary, and a relativistic view must hold that particular ways of setting these parameters are not subject to appraisal (e.g. as true, or justified)

Reprinted, by permission of the publisher and copyright holder, from T. M. Scanlon, "Fear of Relativism," in Rosalind Hursthouse, Gavin Lawrence, and Warren Quinn, *Virtues and Reasons*, pp. 219–245. Oxford: Oxford University Press, 1995.

by the standards appropriate to judgements of the kind in question.[2] I will call this necessary condition for relativism Condition R.

An account of moral judgements can satisfy my Condition R without falling prey to the kind of incoherence that often troubles relativist views. I have in mind the problem that arises, in its simplest form, when one person says, "Every judgement is relative. What is true for you need not be true for me" and someone else replies, "So is *that* judgement just true for you?" The assertion of relativism seems to deprive relativists of the ability to make the very claim they want to assert.[3] Condition R allows for at least two possible routes of escape from this problem. First, it is formulated as a claim about judgments of a certain kind, and the assertion of relativism for judgements of kind A may not itself be a judgement of that kind. An assertion of moral relativism, for example, may not itself be a moral judgement, hence not a judgement to which the asserted relativity applies. Second, suppose that some thesis of relativity (perhaps a higher-order thesis) applies to the claim that judgements of type A are relative to certain parameters. Then the question can be asked, "With respect to what system of parameters is your thesis of relativism for judgements of kind A supposed to be justifiable?" But the relativist may have a reply to this question that is not embarrassing because it does not undercut the claim he or she wishes to make. For example, one possible reply[4] would be to say, "it is justifiable with respect to every evaluative standpoint that I can imagine taking seriously. You are welcome to try to convince me that, given the parameters that describe your situation, the mode of justification for judgements of this higher-order kind that is appropriate for you is one with respect to which the thesis of relativism for judgements of kind A is not justifiable, but I doubt you will succeed in anything except possibly convincing me that your outlook is a very strange one."

What might an account of evaluative judgements satisfying Condition R be like? In formulating R I have referred to the "cardinal virtue" in question as that of "being true or being justified, or some other property," rather than just as "being true," in order to allow for the possibility that the distinction between relativism and non-relativism about a class of judgements can cut across the distinction between non-cognitivist and cognitivist accounts of these judgements. So consider first a non-cognitivist account of some class of evaluative judgements, that is to say, an account according to which these judgements are not to be understood as making factual claims but only as expressing some attitude or emotion.

On such an account, even though these judgements appear to have the form of declarative statements they are not the kind of thing that can be true or false, but only appropriate or inappropriate, justified or not justified. Such a view need not satisfy Condition R. For even if the judgements in question are not properly assessed as true or false, the attitudes they express may be assessable as justified or unjustified, and it may be that there is a single standard of justification for such attitudes, a standard applicable to all agents and societies. If there is, then the account in question is not relativistic, but if there is not—if the justifiability of the attitudes in question is relative to some variable features of the individuals in question and their societies—then we may have an account satisfying Condition R. On such an account, it could be said that "conflicting evaluative judgements of the kind in question can both be justified." These judgements would not "conflict" by making incompatible truth-claims. But they would conflict in a more practical sense by expressing conflicting attitudes that no one could live by at the same time.

Now suppose, alternatively, that the evaluative judgements we are concerned with are best understood as stating facts. The "cardinal virtue" for these judgements will then be truth, so a relativistic account of them must hold that their truth-conditions vary, depending on certain "parameters." For example, a relativistic, but cognitivist, account of moral judgements might hold that "right" and "wrong" are relational in something like the way that "is tall" is. According to a "relational" view of this sort, an act can be called "wrong" only relative to some norms or standards, of which there can be many, and a judgement using this predicate is intelligible only if, in the context, we can identify the norms that the person making that judgement intends to invoke. Alternatively, it might be held that what a judgement of the form "X is morally wrong" asserts is that X is disallowed by norms that bear a certain relation to the person making the judgement (for example, norms that that person accepts or has reason to accept, or norms generally recognized in the society in which that person lives). Assuming that different norms can stand in this relation to different speakers, this "indexical" account of the semantics of "is morally wrong" will satisfy my Condition R.

On either of these accounts, the judgement "Lying is always wrong," made by one speaker, and the judgement "Lying is not always wrong," made by another, could both be quite correct; but if so then these utterances would not make conflicting judgements in the strict cognitivist sense: they can both be true, at the same time, so they are not incompatible. But there are at least two other senses in which the claims that these speakers make could be held to conflict. First, in so far as they invoke different standards of conduct which no one could live by at the same time, they conflict in the practical sense mentioned above. Second, we could say, following Gilbert Harman,[5] that these judgements make claims which would conflict if they were interpreted non-relativistically. I want to explore this idea more fully since it seems to me that something important lies behind it.

Consider the following example. I believe that there is nothing morally objectionable about sexual relations between adults of the same sex. That is to say, I believe that the kind of considerations that I think of as relevant to morality—the kind that back up my judgements that murder and exploitation are wrong, for example—do not support any objection to such conduct. But it is easy to imagine someone, a devoted member of a fundamentalist Christian community, for example, who would hold that homosexual relations are, in themselves, deeply wrong—that they are incompatible with and excluded by that form of life that we are all required to live according to the authoritative teachings laid down in the Bible, which are the basis of all morality. This disagreement fits the pattern of cognitivist relativism just described: I judge a certain form of conduct to be morally permissible, another person judges it morally impermissible, and our judgements refer, implicitly or explicitly, to different standards of conduct. But there is a further element: each of us regards the standards to which we refer as authoritative and binding—as standards which we have good reason to regard as out-weighing all others, and whose violation is proper grounds for feelings of guilt and shame. If we did not so regard them then it would be questionable whether our judgements are properly called moral judgements. So here is, at least potentially, a new kind of conflict: we may disagree over which stan-dards of conduct are authoritative—which have that distinctive importance which the term 'moral' entails. We disagree in part, perhaps, because we dis-agree about what that kind of importance is, or at least about what could or does confer it.[6]

If we are both non-relativists, then we will each hold that the standards which we have in mind have unique claim to this distinctive kind of impor-tance, and our judgements about homosexuality (which presuppose this claim) will thus conflict in this further way. This is a plausible interpretation of what Harman means when he speaks of judgements which would conflict if interpreted non-relativistically. On the other hand, if both parties to the dis-pute I have imagined are relativists, then both may hold that there is no unique set of standards that can claim this importance: it is not something that can be claimed absolutely but only given the setting of certain parame-ters, and, depending on how these parameters are set, many different stan-dards may claim this authority.

It is this idea of the authority or importance of moral considerations which is, I believe, the central problem of relativism for non-relativists and for many relativists as well. It is the central problem for non-relativists because it is the thing which, above all, moral relativism seems to threaten. It is also a central problem for those relativists who do not see their relativism as a form of scepticism.

Relativism is often seen as a self-consciously debunking doctrine, a chal-lenge which might be put in the form: "Morality is merely a matter of social convention. After all, what else *could* it be about?" At least this is the way rel-ativism is often imagined by non-relativists, and no doubt some relativists also have this kind of thing in mind. The proper response to this sceptical form of relativism is a positive account of what the authority of morality could amount to. But such a response might be successful while still leaving *relativism* untouched. That is, one might succeed in fending off scepticism—in showing that morality is not *merely* a matter of social convention, say—while still leaving open the possibility that moral requirements may vary in the way that Condition R describes. In fact it seems to me that many of those who speak in favour of relativism actually take themselves to be defending a view of this kind, a form of non-sceptical, or *benign,* relativism, according to which the requirements of morality vary but are not for that reason to be taken less seriously. Philippa Foot seems to me to put forward a version of benign relativism in the papers I will discuss below, and I believe that

Michael Walzer also sees his view in this way. Outside philosophy, it seems to me that anthropologists, who are some of the most common proponents of relativism, are often best understood as having this benign form of the doctrine in mind: they urge us to respect the moralities of other cultures as "just as good as ours," the suggestion clearly being that both "ours" and "theirs" should be respected. The question that most interests me about relativism, and that I will be mainly concerned with below, is whether and how a form of benign relativism could be true.

I have claimed that Condition R is a *necessary* condition for an account of a class of judgements to count as relativistic. Is it also a *sufficient* condition? This seems unlikely, at least if the line between relativistic and non-relativistic doctrines is supposed to distinguish between those that do and those that do not give rise to fears and objections of the kind that relativism has generally provoked. In order to do that, a definition would have to rule out, more clearly than I have so far done, forms of what might be called "parametric universalism." By this I mean, in the case of morality, views which hold that there is a single standard of validity for moral principles but which leave open the possibility that what valid moral principles allow and require can vary, depending on certain variable conditions. To take the most trivial example, it might be a valid general principle that governments' policies should be responsive to the needs of their citizens, among which is the need for protection against the climate. But this requires different measures in arctic, temperate, and tropical zones. A less trivial example is the general principle that where a just scheme is established to provide an important public good, it is wrong to take advantage of that scheme while ignoring the requirements it imposes on one.[7] This principle also has the consequence that what is morally required of a person will depend on facts about that person's society and its customs, but no one, I think, would call either of these doctrines relativistic. And neither of them satisfies Condition R, since the two principles just described (and the standards of justice alluded to in the second of these principles) are presumably held to be valid on some "universal," non-parametric basis.

Now consider a third example. I have maintained elsewhere[8] that an action is wrong if it would be disallowed by any set of principles for the general regulation of behaviour that no one suitably motivated could reasonably reject. As I will say later, it seems to me that what one can "reasonably reject" may well vary, depending on, among other things, those features of a society that determine which goods and opportunities are essential for the kind of life most people will want to live. Is this a form of relativism? One might argue that it is not, since the contractualist formula just stated is a substantive, universal moral principle, on a par with the two I have mentioned, but more general. But this formula could as well be seen as a characterization of the idea of moral wrongness and of the kind of justification appropriate to claims that certain acts are wrong. As such, it could be seen as on a par with avowedly relativistic claims that acts are wrong simply in virtue of being disallowed by principles that are generally accepted in the society in which those acts are committed. If one of these doctrines is to be counted as relativistic in the sense that people are inclined to fight about it and the other not, this cannot be because one of them, but not the other, makes arguments about wrongness dependent on "parameters"—features of the society in question which are not themselves right or wrong. The difference must lie in what these "parameters" are held to be, and perhaps one cannot tell whether the contractualist account of wrongness is relativistic in a controversial sense until one knows what the features of a society are that are supposed to affect what it is "reasonable to reject." We need to know whether dependence on *these* features is something that we have reason to fear or object to. Let me turn, then, to consider some reasons why relativism has seemed to many people a doctrine that is to be feared and resisted.

3. WHY RESIST RELATIVISM?

Three kinds of reason for fearing or resisting relativism occur to me. First, relativism can be threatening because morality is seen as an important force for keeping people in line, and keeping the rest of us safe from potential wrongdoers. For those who take this view, relativists will seem dangerous in something like the way that Locke thought atheists were. Near the end of his *Letter on Toleration* (1689) after a firm condemnation of seventeenth-century practices of religious intolerance, and a stirring endorsement of toleration, he mentions some exceptions, ending with this one: "Lastly, those are not at all to be tolerated who deny the being of a God. Promises, covenants, and oaths, which are the bonds of human society, can have no hold upon an atheist. The taking away of God, though but even in thought, dissolves all. . . ."[9]

Similarly, by claiming that familiar moral requirements may fail to apply even to cases that seem to us the clearest examples of wrongdoing, relativists may seem to announce that people are free to treat us in ways that these requirements forbid, and they encourage others to believe this as well. This would explain the element of fear in responses to relativism, and to that extent at least would seem to fit the facts. Describing such reactions to relativism, Philippa Foot says, for example, "We are, naturally, concerned about the man who doesn't care what happens to other people, and we want to convict him of irrationality, thinking he will mind about that."[10] She does not say exactly what the nature of this "concern" is, but a natural hypothesis is that it is, at base, a desire to restrain others for the sake of our own protection. This hypothesis is supported by Foot's suggestion, later in the same paragraph, that it would be more honest "to recognize that the 'should' of moral judgment is sometimes merely an instrument by which we (for our own very good reasons) try to impose a rule of conduct even on the uncaring man."

In order for the "should" of moral judgement to be successful in this task (and not merely by deception), it needs to give reasons to (and thus, at least potentially, to motivate) every agent, whatever that agent's desires may happen to be. In addition, that "should" has to have the right content—it has to forbid at least those actions by which we are most clearly threatened. Relativism is a threat on both scores: it threatens to exempt some agents from moral requirements altogether, and it threatens to allow the content of those requirements to vary—even, some fear, to the extent of permitting what we now see as the most heinous crimes.

The prospect of people in general giving no weight to even the most basic moral demands is indeed a frightening one. But relativism, as a philosophical doctrine, does not seem to me likely to lead to this result. So I am not much moved by this reason for resisting relativism. I mention it mainly in order to distinguish it from a second reason, which I take more seriously.

This second reason is grounded in the confidence we have or would like to have in our condemnations of wrongful conduct and of those who engage in it. For example, when Gilbert Harman told us[11] that "ought to do" judgements do not apply to people who lack relevant reasons, and that we therefore cannot say that it was wrong of Hitler to murder the Jews or that he ought not to have done it (even though we can condemn him in other ways), this claim seemed to deprive us of something important. It does this even if we believe that the thought that he was behaving wrongly, in the sense that we want to preserve, would not influence Hitler or others like him at all. What relativism threatens to deprive us of in such a case is not a mode of protection but rather, I would suggest, the sense that our condemnation of certain actions is legitimate and justified.

It may of course be asked why one should care so much about condemnation. This concern is sometimes ridiculed as an idle and self-righteous desire to be able to pass judgement on every agent, even those at great cultural or historical distance from us. So portrayed, it may seem unattractive. But if we give up the idea that an agent can be properly condemned for his action then we must also withdraw the claim, on his victims' behalf, that they were entitled not to be treated in the way that he did, and that it was therefore wrong of him to treat them that way. One need not be excessively judgemental or self-righteous to feel that conceding this would involve giving up something important, and I believe that this feeling, rather than a concern with self-protection or a self-righteous desire to pass judgement, is what lies behind most people's reluctance to accept Harman's claim about Hitler. But while the accusation of self-righteous moralism on the one side and the appeal to the perspective of the victim on the other have a certain rhetorical power, neither captures exactly what is at stake in this reason for resisting relativism. The essential point is that certain moral judgements seem to us clearly true and important (focusing on cases in which there is a clear victim just helps to make this apparent). Relativism is a threat in so far as it would force us to withdraw those judgements, or would undermine their claim to importance.

Different forms of relativism can have these threatening effects to different degrees and in different ways. What Harman calls normative relativism, the view that different agents are subject to different ultimate moral demands, can be threatening in the first way, since if moral demands that we take seriously do not apply to an agent then judgements based on those demands must be withdrawn. What he calls moral judgement relativism is in this respect less threatening. This is the view that moral judgements are to be assessed not absolutely but only relative to the particular standards that they presuppose, and the different judgements (like different utterances of "is tall") presuppose different standards. Recognizing that your favourable judgement of a certain action and my unfavourable one presuppose different standards does not require me to withdraw my judgement. But it may be threatening in another way in so far as it requires me to accept the idea that our judgements are "equally correct." This form of relativity (to the "choice" of standards) may undermine the importance attached to our judgements of right and wrong. Whether it does so or not will depend on the kinds of reason that one can have for adhering to one set of standards rather than another. I will return to this question in Section 4.

Given this account of the interests that lie behind these first two reasons for resisting relativism, let me turn now to consider what would be required to satisfy these interests. If our opposition to relativism were based on the hope that morality will restrain others, then what we would want would be for there to be reasons to be moral which, if presented in the right way, would motivate even a "bad" person, and would be available to restrain the rest of us, should other motives fail. But motivation is less central to the second reason for resisting relativism, which I have just considered. If what we are concerned about, in the first instance, is merely that our moral judgements "apply to" those to whom we take them to apply, even, or especially, when these people care nothing for morality, then we need not be concerned with motivation per se. Motivation becomes an issue only if it is true, as Harman and others[12] have held, that "ought" judgements of the relevant sort can apply to an agent only if he or she has a reason to behave accordingly. "Ought" judgements that are not so grounded are, Williams claims, inappropriate, since, lacking any basis in what the agent cares about, they could not sincerely be offered as advice. But these claims are controversial. Unless they are accepted, the possibility that some agents might not have reasons to care about certain moral judgements, e.g. reasons grounded in their "subjective motivational set," does not mean that those judgements must be withdrawn.

In order to get a clearer view of this problem it will be helpful to consider a related point about the plausibility of a response to relativism put forward by Philippa Foot. She has argued that an unrestricted moral relativism could not be correct because there are "definitional criteria" which limit the content of anything that could be called morality, with the result that, for example, nothing properly called "morality," or "a moral system," or "a moral code" could permit what Hitler did.[13] From the point of view of restraint this may seem small comfort, since it matters little whether Hitler's action can be *said* to be wrong if that judgement will in any event have no motivational effect for people like him. But things look different when we consider the importance of the judgements themselves, as embodied, for example, in the claims of victims. It adds insult to injury to have to admit that the person who attacked you did no wrong, and relativism may be resisted precisely because it seems to force this admission. From this point of view, then, Foot's appeal to definitional criteria has more substance: it preserves the judgement that the victim was wronged, and the further observation that the agent is one who cares nothing for moral considerations may take nothing away from this judgement, or from the importance it has for us. (Whether it does so is something I will consider at length below.)

Let me turn now, finally, to the last of the three reasons for resisting relativism that I said I would consider. Some may fear and resist relativism because it seems to threaten their sense that they have adequate grounds for believing their way of life is justified, and for preferring it to others. Like a concern with condemnation, this reaction to relativism may be regarded with scepticism. Indeed, it is open to attack from two opposing directions. Relativists may see it as involving an inappropriate attitude towards others—an unseemly desire to see other ways of life as inferior. Others (Nietzscheans, I might call them) may see it as involving an inappropriate attitude towards oneself: why, if one finds a certain way of life appealing and wants to live that way, must one need to believe, in addition, that it is "correct" in some deeper sense? Why should one need the support of "objectivity"? Why, Nietzsche asks in a notebook entry,[14] do people think that they can have an ideal only if it is *the ideal?* To think this, he says, is to deprive one's ideal of its own special character. On the contrary, he suggests, "One should have [an ideal] in order to distinguish oneself, not to level oneself."

With respect to those elements of a way of life that might be called "traditions and customs," both of these criticisms seem correct at the same time. Suppose that I attach importance to eating certain foods, dressing in a certain way, observing certain holidays, playing certain sports, supporting a certain team, listening to a certain kind of music, and singing certain songs, all because these are part of the life I have grown up in and I see them as elements of my continuing membership in that life and connection with its, and my, past. This provides me with ample reason for doing these things and for preferring them to others. Perhaps I might like to think that in some way this way of life is "better than all others," but there is no need for me to think this in order to have good reasons for following it. Why think that there is some notion of "getting it right" which is what we should strive for in such matters? To take this seriously would be a sign of insecurity and weakness (as the Nietzscheans would say) and a foolish desire for superiority (as the relativists would add).

This is the best example that I can imagine of clearly benign relativism—relativism that can be accepted without undermining the judgements to which it applies. Following one "way of life" (one set of customs and traditions) is something I have reason to do not absolutely but only relative to certain parameters: in this case my being a person who was brought up in this particular way and for whom these customs therefore have a particular meaning. If I had been born in a different place and had a different life, then I would have had no reason to do the things just listed but would instead have had other, parallel reasons for following different customs. Moreover, acknowledging this parametric dependence does not undermine the force that these reasons have for me, or make these reasons merely a matter of preferences that I "just happen to have." The "parameters" (being a person who has a certain past and for whom these customs therefore have a certain meaning) are mere facts which are themselves not up for justification, but they serve as *grounds* for my preferences, not merely as their causal determinants.

This parametric dependence explains not only why members of two different groups can have reasons for accepting different judgements as justified but also why they would be mistaken in applying these judgements to members of the other group: it would make no sense to say that I have reason to follow the customs of some group to which I have no connection, or that they have such reasons to follow mine.

This is not a case of "parametric universalism," since there is no need to invoke an overarching principle of the form "People whose life and history is of type *A* ought to live according to R(*A*)" and to claim that each of the groups I have imagined is an instance of this principle. The reasons that a person has to follow the traditions that are part of his or her way of life depend on the particular meaning that those actions and that history have for that person. They need not derive this importance from any beliefs about the value of "tradition" in general. In fact, once one reaches that level of abstraction reasons of the kind in question largely lose their force. (When people start talking in general terms about "the value of traditions" they are usually on the edge of ceasing to care about their own.)

It is easy to see why examples of this kind are emphasized by defenders of (at least a qualified) relativism, such as Stuart Hampshire and Michael Walzer.[15] These examples are convincing in themselves, and they illustrate what I take to be the relativists' main point: that those who think we must look to the idea of objectivity in order to account for the importance that our way of life has for us are in fact looking in the wrong place. Many relativists (including Walzer, but not Hampshire) urge us to extend this example, taking it as the model for understanding other modes of moral evaluation, including standards of justice.

How might this extension work? In the example just considered the model was this. We can describe, abstractly, a certain kind of importance, roughly the kind of importance that a form of behaviour has for a person if it defines a community of which he or she feels a part or expresses a connection with a certain history to which the person is attached. We can then see how it can be reasonable for different people, given their different histories and situations, to attach this kind of importance to quite different modes of behaviour. Applied to the case of morality, then, the idea would be first to characterize the kind of importance or authority that moral considerations have, the kinds of reason they give people, and then to show, in the light of this characterization, how different people could, quite reasonably, attach this kind of importance to different forms of conduct.

The kind of moral relativism that this strategy leads to will depend heavily on how the importance or authority of morality is characterized. One possibility is that this account will remain quite close to the example just given, that is that it will take the importance that moral considerations have just to be that importance that attaches to any standards that we are brought up to take seriously, that are part of the life of a community to which we feel attached, and that are enforced within that community by sanctions of approval and disapproval. This yields a form of relativism that has seemed to many people to be threatening in both of the ways I have mentioned above: it gives a deflationary account of the importance of morality and it allows the content of moral rules to vary widely, perhaps even to permit actions that now strike us as very clearly wrong.

Walzer has argued that his view should not be seen as threatening in this latter way, since there are good reasons why any set of standards that are generally accepted in a society will include a common core of basic prohibitions against such things as "murder, deception, betrayal and gross cruelty."[16] I want to focus here, however, on the first of these anti-relativist worries, and less on the fixed than on what is seen as the variable part of morality. In so far as moral standards vary, what kind of importance can they claim?

4. CONTINGENT PRINCIPLES

Some possible answers to this question are suggested by a form of relativism considered by Philippa Foot in "Morality and Art" and in "Moral Relativism." According to this view, moral judgements, like judgements about who is tall or what food tastes good, always presuppose certain standards. A particular moral judgement is to be assessed as true or false by determining how the standards that it presupposes apply to the case in question. But these standards cannot have just any content. As I have said above, Foot holds that there are "definitional starting-points of morality," considerations which must be counted as relevant and given a certain weight by any standards that can properly be called moral.

Relativism remains a possibility, however, because these definitional starting-points may underdetermine the content of morality. There may be "contingent principles" on which different sets of standards could differ while still being fully entitled to be called moral standards. If two sets of standards differ in this way, then moral judgements which implicitly refer to these differing standards could give opposing views about the permissibility of a given action while both remain true. These judgements would not contradict one another, since they refer to different standards. But they would at least conflict in the practical sense I discussed above, and each would be true, since it makes a correct claim about how the standards to which it refers apply to this case. Nor could we claim that one of these sets of *standards* is true and the other false if they are each compatible with the "definitional starting points" and there is no possibility of "proving or showing" on the basis of "criteria internal to the concept of morality" that one of them rather than the other is correct. Foot indicates at least some sympathy for Bernard Williams's claim that truth has no "substantial" application in such cases.[17]

As I have stated it, this hypothesis leaves open the crucial question of where the fixed part of morality ends and the contingent part begins, and Foot expresses uncertainty on this point.[18] It is unclear, she says, how much is determined by the criteria internal to the concept of morality, and how much room is left for relativism. But the examples of possibly contingent principles that she cites in "Morality and Art" give some guidance as to what she had in mind at least at that time.

The first of these is abortion. "Thinking about the problem of abortion," she writes, "I come to the conclusion that there is a genuine choice as to whether or not to count as a human being, with the rights of a human being, what would become a human being but is not yet capable of independent life."[19]

Second, she suggests that something similar may be true in some cases in which the interests of individuals clash with those of the community. "We ourselves," she says, "have a strong objection to the idea of *using* one person for the benefit of others, and it probably guides our intuitions in many cases. It does not seem clear, however, that one could rule out of court the principles of a strict utilitarian who would, at least if he were consistent, allow things that we will not allow in the interests of cancer research."[20]

In another article,[21] Foot suggested that the solidarity shown by the people of Leningrad during the siege was "contingent." She was not there discussing relativism, and she may well have meant to suggest a different form of contingency. But since I find the example a helpful one I want to bear it in mind.

Foot remarks that she thinks it unlikely that many people will be willing to accept even the qualified relativism that this hypothesis suggests where ethics is concerned.[22] Why should this be so? I suggested above that relativism is threatening when it forces us to withdraw moral judgements that strike us as clearly correct, or when, while allowing our judgements to stand, it undermines the importance that they seemed to have. Would Foot's relativism have effects of this kind?

It is not obvious that accepting her hypothesis would require us to withdraw judgements which seem clearly true. To begin with, it would not have this effect where judgements based on "definitional criteria" are concerned. So there would be no problem of the sort that arises with Harman's claim about Hitler. And even in the case of contingent principles, the kind of relativity that is suggested does not, by itself, make it logically inappropriate to pass judgement (based on "our" standards) on the actions of people who live in societies where quite different standards prevail.[23] A Sicilian tourist in Los Angeles who writes on a postcard to his family that almost everyone in California is very tall will be saying something true, even though it would be false by the standards of the Californians. So an analogous relativity would not be a bar to cross-cultural moral judgements. If such judgements are sometimes odd or inappropriate this must be for some further reason. For example, even when it makes sense to criticize the practices of another society—to say, for example, that they are unjust—it may sound odd to criticize an individual in that society for not doing what we would see as the right thing if such an action would have made no sense in that context.

Even if relativism of the kind Foot considers would not force us to withdraw judgements that seem clearly correct, it would require us to accept the idea that other, opposing judgements are equally correct and that there is no question of truth between our standards and the ones reflected in these judgements. As Foot says, this might be resisted on the ground that it involves a "weakening of allegiance" to our own standards.[24] There are two problems here. The first is understanding how the 'contingent' part of one's moral outlook is supposed to be related to the non-contingent, or 'definitional,' part. How can we see some of our principles as "contingent" yet at the same time having the force of morality for us—the same kind of importance that the rest of morality has? Given an answer to this question, we can then go on and inquire whether it is compatible with this kind of allegiance to our contingent principles to say that there is no question of truth as between these principles and the different contingent principles held by others.

Before addressing these questions I need to say more about the status of Foot's definitional criteria. In speaking of the "importance" of morality I do not mean to presuppose that it has the kind of special authority that Foot called into question in "Morality as a System of Hypothetical Imperatives": that is, I do not mean to be assuming that morality "gives reason for acting to any man."[25] Whether it does this or not is a question I mean to be leaving open. The importance I have in mind is the importance that moral considerations have for those who take morality seriously. Even among those for whom it has such importance, however, there may be disagreement about its nature and basis.[26] Some people see morality as depending crucially on the authority of the will of God. For others, it may be based in one or another secular idea of human excellence. Still others may see it as grounded in what Mill calls "the social feelings of mankind; the desire to be in unity with our fellow creatures,"[27] or, in my terminology, the desire to be able to justify our actions to others.[28]

In so far as they are taken to mark the limits of applicability of the concept "morality," Foot's definitional criteria must be common ground for people who disagree in this way. In discussing these criteria she says, "A moral system seems necessarily to be one aimed at removing certain dangers and securing certain benefits, and it would follow that some things do and some do not count as objections from a moral point of view."[29] Here the words "aimed at" can be understood in a stronger or weaker way. On the weaker interpretation the claim that is being made is about the content of morality: anything that is to count as a moral code must recognize our need for protection against certain dangers and the importance for us of certain benefits. On the stronger interpretation, the claim would be that protecting us in these ways and securing these benefits must be the ultimate aim and source of importance of anything that could be called a system of morality. This stronger interpretation seems too strong. Taken strictly, it would rule out the possibility of a religious basis for morality, and even if one thinks religious accounts of morality mistaken it would be excessive to say that calling them "moral views" involved a misuse of the term. On the other hand, the weaker interpretation, taken strictly, seems too weak. We would not count just any code with the relevant minimum content as a moral system, no matter what its rationale might be. (The dictates of a malevolent superbeing would not count as a moral system even if, for some reason related to that being's ultimate purposes but not at all to our good, they forbade us to kill or injure one another.)

So the rationale of anything plausibly called a morality must be related to some conception of how it is good for us to live. But this definitional constraint is compatible with a wide variety of different views of the nature of morality and its distinctive importance, including at least those I have listed above. It follows from this general constraint on its rationale that the content of a morality must include the definitional starting-points Foot mentions, but different accounts of this rationale will explain this content in different ways. Someone who believed that morality derives its importance from God's will could explain its content by arguing that, given the nature of God, any system of commands plausibly attributed to him would have to take account of the needs of human life, and they would offer a specific account of what these are. Millians, contractualists, or Aristotelians would offer other, quite different explanations, and these accounts, while agreeing in a general sense on the "definitional starting-points of morality," are likely to lead to differing interpretations of their content.

Let me return now to the question whether, if we accept the idea that between different sets of contingent principles there can be no question of truth, this would undermine our allegiance to the contingent principles we accept—undermine our grounds for assigning them moral significance and the importance that goes with it. What, then, are these grounds? If we concede that a principle cannot be proved or shown to be correct on the basis of criteria internal to the concept of morality, what ground could we have for giving it the kind of importance that moral principles have as opposed to considering it merely a matter of shared reactions or of custom and tradition? There are a number of possible answers.

One possibility is that the moral standing of contingent principles depends on their relation to the "definitional starting-points" of moral argument, but that there may be room for different sets of such principles because there may be different ways of understanding these starting-points. As Foot says, we may agree that murder must be counted a serious moral wrong, but disagree about exactly what counts as murder.[30] What kind of reasons might one have to accept one definition of murder rather than another as morally determinative? A person might take one definition (or one class of definitions) to be superior on the ground that the others all involved restrictions on the scope of "murder" that seemed arbitrary. It is plausible to suppose that something like this is the reason some people have for thinking that abortion is always, or nearly always, murder. This is certainly not a proof. Is it "showing"? Well, it is at least a consideration capable of determining the mind for a number of people. There are, of course, considerations that can be offered on the other side. Could a person who finds these counter-arguments insufficient, and therefore holds that abortion is nearly always murder, none the less accept the claim that there is no substantial sense in which this principle, but not opposing ones, can be called true?

Such a person could, at least, admit that there is a degree of uncertainty here. That is, they could, while remaining convinced that abortion is wrong, admit that there are reasonable grounds for holding the opposite view. But it is more difficult to see how someone whose reasons for believing abortion to be wrong were of the kind I have mentioned could admit that there is no substantial question of truth between this principle and opposing ones. To make this admission plausible we would need to move beyond mere uncertainty to something more like genuine underdetermination: it is not just that we cannot be certain which way of characterizing murder is in fact morally correct but rather that there is no fact of the matter as to which is correct; moral argument is underdetermined and does not settle this question.

There may be problems about how this idea of underdetermination is to be understood. But, leaving these aside for the moment, there is the question of what reason we could have to regard one of two answers as having moral force if we saw the choice between them as morally underdetermined. It seems that we would have to appeal to reasons of some other sort, for example to considerations like those I discussed above under the heading of "tradition." Suppose that a significant, but not conclusive, moral case can be made for each of two conflicting principles. If one of these principles has long been accepted in my community, then I can have strong reason to be guided by it rather than by the alternative principle for which, I recognize, an equally good abstract case can be made. In such a case I could, without undermining my allegiance to my principle, admit that it had no greater claim than the alternative to moral truth.

But there is, I think, a better explanation. The moral status of contingent principles might depend not on their logical ties to "definitional criteria," understood as fixed points in the content of morality, but rather on their connection with different conceptions of the nature of morality and its authority. This suggests a more plausible understanding both of the nature of the underdetermination and of how it can be filled in in different ways that will seem, to the person who holds them, to be entirely continuous with the core or morality. As I have argued above, the limits on the application of the term "morality" must leave open the possibility of different understandings of its rationale and basis. That the concept of morality underdetermines its content is hardly surprising. But particular understandings of the basis of moral requirements are more determinate. As I have argued above, different ways of understanding the basis of moral requirements can support different interpretations even of what Foot calls definitional criteria, and the case of abortion may be an example of this. Moreover, different moral outlooks may go beyond these definitional criteria in different ways and include different contingent principles because these outlooks are based on different conceptions of the nature and importance of morality, or on different interpretations of the same conception.

Foot's example of utilitarianism can be used to illustrate these two possibilities. Like some contractualists, some utilitarians may locate the ground of morality in what Mill called the desire to be in unity with one's fellow creatures. These contractualists and utilitarians may agree that any principles that can claim to be responsive to this desire must include Foot's definitional starting-points, but beyond this point they may disagree about the content of morality, the utilitarian allowing, as in Foot's second example, greater sacrifice to be imposed on individuals for the sake of the common good. To a utilitarian, a contractualist's interpretation of the "desire for unity" may seem to be narrow and ungenerous and to fail to recognize the full force of this basic moral impulse. Someone might be a convinced utilitarian for this reason, and such a person would hold utilitarian contingent principles for the same reason: not because they follow from the definitional starting-points but because they are supported by the best account of the moral force of those starting-points.

Utilitarians of this kind could recognize contractualists' moral judgements as "true relative to" (i.e. as genuinely following from) contractualists' contingent principles. They also have reasons for finding those principles unappealing. And contractualists have their own objections to utilitarian principles. Indeed, these reasons may be, from their point of view, more exigent, since they may see utilitarian principles as licensing actions that at least come very near to violating definitional starting-points if, for example, they allow medical treatment to be withheld from people who refuse to participate in medical experiments.

Must each of these parties think that the other's principles are *false?* At least they will think them mistaken in so far as they purport to represent the moral consequences of the idea of "unity with one's fellow creatures." Given that each side has these reasons for regarding the other not only as an inferior moral outlook but also as an inferior expression of the shared but disputed idea of "unity with one's fellow creatures," and given that the judgements expressing these views seem to have the logic of ordinary declarative sentences, it seems natural to use the terms "true" and "false" to describe their disagreement.

So let us consider instead the possibility that utilitarians and contractualists are appealing to quite different conceptions of the ground and authority of moral requirements rather than making rival claims about the proper interpretation of the same ground. Some utilitarians see morality as following from a general demand of rationality, that one always chooses the action that one has reason to believe will yield the best consequences, objectively understood.[31] They might also claim that since actions that meet this requirement have the best possible justification they can certainly be "justified to" others. But the idea of justifiability to others does not have the fundamental place in their outlook that it enjoys in contractualist or Kantian accounts of morality. So when utilitarians of this kind make judgements about right and wrong they could be seen as appealing not just to different contingent principles than Kantians or contractualists invoke but also to a conception of the importance and appeal of morality that is quite different from the idea of a "kingdom of ends."

Supposing that moral judgements made by a contractualist and by a utilitarian are understood in this way, could each of these parties admit, without undermining allegiance to his or her own outlook, that what the other says is equally true? At one level it would seem that they could do this, since each can see the other's judgements as being "about" a different subject: what we owe to each other is one thing, what would produce the most valuable state of affairs is something else. But at a higher level, the two parties must see themselves as making conflicting claims about the same subject: about what considerations we have reason to give most weight to in governing our lives. The result is relativism about judgements of right and wrong (because these judgements have varying reference) but not about claims about reasons. This limited relativism does not seem to me to present a threat.

Might it be extended to a more thoroughgoing relativity, according to which the parties to a disagreement like the one I have just described might recognize their opponents' claims about reasons to be "equally correct"? And could they do this without sacrificing allegiance to their own positions? I see two possibilities here. One would be a relativism about reasons, according to which all claims about reasons for action are relative to certain "parameters."[32] This could be threatening in so far as the relativity in question seemed to undermine the force of reasons we take ourselves to have. But it would take me too far afield to explore here the questions whether some such view might be correct and whether it should be seen as threatening. A second possibility is that each of the parties could (without becoming relativists about reasons) recognize the others' outlook as a reasonable alternative worthy of respect, even though it is not one that they themselves would adopt. I believe that this is closer to what many benign relativists have in mind.

This possibility can be illustrated by a revised version of the Leningrad example, which I will take to involve a contrast between a form of liberal contractualism on the one hand and, on the other, what we may imagine to be the moral ideal of solidarity that, we may imagine, moved many of the people of Leningrad during the siege. I will suppose that this ideal demands a greater level of self-sacrifice than contractualism does, but does not license the use of coercion to extract these sacrifices. The people who hold this ideal, we may suppose, see that because of the sacrifices it requires it is something that others could reasonably reject. None the less, it represents the kind of life with others that they want to live. They would not be satisfied with less.

Foot's hypothesis seems plausible in this case. When a citizen of Leningrad says, of a particular act of sacrifice, "This is what I must do," she says something true even though when I say, looking back, "No one is required, morally, to do what they did," I also speak truly. Moreover, when we step back from the "contingent principles" on which these judgements are based, and from the conceptions of morality from which they draw their force, there is much that might be said to explain the appeal of each, but the idea of truth does not seem to have a significant role to play in this discussion. Each can recognize, without sacrifice of allegiance, that the others act on good, respectable reasons.

Could the same be said about the disagreement between secular liberal and conservative Christian views about homosexuality that I mentioned in Section 2? The proposal would be this. When a conservative Christian says, "Homosexuality is a sin," and I say "There is nothing morally objectionable about sexual relations between two men, or between two women," I may hope that the Christian is mistaken even in his own terms, but it is conceivable that we may both be saying something true. The standards that our judgements presuppose make conflicting claims to allegiance: they conflict in a practical sense. Given the very different bases of these claims, however, it might be suggested that the contingent principles that they support are not plausibly understood as making conflicting truth-claims about the same subject.

I have expressed the Christian's claims in terms of "sin" in order to emphasize this divergence. There would be at least the appearance of more direct conflict if we were to imagine instead that he urges on me the claim that "Homosexual conduct is morally wrong." This claim could be understood in two different ways. It might embody the claim that Christianity offers the best, perhaps the only, coherent way of understanding what *I* mean by morality. If so, then the dispute has much the same form as the one between the utilitarian and the contractualist as I first described it. There is a single subject, an allegedly shared idea of morality, about which conflicting claims are being made, and there seems little reason to deny that these claims can be true or false. Alternatively, "Homosexuality is morally wrong" may amount to the same thing as "Homosexuality is a sin," giving added emphasis, perhaps, to the Christian's belief that *these* are the standards worth caring about. In this case, as in the original version of this example and in the case of the people of Leningrad, the question of truth seems less relevant, and my reason for rejecting the Christian's claim is not that it says something false about morality but rather that it expresses a conception of what is important in life that I see no reason to accept (perhaps because it involves factual assumptions which I see as mistaken).

Should we accept this proposal? In one respect there seems to me to be something clarifying about it. We often speak, in moral philosophy, as if there were one subject-matter, *morality*, the domain of one particular kind of reason for action, which we are studying and to which everyone is referring when they make judgements about right and wrong. The present proposal is helpful in suggesting, very plausibly I think, that this is not so, and that different people may have quite different kinds of reason in mind when they use the terms "right," "wrong," and "morality." This much could, I think, be accepted without compromising our allegiance to our own moral views. But it would be much more difficult in this case for either party to accept the further idea that the reasons backing the other side's conception of morality are "just as good as" their own. This was possible in the version of the Leningrad example that I just discussed because the ideals in question there were ones that each side could recognize as alternatives deserving of similar respect. But in the present case we have conflicting outlooks that make stronger claims to unique authority and rest on premises which the opposing side is likely to see as false.

My conclusions are these. The concept of "a morality" or "a moral system" is broad enough to allow variation not only in the content of what is required but also in the reasons seen as supporting these requirements and their claim to importance. Variation of the latter kind explains the former: people who all recognize the same "definitional" principles as morally required, can see different sets of "contingent principles" as having the same status as these shared principles because they have different views about what this status amounts to. Recognizing other people's (definitional plus contingent) principles as constituting "a moral system," and recognizing the judgements they make as true (relative to this system), need not be incompatible with allegiance to our own moral views. Despite the applicability to both of the term "moral," their judgements and ours are properly understood as making claims "about different things." What is more difficult to see is how we might, without sacrificing allegiance to our own principles, regard the reasons others have for following their principles as just as good as our reasons for following our own. I have suggested that this would be possible if we accept the substantive evaluative judgement that both ways of life are worthy of respect and adherence. This seems to me the most plausible way for a benign moral relativism to be realized. So understood, it is not a possibility that there is any reason to fear.

NOTES

The work on relativism from which this paper is derived has been presented in various forms, long and short, to many audiences. I am grateful to participants in all of these occasions for their comments and criticisms, and also to Derek Parfit and Hilary Putnam for their detailed comments on earlier drafts.

1. What Gilbert Harman calls "metaethical relativism." See his "What Is Moral Relativism," in A. Goldman and J. Kim (eds.), *Values and Morals* (Dordrecht: Reidel, 1978), 143 and 146–8.

2. This amounts to what Harman has called "moral judgment relativism" (ibid. 143). My characterization leaves it open how the parameters governing a given moral judgement are set or constrained—whether, for example, they are determined by facts about the speaker's attitudes, or the agent's, or by facts about the societies to which they belong. It is therefore left open whether or not the relativism in question is "normative relativism" in Harman's sense, that is to say, relativism which holds that different agents are subject to different ultimate moral demands. Harman's own view (as expressed in this article and others, such as "Moral Relativism Defended," *Philosophical Review*, 84 (1975), 3–22) is that moral judgements of the "ought to do" variety are relative to attitudes shared by the speaker, the agent, and the intended audience of the judgement.

3. This problem is forcefully presented by Hilary Putnam in ch. 5 of his *Reason, Truth and History* (Cambridge: Cambridge University Press, 1981).

4. I take something like this to be the reason why Nietzsche thinks that he can square his "perspectivism" with his apparently unqualified assertion of this and other doctrines. He would not, however, apply the term "relativist" to his position.

5. Harman "What Is Moral Relativism?," 160.

6. This kind of disagreement would be one version of the phenomenon which David Wong describes by saying that the term "adequate moral system" may have different extensions as used by different people. See his *Moral Relativity* (Berkeley, Calif.: University of California Press, 1984), 45. But some of the other forms of disagreement that I have described may also fall under Wong's description, since it is not clear that he means to restrict disagreement over the extension of "adequate moral system" to disagreement over the source or ground of moral authority.

7. Essentially John Rawls's principle of fairness. See *A Theory of Justice* (Cambridge, Mass.: Harvard University Press, 1971), 111–14.

8. In "Contractualism and Utilitarianism," in A. Sen and B. Williams (eds.), *Utilitarianism and Beyond* (Cambridge: Cambridge University Press, 1982).

9. John Locke, *Letter on Toleration* (1689). Quoted from p. 52 of the Library of Liberal Arts edn. (Indianapolis: Bobbs-Merrill, 1950).

10. Philippa Foot, "Morality and Art," *Proceedings of the British Academy*, 56 (1970), 143.

11. In "Moral Relativism Defended." Harman does allow that we can condemn Hitler in other ways, for example by saying that he was evil.

12. Harman, ibid.; Bernard Williams, in a slightly more qualified way, in "Internal Reasons and the Obscurity of Blame," *LOGOS: Philosophic Issues in Christian Perspective*, 10 (1989), 1–11; see esp. pp. 6–7.

13. See Foot, "Morality and Art," 132, and "Moral Relativism" [reprinted as chap. 13, this book].

14. F. Nietzsche, *The Will to Power*, tr. Walter Kaufmann and R. J. Hollingdale (New York: Vintage Books, 1968), sect. 349.

15. See S. Hampshire, "Morality and Convention," in his *Morality and Conflict* (Cambridge, Mass.: Harvard University Press, 1983), and M. Walzer, *Spheres of Justice* (New York: Basic Books, 1983), esp. chs. 1 and 13.

16. M. Walzer, *Interpretation and Social Criticism* (Cambridge, Mass.: Harvard University Press, 1987), 24.

17. "Moral Relativism," 8. She cites Williams's essays "Consistency and Realism," *Proceedings of the Aristotelian Society*, supp. vol. (1966) and "The Truth in Relativism," in *Moral Luck*, (Cambridge: Cambridge University Press, 1981), 132–43.

18. See pp. 17–19 of "Moral Relativism" and the "Retrospective Note" added to the version of "Morality and Art" repr. in T. Honderich and M. Burnyeat (eds.), *Philosophy As It Is* (New York: Penguin, 1979).

19. Foot, "Morality and Art," 133.

20. Ibid.

21. Philippa Foot, "Morality as a System of Hypothetical Imperatives," *Philosophical Review*, 81/3 (July 1972), 305–16.

22. Foot, "Morality and Art," 139.

23. What we have here is, in Harman's terms, a form of moral judgement relativism, not normative relativism.

24. Foot, "Morality and Art," 139.

25. See generally Foot, "Morality as a System of Hypothetical Imperatives" and "Morality and Art," 142–3.

26. This distinction, between accounts of the content of morality and accounts of its nature and importance, is discussed at greater length in my paper "The Aims and Authority of Moral Theory," *Oxford Journal of Legal Studies,* 12 (1992), 1–23. I am indebted to Angel Oquendo for many discussions of the bearing of this distinction on issues of relativism.

27. J. S. Mill, *Utilitarianism,* ch. 3, para. 10.

28. See my "Contractualism and Utilitarianism," sect. 3.

29. Foot, "Morality and Art," 132.

30. Ibid. 133.

31. Sidgwick gave the classic statement of this rationale for utilitarianism in book IV of his *Methods of Ethics* (Chicago, Ill.: University of Chicago Press, 1962). Foot criticizes modern versions of the idea in her article "Utilitarianism and the Virtues," in S. Scheffler (ed.), *Consequentialism and Its Critics* (Oxford: Oxford University Press, 1988).

32. Bernard Williams's well-known claim that all statements about reasons for action are relative to the agent's "subjective motivational set" would be an example. See "Internal and External Reasons," in *Moral Luck* (Cambridge: Cambridge University Press, 1978). He appears to regard this as what I have been calling a benign view— one we have no good reason to fear. Foot has said (in the postscript to "Reasons for Action and Desires," in *Virtues and Vices* (Oxford: Blackwell, 1978), 156) that she is inclined to the view that at least one class of reasons (those deriving from what is in an agent's best interest) are independent of desires, thus rejecting Williams's extreme position. But she seems there to remain agnostic on the more general question of the relatively of reasons.

PART FOUR

DEFENSE AND CRITICISM

12

Is There a Single True Morality?

GILBERT HARMAN

CONFESSION

I have always been a moral relativist. As far back as I can remember thinking about it, it has seemed to me obvious that the dictates of morality arise from some sort of convention or understanding among people, that different people arrive at different understandings, and that there are no basic moral demands that apply to everyone. For many years, this seemed so obvious to me that I assumed it was everyone's instinctive view, at least everyone who gave the matter any thought "in this day and age."

When I first studied philosophical ethics (in the 1950s), I was not disabused of this opinion. The main issue at the time seemed to be to determine exactly what form of "noncognitivism" was correct. (According to noncognitivism, moral judgments do not function to describe a moral reality but do something else—express feelings, prescribe a course of action, and so forth.)

It is true that many of the philosophers I studied seemed for some reason to want to avoid calling themselves "relativists." This was usually accomplished by defining moral relativism to be an obviously inconsistent position; for example, the view both that there are no universal moral truths and also that everyone ought to follow the dictates of his or her group, where this last claim is taken to be a universal moral truth. I wasn't sure what this verbal maneuver was supposed to accomplish. Why would anyone want to give such a definition of moral relativism? Moral relativism was obviously correct, and the philosophers I was studying seemed all to be moral relativists even if they did not want to describe themselves in that way.

In the 1960s I was distressed to hear from various people teaching ethics that students in their classes tended to proclaim themselves moral relativists until they had been shown how confused they were about ethics. I suspected that what confusions there were were not confusions of the students, but were confusions of their teachers, due perhaps to a faulty definition of moral

Reprinted, by permission of the publisher and copyright holder, from Gilbert Harman, "Is There a Single True Morality?" in David Copp and David Zimmerman, eds., *Morality, Reason, and Truth,* pp. 27–48. Totowa, N.J.: Rowman & Allanheld, 1984.

relativism. It seemed to me that the obvious solution was to show that moral relativism can be consistently defined as a plausible view and that standard objections to moral relativism are mistaken.

So, I eventually wrote and published an essay about this (Harman, 1975), naively thinking it would clear things up and end worries about moral relativism. I was surprised to discover that this did not happen. I was also startled to find that many students in my own ethics courses resisted my attempt to make clear what I thought they instinctively believed. After some study I concluded that in fact only some of the students in my courses were instinctive moral relativists; a significant number of them were instinctive absolutists.

I had known of course that there were philosophers and friends of mine who were not moral relativists. For a long time I attributed this to their perversity and love of the bizarre and attached no significance to it. But then I discovered that some of them thought moral relativism was the perverse view, a kind of philosophical folly like skepticism about other minds or the external world (for example, Nagel, 1980). I was stunned! How could they think that when they knew so many moral relativists (like me) and no epistemological skeptics (at least none who took such skepticism seriously in ordinary life)? It then occurred to me to wonder how I could think of moral absolutism as such a perverse view when I knew so many moral absolutists.

THE ISSUE

It turns out to my surprise that the question whether there is a single true morality is an unresolved issue in moral philosophy. On one side are relativists, skeptics, nihilists, and noncognitivists. On the other side are those who believe in absolute values and a moral law that applies to everyone. Stangely, only a few people seem to be undecided. Almost everyone seems to be firmly on one side or the other, and almost everyone seems to think his or her side is obviously right, the other side representing a kind of ridiculous folly. This is strange since everyone knows, or ought to know, that many intelligent people are on each side of this issue.

Two Approaches

In this essay I want to suggest that part of the explanation for this mutual incomprehension is that there are two different ways to do moral philosophy. If one approach is taken, moral relativism, noncognitivism, or skepticism may seem obviously correct and moral absolutism may seem foolish. If the other approach is taken, absolutism may seem clearly right and skepticism, relativism, and noncognitivism may seem foolish.

The difference in approaches is, to put it crudely, a difference in attitude toward science. One side says we must concentrate on finding the place of value and obligation in the world of facts as revealed by science. The other side says we must ignore that problem and concentrate on ethics proper.

Of course, both sides agree that we must begin at the beginning with our initial beliefs, both moral and nonmoral, and consider possible modifications that will make these beliefs more coherent with each other and with plausible generalizations and other explanatory principles. Eventually, we hope to arrive at a "reflective equilibrium" (Rawls, 1971) when no further modifications seem called for, at least for the time being. This process will inevitably leave many issues unresolved; in particular, we may find ourselves with no account of the place that value and obligation have in the world of facts. This will not dismay someone who is willing to leave that question unanswered, but it will be disturbing to someone who, on the way to "reflective equilibrium," has come to think that the basic issue in moral philosophy is precisely how value and obligation fit into the scientific conception of the world.

I will use the term "naturalism" for an approach to ethics that is in this way dominated by a concern with the place of values in the natural world. I will call any approach that is not so dominated an instance of "autonomous ethics," since such an approach allows us to pursue ethics internally. Of course, autonomous ethics allows that science is relevant to ethics in as much as ethical assessment depends on the facts of the case. But unlike naturalism, autonomous ethics does not take the main question of ethics to be the naturalistic status of values and obligations.

Naturalism

I hope the terms "naturalism" and "autonomous ethics" will not be too misleading. The term "naturalism" is sometimes reserved for the thesis that moral judgments can be analyzed into or reduced to factual statements of a sort clearly compatible with the scientific world view. I am using the term "naturalism" more broadly in a more traditional and accurate sense. Naturalism in this sense does not have to lead to naturalistic reduction, although that is one possibility. Another possibility is that there is no way in which ethics could fit into the scientific conception of the world. In that case naturalism leads to moral nihilism, as in Mackie (1977). Mackie supposes that ethics requires absolute values which have the property that anyone aware of their existence must necessarily be motivated to act morally. Since our scientific conception of the world has no place for entities of this sort, and since there is no way in which we could become aware of such entities, Mackie concludes that ethics must be rejected as resting on a false presupposition. That is a version of naturalism as I am using the term.

Naturalism can also lead one to a noncognitive analysis of moral judgments. In this view, moral judgments do not function to describe the world, but to do something else—to express one's attitudes for and against things, as Stevenson (1963) argues—or to recommend one or another course of action or general policy, as Hare (1952, 1981) proposes. Or a naturalist may decide that moral judgments do make factual claims that fit in with the claims of science. This can be illustrated by some sort of naturalistic reduction. One example would be an analysis that takes moral claims to be claims about the reactions of a hypothetical impartial observer as in Hume (1739) or Firth (1952).

More complex positions are possible. Mackie (1977) argues in Chapter 1 that ethics rests on a false presupposition, but then he goes on in later chapters to discuss particular moral issues. It is almost as if he had first demonstrated that God does not exist and had then gone on to consider whether He is wise and loving. Presumably, Mackie believes that ethics as normally conceived must be or can be replaced with something else. But he does not indicate exactly what sort of replacement he has in mind—whether it is an institution of some sort, for example. Nor does he say how moral claims made within this replacement fit in with the claims of science. I suspect he would accept some sort of noncognitivist account of the judgments that are to replace the old moral judgments.

It is possible to be both a naturalist and an absolutist, although this is not very common. Firth (1952) defends an absolutist version of the ideal-observer theory and Hare (1981) defends an absolutist version of noncognitivism. But I will argue that the most plausible versions of naturalism involve a moral relativism that says different agents are subject to different basic moral requirements depending on the moral conventions in which they participate.

AUTONOMOUS ETHICS

Naturalism tends toward relativism. What I am calling autonomous ethics, on the other hand, can have a very different tendency. In this approach, science is relevant, since our moral judgments depend on what we take the facts to be; but we attach no special importance to saying how obligations and values can be part of the world revealed by science. Rather, we do ethics internally. We begin with our initial moral beliefs and search for general principles. Our initial opinions can be changed to some extent so as to come into agreement with appealing general principles and our beliefs about the facts, but an important aspect of the appeal of such principles will be the way in which they account for what we already accept.

This approach normally (but not always) involves an initial assumption of moral absolutism, which in this context is of course not the thesis that there are simple moral principles that hold absolutely without exceptions, but rather the thesis that there are basic moral demands that apply to all moral agents. Autonomous ethics tends to retain that absolutist thesis. It may also involve some sort of intuitionism, claiming that each of us has immediate insight into the truths of certain moral principles. It sometimes leads to a fairly conservative morality, not much different from one's initial starting point. That is not surprising given the privileged position assigned to our initial moral beliefs.

But let me stress that conservatism is not inevitable, and autonomous ethics can and often does lead to more radical moralities too. It leads some philosphers to a radical utilitarianism, for example. It leads Rawls (1971) to principles of social justice that appear to be considerably more egalitarian than those most people accept. And Nozick (1974), using the same general approach, comes out at a very different place, in which he ends up denying that any sort of egalitarian redistribution by governments is ever morally justified. (However, the moral theory in Nozick, 1981, as contrasted with the political theory in Nozick, 1974, insists on the moral requirement of helping others.) Indeed, there are many different ways in which ethics can be pursued as an autonomous discipline with its own principles that are not reducible to the principles of any science. I can illustrate this variety by mentioning a few of the many other contemporary philosophers who accept some form of autonomous ethics: Baier (1958), Darwall (1983), Donagan (1977), Frankena (1976), Fried (1978), Gewirth (1978), Grice (1967), Nagel (1970, 1980), and Richards (1971). Each of these philosophers has a somewhat different approach, although all are absolutists who rely on some form of autonomous ethics.

I should say that it is possible to believe in autonomous ethics without being an absolutist. One might be impressed by the variety of views held by those who accept autonomous ethics and so be led to allow for relativism while continuing to accept the method of autonomous ethics, believing that naturalism must be rejected. A possible example is McDowell (1978, 1979, 1981). But the tendency of autonomism in ethics is toward absolutism. In what follows I will restrict my discussion to absolutist versions of autonomous ethics and to relativistic versions of naturalism.

TEACHERS OF ETHICS

I might also mention that ethics pursued internally, as in autonomous ethics, is more interesting to many people than ethics as pursued by naturalism. That is because autonomous ethics allows one to spend more of one's time thinking about interesting complicated moral puzzles than naturalistic ethics does, and many people find moral puzzles more interesting than "abstract" questions about the objectivity of value and its place in nature. Philosophers attracted by naturalism tend not to find ethics as interesting a subject as do philosphers attracted by autonomous ethics. So, relativists tend to be less interested in ethics than absolutists are. For example, logicians, philosphers of science, and philosophers of mathematics, who tend toward naturalism, are usually not moral absolutists and are not very interested in ethics as a philosophical subject. Philosophers who are relatively interested in ethics tend to be those who favor autonomous ethics and therefore tend to be absolutists. This is why teachers of ethics tend more than their students to be absolutists. It is not merely, as they sometimes suppose, that ethics teachers have seen through confusions that affect their students. A more important factor is that relativists tend not to become teachers of ethics.

WHY DO WE BELIEVE WHAT WE BELIEVE?

Autonomous ethics and naturalism represent very different attitudes toward the relation between science and ethics. Consider, for example, the question of what explains our believing what we in fact believe. Naturalists see an important difference between our factural beliefs and our moral beliefs. Our ordinary factual beliefs provide us with evidence that there is an independent world of objects because our having those beliefs cannot be plausibly explained without assuming we interact with an independent world of objects external to ourselves, objects we perceive and manipulate. But our having the moral beliefs we have can be explained entirely in terms of our upbringing and our psychology, without any appeal to an independent realm of values and obligations. So our moral beliefs do not provide us with evidence for such an independent realm of values and obligations, and we must choose between skepticism, noncognitivism, and relativism (Harman, 1977, chapter 1).

Autonomists disagree with this. They claim we often believe that something is good or right or obligatory in part because it *is* good or right or obligatory. They accuse naturalists of begging the question. When naturalists say that a belief cannot be explained by virtue of something's being right, unless that thing's being right consists in some psychological or sociological fact, they simply assume that all explanatory factors are part of the world revealed by science. But this is the point at issue. Autonomists argue that it is more obvious that we sometimes recognize what is right than that naturalism is correct. True, we may be unable to say how a given "moral fact" and someone's recognition of it fit into the world of facts as revealed by science. But there are always unanswered questions. To jump from our current inability to answer this question to skepticism, relativism, or noncognitivism is to make a more drastic move than this puzzle warrants, from the point of view of autonomous ethics.

EXPLANATION AND REDUCTION

The naturalist seeks to locate the place of value, justice, right, and wrong, and so forth in the world in a way that makes clear how they might explain what we take them to explain. A naturalist cannot understand how value, justice, right, and wrong might figure in explanations without having some sense of their "location" in the world. We can say that this involves "naturalistic reduction," but it need not involve reductive definitions of a serious sort. Indeed, reduction rarely (if ever) involves serious reductive definitions. We identify tables with clusters of atoms in a way that allows us to understand how tables can hold up the things they hold up without having to suppose the word *table* is definable using only the concepts of physics! Similarly, we identify colors with dispositional properties of objects, namely, their tendencies to look in certain ways to certain sorts of observers in certain conditions, without having to suppose there is a satisfactory definition in these terms. Similarly for temperatures, genes, and so on. What a naturalist wants is to be able to locate value, justice, right, wrong, and so forth in the world in the way that tables, colors, genes, temperatures, and so on can be located in the world.

What is at issue here is understanding *how* moral facts might explain something, how the badness of someone's character might explain why that person acts in a certain way, to take an example from Sturgeon's essay. It is not sufficient that one be prepared to accept the counterfactual judgment that the person would not have acted in that way if the person had not had a bad character, if one does not see how the *badness* of the person's character could have such an effect. A naturalist believes one can see that only by locating badness of character in aspects of the world which one sees can have that effect.

Notice that a "naturalist" as I am here using the term is not just someone who supposes that all aspects of the world have a naturalistic location in this way, but rather someone who takes it to be of overriding importance in doing moral philosophy actually to attempt to locate moral properties. My claim is that, when one takes this attempt seriously, one will tend to become skeptical or relativistic. Sturgeon is not a naturalist in my sense, despite his insistence that he takes moral facts to be natural facts.

MORAL ABSOLUTISM DEFINED

I now want to be more specific about what is to count as moral absolutism. Various things might be meant by the claim that there are absolute values and one true morality. Moral absolutists in one sense might not be moral absolutists in other senses. We must be careful not to mix up real issues with purely verbal issues. So let me stipulate that I will take moral absolutism to be a view about the moral reasons people have to do things and to want or hope for things. I will understand a belief about absolute values to be a belief that there are things that everyone has a reason to hope or wish for. To say that there is a moral law that "applies to everyone" is, I hereby stipulate, to say that everyone has sufficient reasons to follow that law.

It is true that many philosophers pursue something that resembles autonomous ethics when they ask what principles an "ideal" moral code of one or another sort would have, quite apart from the question whether people now have any reason to follow that code. Depending on what sort of idealization is being considered, there may or may not be a unique "ideal" code of that sort. But I am not going to count as a form of moral absolutism the claim that there is a unique ideal moral code of such and such a type. Relativists and absolutists in my sense might very well agree about this claim without that having any effect at all on what I take to be the basic issue that separates them, since this claim has no immediate relevance to questions about what reasons people actually have to hope for certain things or do certain things.

Similarly, I am not going to count as a form of moral absolutism the claim that there is one true morality that applies to everyone in that everyone ought to follow it, if this is not taken to imply that everyone has a sufficient reason to follow it. I am not sure what *ought* is supposed to mean if it is disconnected in this way from reasons to do things. If what is meant is that it ought to be the case that everyone followed the one true morality—in other words that it would be a good thing if they did—then this is a version of the view that there is a unique "ideal" moral code. I am not sure what else might be meant, although a great deal more could be said here (Harman 1978). Rather than try to say it, however, I simply stipulate that this sort of claim is not a version of what I am counting as moral absolutism.

I should note that, of the contemporary philosophers I have identified as absolutists, Baier, Darwall, Donagan, Frankena, Gewirth, Grice, Nagel, and Richards, clearly advocate moral absolutism in this sense. They all think that there are basic moral demands that in some sense every competent adult has reasons to adhere to. I *believe* the others I mentioned—namely Rawls, Nozick, and Fried—also agree with this, although they do not explicitly say so in the works I have cited.

DOES A SINGLE MORAL LAW APPLY TO EVERYONE?

Consider the issue between absolutism and relativism concerning reasons people have for doing things. According to moral absolutism about this, there is a single moral law that applies to everyone; in other words, there are moral demands that everyone has sufficient reasons to follow, and these demands are the source of all moral reasons. Moral relativism denies that there are universal basic moral demands and says different people are subject to different basic moral demands depending on the social customs, practices, conventions, values, and principles that they accept.

For example, a moral absolutist might suppose there is a basic moral prohibition on causing harm or injury to other people. This prohibition is in one sense not absolute, since it can be overridden by more compelling considerations and since it allows exceptions in order to punish criminals, for instance. But the prohibition is supposed to be universal in the sense that it applies to absolutely all agents and not just to those who happen to participate in certain conventions. The absolutist claims that absolutely everyone has sufficient reasons to observe this prohibition and to act as it and other basic moral requirements dictate.

A moral relativist denies this and claims that many people have no reasons to observe this prohibition. Many people participate in moralities that sharply distinguish insiders and outsiders and do not prohibit harm or injury to outsiders, except perhaps as this is likely to lead to retaliation against insiders. A person participating in such a morality has no reason to avoid harm or injury to outsiders, according to the relativist, and so the general prohibition does not apply to that person. Such a person may be a member of some primitive tribal group, but he or she need not be. He or she might also be part of contemporary society, a successful professional criminal, say, who recognizes various obligations to other members of a criminal organization but not to those on the outside. According to the moral relativist, the successful criminal may well have no reason at all not to harm his or her victims.

An Argument for Relativism

Let us concentrate on this case. The moral absolutist says the demands of the one true morality apply as much to this successful criminal as to anyone else, so this criminal does have a reason not to harm a given victim. The relativist denies the criminal has any such reason and so denies the relevant moral demand is a universal demand that applies to everyone. Here naturalism tends to support relativism in the following way.

Consider what it is for someone to have a sufficient reason to do something. Naturalism requires that this should be explained in terms congenial to science. We cannot simply treat this as irreducibly normative, saying, for example, that someone has a sufficient reason to do something if and only if he or she ought to do it. Now, presumably, someone has a sufficient reason to do something if and only if there is warranted reasoning that person could do which would lead him or her to decide to do that thing. A naturalist will suppose that a person with a sufficient reason to do something might fail to reason in this way to such a decision only because of some sort of empirically discoverable failure, due to inattention, or lack of time, or failure to consider or appreciate certain arguments, or ignorance of certain available evidence, or an error in reasoning, or some sort of irrationality or unreasonableness, or weakness of will. If the person does not intend to do something and that is not because he or she has failed in some such empirically discoverable way to reason to a decision to do that thing, then, according to the naturalist, that person cannot have a sufficient reason to do that thing. This is the first premise in a naturalistic argument in support of the relativist.

The other premise is that there are people, such as certain professional criminals, who do not act in accordance with the alleged requirement not to harm or injure others, where this is not due to inattention or failure to consider or appreciate certain arguments, or ignorance of certain evidence, or any errors in reasoning, or any sort of irrationality or unreasonableness, or weakness of will. The argument for this is simply that there clearly are people who do not adhere to the requirement in question and who do not *seem* to have failed in any of these ways. So, in the absence of special theoretical reasons, deriving, say, from psychology, to think these people must have failed in one of the specified ways, we can conclude they have not done so.

From these two premises it follows that there are people who do not have sufficient reasons, and therefore do not have sufficient moral reasons, to adhere to the general prohibition against harming or injuring others. In particular, a successful criminal may not have a sufficient reason not to harm his or her victims. The moral prohibition against harming others may simply fail to apply to such a person. It may fail to apply in the relevant sense, which is of course not to say that the principle makes an explicit exception for criminals, allowing them but not others to injure and harm people without restraint. Rather, the principle may fail to apply in the sense that the criminal in question may fail to have sufficient reason to act in accordance with the principle.

An Absolutist Reply

Moral absolutism must reject this argument. It can do so by invoking autonomous ethics at the place at which moral relativism invokes naturalism. Autonomous ethics does not suppose that we must give some sort of naturalistic account of having a sufficient reason to do something, nor does it suppose that only a science like psychology can discover the conditions under which someone has failed to reason in a certain way because of inattention, irrationality, unreasonableness, or any of the other causes of failure mentioned in the relativistic argument.

Autonomous ethics approaches this issue in the following way. We begin with certain beliefs. Presumably these imply that everyone has a sufficient reason to observe the prohibition against harm to others, including, in particular, the successful criminal who does not participate in or accept any practice of observing this general prohibition. At the start we therefore believe that the criminal does have sufficient reason not to harm his or her victims. Following autonomous ethics, then, we should continue to believe this unless such continued belief conflicts with generalizations or other theoretical principles internal to ethics that we find attractive because they do a better job at making sense of most of the things we originally believe. Taking this approach, the absolutist must claim that the relativistic argument does not provide sufficient reason to abandon our original absolutism. It is more plausible, according to the absolutist, that at least one of the premises of the relativistic argument is false than that its conclusion is true.

Assessing the First Premise

The first premise of the relativistic argument is that for someone to have a sufficient reason to do something there must be warranted reasoning available to that person that leads to a decision to do that thing, so that if the person fails to intend to do that thing it must be because of inattention, lack of time, failure to consider or appreciate certain arguments, ignorance of relevant evidence, an error in reasoning, irrationality, unreasonableness, or weakness of will. The absolutist might object that this is oversimplified. If a person with sufficient reason to do something does not do it, then something has gone wrong, and it might be one of the things the relativist mentions, but it might be something else as well. There might be something wrong with the *person* in question. That person might be bad, immoral. The failure might simply be a failure not to care enough about other people. A person ought to care about others and there is something wrong with a person who does not care, even if that person is not inattentive, ignorant, rushed, or defective in any other of the particular ways the relativist mentions. So, even if some people fail to observe the prohibition against harming others not because of inattention, lack of time, and so forth, but simply because of lack of concern and respect for others, such people still do have sufficient reason not to harm others. (This response on behalf of absolutism was suggested to me by Thomas M. Scanlon.)

This response to the relativistic argument is a response within autonomous ethics. It does not explain having a sufficient reason to do something in terms that are acceptably factual from a naturalistic perspective. It appeals also to the notion of something's being wrong with someone, where what might be wrong is simply that the person is bad or immoral. It is like saying one has a sufficient reason to do something if and only if one ought to do it, or if and only if it would be wrong not to do it.

The relativist claims that the only plausible accounts of these normative notions are relativistic ones. There is no prohibition on harm to outsiders in the criminals' morality. There is such a prohibition only in some other morality. In that other morality something is wrong with a person who has no compunction about injuring someone else; but nothing is wrong with such a person with respect to the criminal morality, as long as those injured are outsiders. But how can it be a sufficient reason for the criminal not to harm his or her victims that this is prohibited by somebody else's morality? How can its being bad, immoral, or wrong in this other morality not to care about and respect others give the criminal, who does not accept that morality, a sufficient reason to do anything?

The absolutist's answer is that failure to respect others is not just wrong according to some morality the criminal does not accept, it is also wrong, period. Something is really wrong with lack of respect and concern for others. It is not just wrong in relation to one or another morality. Of course, the relativist will not be satisfied with this answer and, appealing to naturalism, will ask what it is for something to be wrong in this way. The absolutist supposes that the failure to care about and respect others does involve something the absolutist points to by saying this failure is wrong. But what is this thing that is true of such a failure to care and that can give the criminal a sufficient reason not to harm and injure others? The relativist can see no aspect of such a failure that could provide such a reason. This of course is because the relativist, as a naturalist, considers only aspects of the failure that are clearly compatible with a scientific world view. The relativist disregards putative aspects that can be specified only in normative terms. But the absolutist, as an autonomist, can specify the relevant aspect of such a failure to care about others: It is bad, immoral, wrong not to care; the criminal ought to have this concern and respect and so ought not to harm and injure others, and therefore has a sufficient reason not to harm and injure them.

ASSESSING THE SECOND PREMISE

We have been discussing an argument for relativism concerning moral reasons. We have seen that naturalism supports the first premise of this argument and that autonomous ethics allows the rejection of this premise. The same thing is true of the second premise, which says that there are people, such as the successful criminal, who do not observe the alleged requirement not to harm or injure others and this is not due to inattention, failure to consider or appreciate certain arguments, ignorance of relevant evidence, errors in reasoning, irrationality, unreasonableness, or weakness of will. Naturalism supports this because there do seem to be such people, and no scientifically acceptable grounds exist for thinking this is an illusion. On the other hand, autonomous ethics allows other grounds, not reducible to scientific grounds, for thinking this is an illusion. In autonomous ethics we begin by supposing that we recognize the wrongness of harming others, where this is to recognize a sufficient reason not to harm others. If that is something we recognize, then it must be there to be recognized, so the successful criminal in question must be failing to recognize and appreciate something that is there.

The absolutist might argue that the criminal must be irrational or at least unreasonable. Seeing that a proposed course of action will probably cause serious injury to some outsider, the criminal does not treat this as a reason not to undertake that course of action. This must be irrational or unreasonable, because such a consideration simply is such a reason and indeed is an obvious reason, a basic reason, not one that has to be derived in some complex way through arcane reasoning. But then it must be irrational or at least unreasonable for the criminal not to care sufficiently about others, since the criminal's lack of concern for others is what is responsible for the criminal's not taking the likelihood of harm to an outsider to be a reason against a proposed course of action. This is one way an absolutist might argue.

The relativist's reply to such an argument is that, on any plausible characterization of reasonableness and unreasonableness (or rationality and irrationality) as notions that can be part of the scientific conception of the world, the absolutist's claim is just false. Someone can be completely rational without feeling concern and respect for outsiders. But of course this reply appeals to naturalism. The absolutist who rejects naturalism in favor of autonomous ethics relies on an unreduced normative characterization of rationality and irrationality (or reasonableness and unreasonableness).

Now the argument continues as before. The relativist argues that, if rationality and irrationality (or reasonableness and unreasonableness) are conceived normatively, they become relative notions. What one morality counts as irrational or unreasonable, another does not. The criminal is not irrational or unreasonable in relation to criminal morality, but only in relation to a morality the criminal rejects. But the fact that it is irrational or unreasonable in relation to this other morality not to have concern and respect for others does not give the criminal who rejects that morality any reason to avoid harming or injuring others. The absolutist replies that relative irrationality or unreasonableness is not what is in question. The criminal is irrational or at least unreasonable, period. Not just irrational or unreasonable in relation to a morality he or she does not accept. Since it is irrational or unreasonable for anyone not to care sufficiently about others, everyone has a sufficient reason not to injure others, whether he or she recognizes this reason or, through irrationality or unreasonableness, does not recognize it.

The naturalist is unconvinced by this because the naturalist can find no aspect of the criminal the absolutist might be referring to in saying the criminal is "irrational" or "unreasonable," if this aspect is to give the criminal any reason to care about others. This of course is because the naturalist is considering only naturalistic aspects of the criminal, whereas the absolutist, as an autonomist, is thinking about an unreduced normative aspect, something the naturalist cannot appeal to.

So, as was true of the first premise of the relativistic argument about reasons, the second premise depends on an assumption of naturalism. By appealing to autonomous ethics, an absolutist can reject this premise.

An absolutist may in fact actually accept one or the other of the premises of the relativistic argument (although of course not both). A given absolutist might reject either the first premise or the second or both premises. An absolutist might even be undecided, holding merely that one or the other premise must be rejected, without saying which. There is nothing wrong with being undecided about this. Reflective equilibrium leaves many issues unresolved.

ARE THERE ABSOLUTE MORAL VALUES?

The situation is similar in the theory of value. Naturalism tends to support the conclusion that all value is relative and that something is always good for one or another person or group of people or in relation to a specified set of purposes or interests or aims. Autonomous ethics allows also for absolute values, things that are good, period, and not just good for someone or some group or for some purpose.

The issue here concerns the goodness or value of a possible state of affairs, not the goodness or value of something as a thing of a given sort. The issue is not what it is for something to be a good thing of a kind, a good knife, a good watch, a good backswing, a good apple, a good farmer, a good poem. The issue is rather what it is for an event or situation to be a good thing; what is it, for example, to be a good thing that it is raining or that Egypt and Israel signed a peace treaty.

It is uncontroversial that this sort of goodness is sometimes relational. A situation is good for someone or some group of people, good from a certain point of view, in relation to certain purposes or interests. That it is raining is a good thing for the farmer, but not for the vacationer. That Egypt and Israel signed a peace treaty might be good from their point of view, but not from the point of view of the PLO. Given a fixed point of reference, we can evaluate states of affairs as better or worse. The value of a state of affairs in relation to that reference point represents the degree to which someone with the relevant purposes and interests has a reason to try to bring about, or want, or at least hope for that state of affairs.

Now it can be argued that there is also a kind of absolute value. The claim is that states of affairs can be good or bad, period, and not merely good or bad for someone or in relation to given purposes or interests. On hearing of pointless painful experiments on laboratory animals, for example, one immediately reacts with the thought that this is bad and it would be good to eliminate such practices. Clearly, one does not simply mean that these tortures are bad for the animals involved and that these animals would benefit if such experiments were ended. A heartless experimenter might agree that what he does is bad for the animals without having to agree that it would be a good thing to eliminate this sort of experimentation. Similarly, it seems intelligible to suppose that it would be better if there were no inequalities of wealth and income in the world even though this would not be better for everyone, not for those who are now relatively wealthy, for instance. And this seems to say more, for example, than that the average person would be better off if there were no such inequalities, since an elitist might agree with that but not agree that the envisioned state of affairs would be better, period, than our present situation. Again, we can consider which of various population policies would lead to the best resulting state of affairs even though these policies would result in different populations, so that we cannot be simply considering the interests and purposes of some fixed group. It may seem, then, that we can consider the absolute value of a possible state of affairs.

Skepticism about Absolute Values

The relative value of a possible state of affairs in relation to given purposes and interests is a measure of the extent to which someone with those purposes and interests has a reason to try to bring about, or want, or hope for that state of affairs. The absolute value of a possible state of affairs is a measure of the extent to which anyone, apart from having a personal stake in the matter, has a reason to try to bring about, or want, or hope for that state of affairs. Naturalism leads to skepticism at this point. How could we ever be aware of absolute values? How could we ever know that everyone has a reason to want a certain possible state of affairs?

Further reflection along naturalistic lines suggests that apparent absolute values are often illusory projections of one's personal values onto the world. Sometimes this sort of projection yields plausible results, but usually it does not. To begin with the most plausible sort of case, in hearing about the pain involved in animal experimentation, our sympathies are immediately and vividly engaged; we immediately side with the animals against the experimenters. In saying "That is awful!" we are not just saying "That is awful for the animals," since our remark expresses our sympathetic identification with the point of view of the animals. We do not merely state a fact, we express our feelings and we expect an awareness of this state of affairs to call forth the same feelings of dismay in everyone. This expectation seems reasonable enough in this case, since it may well be, as Brandt argues, that everyone has a sympathetic reaction to suffering (1976, p. 450).

But plausibility vanishes as soon as the case becomes even a little complex. Suppose the animal experiments are not pointless but are an essential part of a kind of medical research that promises to alleviate a certain amount of human suffering. Or suppose that, although the experiments promise no practical benefit of this sort, they are relevant to a theoretical issue in psychology. A given person may still feel that it is bad that the experiments should occur and that it would be good if they were not done, the gain not being worth the cost. Again, the person is not just saying that the experiments are bad for the animals, something to which everyone would agree. He or she is also expressing overall disapproval of the experiments, expecting others also to disapprove if they consider the issue in an impartial way. The trouble is that people react differently to these cases.

Consider the question whether it is good or bad to experiment painfully on animals in order to resolve certain theoretical issues in psychology. The extent to which this is (absolutely) good is the extent to which everyone (apart from any personal stake in the matter) has a reason to try to bring it about that such experiments are done, or to want them to be done, or hope that they are done. The extent to which this is (absolutely) bad is the extent to which everyone (apart from any personal stake) has a reason to try to end the experiments, or want them to end, or hope they end. But naturalism suggests that there is no unique answer here and that what a person has a reason to want will depend on the relative value he or she attaches to animal suffering, to using animals as means, and to theoretical progress in psychology. Different people attach different values to these things without having overlooked something, without being irrational or unreasonable, and so on. So it seems that some people will have reason to be in favor of the experiments and others will have reason to be opposed to the experiments, where this is determined by the personal values of those people. If we suppose that our answer is the right answer, we are merely projecting our own values onto the world.

The Issue Joined

Of course, autonomous ethics sees nothing wrong with projecting our own values onto the world, holding in fact that that is exactly the right method! We should begin with our initial valuations and modify them only in the interests of theoretical simplicity. If we start out believing in absolute values, we should continue believing this until forced to believe otherwise.

Clearly the controversy over absolute values parallels the controversy about reasons to do things. The argument against absolute values has the same structure as the relativistic argument about reasons to do things. Its first premise is that a person has a reason to want or hope for or try to bring about a particular state of affairs only to the extent that he or she would be irrational or unreasonable not to want that state of affairs unless he or she was unaware of some relevant consideration, was confused, or had some other specified defect. Its second premise is that, except for the simplest cases, a person can fail to want a given state of affairs without being irrational or unreasonable or ignorant or whatever. The conclusion is that, except possibly for simple cases, where, for example, the only thing relevant is that a creature suffers, there are no reasons everyone has to want or hope for or try to bring about a given state of affairs. So there are no nontrivial absolute values.

As before, the two premises are defended in each case by an appeal to naturalism: We must give a naturalistic account of reasons and we must give empirical grounds for supposing someone to be irrational or unreasonable. The absolutist rejects the argument as before by invoking autonomous ethics, perhaps by rejecting the naturalistic account of reasons, perhaps by rejecting the requirement that scientific grounds must be given for a judgment of irrationality or unreasonableness, possibly remaining undecided between these alternatives.

NATURALISM VERSUS AUTONOMOUS ETHICS

So the issue between relativism and absolutism comes down to the dispute between naturalism and autonomous ethics. Which is the best approach in moral philosophy? Should we concentrate on the place of values and reasons in the world of scientific fact, as naturalism recommends, or should we start with our initial moral beliefs and look for general principles and moral theories that will eventually yield a reflective equilibrium, not putting too much weight on the question of the place of value in the world of facts.

Religious Beliefs

In thinking of the issue between naturalism and autonomous ethics, it is useful to consider analogous issues that arise in other areas. Consider religious beliefs. Our scientific conception of the world has no place for gods, angels, demons, or devils. Naturalists hold that there is no empirical evidence for the existence of such beings nor for any sort of divine intervention in human history. Naturalists say that people's religious beliefs can be explained in terms of their upbringing and psychology without any supernatural assumptions, so these beliefs provide no evidence whatsoever for the truth of religious claims. Naturalists therefore incline toward skepticism and atheism, although naturalism might also lead to a kind of religious noncognitivism which supposes that religious language makes no factual claims about a supernatural realm but has a different function, for example, in religious ritual.

Another approach to religion is for a believer to start with his or her initial religious beliefs, including beliefs in the authority of certain writings, and then to develop general principles and theories that would accommodate these beliefs, allowing modifications in the interest of more plausible general principles. This will continue until no further modifications seem useful in improving the organization and coherence of that person's views. Inevitably, many questions will remain unanswered, and these will include issues concerning the relation between that person's religious views and his or her scientific views, for example, as regards creation. But this is not a serious worry for autonomous religion, which will say this shows merely that science is not everything, or at least that there are things we do not now and perhaps never will understand.

Naturalists say there is no reason to accept religious claims, because the fact that people have the religious beliefs they have can be explained without any supernatural assumptions. Religious autonomists say there is reason to accept religious claims, at least for someone who begins with religious beliefs, since the process of generalization, systematization, and theory construction internal to religion will give that person no reason to abandon more than a few, if any, of those religious beliefs. Furthermore, certain supernatural events might be part of the correct explanation of the appearance of sacred texts, the occurrence of miracles, and particular religious experiences. There is at present no way to say how these religious explanations mesh with ordinary scientific conceptions, but that by itself is no more an objection to religion that it is an objection to science.

Naturalists in ethics might urge this religious analogy as an *ad hominem* argument against those defenders of autonomous ethics who are not willing to take the same line with respect to religion.

Beliefs about the Mind

There is another sort of issue in which an autonomous position comes off looking rather good, even in an irreligious age, namely, the so-called mind-body problem. Here the naturalistic position corresponds to the thesis of physicalism, according to which all real aspects of mind must be features of the physical brain and central nervous system, its atomic or neural structure, or some more complex structure that the brain and nervous system instantiate. This may involve behaviorism or some sort of functionalism that treats the brain as an information-processing system like a computer in a robot. A few defenders of this approach, like Skinner (1974), conclude that there are no mental events, no mind, no consciousness, no sensation. (Rorty, 1965, sympathetically describes a similar view, "eliminative materialism.") But most physicalists suppose that mental events and other aspects of mind do exist and can be identified with certain physical or structural or functional aspects of the brain and central nervous system.

On the other side is autonomous mentalism, which holds that the physicalist hypothesis clearly leaves something out. In this view we clearly know we are conscious, can initiate action, and have experiences of a distinctive phenomenological character and feeling. The physicalist hypothesis does not account for this. A computer or robot is not conscious. Although a robot can move, it does not *act* in the way people can act. And a robot has no sensuous experience. Indeed, something could have exactly the functional structure of the human brain and nervous system without being conscious. Block (1978) describes a case in which one billion people in radio communication with each other model a particular brain for an hour, each person corresponding to a particular neuron in the brain. Block takes it to be absurd to suppose that this vast collection of people would have a group consciousness that was phenomenologically the same as the consciousness of the person whose brain and central nervous system was being modeled. Nagel (1979) observes that we might know everything there was to know about the neurophysiological structure and functioning of the brain and central nervous system of a bat without knowing what the experience of the bat was like. Defenders of autonomous mentalism agree that this leaves a mind-body problem, since they are unable to say how consciousness, free will, and sensory experience can be part of the world described by physics. But they deny that this means we must stop believing in consciousness or must identify it with some aspect of physical or functional structure. For they claim, with considerable plausibility, that it is much more reasonable to believe in consciousness, free will, and sensory experience, and to believe that these are not aspects of neurophysiological functional structure, than it is to believe in physicalism.

I am not saying that autonomous mentalism *is* more plausible than physicalism. After all is said and done, I find a physicalistic functionalism more plausible than autonomous mentalism. My point is that autonomous mentalism is a perfectly respectable philosophical position.

A defender of autonomous ethics might even argue that naturalism in ethics loses much of its plausibility once autonomous mentalism is recognized as plausible. For that casts doubt on the universal applicability of the naturalistic approach and therefore casts doubt on the naturalist's argument that a belief that something is right cannot be explained by that thing's being actually right unless that thing's being right consists in some psychological or sociological fact. The naturalist's only argument for this, it might be said, depends on accepting the general applicability of naturalism. But it is not obvious that this approach is generally applicable, since it is not obviously correct as compared with autonomous mentalism. There is at least some plausibility to the claim that one's awareness of what red looks like is to be explained by appeal to an experience of redness that does not consist entirely in some neurophysiological event. It might be said that the naturalist has no argument against autonomous ethics, since the naturalist cannot take for granted the general applicability of naturalism.

ETHICS

Defenders of autonomous ethics argue that their approach represents the only undogmatic way to proceed. They say that naturalism begs the question in supposing that everything true must fit into a scientific account of the world and by supposing that the central question about morality is how, if at all, morality fits into such a scientific account.

Defenders of naturalism reply that naturalism itself is the result of following the method of reflective equilibrium, and that autonomous ethics begs the question by assigning a specially protected status to initial moral beliefs as compared, say, with initial beliefs about the flatness of the earth or the influence of the stars on human history. Naturalists say that, starting with our initial beliefs, we are led to develop a scientific conception of the world as an account of everything there is. In doing so, we also acquire beliefs about how we learn about the world and about how errors can arise in our thinking. We come to see how superstition arises. We begin to worry about our moral views: Are they mere superstitions? We note certain sorts of disagreement in morality and extreme differences in moral customs. We observe that some people are not much influenced by what we consider important moral considerations. All this leads us to raise as a central question about morality how morality fits in with our scientific conception of the world. Naturalism is no mere prejudice in favor of science; it is an inevitable consequence of intelligent thought. This, at least, is what a defender of naturalism will say.

A defender of autonomous ethics will reply that moral disagreements, differences in custom, and the behavior of criminals prove nothing. All these things are compatible with moral absolutism.

The naturalist retorts that any view can be made *compatible* with the evidence; astrology, for example, is perfectly compatible with the evidence. The issue is not what is compatible with the evidence, but what best accounts for it. The naturalist argues that relativism accounts for the evidence better than absolutism does, since relativism is able to say how reasons and values are part of the world science describes, whereas absolutism is not able to do that.

The defender of autonomous ethics replies that such an argument is no better than the corresponding argument for behaviorism. Behaviorism is able to say how mental states (as it conceives them) are part of the world physics describes and autonomous mentalism is not able to say how mental states (as *it* conceives them) are part of the world physics describes; but one should not for this reason alone abandon one's initial view that one is conscious, makes decisions, has feelings, and so on, where this is not just being disposed to act in various ways (since something could have the dispositions without being conscious and could be conscious without having the dispositions). Similarly, one should not accept the naturalistic argument and give up one's belief in absolute values and universal moral reasons.

I see no knockdown argument for either side. A question of judgment is involved, "Which view is more plausible, all things considered?" To me, the relativistic naturalist position seems more plausible. Others find the absolutist position of autonomous ethics more plausible. I have not tried to show that one side is correct. I have tried to bring out the central issue.

REFERENCES

Baier, Kurt. 1958. *The Moral Point of View.* Ithaca, NY: Cornell University Press, 1965.

Block, Ned. 1978. "Troubles with Functionalism." In *Perception and Cognition: Issues in the Foundations of Psychology,* ed. C. Wade Savage. Minnesota Studies in the Philosophy of Science, vol. 9. Minneapolis: University of Minnesota Press.

Brandt, Richard B. 1976. "The Psychology of Benevolence and Its Implications for Philosophy." *The Journal of Philosophy* 73: 429–453.

Darwall, Stephen L. 1983. *Impartial Reason.* Ithaca, NY: Cornell University Press.

Donagan, Alan. 1977. *The Theory of Morality.* University of Chicago Press.

Firth, Roderick. 1952. "Ethical Absolutism and the Ideal Observer." *Philosophy and Phenomenological Research* 12: 317–345.

Frankena, William. 1976. In *Perspectives on Morality,* ed. K. E. Goodpaster, Notre Dame, IN: University of Notre Dame Press.

Fried, Charles. 1978. *Right and Wrong.* Cambridge, MA: Harvard University Press.

Gewirth, Alan. 1978. *Reason and Morality.* University of Chicago Press.

Grice, Geoffrey Russell. 1967. *The Grounds of Moral Judgment.* Cambridge: Cambridge University Press.

Hare, R. M. 1952. *The Language of Morals.* Oxford: The Clarendon Press.

———. 1981. *Moral Thinking: Its Levels, Method and Point.* Oxford: The Clarendon Press.

Harman, Gilbert. 1975. "Moral Relativism Defended." *The Philosophical Review* 84: 3–22.

———. 1977. *The Nature of Morality: An Introduction to Ethics.* New York: Oxford University Press.

———. 1978. "Relativistic Ethics: Morality as Politics." In *Midwest Studies in Philosophy,* vol. 3, *Studies in Ethical Theory,* ed. Peter A. French, Theodore E. Uehling, Jr., and Howard K. Wettstein, pp. 109–121. The University of Minnesota, Morris.

Hume, David. 1739. *Treatise of Human Nature,* ed. L. A. Selby-Bigge. Oxford: The Clarendon Press, 1978.

Mackie, John L. 1977. *Ethics: Inventing Right and Wrong.* Harmondsworth, England: Penguin.

McDowell, John. 1978. "Are Moral Requirements Hypothetical Imperatives?" *Proceedings of the Aristotelian Society, Supplementary Volume* 52: 13–29.

———. 1979: "Virtue and Reason." *The Monist* 62: 331–350.

———. 1981: "Noncognitivism and Rule Following." In *Wittgenstein: To Follow a Rule,* ed. Steven H. Holtzman and Christopher M. Leich, pp. 141–162. London: Routledge and Kegan Paul.

Nagel, Thomas. 1970. *The Possibility of Altruism.* Oxford: Oxford University Press.

———. 1979. "What Is It Like to Be a Bat?" In *Mortal Questions,* pp. 165–180. Cambridge: Cambridge University Press.

———. 1980. "The Limits of Objectivity." In *The Tanner Lectures on Human Values,* ed. Sterling M. McMurrin, pp. 77–139. Salt Lake City: University of Utah Press; Cambridge: Cambridge University Press.

Nozick, Robert. 1974. *Anarchy, State and Utopia.* New York: Basic Books.

———. 1981. *Philosophical Explanations.* Cambridge, MA: Harvard University Press.

Rawls, John. 1971. *A Theory of Justice.* Cambridge, MA: Belknap Press of Harvard University Press.

Richards, David A. J. 1971. *A Theory of Reason for Action.* Oxford: Oxford University Press.

Rorty, Richard. 1965. "Mind-Body Identity, Privacy, and Categories," *Review of Metaphysics* 19: 24–54.

Skinner, B. F. 1974. *About Behaviorism.* New York: Alfred A. Knopf.

Stevenson, Charles L. 1963. *Facts and Values.* New Haven, CT: Yale University Press.

13   *Moral Relativism*

PHILIPPA FOOT

Some philosophical questions interest only philosophers: they would never occur to the plain man, and if he hears of them he may very well think that those who spend their time on philosophy must be a trifle mad. There are, however, other problems, no less philosophical and just as important, that are apt to present themselves to any enquiring mind. One does not have to be a philosopher by trade or training to have doubts, for instance, about freewill; and it has even struck many innocent of philosophy that perhaps the world looks undetectably different to different persons, one man systematically seeing as red what the other sees as green. The thesis of moral relativism is one of these natural philosophical thoughts. Very many students, beginning philosophy, are sure that relativism is true; and although they are often taken aback when reminded that it is, for example, common for members of our materialistic society to criticise this society for its materialism they usually think that some adjustments will save the theory. One might therefore expect that moral relativism would be a central topic among those discussed in classes and in the journals. Surprisingly, however, the truth has for long been quite otherwise. Many recent books on moral philosophy ignore the problem or give it perfunctory treatment, and it is only in the last two or three years that strong, interesting, articles have begun to appear in print.[1]

Why was the subject so long neglected? Probably it was because few of those teaching, and writing, philosophy believed moral relativism to be anything they need worry about: some thought they knew how to discredit it in a few easy moves, and others supposed vaguely that it had been done. In fact, as we shall see, there were elements in the prevailing theories of ethics—in emotivism for instance—that made it seem difficult even to formulate relativism except in a version that was indeed easy to refute.

C. L. Stevenson is one of the few influential moral philosophers of the past thirty or forty years to have treated the subject of relativism at any length. He argued, in an essay called "Relativism" printed in *Facts and Values* in 1963, that his own "emotivist" theory of moral judgement gave a basis for the refutation of moral relativism. Now what Stevenson actually says about

Reprinted, by permission of the publisher and copyright holder, from Philippa Foot, "Moral Relativism," The Lindley Lecture, University of Kansas, 1978.

relativism, what he takes it to be, is rather odder than most people remember if they have not been reading him lately: he says, for instance, that an account of moral judgement taking "X is good" to mean the same as "I approve of X" is not relativistic, whereas the same theory would be relativistic if requiring the speaker's name to be inserted instead of "I." The interest of Stevenson's discussion is not, however, in these details but rather in a certain assumption; namely the assumption that a relativistic theory identifies a moral utterance with an assertion of psychological or sociological fact. The relativist is supposed to identify the thought that a given action is morally good or bad with some proposition about the reactions that people have to it; and it is on this that Stevenson's "refutation" depends. He points out that the identification must be mistaken because the two types of propositions are backed up in different ways. If someone is asked why he thinks certain things morally good or bad he does not set out to show that some individual or group really does have this or that reaction to it, but tries to bring forward facts about the action itself. Moreover, in putting forward his moral views he expresses feelings or attitudes and tries to change the feelings and attitudes of others, whereas a statement of psychological or sociological fact lacks this dynamic aspect.

One does not have to share Stevenson's emotivism to agree that moral judgements are not descriptions of reactions, since his first argument seems sufficient for the proof. Stevenson will, however, have refuted moral relativism only if his assumption is true of all its versions. And it seems implausible to deny that other models are possible. For outside ethics we actually find judgements that do appear to be relativistic but not in Stevenson's sense.

It will be worth spending a little time considering what might be meant by calling certain types of judgements relativistic: and what relativism amounts to in those areas in which it seems to belong. I am thinking, for instance, of certain judgements of "taste," such as those asserting that some people but not others are good-looking, that some food or drink is appetising or delicious, or that certain colours go well together for furnishings or clothes. Here, it seems, we find wide variations in judgements between different cultures and different generations. One does not have to go as far as ancient Mexico to find a set of faces that we find ugly while supposing that they were once admired, and while we think Nureyev's a better looking face than Valentino's there was a time when the verdict would probably have gone the other way. It is obvious that there is the same kind of disagreement about the palatability of food and drink; and combinations of colors once declared deplorable are now thought particularly good. The old rhyme said that "blue and green should never be seen," and black and brown were once seen as colours that killed each other as we should say that navy blue kills black.

The reason why such judgements seem undoubtedly relativistic is not, of course, that a wide variety of opinions exist, but rather that no one set of these opinions appears to have any more claim to truth than any other. But there is a problem here. For if the differences in the application of concepts such as "good-looking" are as great as this, why are we so confident that at different times or in different places the judgements are *about the same thing?* This difficulty must be taken seriously, and may lead us to cut down the number of judgements that we would count as certainly relativistic, even in the area of "taste." Perhaps some kind of relativism is true of many other judgements, but relativism is most obviously true where we need set no limit to the variations in the application of an expression, or rather no limits to its application within a given domain. This condition seems to be fulfilled for our examples, but it would not have been fulfilled had we been operating with concepts such as *prettiness*, or even *handsomeness*. It makes sense to speak of another society as thinking good-looking just the faces we think not good-looking, but not as thinking pretty just the faces we think not pretty. The examples most suitable for the present purposes are those that are rather general, and this is why I suggested considering the good-looking, the good-tasting, and the good combinations of colours.

Let us suppose then that there are in different communities divergent sets of such judgements which we have no hope of reconciling, and that in this area we also have no thought of distinguishing the opinions of one group of people as right and those of the others as wrong. Shall we say that this is because the judgements describe reactions such as admiration and liking, and that reactions vary from place to place and time to time? This, which fits Stevenson's version of relativism, is not, in the area we are now discussing, the truth. To say that someone is good-looking is not to say that his looks are admired, any more than to say that someone is likeable is to say that he is well-liked. No doubt it is true that the concept *likeable* depends on reactions of liking. And no doubt it can operate as it does only on account of shared reactions of liking. Shared reactions are also necessary if the language of a particular community is to contain a word like "elegant," or if it is to be possible to say in it that certain colours go well together. But there is no reason to think that the judgements describe the reactions. One might as well think that "is red" means the same as "seems red to most people," forgetting that when asked if an object is red we look at it to see if it is red, and not in order to estimate the reaction that others will have to it. That one does not describe one's own reaction of admiration in saying that someone is good-looking is shown by the fact that one may admit a mistake. That one does not describe the reactions of others in one's community is shown by the fact that one may accuse them of mistake. Nor is this kind of language empty, the mere reiteration of the expression of one's own reaction. There is room here for the idea of showing, even if not of proving or demonstrating. An individual who makes some very idiosyncratic judgement may simply be ignored or told that he is out of his mind. But he may say something that his fellows find instructive, either with an explanation or without it. I do not want to attribute to any particular type of judgement one jot of (local) objectivity that does not really belong to it, or any method for bringing agreement that does not really go along with it. But distinctions are there to be made. It will not do for one of us to say that Charles Laughton got up as the Hunchback of Notre Dame presented the appearance of a good-looking man; but Laughton's brother's suggestion that he was, in his own person, good-looking was a surprising but possible corrective idea.

What this discussion shows is that if a relativistic thesis is true of the judgements under scrutiny it does not assert relativism as understood by Stevenson. And yet it is certainly relativism. For the key concepts will work as they do work—with a kind of objectivity and the attribution of truth—only where there are shared reactions. Once this background is left behind it is impossible to speak of "right" and "wrong," "mistaken" and "correct," as we commonly do. And therefore it is empty to say of the judgements of another group whose reactions are very different from ours that their opinions are wrong. Our own discussions of these matters of "taste" implicitly invoke the standards set by our paradigms and our way of going on from them, and here we can speak of right and wrong. But if we are talking of the views of another society we shall speak of what is true by their standards and by our standards, without the slightest thought that our standards are "correct." If the ancient Mexicans admired the looks of someone whose head had been flattened, a proposition not *about* this admiration may have been true as spoken by them, though it is false as spoken by us.

We have, then, a version of relativism true of some judgements and not vulnerable to a Stevensonian type of refutation. The question is whether moral assertions might similarly admit only of relative truth. It will probably be objected that this is impossible because moral judgements do not depend on local moral standards as our judgements of taste were thought to depend on local standards of taste. The thought behind this objection is that a challenge to a moral judgement or moral system can be made "out in the open" as it were, with no agreed method, formal or informal, for showing that the challenge is justified. The idea is that there can be disagreement, with each party thinking the other mistaken, even if there is in principle no way of setting the "dispute." It is therefore supposed that an individual can challenge the views of his own society not just in the way that we think it possible for someone to query some judgement of taste, but more radically. He is to be able to say anything he likes about what is morally good and bad, so long as he is consistent, and is to be taken seriously as a man of very eccentric taste would not be. It follows also that the members of one society may similarly challenge the moral view of another society. No common starting point is necessary, and nothing to back up an accusation of falsity or mistake.

Anyone taking this position will insist that moral assertions do not have merely relative truth. Local standards are supposed to be irrelevant, and there is to be no point at which a set of moral opinions inconsistent with one's own are to be admitted to have just as much truth. This is an argument that we should examine carefully; it is perhaps not as powerful as it looks.

The case against construing moral judgements as relativistic along the lines that fit judgements of taste has been made to depend, it seems, on some points of linguistic usage. It was thought crucial that we can say of the moral opinions of our own society, or of some other society, that they are "mistaken" or "false," and this was described in terms of a "challenge" to moral views that differ from our own. The question is whether "challenge" is the right description if words such as "true" and "false" are used as they are supposed to be used here; and in general whether it is important that these words are or are not so employed. It will be remembered that by our hypothesis talk of truth and falsity was to go on even in the absence of any kind of proving or showing, or any *possibility* of proving or showing, that one view rather than the other was in fact true. And this is, of course, a situation very different from that in which the vocabulary of "true" and "false" is used in discussing ordinary matters of fact, in everyday life or in science or history, or even literary criticism. Using Bernard Williams' terminology one might say that words such as "true" and "false" are not used "substantially" when used like this.[2] This is not, of course, to say that there is something wrong with the usage, but it does raise doubts about the weight that can be placed on it in discussions of relativism. The linguistic facts were appealed to in the attempt to show that moral judgements could not be relativistic as some judgements of taste seem to be. Yet if we suppose, as a kind of thought experiment, that the same linguistic possibilities exist in the case of these other judgements we see that their relativism is left unchanged. In this new situation it would be possible for an individual to reject as "false" everything that other members of his society said about good-looking faces, and such things, and it would be possible for one society so to describe the views of another society however far apart their judgements. The important point is that substantial truth would still belong only where common standards were in some sense presupposed; it would still be right to deny that there was any substantial truth belonging to the standards of any particular community.

According to the argument just presented relativism is true in a given area if in that area all *substantial* truth is truth relative to one or other of a set of possible standards. And it is now possible to see that individualistic subjectivism may itself be a form of moral relativism. (Perhaps we would call it a limiting case.) For even if the truth of moral judgements is not relative to local community standards it (the substantial truth) could still be relative to the standards of the individual. This is how it is, in effect, in emotivist and prescriptivist theories, since these theories deny the presence of objective criteria, or any objective method by which differences between individuals with radically different basic moral principles could in principle be resolved. If these theories are correct, anyone who queries the truth of a moral judgement, and still possesses the resource of testing it by his more basic moral principles, uses "true" substantially; but beyond this point he does not. It follows that the emotivist or prescriptivist is committed to a form of relativism, however little he may like the label. Stevenson, who claimed to have refuted moral relativism, turns out to be himself a kind of moral relativist.

This account of relativism is gravely deficient in so far as it depends on the idea of substantial truth, and gives only merest indication of what this is. Nevertheless there is enough in what has been said about that, and in the comparison with judgements of taste, to make it possible to enquire further into the implications of moral relativism; and at this point I want to refer to a discussion of the topic appearing in Walter Stace's book *The Concept of Morals* in 1937.

Stace takes the relativist to be one who denies that there is any single objective standard of morals, and this is, of course, in line with what we have just been saying. But he also attributes to him two other beliefs: firstly that the very same action that is right in one country or at one period may be wrong in another and secondly that if a man thinks something right it is right for him.

Let us consider the first proposition, once more thinking about the analogy provided by our relativistic judgements of taste. It was seen that such assertions may be true by the standards in operation in one social context and false by those equally well established in another; but it would be wrong to infer, for example, that some men are good-looking in a certain place but not elsewhere, as if their complexions suffered when they moved. And it would be similarly misleading to say that a man might become less good-looking as time went on not because he got older but because standards changed. Nor could two sets of standards be employed simultaneously, to make the same man at the same time both good-looking and ugly. This would be no better than declaring in mid Atlantic, half way between Southern Italy and the U.S., that a man of a certain height was both tall and short. If, for a certain type of judgement, a local standard automatically comes into force, every proposition of this form will presuppose one rather than another. Even with the limiting case of relativism, where the reference is supposed to be only to the standards of the speaker, it will be impossible to employ two sets of standards at once.

Stace is wrong, then, in thinking that the moral relativist is committed to the first of the two propositions listed above. But is he wrong also about the second? This is much more interesting, and more debatable, but we have first to try to get clear about what it means to say that if a man thinks something right it is right for him. It could, I suppose, be taken as denying any distinction between "A thinks it right to do X" and "It is right for A to do X," rather as we might deny the distinction between "A thinks the temperature in the room pleasant" and "The temperature in the room is pleasant for A." So interpreted the proposition would deny the possibility of error about matters of right and wrong, and this would seem to make it obviously false. For even on subjectivist theories a man may apply his own standards wrongly, and hence there is a possibility of "correction" that is not simply a change of mind. There is, however, another interpretation, starting from the thought that if we say "X is right for A" we are committed to a favorable judgement on the doing of X by A, and going on to assert that this is the judgement to be made wherever A is following his conscience in doing X. It is usually supposed, I think, that it is absurd to think this implied by moral relativism as we have so far discussed it, but I am inclined to believe that something like it is true.

Let us consider the thought that if a man follows his conscience he will act well, and first its relation to the proposition that if he goes against his conscience he will act badly. It seems to be taken for granted by contemporary moralists that the two propositions are on the same footing, and do not need to be considered separately, but this is curious given that Aquinas, who would strenuously have disagreed, wrote powerfully against this view.³ Aquinas argues that a man acts badly if he goes against his conscience, whatever it may be that his conscience tells him to do, so that even the erring conscience "binds." It does not follow, however, that anyone who follows his conscience necessarily acts well: he will also act badly when he intentionally does the things that are evil, even if he thinks them good. Of a man such as Himmler, who seems to have believed that he *should* gas Jewish men, women and children (and therefore indisputably innocent human beings), Aquinas would have said that so long as he thought as he did he could not but act badly. For either he would spare the lives of those in the concentration camps and so go against his conscience or else he would kill them and so do an evil deed. To the suggestion that a parallel argument could be used to show that whatever Himmler did he would act well, since either he would follow his conscience or else do something good, Aquinas would have replied that good and evil are not symmetrical, as the argument requires. If a man's action is bad in that he is going against his conscience, and good in that he is sparing or saving lives, he acts badly. And he also acts badly if he follows his conscience and does something that is bad. For a single defect is enough to make anything defective whereas a single merit does not suffice to make it good. This surprising principle turns out to be one with which we must agree, and agree quite generally. A house is a bad house if it is either badly designed or badly built; it is a good house only if good in both ways. An apple is bad if it is either worm-ridden or tasteless, and good only if free from either defect. This is not to say that any small defect is enough to make us call something bad: the point is that there is substantial asymmetry of the kind that Aquinas requires.

It is possible, therefore, to maintain with Aquinas that although the erring conscience binds it does not excuse. One may consistently say that if a man thinks he is doing wrong he is doing wrong, but that he may also be doing wrong when he thinks he is doing right. The case is parallel to that of any judge, who has two ways of giving an unjust judgement, firstly by giving one that he believes to be unjust, and secondly by giving one that really is. And similarly anyone has two ways of demeaning himself: he can do what he sees as low or unworthy or demeaning, or he can do something to which these terms do, though he does not see it, apply.

If follows that in discussing the implications of relativism one must deal separately with the two propositions "If he thinks he is acting badly he is acting badly" and "If he thinks he is acting well he is acting well."

That someone who goes against his conscience ipso facto acts badly cannot, I think, be denied. One might say that there could not be a more radical moral defect than that of being prepared to do what one believes to be wrong. A man of whom this is true is like an archer who does not even aim at the target, it will be the merest chance if he does what *is* good when he is doing what he *sees* as bad. His will is following evil and is therefore an evil will. This thesis has, however, nothing to do with relativism: it must be accepted by non-relativist and relativist alike.

Can a relativist also agree with a non-relativist in thinking that a man may act badly when he believes he is acting well? This is more doubtful. He can, of course, allow the case of one who misapplies his own principles, so that there is no question of adopting the slogan "What he thinks is right is right." But let us put this aside, and ask what the relativist can consistently say about one who reasons correctly from his own moral principles, and does what his conscience tells him to do. If our relativist (B) has moral principles telling him that it is wrong to do action X, but X is what is required by the morality of another man (A), what will B be able to say about the doing of X by A? We will suppose that there are no circumstances other than the fact that A thinks X required of him that could make B say that X *as done by A* was right rather than wrong, or good rather than bad. How will A's conscience affect B's judgement in such a case? Aquinas would be free to say that A acted badly because of the action A was doing; but could a relativist say this too?

The issue hangs, I think, on the question of the innocence or culpability of a man who holds particular moral views. Aquinas, like Aristotle, makes a distinction between ignorance of matters of fact, which is often not culpable, and ignorance of the moral law, which always is.[4] It is within anyone's power to put aside his erring conscience, and if he continues in it this is because he does not want to know the truth. He can therefore be blamed even when he follows his conscience, because he is at fault in having this conscience. But now consider our relativist. Unlike Aquinas he cannot say that the truth is there to be seen by anyone who wants to see it, because as a relativist he has denied the existence of objective universal criteria of moral truth. So if he says that A will act badly in doing X, after already agreeing that A will act badly if he goes against his conscience and does not do X, he must think that although A can only act badly he is in this moral trap through no fault of his own. A could, we may suppose, have changed his moral opinions, and perhaps he could still change them, but B cannot say that he should change them or should have changed them. Unlike Aquinas he cannot insist that someone with these opinions must have wanted not to know the truth, or not wanted to know it enough to discover it. Therefore A was not morally at fault in holding his opinions, and it is for this reason that he is in the moral trap through no fault of his own.

It is the objection to the idea that a man can be in this kind of situation that seems to me to tell against the possibility that a relativist can judge him adversely when he follows his conscience. Nor am I impressed by the suggestion that the innocent man who can only act badly is a figure with whom we are familiar from the consideration of the (quite different) case of conflicting duties. The arguments supposed to show that someone breaking a promise to avert some great evil does what he "ought not" to do in spite of doing the best he can in the circumstances seem to me specious, relying on a somewhat romantic admiration for one who is ready to turn regret into the semblance of remorse. This must, of course, be shown, not here, but elsewhere; I mention it only because otherwise I shall probably be accused of forgetting it.

Meanwhile the objection stands to the idea that one may be bad whatever one does, though through no fault of one's own.

It has been argued in the preceding paragraphs that relativism as a theory of the logical status of moral judgement does not leave the practice of making moral judgements unaffected. In terms of the usual jargon, metaethical relativism may be said to imply some measure of normative relativism. This thesis must not, however, be confused with the proposition that no one who holds a relativistic moral theory can consistently make moral judgements at all. This quite different idea comes from the thought that a moral relativist is one who denies that any one moral assertion is any truer than any others, and who therefore can *have no moral opinions of his own*. Is this a consequence of relativism? It seems that it is not. For looking to our old model we observe that opinions about matters of taste are not disturbed by the belief that judgements of taste (or the particular judgements of taste that we considered) have only relative truth. We say that Nureyev is good-looking, that oysters are delicious, and that blue and green go well together, without worrying about the fact that by the standards of some other society these things might be false, and that our standards are no better than theirs. Local truth is the only substantive truth that we have, and it is this truth that we tacitly claim for our opinions when we express them. If there is something that makes this kind of accommodation impossible in the case of moral opinions it must be brought to light. Why is it not enough that we should claim relative truth for our moral judgements, taking it as truth relative either to local standards or to individual standards, according to our theory of moral judgement?

Some will no doubt argue that moral judgements are different from judgements of taste in so far as we must wish to see others adopt our own moral system, whereas we do not mind what they think about good looking faces and other matters of "taste." Everyone must necessarily preach his own moral opinions, refusing to live and let live, and he therefore cannot say that opposing views are as good as his own. That this is an invalid argument can be seen, I think, by considering the case of imperatives. If two men give opposite instructions each will, in general, want his own order obeyed and the other disregarded. This does not, however, mean that the other order must be seen as in some way invalid or defective: it can be allowed to have equal status even while one urges that one's own should be obeyed. It might be considered a linguistic accident that we do not use "true" of the imperatives we issue or support and "false" of those we oppose: if we did do so it would leave the differences between imperatives and assertions as they are, and it would be quite wrong to think that we should be supporting some imperatives *as* we support some propositions in the empirical sciences or in everyday matters of fact because we supported them and used the word "true." If we wanted to say in these circumstances that no one imperative was any truer than any other this would make a valid point, and be perfectly consistent with our wish to see our own imperatives carried out. We could also, if we liked, go on calling some imperatives and not others "true." With moral

judgements it is the same. If there are good reasons for accepting moral relativism (and we have yet to ask about that) then we have to admit that moral
judgements opposed to our own are true by some other peoples' standards as
ours are true by ours, and that there is no choosing between them on objective grounds. If we believed this we could with perfect consistency put our
weight behind our own moral directives, but would have to recognize that if
we called them "truer" than some judgements from another system this truth
would not be substantial truth.

So much for the implications of moral relativism. I must now approach,
with some trepidation, the extremely difficult question whether relativism is
a correct theory of moral judgement.

Let me ask, first, whether we have the same reason to accept moral relativism as we had to accept relativism for our handpicked bunch of judgements of taste? This, it seems to me, we do not. For our starting point there
was the thought that some rather general judgements of taste could be identified through any amount of variation in the application of the key concepts
through the relevant domain. I myself have frequently argued that such variation cannot be postulated in the case of moral judgement, because the
thought of moral goodness and badness cannot be held steady through any
and every change in the codes of behaviour taught, and in their grounds.[5]
From this it follows that not everything that anyone might want to call a
"moral code" should properly be so described. And this shows, incidentally,
that hypotheses about "cultural relativism" are not totally independent of
moral theory. Even if an anthropologist is inclined to call a certain code a
moral code, and to go on to talk about a morality radically different from our
own, it does not follow that we should accept this way of describing the phenomena. An anthropologist may be as confused or prejudiced as anyone else
in applying words such as "morality" to the teachings of an alien culture.

I shall assume that even general moral terms such as "right" or "ought"
are restricted, to a certain degree, in their extension, at least at the level of
basic principles. It is not possible that there should be two moral codes the
mirror images of each other, so that what was considered fundamentally
right in one community would be considered wrong at the same level in the
other. It seems that some considerations simply are and some are not evidence for particular moral assertions. Nevertheless it does not look as if a correct account of what it is to have a moral thought, or a moral attitude, or to
teach a moral code, will suffice to dismiss relativism out of hand. Even if
some moral judgements are perfectly objective, there may be others whose
truth or falsity is not easily decidable by criteria internal to the subject of
morality. We may suppose, I think, that it is clearly an objective moral fact
that the Nazi treatment of the Jews was morally indefensible, given the facts
and their knowledge of the facts. The Nazis' moral opinions had to be held on
grounds either false or irrelevant or both, as on considerations about Ger-
many's "historic mission," or on the thought that genocide could be a necessary form of self-defence. It was impossible, logically speaking, for them to
argue that the killing of millions of innocent people did not need any moral

justification, or that the extension of the German Reich was in itself a morally desirable end. Yet after such things have been said the problem of moral relativism is still with us.[6] Even if the fact that it is morality that is in question gives us some guaranteed starting points for arguments about moral right or wrong, how much is this going to settle? Are there not some moral matters on which, even within our own society, disagreement may be irreducible? And is it not possible that some alien moral systems cannot be faulted by us on any objective principles, while our moral beliefs can also not be faulted by theirs? May there not be places where societies simply confront each other, with no rational method for settling their differences?

In the most penetrating critique of relativism that has appeared for many years Bernard Williams has recently argued that this is so, and he bases his belief in moral relativism on this possibility.[7] He thinks that although the vocabulary of appraisal can be used "substantially" in the consideration of the moral beliefs of some alien cultures, this is not always the case. Is he right about this? He supposes that "substantial" employment of terms such as "true" or "false" can occur only where a system is in "real confrontation" with our own; and real confrontation turns out to be given by the fact that we could, without suffering hallucination or otherwise losing our grip on reality and rationality, come to hold those beliefs. What is puzzling is why he thinks this relationship to be either necessary or sufficient to give substance (he says, perhaps significantly, "point or substance") to the vocabulary of appraisal. If we think back to the judgements of taste discussed earlier in this lecture we see that anything of this kind would be irrelevant there. By some process of acculturation we could, no doubt, come to hold quite different opinions about good-looking faces, delicious foods, and combinations of colors. But this does not mean that we can *criticise* the systems which are a real option for us. "True" and "false" get a substantial use where there are objective criteria, or at least methods of some kind for settling disputes, and this seems to have nothing to do with "real confrontation" as defined by Williams.

Nevertheless Williams is surely right in thinking that if some societies with divergent moral systems merely confront each other, having no use for the assertion that their own systems are true and the others false except to mark the system to which they adhere, then relativism is a true theory of morality. Yet at this point one may become uneasy about his reasons for saying that relativism is true. For it seems strange to suggest that there is any society whose values we can identify without being able to set them critically beside our own, and our own beside theirs. Some parts of the moral vocabulary do indeed seem unusable when we are considering very alien and distant communities. For instance it would be odd then to talk in terms of the permissible and the impermissible, simply because language of this kind cannot venture very far from actual sets of permissions and prohibitions. But this does not mean that we cannot in any way judge the moral rules and values of societies very different in this respect from our own. Granted that it is wrong to assume identity of aim between peoples of different cultures; nevertheless there is a great deal that all men have in common. All need affection, the cooperation of others, a place in a community, and help in trouble. It isn't true to suppose that human beings can flourish without these things—being isolated, despised or embattled, or without courage or hope. We are not, therefore, simply expressing values that we happen to have if we think of some moral systems as good moral systems and others as bad. Communities as well as individuals can live wisely or unwisely, and this is largely the result of their values and the codes of behavior that they teach. Looking at these societies, and critically also at our own, we surely have some idea of how things work out and why they work out as they do. We do not have to suppose it is just as good to promote pride of place and the desire to get an advantage over other men as it is to have an ideal of affection and respect. These things have different harvests, and unmistakably different connexions with human good.

No doubt it will be argued that even if all this is true it leaves moral relativism substantially intact, since objective evaluation of moral systems can go only a little way, and will come to an end before all the radical disagreements are resolved. One wonders, however, why people who say this kind of thing are so sure that they know where discussions will lead and therefore where they will end. It is, I think, a fault on the part of relativists, and subjectivists generally, that they are ready to make pronouncements about the later part of moral arguments, and moral reviews, without being able to trace the intermediate steps. Nor is it that they just do not bother to take the whole journey; for there are reasons why they are not able to. One of these has to do with conventions about moral philosophy, conventions that forbid the philosopher to fill chapters with descriptive material about human nature and human life. It isn't supposed to be part of his work to think in the somewhat discursive way that is suitable to reflections about the human heart, and the life of men in society. It is, of course, a kind of decency that keeps moral philosophers in the analytic tradition away from the pseudo-profundity that is found in some philosophies as well as in vulgar preachers. Yet it may be that they have to do this work, and do it properly, before they will know the truth about divergent moralities and values. And we have, after all, a rich tradition of history and literature on which to draw.

There is, however, another reason why moral philosophers tend to give only a sketch of the beginning and end of discussions of the values of different societies; and this has to do with a gap in our philosophical understanding. Perhaps it would be better to speak of a series of gaps, of which I shall give instances in the next few paragraphs. My thought is that there are some concepts which we do not understand well, and cannot employ competently in an argument, that are, unfortunately, essential to genuine discussions of the merits of different moral systems.

Let me give some examples of the kind of thing that I have in mind. I would suppose, for instance, that in some fundamental moral enquiries we might find ourselves appealing to the fact that human life is of value. But do we really understand this thought? Do we know what we mean by saying that *anything* has value, or even that we value it, as opposed to wanting it or being prepared to go to trouble to get it? I do not know of any philosopher living or dead who has been able to explain this idea. And then again we are likely to find ourselves talking about happiness, which is a most intractable concept. To realize that one does not understand it one has only to try to explain why, for instance, the contented life of someone on whom a prefrontal lobotomy has been performed is not the happy life, or why we would count someone as unfortunate rather than endowed with happiness if he were tricked into thinking he was successfully spending his life on important work when he was really just messing around. That we do not understand the concept of happiness is shown, once more, by the fact that we are inclined to think stupid thoughts about the idea of great happiness, as if it were simply extreme and prolonged euphoria. That great happiness depends on its objects is a surprising idea once we understand this, as it should be understood, as a conceptual not a causal matter. It seems that great happiness, unlike euphoria or even great pleasure, must come from something related to what is deep in human nature, and fundamental in human life, such as affection for children and friends, and the desire to work, and love of freedom and truth. But what do we mean by calling some things in human nature deep, and some things in life fundamental? In one way we know this, because we are able, for instance, to understand a man who says at the end of his life that he has wasted his time on "things that don't matter." But what are things that "matter" if they are not the trivial things on which we spend so much time? Clearly such questions are relevant to fundamental discussions of the moralities of other societies and our own. It is impossible to judge a society's morality if we cannot talk about its values, and we must be able to handle the thought of false values if we are to say what is wrong with a materialistic society such as ours. But what is it to have false values if it is not to think too highly of things that do not matter very much?

It seems, then, that we are all at sea with some of the ideas that we are bound to employ in any real discussion of divergent moralities. What we tend to do is to ignore these ideas, and pretend that the debate can be carried on in other terms. But why should this be supposed possible? With other, more jejune, concepts we shall get another discussion, and from it we cannot draw conclusions about how the first would end. Moving from one to the other we are merely guessing at results, and this is, I think, exactly what happens in many arguments about moral relativism. Personally I feel uncomfortable in these arguments, and perhaps this is because I am advancing opinions on the basis of a guess. The practical conclusion may be that we should not at the moment try to say whether moral relativism is true or false, but should start the work farther back.

NOTES

1. See, for instance, Bernard Williams, "The Truth in Relativism," *Proceedings of the Aristotelian Society* (1974–75); Gilbert Harman, "Moral Relativism Defended," *Philosophical Review* (1975) and remarks in David Wiggins, "Truth, Invention, and the Meaning of Life." *Proceedings of the British Academy* (1976).

2. "Consistency and Realism," *Aristotelian Society Supplementary Volume* (1966). Also "The Truth in Relativism."

3. *Summa Theologica* 1a 2ae. Q.19, a 5 and 6.

4. Op. cit. 1a 2ae Q.6, a 8, and Q.19, a 6.

5. See, e.g., P. R. Foot, "Moral Arguments," *Mind* 1958, and "Moral Beliefs," *Proceedings of the Aristotelian Society* 1958–59.

6. Compare P. R. Foot "Morality and Art," *Proceedings of the British Academy* 1970.

7. "The Truth in Relativism."

14   *Non-Relative Virtues*

MARTHA NUSSBAUM

All Greeks used to go around armed with swords.

THUCYDIDES, *HISTORY OF THE PELOPONNESIAN WAR*

The customs of former times might be said to be too simple and bar-baric. For Greeks used to go around armed with swords; and they used to buy wives from one another; and there are surely other ancient cus-toms that are extremely stupid. (For example, in Cyme there is a law about homicide, that if a man prosecuting a charge can produce a cer-tain number of witnesses from among his own relations, the defendant will automatically be convicted of murder.) In general, all human beings seek not the way of their ancestors, but the good.

ARISTOTLE, *POLITICS*, 1268A39 FF.

One may also observe in one's travels to distant countries the feelings of recognition and affiliation that link every human being to every other human being.

ARISTOTLE, *NICOMACHEAN ETHICS*, 1155A21-2

1

The virtues are attracting increasing interest in contemporary philosophical debate. From many different sides one hears of a dissatisfaction with ethical theories that are remote from concrete human experience. Whether this remoteness results from the utilitarian's interest in arriving at a universal cal-culus of satisfactions or from a Kantian concern with universal principles of broad generality, in which the names of particular contexts, histories, and persons do not occur, remoteness is now being seen by an increasing number of moral philosophers as a defect in an approach to ethical questions. In the search for an alternative approach, the concept of virtue is playing a promi-nent role. So, too, is the work of Aristotle, the greatest defender of an ethical

Reprinted, by permission of the publisher and copyright holder, from Martha Nussbaum, "Non-Relative Virtues: An Aristotelian Approach," in Nussbaum and Amartya Sen, eds., *The Quality of Life*, pp. 242–269. Oxford: Clarendon Press, 1993.

approach based on the concept of virtue. For Aristotle's work seems, appealingly, to combine rigour with concreteness, theoretical power with sensitivity to the actual circumstances of human life and choice in all their multiplicity, variety, and mutability.

But on one central point there is a striking divergence between Aristotle and contemporary virtue theory. To many current defenders of an ethical approach based on the virtues, the return to the virtues is connected with a turn towards relativism—towards, that is, the view that the only appropriate criteria of ethical goodness are local ones, internal to the traditions and practices of each local society or group that asks itself questions about the good. The rejection of general algorithms and abstract rules in favour of an account of the good life based on specific modes of virtuous action is taken, by writers as otherwise diverse as Alasdair MacIntyre, Bernard Williams, and Philippa Foot,[1] to be connected with the abandonment of the project of rationally justifying a single norm of flourishing life for all human beings and a reliance, instead, on norms that are local both in origin and in application.

The position of all these writers, where relativism is concerned, is complex; none unequivocally endorses a relativist view. But all connect virtue ethics with a relativist denial that ethics, correctly understood, offers any transcultural norms, justifiable by reference to reasons of universal human validity, by reference to which we may appropriately criticize different local conceptions of the good. And all suggest that the insights we gain by pursuing ethical questions in the Aristotelian virtue-based way lend support to relativism.

For this reason it is easy for those who are interested in supporting the rational criticism of local traditions and in articulating an idea of ethical progress to feel that the ethics of virtue can give them little help. If the position of women, as established by local traditions in many parts of the world, is to be improved, if traditions of slave-holding and racial inequality, religious intolerance, aggressive and warlike conceptions of manliness, and unequal norms of material distribution are to be criticized in the name of practical reason, this criticizing (one might easily suppose) will have to be done from a Kantian or utilitarian viewpoint, not through the Aristotelian approach.

This is an odd result, as far as Aristotle is concerned. For it is obvious that he was not only the defender of an ethical theory based on the virtues, but also the defender of a single objective account of the human good, or human flourishing. This account is supposed to be objective in the sense that it is justifiable by reference to reasons that do not derive merely from local traditions and practices, but rather from features of humanness that lie beneath all local traditions and are there to be seen whether or not they are in fact recognized in local traditions. And one of Aristotle's most obvious concerns was the criticism of existing moral traditions, in his own city and in others, as unjust or repressive, or in other ways incompatible with human flourishing. He uses his account of the virtues as a basis for this criticism of local traditions: prominently, for example, in Book II of the *Politics*, where he frequently argues against existing social forms by pointing to ways in which they neglect or hinder the development at some important human virtue.[2] Aristotle evidently believed that there is no incompatibility between basing an ethical theory on the virtues and defending the singleness and objectivity of the human good. Indeed, he seems to have believed that these two aims are mutually supportive.

Now the fact that Aristotle believed something does not make it true (though I have sometimes been accused of holding that position!). But it does, on the whole, make that something a plausible *candidate* for the truth, one deserving our most serious scrutiny. In this case, it would be odd indeed if he had connected two elements in ethical thought that are self-evidently incompatible, or in favour of whose connectedness and compatibility there is nothing interesting to be said. The purpose of this paper is to establish that Aristotle did indeed have an interesting way of connecting the virtues with a search for ethical objectivity and with the criticism of existing local norms, a way that deserves our serious consideration as we work on these questions. Having described the general shape of the Aristotelian approach, we can then begin to understand some of the objections that might be brought against such a non-relative account of the virtues, and to imagine how the Aristotelian could respond to those objections.

2

The relativist, looking at different societies, is impressed by the variety and the apparent non-comparability in the lists of virtues she encounters. Examining the different lists, and observing the complex connections between each list and a concrete form of life and a concrete history, she may well feel that any list of virtues must be simply a reflection of local traditions and values, and that, virtues being (unlike Kantian principles or utilitarian algorithms) concrete and closely tied to forms of life, there can in fact be no list of virtues that will serve as normative for all these varied societies. It is not only that the specific forms of behaviour recommended in connection with the virtues differ greatly over time and place, it is also that the very areas that are singled out as spheres of virtue, and the manner in which they are individuated from other areas, vary so greatly. For someone who thinks this way, it is easy to feel that Aristotle's own list, despite its pretensions to universality and objectivity, must be similarly restricted, merely a reflection of one particular society's perceptions of salience and ways of distinguishing. At this point, relativist writers are likely to quote Aristotle's description of the "great-souled" person, the *megalopsuchos,* which certainly contains many concrete local features and sounds very much like the portrait of a certain sort of Greek gentleman, in order to show that Aristotle's list is just as culture-bound as any other.[3]

But if we probe further into the way in which Aristotle in fact enumerates and individuates the virtues, we begin to notice things that cast doubt upon the suggestion that he simply described what was admired in his own society. First of all, we notice that a rather large number of virtues and vices (vices especially) are nameless, and that, among the ones that are not nameless, a good many are given, by Aristotle's own account, names that are somewhat arbitrarily chosen by Aristotle, and do not perfectly fit the behaviour he is trying to describe.[4] Of such modes of conduct he writes, "Most of these are nameless, but we must try . . . to give them names in order to make our account clear and easy to follow" (*NE* 1108a 6–19). This does not sound like the procedure of someone who is simply studying local traditions and singling out the virtue-names that figure most prominently in those traditions.

What *is* going on becomes clearer when we examine the way in which he does, in fact, introduce his list. For he does so, in the *Nicomachean Ethics*,[5] by a device whose very straight-forwardness and simplicity has caused it to escape the notice of most writers on this topic. What he does, in each case, is to isolate a sphere of human experience that figures in more or less any human life, and in which more or less any human being will have to make *some* choices rather than others, and act in *some* way rather than some other. The introductory chapter enumerating the virtues and vices begins with an enumeration of these spheres (*NE* II. 7); and each chapter on a virtue in the more detailed account that follows begins with "Concerning X . . . ," or words to this effect, where X names a sphere of life with which all human beings regularly and more or less necessarily have dealings.[6] Aristotle then asks, what is it to choose and respond well within that sphere? And what is it to choose defectively? The "thin account" of each virtue is that it is whatever being stably disposed to act appropriately in that sphere consists in. There may be, and usually are, various competing specifications of what acting well, in each case, in fact comes to. Aristotle goes on to defend in each case some concrete specification, producing, at the end, a full or "thick" definition of the virtue.

Here are the most important spheres of experience recognized by Aristotle, along with the names of their corresponding virtues:[7]

Sphere	Virtue
1. Fear of important damages, especially death	Courage
2. Bodily appetites and their pleasures	Moderation
3. Distribution of limited resources	Justice
4. Management of one's personal property, where others are concerned	Generosity
5. Management of personal property, where hospitality is concerned	Expansive hospitality
6. Attitudes and actions with respect to one's own worth	Greatness of soul
7. Attitude to slights and damages	Mildness of temper
8. "Association and living together and the fellowship of words and actions"	

a. Truthfulness in speech	Truthfulness
b. Social association of a playful kind	Easy grace, (contrasted with coarseness, rudeness, insensitivity)
c. Social association more generally	Nameless, but a kind of friendliness (contrasted with irritability and grumpiness)
9. Attitude to the good and ill fortune of others	Proper judgement (contrasted with enviousness, spitefulness, etc.)
10. Intellectual life	The various intellectual virtues, such as perceptiveness, knowledge, etc.
11. The planning of one's life and conduct	Practical wisdom

There is, of course, much more to be said about this list, its specific members, and the names Aristotle chose for the virtue in each case, some of which are indeed culture-bound. What I want to insist on here, however, is the care with which Aristotle articulates his general approach, beginning from a characterization of a sphere of universal experience and choice, and introducing the virtue-name as the name (as yet undefined) of whatever it is to choose appropriately in that area of experience. On this approach, it does not seem possible to say, as the relativist wishes to, that a given society does not contain anything that corresponds to a given virtue. Nor does it seem to be an open question, in the case of a particular agent, whether a certain virtue should or should not be included in his or her life—except in the sense that she can always choose to pursue the corresponding deficiency instead. The point is that everyone makes some choices and acts somehow or other in these spheres: if not properly, then improperly. Everyone has *some* attitude, and corresponding behaviour, towards her own death; her bodily appetites and their management; her property and its use; the distribution of social goods; telling the truth; being kind to others; cultivating a sense of play and delight, and so on. No matter where one lives one cannot escape these questions, so long as one is living a human life. But then this means that one's behaviour falls, willy-nilly, within the sphere of the Aristotelian virtue, in each case. If it is not appropriate, it is inappropriate; it cannot be off the map altogether. People will of course disagree about what the appropriate ways of acting and reacting in fact *are*. But in that case, as Aristotle has set things up, they are arguing about the same thing, and advancing competing specifications of the same virtue. The reference of the virtue term in each case is fixed by the sphere of experience—by what we shall from now on call the "grounding experiences." The thin or "nominal" definition of the virtue will be, in each case, that it is whatever being disposed to choose and respond well consists in, in that sphere. The job of ethical theory will be to search for the best further specification corresponding to this nominal definition, and to produce a full definition.

3

We have begun to introduce considerations from the philosophy of language. We can now make the direction of the Aristotelian account clearer by considering his own account of linguistic indicating (referring) and defining, which guides his treatment of both scientific and ethical terms, and of the idea of progress in both areas.[8]

Aristotle's general picture is as follows. We begin with some experiences—not necessarily our own, but those of members of our linguistic community, broadly construed.[9] On the basis of these experiences, a word enters the language of the group, indicating (referring to) whatever it is that is the content of those experiences. Aristotle gives the example of thunder.[10] People hear a noise in the clouds, and they then refer to it, using the word "thunder." At this point, it may be that nobody has any concrete account of the noise or any idea about what it really is. But the experience fixes a subject for further inquiry. From now on, we can refer to thunder, ask "What is thunder?," and advance and assess competing theories. The thin or, we might say, "nominal" definition of thunder is "That noise in the clouds, whatever it is." The competing explanatory theories are rival candidates for correct full or thick definition. So the explanatory story citing Zeus' activities in the clouds is a false account of the very same thing of which the best scientific explanation is a true account. There is just one debate here, with a single subject.

So too, Aristotle suggests, with our ethical terms. Heraclitus, long before him, already had the essential idea, saying, "They would not have known the name of justice, if these things did not take place."[11] "These things," our source for the fragment informs us, are experiences of injustice—presumably of harm, deprivation, inequality. These experiences fix the reference of the corresponding virtue word. Aristotle proceeds along similar lines. In the *Politics* he insists that only human beings, and not either animals or gods, will have our basic ethical terms and concepts (such as just and unjust, noble and base, good and bad), because the beasts are unable to form the concepts, and the gods lack the experiences of limit and finitude that give a concept such as justice its points.[12] In the enumeration of the virtues in the *Nicomachean Ethics,* he carries the line of thought further, suggesting that the reference of the virtue terms is fixed by spheres of choice, frequently connected with our finitude and limitation, that we encounter in virtue of shared conditions of human existence.[13] The question about virtue usually arises in areas in which human choice is both non-optional and somewhat problematic. (Thus, he stresses, there is no virtue involving the regulation of listening to attractive sounds, or seeing pleasing sights.) Each family of virtue and vice or deficiency words attaches to some such sphere. And we can understand progress in ethics, like progress in scientific understanding, to be progress in finding the correct fuller specification of a virtue, isolated by its thin or nominal definition. This progress is aided by a perspicuous mapping of the sphere of the grounding experiences. When we understand more precisely what problems human beings encounter in their lives with one another, what circumstances they face in which choice of some sort is required, we will have a way of assessing competing responses to those problems, and we will begin to understand what it might be to act well in the face of them.

Aristotle's ethical and political writings provide many examples of how such progress (or, more generally, such a rational debate) might go. We find argument against Platonic asceticism, as the proper specification of moderation (appropriate choice and response vis à vis the bodily appetites), and in favour of a more generous role for appetitive activity in human life. We find argument against the intense concern for public status and reputation, and the consequent proneness to anger over slights, that was prevalent in Greek ideals of maleness and in Greek behaviour, together with a defence of a more limited and controlled expression of anger, as the proper specification of the virtue that Aristotle calls "mildness of temper." (Here Aristotle evinces some discomfort with the virtue term he has chosen, and he is right to do so, since it certainly loads the dice heavily in favour of his concrete specification and against the traditional one.)[14] And so on for all the virtues.

In an important section of *Politics* II, part of which forms one of the epigraphs to this paper, Aristotle defends the proposition that laws should be revisable and not fixed, by pointing to evidence that there is progress towards greater correctness in our ethical conceptions, as also in the arts and sciences. Greeks used to think that courage was a matter of waving swords around; now they have (the *Ethics* informs us) a more inward and a more civic and communally attuned understanding of proper behaviour towards the possibility of death. Women used to be regarded as property, to be bought and sold; now this would be thought barbaric. And in the case of justice as well we have, the *Politics* passage claims, advanced towards a more adequate understanding of what is fair and appropriate. Aristotle gives the example of an existing homicide law that convicts the defendant automatically on the evidence of the prosecutor's relatives (whether they actually witnessed anything or not, apparently). This, Aristotle says, is clearly a stupid and unjust law; and yet it once seemed appropriate—and, to a tradition-bound community, must still be so. To hold tradition fixed is then to prevent ethical progress. What human beings want and seek is not conformity with the past, it is the good. So our systems of law should make it possible for them to progress beyond the past, when they have agreed that a change is good. (They should not, however, make change too easy, since it is no easy matter to see one's way to the good, and tradition is frequently a sounder guide than current fashion.)

In keeping with these ideas, the *Politics* as a whole presents the beliefs of the many different societies it investigates not as unrelated local norms, but as competing answers to questions about justice and courage (and so on) with which all societies are (being human) concerned, and in response to which they all try to find what is good. Aristotle's analysis of the virtues gives him an appropriate framework for these comparisons, which seem perfectly appropriate inquiries into the ways in which different societies have solved common human problems.

In the Aristotelian approach it is obviously of the first importance to distinguish two stages of the inquiry: the initial demarcation of the sphere of choice, of the "grounding experiences" that fix the reference of the virtue term; and the ensuing more concrete inquiry into what the appropriate choice, in that sphere, *is*. Aristotle does not always do this carefully; and the language he has to work with is often not helpful to him. We do not have much difficulty with terms like "moderation" and "justice" and even "courage," which seem vaguely normative, but relatively empty, so far, of concrete moral content. As the approach requires, they can serve as extension-fixing labels under which many competing specifications may be investigated. But we have already noticed the problem with "mildness of temper," which seems to rule out by fiat a prominent contender for the appropriate disposition concerning anger. And much the same thing certainly seems to be true of the relativists' favourite target, *megalopsuchia*, which implies in its very name an attitude to one's own worth that is more Greek than universal. (A Christian, for example, will feel that the proper attitude to one's own worth requires an understanding of one's lowness, frailty, and sinfulness. The virtue of humility requires considering oneself *small*, not great.) What we ought to get at this point in the inquiry is a word for the proper attitude towards anger and offence, and for the proper attitude towards one's worth, that are more truly neutral among the competing specifications, referring only to the sphere of experience within which we wish to determine what is appropriate. Then we could regard the competing conceptions as rival accounts of one and the same thing, so that, for example, Christian humility would be a rival specification of the same virtue whose Greek specification is given in Aristotle's account of *megalopsuchia*, namely, the proper attitude towards the question of one's own worth.

In fact, oddly enough, if one examines the evolution in the use of this word from Aristotle through the Stoics to the Christian fathers, one can see that this is more or less what happened, as "greatness of soul" became associated, first, with the Stoic emphasis on the supremacy of virtue and the worthlessness of externals, including the body, and, through this, with the Christian denial of the body and of the worth of earthly life.[15] So even in this apparently unpromising case, history shows that the Aristotelian approach not only provided the materials for a single debate but actually succeeded in organizing such a debate, across enormous differences of both place and time.

Here, then, is a sketch for an objective human morality based upon the idea of virtuous action—that is, of appropriate functioning in each human sphere. The Aristotelian claim is that, further developed, it will retain the grounding in actual human experiences that is the strong point of virtue ethics, while gaining the ability to criticize local and traditional moralities in the name of a more inclusive account of the circumstances of human life, and of the needs for human functioning that these circumstances call forth.

4

The proposal will encounter many objections. The concluding sections of this paper will present three of the most serious and will sketch the lines along which the Aristotelian might proceed in formulating a reply. To a great extent these objections were not imagined or confronted by Aristotle himself, but his position seems capable of confronting them.

The first objection concerns the relationship between singleness of problem and singleness of solution. Let us grant for the moment that the Aristotelian approach has succeeded in coherently isolating and describing areas of human experience and choice that form, so to speak, the *terrain* of the virtues, and in giving thin definitions of each of the virtues as whatever it is that choosing and responding well within that sphere consists in. Let us suppose that the approach succeeds in doing this in a way that embraces many times and places, bringing disparate cultures together into a single debate about the good human being and the good human life. Different cultural accounts of good choice within the sphere in question in each case are now seen not as untranslatably different, but as competing answers to a single general question about a set of shared human experiences. Still, it might be argued, what has been achieved is, at best, a single discourse or debate about virtue. It has not been shown that this debate will have, as Aristotle believes, a single answer. Indeed, it has not even been shown that the discourse we have set up will have the form of a *debate* at all—rather than a plurality of culturally specific narratives, each giving the thick definition of a virtue that corresponds to the experience and traditions of a particular group. There is an important disanalogy with the case of thunder, on which the Aristotelian so much relies in arguing that our questions will have a single answer. For in that case what is given in experience is the definiendum itself, so that experience establishes a rough extension, to which any good definition must respond. In the case of the virtues, things are more indirect. What is given in experience across groups is only the *ground* of virtuous action, the circumstances of life to which virtuous action is an appropriate response. Even if these grounding experiences are shared, that does not tell us that there will be a shared appropriate response.

In the case of thunder, furthermore, the conflicting theories are clearly put forward as competing candidates for the truth; the behaviour of those involved in the discourse about virtue suggests that they are indeed, as Aristotle says, searching "not for the way of their ancestors, but for the good." And it seems reasonable in that case for them to do so. It is far less clear, where the virtues are concerned (the objector continues), that a unified practical solution is either sought by the actual participants or a desideratum for them. The Aristotelian proposal makes it possible to conceive of a way in which the virtues might be non-relative. It does not, by itself, answer the question of relativism.

The second objection goes deeper. For it questions the notion of spheres of shared human experience that lies at the heart of the Aristotelian approach. The approach, says this objector, seems to treat the experiences that ground the virtues as in some way primitive, given, and free from the cultural variation that we find in the plurality of normative conceptions of virtue. Ideas of proper courage may vary, but the fear of death is shared by all human beings. Ideas of moderation may vary, but the experiences of hunger, thirst, and sexual desire are (so the Aristotelian seems to claim) invariant. Normative conceptions introduce an element of cultural interpretation that is not present in the grounding experiences, which are, for that very reason, the Aristotelian's starting point.

But, the objector continues, such assumptions are naive. They will not stand up either to our best account of experience or to a close examination of the ways in which these so-called grounding experiences are in fact differently constructed by different cultures. In general, first of all, our best accounts of the nature of experience, even perceptual experience, inform us that there is no such thing as an "innocent eye" that receives an uninterpreted "given." Even sense-perception is interpretive, heavily influenced by belief, teaching, language, and in general by social and contextual features. There is a very real sense in which members of different societies do not see the same sun and stars, encounter the same plants and animals, hear the same thunder.

But if this seems to be true of human experience of nature, which was the allegedly unproblematic starting point for Aristotle's account of naming, it is all the more plainly true, the objector claims, in the area of the human good. Here it is only a very naive and historically insensitive moral philosopher who would say that the experience of the fear of death, or of bodily appetites, is a human constant. Recent anthropological work on the social construction of the emotions,[16] for example, has shown to what extent the experience of fear has learned and culturally variant elements. When we add that the object of the fear in which the Aristotelian takes an interest is death, which has been so variously interpreted and understood by human beings at different times and in different places the conclusion that the "grounding experience" is an irreducible plurality of experiences, highly various and in each case deeply infused with cultural interpretation, becomes even more inescapable.

Nor is the case different with the apparently less complicated experience of the bodily appetites. Most philosophers who have written about the appetites have treated hunger, thirst, and sexual desire as human universals, stemming from our shared animal nature. Aristotle himself was already more sophisticated, since he insisted that the object of appetite is "the apparent good" and that appetite is therefore something interpretive and selective, a kind of intentional awareness.[17] But he does not seem to have reflected much about the ways in which historical and cultural differences could shape that awareness. The Hellenistic philosophers who immediately followed him did so reflect, arguing that the experience of sexual desire and of many forms of the desire for food and drink are, at least in part, social constructs, built up over time on the basis of a social teaching about value; this is external to start with, but it enters so deeply into the perceptions of the individual that it actually forms and transforms the experience of desire.[18] Let us take two Epicurean examples. People are taught that to be well fed they require luxurious fish and meat, that a simple vegetarian diet is not enough. Over time, the combination of teaching with habit produces an appetite for meat, shaping the individual's perceptions of the objects before him. Again, people are taught that what sexual relations are all about is a romantic union or fusion with an object who is seen as exalted in value, or even as perfect. Over time, this teaching shapes sexual behaviour and the experience of desire, so that sexual arousal itself responds to this culturally learned scenario.[19]

This work of social criticism has recently been carried further by Michel Foucault, in his *History of Sexuality*.[20] This work has certain gaps as a history of Greek thought on this topic, but it does succeed in establishing that the Greeks saw the problem of the appetites and their management in an extremely different way from that of twentieth-century Westerners. To summarize two salient conclusions of his complex argument: first, the Greeks did not single out the sexual appetite for special treatment; they treated it alongside hunger and thirst, as a drive that needed to be mastered and kept within bounds. Their central concern was with self-mastery, and they saw the appetites in the light of this concern. Furthermore, where the sexual appetite is concerned, they did not regard the gender of the partner as particularly important in assessing the moral value of the act. Nor did they treat as morally salient a stable disposition to prefer partners of one sex rather than the other. Instead, they focused on the general issue of activity and passivity, connecting it in complex ways with the issue of self-mastery.

Work like Foucault's—and there is a lot of it in various areas, some of it very good—shows very convincingly that the experience of bodily desire, and of the body itself, has elements that vary with cultural and historical change. The names that people call their desires and themselves as subjects of desire, the fabric of belief and discourse into which they integrate their ideas of desiring: all this influences, it is clear, not only their reflection about desire, but also their experience of desire itself. Thus, for example, it is naive to treat our modern debates about homosexuality as continuations of the very same debate about sexual activity that went on in the Greek world.[21] In a very real sense there was no "homosexual experience" in a culture that did not contain our emphasis on the gender of the partner, the subjectivity of inclination, and the permanence of appetitive disposition, nor our particular ways of problematizing certain forms of behaviour.

If we suppose that we can get underneath this variety and this constructive power of social discourse in at least one case—namely, with the universal experience of bodily pain as a bad thing—even here we find subtle arguments against us. For the experience of pain seems to be embedded in a cultural discourse as surely as the closely related experiences of the appetites, and significant variations can be alleged here as well. The Stoics had already made this claim against the Aristotelian virtues. In order to establish that bodily pain is not bad by its very nature, but only by cultural tradition, the Stoics had to provide some explanation for the ubiquity of the belief that pain is bad and of the tendency to shun it. This explanation would have to show that the reaction is learned rather than natural, and to explain why, in the light of this fact, it is learned so widely. This they did by pointing to certain features in the very early treatment of infants. As soon as an infant is born, it cries. Adults, assuming that the crying is a response to its pain at the unaccustomed coldness and harshness of the place where it finds itself, hasten to comfort it. This behaviour, often repeated, teaches the infant to regard its pain as a bad thing—or, better, teaches it the concept of pain, which includes the notion of badness, and teaches it the forms of life its society shares concerning pain. It is all social teaching, they claimed, though this usually escapes our notice because of the early and non-linguistic nature of the teaching.[22]

These and related arguments, the objector concludes, show that the Aristotelian idea that there can be a single, non-relative discourse about human experiences such as mortality or desire is a naive one. There is no such bedrock of shared experience, and thus no single sphere of choice within which the virtue is the disposition to choose well. So the Aristotelian project cannot even get off the ground.

Now the Aristotelian confronts a third objector, who attacks from a rather different direction. Like the second, she charges that the Aristotelian has taken for a universal and necessary feature of human life an experience that is contingent on certain non-necessary historical conditions. Like the second, she argues that human experience is much more profoundly shaped by non-necessary social features than the Aristotelian has allowed. But her purpose is not simply, like the second objector's, to point to the great variety of ways in which the "grounding experiences" corresponding to the virtues are actually understood and lived by human beings. It is more radical still. It is to point out that we could imagine a form of human life that does not contain these experiences—or some of them—at all, in any form. Thus the virtue that consists in acting well in that sphere need not be included in an account of the human good. In some cases, the experience may even be a sign of *bad* human life, and the corresponding virtue therefore no better than a form of non-ideal adaptation to a bad state of affairs. The really good human life, in such a case, would contain neither the grounding deficiency nor the remedial virtue.

This point is forcefully raised by some of Aristotle's own remarks about the virtue of generosity. One of his arguments against societies that eliminate private ownership is that they thereby do away with the opportunity for generous action, which requires having possessions of one's own to give to others.[23] This sort of remark is tailor-made for the objector, who will immediately say that generosity, if it really rests upon the experience of private possession, is a dubious candidate indeed for inclusion in a purportedly non-relative account of the human virtues. If it rests upon a grounding experience that is non-necessary and is capable of being evaluated in different ways, and of being either included or eliminated in accordance with that evaluation, then it is not the universal the Aristotelian said it was.

Some objectors of the third kind will stop at this point, or use such observations to support the second objector's relativism. But in another prominent form this argument takes a non-relativist direction. It asks us to assess the grounding experiences against an account of human flourishing, produced in some independent manner. If we do so, the objector urges, we will discover that some of the experiences are remediable deficiencies. The objection to Aristotelian virtue ethics will then be that it limits our social aspirations, encouraging us to regard as permanent and necessary what we might in fact improve to the benefit of all human life. This is the direction in which the third objection to the virtues was pressed by Karl Marx, its most famous proponent.[24] According to Marx's argument, a number of the leading bourgeois virtues are responses to defective relations of production. Bourgeois justice, generosity, etc., presuppose conditions and structures that are not ideal and that will be eliminated when communism is achieved. And it is not only the current *specification* of these virtues that will be superseded with the removal of the deficiency. It is the virtues themselves. It is in this sense that communism leads human beings beyond ethics.

The Aristotelian is thus urged to inquire into the basic structures of human life with the daring of a radical political imagination. It is claimed that when she does so she will see that human life contains more possibilities than are dreamed of in her list of virtues.

5

Each of these objections is profound. To answer any one of them adequately would require a treatise. But we can still do something at this point to map out an Aristotelian response to each one, pointing the direction in which a fuller reply might go.

The first objector is right to insist on the distinction between singleness of framework and singleness of answer, and right, again, to stress that in constructing a debate about the virtues based on the demarcation of certain spheres of experience we have not yet answered any of the "What is X?" questions that this debate will confront. We have not even said much about the structure of the debate itself, beyond its beginnings—about how it will both use and criticize traditional beliefs, how it will deal with conflicting beliefs, how it will move critically from the "way of one's ancestors" to the "good"—in short, about whose judgements it will trust. I have addressed some of these issues, again with reference to Aristotle, in two other papers;[25] but much more remains to be done. At this point, however, we can make four observations to indicate how the Aristotelian might deal with some of the objector's concerns here. First, the Aristotelian position that I wish to defend

need not insist, in every case, on a single answer to the request for a specification of a virtue. The answer might well turn out to be a disjunction. The
process of comparative and critical debate will, I imagine, eliminate numerous contenders—for example, the view of justice that prevailed in Cyme.*
But what remains might well be a (probably small) plurality of acceptable
accounts. These accounts may or may not be capable of being subsumed
under a single account of greater generality. Success in the eliminative task
will still be no trivial accomplishment. If we should succeed in ruling out conceptions of the proper attitude to one's own human worth that are based on
a notion of original sin, for example, this would be moral work of enormous
significance, even if we got no further than that in specifying the positive
account.

Second, the general answer to a "What is X?" question in any sphere may
well be susceptible of several or even of many concrete specifications, in connection with other local practices and local conditions. The normative
account where friendship and hospitality are concerned, for example, is
likely to be extremely general, admitting of many concrete "fillings." Friends
in England will have different customs, where regular social visiting is concerned, from friends in ancient Athens. Yet both sets of customs can count as
further specifications of a general account of friendship that mentions, for
example, the Aristotelian criteria of mutual benefit and well-wishing, mutual
enjoyment, mutual awareness, a shared conception of the good, and some
form of "living together."[26] Sometimes we may want to view such concrete
accounts as optional alternative specifications, to be chosen by a society on
the basis of reasons of ease and convenience. Sometimes, on the other hand,
we may want to insist that a particular account gives the only legitimate specification of the virtue in question for that concrete context; in that case, the
concrete account could be viewed as a part of a longer or fuller version of the
single normative account. The decision between these two ways of regarding
it will depend upon our assessment of its degree of non-arbitrariness for its
context (both physical and historical), its relationship to other non-arbitrary
features of the moral conception of that context, and so forth.

Third, whether we have one or several general accounts of a virtue, and
whether this/these accounts do or do not admit of more concrete specifications relative to ongoing cultural contexts, the particular choices that the virtuous person, under this conception, makes will always be a matter of being
keenly responsive to the local features of his or her concrete context. So in this
respect, again, the instructions the Aristotelian will give to the person of
virtue do not differ from part of what a relativist would recommend. The
Aristotelian virtues involve a delicate balancing between general rules and a
keen awareness of particulars, in which process, as Aristotle stresses, the per-

*Editors' note: Cyme was a Greek City in Asia Minor. Aristotle criticized the laws regarding mur-
der in Cyme because they included the following provision: "If the accuser produce a certain
number of witnesses from among his own kinsman, the accused shall be held guilt" (Aristotle
Politics 1268b40).

ception of the particular takes priority. It takes priority in the sense that a good rule is a good summary of wise particular choices, and not a court of last resort. Like rules in medicine and navigation, ethical rules should be held open to modification in the light of new circumstances; and the good agent must therefore cultivate the ability to perceive and correctly describe his or her situation finely and truly, including in this perceptual grasp even those features of the situation that are not covered under the existing rule.

I have written a good deal elsewhere on this idea of the "priority of the particular," exactly what it does and does not imply, in exactly what ways that particular perception is and is not prior to the general rule. Those who want clarification on this central topic will have to turn to those writings.[27]

What I want to stress here is that Aristotelian particularism is fully compatible with Aristotelian objectivity. The fact that a good and virtuous decision is context-sensitive does not imply that it is right only *relative to,* or *inside,* a limited context, any more than the fact that a good navigational judgement is sensitive to particular weather conditions shows that it is correct only in a local or relational sense. It is right absolutely, objectively, anywhere in the human world, to attend to the particular features of one's context; and the person who so attends and who chooses accordingly is making, according to Aristotle, the humanly correct decision, period. If another situation should ever arise with all the same ethically relevant features, including contextual features, the same decision would again be absolutely right.[28]

It should be stressed that the value of contextual responsiveness and the value of getting it right are seen by the Aristotelian as mutually supportive here, rather than in tension. For the claim is that only when we have duly responded to the complexities of the context, seeing it for the very historical situation it is, will we have any hope of making the right decision. Short of that, the importation of plausible general values, however well intentioned, may do no good at all, and may actually make things worse. Nor, the Aristotelian argues, have we been sufficiently responsive to the context before us if we do not see the humanity in it: do not, that is, respond to the claims of human need, the strivings towards the good, the frustrations of human capability, that this situation displays to the reflective person. To study it with detached scientific interest, as an interesting set of local traditions, is not to respond sufficiently to the concrete situation it is; for whatever it is, it is concretely human.

An example from the development context will illustrate this mutual support. In *A Quiet Revolution,* an eloquent study of women's education in rural Bangladesh,[29] Martha Chen describes the efforts of a government development group, the Bangladesh Rural Advancement Committee, to increase the rate of female literacy in certain rural areas. The project began from a conviction that literacy is an important ingredient in the development of these women towards greater capability to live well. It was seen as closely linked with other important values, such as economic flourishing, autonomy, and self-respect. This conviction did not derive from the local traditions of the villages, where women had in fact little autonomy and no experience of education; it derived from the experiences and reflections of the development workers, who were themselves from many different backgrounds and two nationalities. (Chen herself is an American with a Ph.D. in Sanskrit.) The group as a whole lacked experience of the concrete ways of life of rural women, and thus had, as Chen says, "no specific concepts or strategies"[30] for working with them. In the first phase of the programme, then, the development workers went directly to the rural villages with their ideas of literacy and its importance, offering adult literacy materials borrowed from another national programme, and trying to motivate the women of the communities they entered to take them on.

But their lack of contextual knowledge made it impossible for them to succeed, in this first phase. Women found the borrowed literacy materials boring and irrelevant to their lives. They did not see how literacy would help them; even the accompanying vocational training was resisted, since it focused on skills for which there was little demand in that area. Thus failure led the agency to rethink their approach. On the one hand, they never abandoned their basic conviction that literacy was important for these women; their conclusion, based on wide experience and on their picture of what the women's lives might be, still seemed sound. On the other hand, they recognized that far more attention to the lives and thoughts of the women involved would be necessary if they were going to come up with an understanding of what literacy might do and be for them. They began to substitute for the old approach a more participatory one, in which local co-operative groups brought together development workers with local women, whose experience and sense of life were regarded as crucial. This concept of the co-operative group led to a much more complex understanding of the situation, as the development workers grasped the network of relationships within which the women had to function and the specific dimensions of their poverty and constraints, and as the women grasped the alternative possibilities and began to define for themselves a set of aspirations for change. The result, which continues, has been a slow and complex evolution in the role of women in the villages. A visiting journalist wrote, some years later:

> I saw the seeds of the quiet revolution starting in village women's lives. At the meeting houses BRAC has built, the wives, young and old, are learning to read and write. Forbidden from doing marketing, they now at least can keep the accounts . . . In one fishing village, the women have even become the bankers, saving over $2000 and lending it to their men to buy better equipment. It started in the simplest way—they collected a handful of rice a week from each family, stored it, and sold it in the market. About 50 villages from each area have thriving women's cooperatives, investing in new power-pumps or seed, and winning respect for their members.[31]

This is how the Aristotelian approach works—hanging on to a general (and open-ended) picture of human life, its needs and possibilities, but at every stage immersing itself in the concrete circumstances of history and culture. Chen's detailed narrative—which in its very style manifests a combination of Aristotelian commitment to the human good and Aristotelian contextual sensitivity—shows that the two elements go, and must go, together. If the development workers had approached these women as alien beings whose ways could not be compared with others and considered with a view to the human good, no change would have taken place—and the narrative convinces the reader that these changes have been good. On the other hand, general talk of education and self-respect did nothing at all until it came from within a concrete historical reality. Immersion made it possible to get the choice that was humanly right.

Thus the Aristotelian virtue-based morality can capture a great deal of what the relativist is after, and still make a claim to objectivity, in the sense we have described. In fact, we might say that the Aristotelian virtues do better than the relativist virtues in explaining what people are actually doing when they scrutinize the features of their context carefully, looking at both the shared and the non-shared features with an eye to what is best. For, as Aristotle says, people who do this are usually searching for the good, not just for the way of their ancestors. They are prepared to defend their decisions as good or right, and to think of those who advocate a different course as disagreeing about what is right, not just narrating a different tradition.

Finally, we should point out that the Aristotelian virtues, and the deliberations they guide, unlike some systems of moral rules, remain always open to revision in the light of new circumstances and new evidence. In this way, again, they contain the flexibility to local conditions that the relativist would desire—but, again, without sacrificing objectivity. Sometimes the new circumstances may simply give rise to a new concrete specification of the virtue as previously defined; in some cases it may cause us to change our view about what the virtue itself is. All general accounts are held provisionally, as summaries of correct decisions and as guides to new ones. This flexibility, built into the Aristotelian procedure, will again help the Aristotelian account to answer the questions of the relativist, without relativism.

6

We must now turn to the second objection. Here, I believe, is the really serious threat to the Aristotelian position. Past writers on virtue, including Aristotle himself, have lacked sensitivity to the ways in which different traditions of discourse, different conceptual schemes, articulate the world, and also to the profound connections between the structure of discourse and the structure of experience itself. Any contemporary defence of the Aristotelian position must display this sensitivity, responding somehow to the data that the relativist historian or anthropologist brings forward.

The Aristotelian should begin, it seems to me, by granting that with respect to any complex matter of deep human importance there is no 'innocent eye', no way of seeing the world that is entirely neutral and free of cultural shaping. The work of philosophers such as Putnam, Goodman, and Davidson[32]—following, one must point out, from the arguments of Kant and, I believe, from those of Aristotle himself[33]—have shown convincingly that even where sense-perception is concerned, the human mind is an active and interpretative instrument, and that its interpretations are a function of its history and its concepts, as well as of its innate structure. The Aristotelian should also grant, it seems to me, that the nature of human world interpretations is holistic and that the criticism of them must, equally, be holistic. Conceptual schemes, like languages, hang together as whole structures, and we should realize, too, that a change in any single element is likely to have implications for the system as a whole.

But these two facts do not imply, as some relativists in literary theory and in anthropology tend to assume, that all world interpretations are equally valid and altogether non-comparable, that there are no good standards of assessment and "anything goes." The rejection of the idea of ethical truth as correspondence to an altogether uninterpreted reality does not imply that the whole idea of searching for the truth is an old-fashioned error. Certain ways in which people see the world can still be criticized exactly as Aristotle criticized them: as stupid, pernicious, and false. The standards used in such criticisms must come from inside human life. (Frequently they will come from the society in question itself, from its own rationalist and critical traditions.) And the inquirer must attempt, prior to criticism, to develop an inclusive understanding of the conceptual scheme being criticized, seeing what motivates each of its parts and how they hang together. But there is so far no reason to think that the critic will not be able to reject the institution of slavery, or the homicide law of Cyme, as out of line with the conception of virtue that emerges from reflection on the variety of different ways in which human cultures have had the experiences that ground the virtues.

The grounding experiences will not, the Aristotelian should concede, provide precisely a single, language-neutral bedrock on which an account of virtue can be straightforwardly and unproblematically based. The description and assessment of the ways in which different cultures have constructed these experiences will become one of the central tasks of Aristotelian philosophical criticism. But the relativist has, so far, shown no reason why we could not, at the end of the day, say that certain ways of conceptualizing death are more in keeping with the totality of our evidence and the totality of our wishes for flourishing life than others; that certain ways of experiencing appetitive desire are for similar reasons more promising than others.

Relativists tend, furthermore, to understate the amount of attunement, recognition, and overlap that actually obtains across cultures, particularly in the areas of the grounding experiences. The Aristotelian, in developing her conception in a culturally sensitive way, should insist, as Aristotle himself does, upon the evidence of such attunement and recognition. Despite the evident differences in the specific cultural shaping of the grounding experiences, we do recognize the experiences of people in other cultures as similar to our own. We do converse with them about matters of deep importance, understand them, allow ourselves to be moved by them. When we read Sophocles' *Antigone,* we see a good deal that seems strange to us; and we have not read the play well if we do not notice how far its conceptions of death, woman-hood, and so on differ from our own. But it is still possible for us to be moved by the drama, to care about its people, to regard their debates as reflections upon virtue that speak to our own experience, and their choices as choices in spheres of conduct in which we too must choose. Again, when one sits down at a table with people from other parts of the world and debates with them concerning hunger, or just distribution, or in general the quality of human life, one does find, in spite of evident conceptual differences, that it is possible to proceed as if we were all talking about the same human problem; and it is usually only in a context in which one or more of the parties is intellectually committed to a theoretical relativist position that this discourse proves impossible to sustain. This sense of community and overlap seems to be especially strong in the areas that we have called the areas of the grounding experiences. And this, it seems, supports the Aristotelian claim that those experiences can be a good starting point for ethical debate.

Furthermore, it is necessary to stress that hardly any cultural group today is as focused upon its own internal traditions and as isolated from other cultures as the relativist argument presupposes. Cross-cultural communication and debate are ubiquitous facts of contemporary life, and our experience of cultural interaction indicates that in general the inhabitants of different conceptual schemes do tend to view their interaction in the Aristotelian and not the relativist way. A traditional society, confronted with new technologies and sciences, and the conceptions that go with them, does not in fact simply fail to understand them, or regard them as totally alien incursions upon a hermetically sealed way of life. Instead, it assesses the new item as a possible contributor to flourishing life, making it comprehensible to itself, and incorporating elements that promise to solve problems of flourishing. Examples of such assimilation, and the debate that surrounds it,[34] suggest that the parties do in fact recognize common problems and that the traditional society is perfectly capable of viewing an external innovation as a device to solve a problem that it shares with the innovating society. The village woman of Chen's narrative, for example, did not insist on remaining illiterate because they had always been so. Instead, they willingly entered into dialogue with the international group, viewing co-operative discussion as a resource towards a better life. The parties do in fact search for the good, not the way of their ancestors; only traditionalist anthropologists insist, nostalgically, on the absolute preservation of the ancestral.

And this is so even when cross-cultural discourse reveals a difference at the level of the conceptualization of the grounding experiences. Frequently the effect of work like Foucault's, which reminds us of the non-necessary and non-universal character of one's own ways of seeing in some such area, is precisely to prompt a critical debate in search of the human good. It is difficult, for example, to read Foucault's observations about the history of our

sexual ideas without coming to feel that certain ways in which the Western
contemporary debate on these matters has been organized, as a result of
some combination of Christian moralism with nineteenth-century pseudo-
science, are especially silly, arbitrary, and limiting, inimical to a human search
for flourishing. Foucault's moving account of Greek culture, as he himself
insists in a preface,[35] provides not only a sign that someone once thought differently, but also evidence that it is possible for *us* to think differently.
(Indeed, this was the whole purpose of genealogy as Nietzsche, Foucault's
precursor here, introduced it: to destroy idols once deemed necessary, and to
clear the way for new possibilities of creation.) Foucault announced that the
purpose of his book was to 'free thought' so that it could think differently,
imagining new and more fruitful possibilities. And close analysis of spheres
of cultural discourse, which stresses cultural differences in the spheres of the
grounding experiences, is being combined, increasingly, in current debates
about sexuality and related matters, with a critique of existing social arrangements and attitudes, and an elaboration of new norms of human flourishing.
There is no reason to think this combination incoherent.[36]

As we pursue these possibilities, the basic spheres of experience identified in the Aristotelian approach will no longer, we have said, be seen as
spheres of *uninterpreted* experience. But we have also insisted that there is
much family relatedness and much overlap among societies. And certain
areas of relatively greater universality can be specified here, on which we
should insist as we proceed to areas that are more varied in their cultural
expression. Not without a sensitive awareness that we are speaking of something that is experienced differently in different contexts, we can none the
less identify certain features of our common humanity, closely related to Aristotle's original list, from which our debate might proceed.

1. *Mortality.* No matter how death is understood, all human beings face
it and (after a certain age) know that they face it. This fact shapes every aspect
of more or less every human life.

2. *The body.* Prior to any concrete cultural shaping, we are born with
human bodies, whose possibilities and vulnerabilities do not as such belong
to any culture rather than any other. Any given human being might have
belonged to any culture. The experience of the body is culturally influenced;
but the body itself, prior to such experience, provides limits and parameters
that ensure a great deal of overlap in what is going to be experienced, where
hunger, thirst, desire, and the five senses are concerned. It is all very well to
point to the cultural component in these experiences. But when one spends
time considering issues of hunger and scarcity, and in general of human misery, such differences appear relatively small and refined, and one cannot fail
to acknowledge that 'there are no known ethnic differences in human physi-
ology with respect to metabolism of nutrients. Africans and Asians do not
burn their dietary calories or use their dietary protein any differently from
Europeans and Americans. It follows then that dietary requirements cannot
vary widely as between different races.'[37] This and similar facts should surely

be focal points for debate about appropriate human behaviour in this sphere. And by beginning with the body, rather than with the subjective experience of desire, we get, furthermore, an opportunity to criticize the situation of people who are so persistently deprived that their *desire* for good things has actually decreased. This is a further advantage of the Aristotelian approach, when contrasted with approaches to choice that stop with subjective expressions of preference.

3. *Pleasure and pain.* In every culture, there is a conception of pain; and these conceptions, which overlap very largely with one another, can plausibly be seen as grounded in universal and pre-cultural experience. The Stoic story of infant development is highly implausible; the negative response to bodily pain is surely primitive and universal, rather than learned and optional, however much its specific "grammar" may be shaped by later learning.

4. *Cognitive capability.* Aristotle's famous claim that "all human beings by nature reach out for understanding"[38] seems to stand up to the most refined anthropological analysis. It points to an element in our common humanity that is plausibly seen, again, as grounded independently of particular acculturation, however much it is later shaped by acculturation.

5. *Practical reason.* All human beings, whatever their culture, participate (or try to) in the planning and managing of their lives, asking and answering questions about how one should live and act. This capability expresses itself differently in different societies, but a being who altogether lacked it would not be likely to be acknowledged as a human being, in any culture.[39]

6. *Early infant development.* Prior to the greater part of specific cultural shaping, though perhaps not free from all shaping, are certain areas of human experience and development that are broadly shared and of great importance for the Aristotelian virtues: experiences of desire, pleasure, loss, one's own finitude, perhaps also of envy, grief, and gratitude. One may argue about the merits of one or another psychoanalytical account of infancy. But it seems difficult to deny that the work of Freud on infant desire and of Klein on grief, loss, and other more complex emotional attitudes has identified spheres of human experience that are to a large extent common to all humans, regardless of their particular society. All humans begin as hungry babies, perceiving their own helplessness, their alternating closeness to and distance from those on whom they depend, and so forth. Melanie Klein records a conversation with an anthropologist in which an event that at first looked (to Western eyes) bizarre was interpreted by Klein as the expression of a universal pattern of mourning. The anthropologist accepted her interpretation.[40]

7. *Affiliation.* Aristotle's claim that human beings as such feel a sense of fellowship with other human beings, and that we are by nature social animals, is an empirical claim; but it seems to be a sound one. However varied our specific conceptions of friendship and love are, there is a great point in seeing them as overlapping expressions of the same family of shared human needs and desires.

8. *Humour.* There is nothing more culturally varied than humour; and
yet, as Aristotle insists, some space for humour and play seems to be a need
of any human life. The human being is not called the "laughing animal" for
nothing; it is certainly one of our salient differences from almost all other animals, and (in some form or other) a shared feature, I somewhat boldly assert,
of any life that is going to be counted as fully human.

This is just a list of suggestions, closely related to Aristotle's list of common experiences. One could subtract some of these items and/or add others.[41] But it seems plausible to claim that in all these areas we have a basis for
further work on the human good. We do not have a bedrock of completely
uninterpreted "given" data, but we do have nuclei of experience around
which the constructions of different societies proceed. There is no Archi-
medean point here, no pure access to unsullied "nature"—even, here, human
nature—as it is in and of itself. There is just human life as it is lived. But in life
as it is lived, we do find a family of experiences, clustering around certain
focuses, which can provide reasonable starting points for cross-cultural
reflection.

This paper forms part of a larger project. The role of the preliminary list proposed in this section can be better understood if I briefly set it in the context
of this more comprehensive enterprise, showing its links with other arguments. In a paper entitled "Nature, Function, and Capability: Aristotle on
Political Distribution,"[42] I discuss an Aristotelian conception of the proper
function of government, according to which its task is to make available to
each and every member of the community the basic necessary conditions of
the capability to choose and live a fully good human life, with respect to each
of the major human functions included in that fully good life. I examine sympathetically Aristotle's argument that, for this reason, the task of government
cannot be well performed, or its aims well understood, without an understanding of these functionings. A closely connected study, "Aristotelian
Social Democracy,"[43] shows a way of moving from a general understanding
of the circumstances and abilities of human beings (such as this list provides)
to an account of the most important human functions that it will be government's job to make possible. It shows how this understanding of the human
being and the political task can yield a conception of social democracy that is
a plausible alternative to liberal conceptions.

Meanwhile, in a third paper, "Aristotle on Human Nature and the Foundations of Ethics,"[44] I focus on the special role of two of the human capabili-
ties recognized in this list: affiliation (or sociability) and practical reason. I
argue that these two play an architectonic role in human life, suffusing and
also organizing all the other functions—which will count as truly human
functions only in so far as they are done with some degree of guidance from
both of these. Most of the paper is devoted to an examination of Aristotle's
arguments for saying that these two elements are parts of "human nature." I
argue that this is not an attempt to base human ethics on a neutral bedrock of

scientific fact outside of human experience and interpretation. I claim that Aristotle seeks, instead, to discover, among the experiences of groups in many times and places, certain elements that are especially broadly and deeply shared. And I argue that the arguments justifying the claims of these two to be broad and deep in this way have a self-validating structure: that is, anyone who participates in the first place in the inquiry that supports them affirms, by that very fact, her own recognition of their salience. This is an important continuation of the project undertaken in this paper, since it shows exactly how Aristotle's "foundation" for ethics can remain inside human history and self-interpretation, and yet still claim to be a foundation.

7

The third objection raises, at bottom, a profound conceptual question: What is it to inquire about the *human* good? What circumstances of existence go to define what it is to live the life of a *human being,* and not some other life? Aristotle likes to point out that an inquiry into the human good cannot, on pain of incoherence, end up describing the good of some other being, say a god—a good that, on account of our circumstances, it is impossible for us to attain.[45] What circumstances then? The virtues are defined relatively to certain problems and limitations, and also to certain endowments. Which ones are sufficiently central that their removal would make us into different beings, and open up a wholly new and different debate about the good? This question is itself part of the ethical debate we propose. For there is no way to answer it but to ask ourselves which elements of our experience seem to us so important that they count, for us, as part of who we are. I discuss Aristotle's attitude to this question elsewhere, and I shall simply summarize here.[46] It seems clear, first of all, that our mortality is an essential feature of our circumstances as human beings. An immortal being would have such a different form of life, and such different values and virtues, that it does not seem to make sense to regard that being as part of the same search for good. Essential, too, will be our dependence upon the world outside us: some sort of need for food, drink, the help of others. On the side of abilities, we would want to include cognitive functioning and the activity of practical reasoning as elements of any life that we would regard as human. Aristotle argues, plausibly, that we would want to include sociability as well, some sensitivity to the needs of and pleasure in the company of other beings similar to ourselves.

But it seems to me that the Marxist question remains, as a deep question about human forms of life and the search for the human good. For one certainly can imagine forms of human life that do not contain the holding of private property—nor, therefore, those virtues that have to do with its proper management. And this means that it remains an open question whether these virtues ought to be regarded as virtues, and kept upon our list. Marx wished to go much further, arguing that communism would remove the need for justice, courage, and most of the bourgeois virtues. I think we might be sceptical here. Aristotle's general attitude to such transformations of life is to suggest that they usually have a tragic dimension. If we remove one sort of problem—say, by removing private property—we frequently do so by introducing another—say, the absence of a certain sort of freedom of choice, the freedom that makes it possible to do fine and generous actions for others. If things are complex even in the case of generosity, where we can easily imagine the transformation that removes the virtue, they are surely far more so in the cases of justice and courage. And we would need a far more detailed description than Marx ever gives us of the form of life under communism, before we could even begin to see whether it would in fact transform things where these virtues are concerned, and whether it would or would not introduce new problems and limitations in their place.

In general it seems that all forms of life, including the imagined life of a god, contain boundaries and limits.[47] All structures, even that of putative limitlessness, are closed to something, cut off from something—say, in that case, from the specific value and beauty inherent in the struggle against limitation. Thus it does not appear that we will so easily get beyond the virtues. Nor does it seem to be so clearly a good thing for human life that we should.

8

The best conclusion to this sketch of an Aristotelian programme for virtue ethics was written by Aristotle himself, at the end of his discussion of human nature in *Nicomachean Ethics* I:

> So much for our outline sketch for the good. For it looks as if we have to draw an outline first, and fill it in later. It would seem to be open to anyone to take things further and to articulate the good parts of the sketch. And time is a good discoverer or ally in such things. That's how the sciences have progressed as well: it is open to anyone to supply what is lacking. (*NE* 1098a 20-6)

NOTES

This paper was originally motivated by questions discussed at the WIDER Conference on Value and Technology, summer 1986, Helsinki. I would like to thank Steve and Frédérique Marglin for provoking some of these arguments, with hardly any of which they will agree. I would also like to thank Dan Brock for his helpful comments, Amartya Sen for many discussions of the issues, and the participants in the WIDER conference for their helpful questions and comments. Earlier versions of the paper were presented at the University of New Hampshire and at Villanova University; I am grateful to the audiences on those occasions for stimulating discussion. An earlier version of the paper was published in *Midwest Studies in Philosophy*, 1988.

1. A. MacIntyre, *After Virtue* (Notre Dame, IN, 1981); P. Foot, *Virtues and Vices* (Los Angeles, 1978); B. Williams, *Ethics and the Limits of Philosophy* (Cambridge, MA,

1985) and Tanner Lectures, Harvard, 1983. See also M. Walzer, *Spheres of Justice* (New York, 1983) and Tanner Lectures, Harvard, 1985.

2. For examples of this, see Nussbaum, "Nature, Function, and Capability: Aristotle on Political Distribution," circulated as a WIDER working paper, and in *Oxford Studies in Ancient Philosophy*, 1988, and also, in an expanded version, in the Proceedings of the 12th Symposium Aristotelicum.

3. See, for example, Williams, *Ethics and the Limits*, 34–36; Stuart Hampshire, *Morality and Conflict* (Cambridge, MA, 1983), 150 ff.

4. For "nameless" virtues and vices, see *NE* 1107b1–2, 1107b8, 1107b30–31, 1108a17, 1119a10–11, 1126b20, 1127a12, 1127a14; for recognition of the unsatisfactoriness of names given, see 1107b8, 1108a5–6, 1108a20 ff. The two categories are largely overlapping, on account of the general principles enunciated at 1108a16–19, that where there is no name a name should be given, unsatisfactory or not.

5. It should be noted that this emphasis on spheres of experience is not present in the *Eudemian Ethics*, which begins with a list of virtues and vices. This seems to me a sign that that treatise expresses a more primitive stage of Aristotle's thought on the virtues—whether earlier or not.

6. For statements with *peri*, connecting virtues with spheres of life, see 1115a6–7, 1117a29–30, 1117b25, 27, 1119b23, 1122a19, 1122b34, 1125b26, 1126b13; and *NE* 2.7 throughout. See also the related usages at 1126b11, 1127b32.

7. My list here inserts justice in a place of prominence. (In the *NE* it is treated separately, after all the other virtues, and the introductory list defers it for that later examination.) I have also added at the end of the list categories corresponding to the various intellectual virtues discussed in *NE* 6, and also to *phronesis* or practical wisdom, discussed in 6 as well. Otherwise the order and wording of my list closely follows 2.7, which gives the program for the more detailed analyses of 3.5–4.

8. For a longer account of this, with references to the literature and to related philosophical discussions, see Nussbaum, *The Fragility of Goodness* (Cambridge, MA, 1986), chap. 8.

9. Aristotle does not worry about questions of translation in articulating this idea; for some worries about this, and an Aristotelian response, see below sections IV and VI.

10. *Posterior Analytics*, 2.8, 93a21 ff.; see *Fragility*, chap. 8.

11. Heraclitus, fragment DK B23; see Nussbaum, "*Psuche* in Heraclitus, II," *Phronesis* 17 (1972): 153–70.

12. See *Politics* 1.2. 1253a1–18; that discussion does not deny the virtues to gods explicitly, but this denial is explicit at *NE* 1145a25–7 and 1178b10 ff.

13. Aristotle does not make the connection with his account of language explicit, but his project is one of defining the virtues, and we would expect him to keep his general view of defining in mind in this context. A similar idea about the virtues, and experience of a certain sort as a possible basis for a non-relative account, is developed, without reference to Aristotle, in a review of P. Foot's *Virtues and Vices* by N. Sturgeon, *Journal of Philosophy* 81 (1984): 326–33.

14. 1108a5, where Aristotle says that the virtues and the corresponding person are "pretty much nameless," and says "Let us call . . " when he introduces the names. See also 1125b29, 1126a3–4.

15. See John Procope, *Magnanimity* (1987); also R.-A. Gauthier, *Magnanimité* (Paris, 1951).

16. See, for example, *The Social Construction of the Emotions*, edited by Rom Harré (Oxford, 1986).

17. See Nussbaum, *Aristotle's De Motu Animalium* (Princeton, NJ, 1976), notes on chap. 6, and *Fragility*, chap. 9.

18. A detailed study of the treatment of these ideas in the three major Hellenistic schools was presented in Nussbaum, *The Therapy of Desire: Theory and Practice in Hellenistic Ethics*, The Martin Classical Lectures 1986, (Princeton, 1994).

19. The relevant texts are discussed in Nussbaum, *The Therapy*, chaps. 4–6. See also Nussbaum, "Therapeutic Arguments: Epicurus and Aristotle," in *The Norms of Nature*, edited by M. Schofield and G. Striker (Cambridge, 1986), 31–74.

20. M. Foucault, *Histoire de la sexualité*, vols. 2 and 3 (Paris, 1984).

21. See the papers by D. Halperin and J. Winkler in *Before Sexuality*, edited by D. Halperin, J. Winkler, and F. Zeitlin, (Princeton, 1990).

22. The evidence for this part of the Stoic view is discussed in Nussbaum, *The Therapy*.

23. *Politics* 1263b11 ff.

24. For a discussion of the relevant passages, see S. Lukes, *Marxism and Morality* (Oxford, 1987). For an acute discussion of these issues I am indebted to an exchange between Alan Ryan and Stephen Lukes at the Oxford Philosophical Society, March 1987.

25. *Fragility*, chap. 8, and "Internal Criticism and Indian Rationalist Traditions," the latter coauthored with Amartya Sen, in *Relativism*, edited by M. Krausz (Notre Dame, IN, 1988) and a WIDER Working Paper.

26. See *Fragility*, chap. 12.

27. *Fragility*, chap. 10; "The Discernment of Perception," *Proceedings of the Boston Area Colloquium in Ancient Philosophy* 1 (1985): 151–201; "Finely Aware and Richly Responsible: Moral Awareness and the Moral Task of Literature," *Journal of Philosophy* 82 (1985): 516–29, reprinted in expanded form in *Philosophy and the Question of Literature*, edited by A. Cascardi (Baltimore, 1987).

28. I believe, however, that some morally relevant features, in the Aristotelian view, may be features that are not, even in principle, replicable in another context. See "The Discernment," and *Fragility*, chap. 10.

29. Martha Chen, *A Quiet Revolution* (Dhaka, Bangladesh, 1986).

30. Chen, *A Quiet Revolution*, ix.

31. Cited in Chen, *A Quiet Revolution*, 4–5. Chen stresses that one important factor in this later success was that the group had no dogmatic adherence to an abstract theory of development, but had a flexible and situation-guided approach.

32. See H. Putnam, *Reason, Truth, and History* (Cambridge, 1981); *The Many Faces of Realism*, The Carus Lectures (LaSalle, Ill., 1987); and *Meaning and the Moral Sciences* (London, 1979); N. Goodman, *Languages of Art* (Indianapolis, 1968) and *Ways of World-Making* (Indianapolis, 1978); D. Davidson, *Inquiries into Truth and Interpretation* (Oxford, 1984).

33. On his debt to Kant, see Putnam, *The Many Faces*; on Aristotle's "internal realism," see Nussbaum, *Fragility*, chap. 8.

34. C. Abeysekera, paper presented at Value and Technology Conference, WIDER 1986.

35. Foucault, *Histoire,* vol. 2, preface.

36. This paragraph expands remarks made in a commentary on papers by D. Halperin and J. Winkler at the conference on "Homosexuality in History and Culture" at Brown University, February 1987. The combination of historically sensitive analysis with cultural criticism was forcefully developed at the same conference in Henry Abelove's "Is Gay History Possible?," forthcoming.

37. C. Gopalan, "Undernutrition: Measurement and Implications," paper prepared for the WIDER Conference on Poverty, Undernutrition, and Living Standards, Helsinki, 27–31 July 1987, and forthcoming in the volume of Proceedings, edited by S. Osmani.

38. *Metaphysics* 1.1.

39. See Nussbaum, "Nature, Function, and Capability," where this Aristotelian view is compared with Marx's views on human functioning.

40. M. Klein, in Postscript to "Our Adult World and Its Roots in Infancy," in *Envy, Gratitude and Other Works 1946–1963* (London, 1984), 247–63.

41. See Nussbaum, "Aristotelian Social Democracy," in *Liberalism and the Good,* ed. R. B. Douglass (New York, 1990), for a slightly longer list, including discussion of our relationship to other species and to the world of nature. It is very interesting to notice that three other lists in that volume, prepared independently, contain almost the same items as this one: Dan Brock's list of basic human functions used in quality of life measures in medical ethics; Erik Allardt's enumeration of the functions observed by Finnish social scientists; and Robert Erikson's list of functions measured by the Swedish group. Only the last two may show mutual influence. So much independent convergence testifies to the ubiquity of these concerns and to their importance.

42. See note 2 above.

43. See note 41 above.

44. "Aristotle on Human Nature and the Foundations of Ethics," in *World, Mind, and Ethics,* edited by R. Harrison and J. Altham (Cambridge, 1995). This paper will be a WIDER Working Paper.

45. Cf. *NE* 1159a 10–12, 1166a 18–23.

46. See note 44, above.

47. See *Fragility,* chap. 11.

15   *Tolerance, Pluralism, and Relativism*

GORDON GRAHAM

What is the connection between a belief in toleration, the fact of pluralism, and the metaethical thesis of relativism? It is commonly supposed that in some way or other these three go together and stand allied in opposition to moral absolutism, metaethical objectivism, and a failure to recognize cultural incommensurability. But what *precisely* are the connections here? Implicit in much moral argument, it seems to me, is the following picture.

On one side, the fact of pluralism supports the contentions of the relativist, and because relativism holds that unconditional truth cannot be ascribed to any one moral or political view, relativism in turn provides support for toleration; if no one belief or set of beliefs is superior to any other in terms of truth, all must be accorded equal respect.[1] Conversely, an objectivist metaethics implies the endorsement of just one set of proscriptions and prescriptions as true, which are thus regarded as absolutely forbidden or required. This in turn legitimizes suppressing other erroneous views. Thus a belief in toleration requires us to subscribe to relativism; conversely, the rejection of relativism licenses suppressing moral variation on the general ground that "error has no rights."

In this essay I argue that none of these connections holds and that, contrary to common belief, it is subscription to objectivism that sits best with a belief in toleration. We begin with objectivity and absolutism.

I

Is an objectivist in ethics committed to moral absolutism? By moral absolutism I mean the belief that there are some action types that ought never to be performed, irrespective of context or consequence. Just what these actions are will vary, of course, according to specific moral codes. Some, like Kant, might hold that it is always and everywhere wrong to lie, a view that is unlikely to attract very widespread support nowadays, but equally absolutist is the view that it is always and everywhere wrong to have sexual congress with children, a view more likely to resonate with the modern moral consciousness. A consequentialist will hold, by contrast, that we can always imagine circumstances in which the consequences of not performing such an act are so horrific that any consistent ethics must license its performance. Consequentialism is thus highly flexible and commends itself to many in large part just because of the unattractive inflexibility of absolutism. But whatever is to be said about the respective merits of each side of this comparison, it is not hard to see that the arguments to be adduced here are different from the arguments that rage between objectivist and relativist. The best-known form of consequentialism is utilitarianism, but utilitarian ethics is as objectivist as any ethics can be. Because it holds that the rightness or wrongness of an action is a function of the happiness it produces or fails to produce, and because consequences for happiness are in principle empirically determinable, whether an action is right or wrong is, for utilitarianism, a question of empirical truth and falsehood. If there are difficulties with the notion of happiness, the same point can be made about the variety of utilitarianism that operates with preference satisfaction; what the relevant preferences are and whether they are satisfied or not are empirically determinable questions. But if this is correct, it follows that objectivism does not imply absolutism, because utilitarianism combines objectivism and the rejection of absolutism.

There are, it is true, complications here. A question arises as to whether the judgment that an action is right or wrong is to be based on estimated likely consequences or on a retrospective assessment of actual consequences. This is a very important issue but, depending on what we say about the estimation of probabilities, it need not affect the general point about separating absolutism and objectivism. Whether we are talking about actual or likely consequences, the determination of right and wrong can still be construed as an empirical question.

A further and more troubling question arises over whether utilitarian ethics is empirical (and hence objectivist), or for that matter consequentialist, all the way down, so to speak. What about its fundamental principle, "The best action is that which maximizes happiness"; does this admit of truth or falsity? David O. Brink has argued that an objectivist construal of utilitarianism is not only possible but attractive, and he calls on naturalism and coherentism to sustain this view.[2] In doing so, he is arguing against the persuasive lines of thought developed by Williams, Nagel, and Taylor, part of whose object is to argue against the impartialism that this seems to imply. But even if we side with them and accept their reservations, the main point I am making is again unaffected. It is not the fact, if it is one, that at bottom utilitarianism must rest on a subjective commitment that makes it nonabsolutist, but the fact that its basic principle characterizes a *class* of actions and not an action *type*.

This conclusion rests on a slightly contentious interpretation of "absolutism."[3] But clearly the labels we use are not a matter of fundamental importance. We can even say, if we like, that utilitarianism is absolutist with respect to this one fundamental principle (meaning by absolutism here that it admits of no qualification), but, unlike Kantian deontology, it still allows for the correctness of any specific course of action. Of course, "those that maximize the best consequences" picks out a kind of action, as does "those that take five minutes to complete," but there is still a distinction to be drawn between types of action and classes of action, otherwise the dispute between deontologists could not even be stated. In terms of this distinction and my use of the term, consequentialism is nonabsolutist. In short, whether we hold that utilitarianism is an objectivist ethics through and through, the contrast with absolutism as I have characterized it still holds.

If this is correct, the first connection in the familiar picture I am examining fails; although they commonly go together, there is no necessary link between absolutism and objectivism.

II

Equally specious is any supposed connection between relativism and toleration. Indeed, as Nietzsche's writings demonstrate, even radical subjectivism need not issue in toleration. Nietzsche believes realism and arguably objectivism in ethics to be an illusion, but this leads him not to the conclusion that all moral views are worthy of equal respect, but that in matters of the moral will might is right (though not, of course, *objectively* right). If there is no truth, what other mark of discrimination or superiority can there be but the brute assertion of a heroic will? Thus Nietzsche supposes, with Thrasymachus in the *Republic,* that in matters of value justice cannot be more than the assertion of the will of the stronger, or perhaps, in view of the possible variations in interpretation that Nietzsche's deliberately suggestive rather than systematic thought allows, we should follow Thomas Hurka in rejecting the straightforwardly egoistic account and say that perfection lies in the assertion of the heroic will.[4] Against this background, it seems implausible to expect either the Nietzschean Übermensch or the Thrasymachean ruler to be models of toleration. It is true that in places Nietzsche seems to suggest that the true Übermensch will be so supremely confident in his own will that he can afford to tolerate the wills and beliefs of lesser beings. Indeed, at least on occasion, tolerance might be thought to be the very mark of his strength of will. But it is evident that this is not a logical requirement. There is nothing inconsistent in an expression of dominant will through the suppression of others, and the fact that this is a more natural reading of superiority might explain the ease with which connections have been forged between Nietzsche's philosophy and the creeds of Nazism.

In similar fashion, accepting cultural relativism could result in intolerance. Mussolini (or Gentile) believed that war, not truth or reason, was the adjudicator between cultures. This view is not familiar among, or likely to commend itself to, many modern cultural relativists, but it is nonetheless consistent. Respect in the sense of toleration is only one attitude among many that can accompany the perception of cultural incommensurability, and truth is not the only criterion by which cultures can be judged. Those who hold that there is no truth in these matters might still regard some cultures as admirable and others as contemptible, and to be defended or suppressed for these reasons. Whether we take a subjectivist or relativist reading of "admirable" and "contemptible" here is of no significance. Slav culture might appear contemptible only to those of an Aryan culture, but that is still the way they see it. Brink makes this point effectively:

> [N]either noncognitivism nor relativism seems to have any special commitment to tolerance. If no one moral judgement is more correct than another, how can it be that I should be tolerant? Someone with well informed and consistent attitudes might be intolerant, and neither the noncognitivist nor the relativist can complain that his attitude is mistaken (although, of course, many noncognitivists and relativists will hold different attitudes and may express them in his presence). Thus, one person's intolerance is no less justified than the tolerance of others, on these antirealist claims, and the acceptance of these antirealist claims provides no reason for the intolerant person to change his attitude.[5]

Conversely, it is clear that objectivism as such requires no accompanying intolerance. Being true of objectivism, this is obviously true of moral objectivism also, but it is perhaps easier to make the point in other spheres. Take, for instance, mathematics. The practice of mathematics encourages criticism and dispute at the higher levels. The interpretation of mathematics, like the interpretation of morality, admits of disagreement between realists and intuitionists, but whichever side we take it is clear that we must give some account of the possibility of criticism, dispute, and resolution, because these are facts about the practice we are seeking to understand. A thoroughgoing realist about mathematics can consistently hold that there is a transcendent truth in these matters but that proof and refutation of the sort identified by intuitionism are the sole methods of arriving at it. Realism can also hold that dispute and disagreement must, in the interests of truth, be tolerated, even that it must be encouraged. Similarly, those, like Popper, who take a falsificationist view of natural science might think that progress toward the truth depends on conjecture and refutation, and so commitment to the practice of scientific investigation, if it does not depend on tolerating any and every view, nonetheless depends on tolerating many views that are held to be erroneous.

So, too, with morality. We could hold, as Mill did, that tolerating the public expression of what we believe to be error is an ineliminable part of the public process of arriving at what we hold to be the truth. This is a point to which I will return, but it is worth observing here perhaps that this sort of endorsement of toleration is more than the recognition that error has rights. Whether error has rights or not, if the possibility of error is a necessary accompaniment to the possibility of achieving truth, then the pursuit of truth has, so to speak, a self-interested motive in tolerating expressions of error.

III

It seems then that objectivism and toleration not only are consistent but can go together, even that they must go together. There are two ways we might read this: that a belief in objectivism is intelligible only alongside a belief in toleration, or that a belief in the virtues of toleration is intelligible only against a background of objectivism. We have seen some support for both contentions, it seems to me, but the brief argument I have adduced might not be regarded as a very strong one, because the parallels among science, mathematics, and morality I have been using are contentious. Indeed, to some it is a very superficial one, because a closer look at the facts reveals more differences than similarities. Famously, this is the view of J. L. Mackie in *Ethics: Inventing Right and Wrong,* where he says,

> [I]t is not the mere existence of disagreement that tells against the objectivity of values. Disagreement on questions in history or biography or cosmology does not show that there are no objective issues in these fields for investigators to disagree about. But such scientific disagreement results from speculative inferences or explanatory hypotheses based on inadequate evidence, and it is hardly plausible to interpret moral disagreement in the same way. Disagreement about moral codes seems to reflect people's adherence to and participation in different ways of life. The causal connection seems to be mainly that way round: it is that people approve of monogamy because they participate in a monogamous way of life rather than that they participate in a monogamous way of life because they approve of monogamy. . . .
>   . . . In short, the argument from relativity has some force simply because the actual variations in the moral codes are more readily explained by the hypothesis that they reflect ways of life than that they express perceptions, most of them seriously inadequate and badly distorted.[6]

This argument has been widely rehearsed in favor of subjectivism or some related thesis that right and wrong are invented rather than discovered. And yet it seems to me a very weak one. To begin with, Mackie supposes that the extent of moral disagreement is more striking than disagreement in other spheres. This can be contested on the grounds that like is not being compared with like; Peter Railton makes this point. Accepting, with Mackie, that "'the phenomenon of moral disagreement' refers not to a philosophical thesis about the impossibility of rational resolution in ethics but to the actual character and extent of moral disagreement," he says,

> It is for various reasons easy to overstate the extent and depth of moral disagreement. Points of moral disagreement tend to make for social conflict, which is more conspicuous than humdrum social peace. And though we sometimes call virtually any social norms "moral," this does not mean that we really consider these norms to be serious competitors for moral standing in our communities. If, in any area of inquiry, including empirical science, we were to survey not only all serious competitors, but also all views which cannot be refuted, or whose proponents could not be convinced on non-

question-begging grounds to share our view, we would find that area riven
with deep and irremediable disagreement.[7]

But Mackie does not rely solely on the simple *observation* of moral disagreement. The heart of his argument also rests on the *explanation* of this
"fact." Let us suppose that he is correct in his ambitious sociological generalization about the nature and genesis of moral belief. What is explained by this
generalization, if anything is, is the state of moral consciousness on the part
of the members of a culture. But unless we straight-forwardly invoke the
genetic fallacy, which mistakenly tries to reason about the truth and falsehood of beliefs on the basis of their causal origin, there is not much to be
drawn from the truth of this generalization. Indeed, an objectivist might
argue that it is precisely a tendency on the part of human beings to base their
beliefs uncritically on received practices that explains the widespread existence of moral error and distortion. But so long as we can point to a long-term
underlying convergence between cultures, which plausibly we can, we can
continue to hold that the facts of moral variation are wholly consistent with a
realistic objectivism.

   This point needs some amplification perhaps. It is true that there is considerable variation between moral and religious practices over place and time.
Let us suppose that, as in most other spheres, the first efforts of humans in
morality and religion are fumbling and that among human beings there is
indeed a fundamental uncritical conservatism. If so, we will expect the widespread existence of entrenched, but rationally indefensible positions. But so
long as we can detect emergent norms that slowly command universal assent,
as we can in the rejection of human sacrifice and slavery, for instance, we will
have explained all the facts that Mackie seeks to explain without recourse to
the metaethical thesis that morality is a matter of human invention.

   Mackie himself observes that the existence of moral reformers is another
fact that metaethics must accommodate. He suggests that we can understand
moral reform as the pursuit of greater consistency among the elements of a
morality. But this can at best be only part of the story. Why should the pursuit
of greater consistency carry any force if it is not a part of a general endeavor
to make our beliefs and practices conform with universal, that is nonrelativistic, standards of rationality? A simple account of moral reformers is that
they apply the methods of reason all moral agents ought to apply, but which
few do. It is, admittedly, a further step to claim that these methods of reason
result in the apprehension of universally valid truth, but whether this is
really required for metaethical objectivism is a matter to which I will return.

   Before moving on, however, it might be valuable to take stock. I have
argued that though the ideas of pluralism, relativism, and toleration are commonly thought to be associated in some way, this is not so. If and when they
are, this is a purely contingent matter, and, as far as the beliefs and concepts
these ideas invoke are concerned, there are no necessary links between them.
Conversely, metaethical objectivism is a position quite distinct from moral
absolutism and can in fact be quite intimately connected with toleration. The

parallel with mathematics and science suggests this, but it is a parallel that many writers, including John Mackie, have rejected. But Mackie's argument from relativity, I have claimed, is a very weak one, and there is more to be said for the thesis that moral variation is to be explained as the outcome of distorted perceptions that are uncritically held than he allows.

This argument from relativity is not the only one Mackie employs. Equally well known is his "argument from queerness," according to which the postulation of moral and evaluative properties generally is the postulation of properties of a very peculiar kind, properties that, unlike the properties history and science deal with, would have to have the unerring ability to motivate. This is generally known as an argument, but it seems to me more in the way of an expression of puzzlement and assertion. But something more of an argument with a similar conclusion is to be found in Gilbert Harman's *Nature of Morality:*

> [O]bservation plays a role in science that it does not seem to play in ethics. The difference is that you need to make assumptions about certain physical facts to explain the occurrence of the observations that support a scientific theory, but you do not seem to make assumptions about any moral facts to explain the occurrence of so-called moral observations. . . . In the moral case, it would seem that you need only make assumptions about the psychology or moral sensibility of the person making the moral observation. In the scientific case, theory is tested against the world. . . .
>
> The observation of an event can provide observational evidence for or against a scientific theory in the sense that the truth of that observation can be relevant to a reasonable explanation of why that observation was made. A moral observation does not seem, in the same sense, to be observational evidence for or against any moral theory, since the truth or falsity of the moral observation seems to be completely irrelevant to any reasonable explanation of why that observation was made.[8]

Harman considers as a separate question whether there is a parallel between ethics and mathematics, but he concludes that modern mathematics and physics cannot be separated and that the difference between moral theories and observational theories still stands.

In explaining the observations that support a physical theory, scientists typically appeal to mathematical principles. On the other hand, one never seems to need to appeal in this way to moral principles. Because an observation is evidence for what best explains it, and because mathematics often figures in the explanations of scientific observations, there is indirect observational evidence for mathematics.[9]

Harman's contentions about the testability of moral claims have been the subject of extended discussion, especially between him and Nicholas Sturgeon, and it is instructive to see just how hard it is to state precisely the "obvious" distinction that Harman is invoking.[10] However, let us suppose that what he claims is broadly correct, that moral beliefs and principles are not rooted in empirical observation, that their "truth" does not figure in causal explanations of behavior except by way of some sort of reductionism, and that what people commonly refer to as "moral observations" can be given a wholly emotivist interpretation. A parallel with science and mathematics relevant to the concerns of this essay might nevertheless remain. Rawls has made the method of "reflective equilibrium" a familiar one in moral philosophy. This is the method by which moral principles are tested against considered moral judgments and mutual adjustments are made to both judgments and principles until an equilibrium between the two is arrived at. It is well known, however, that in invoking this method in ethics Rawls is merely deploying a device that Goodman earlier detected at work in both science and logic, which is to say, the pursuit of consistency between general principles of logic and particular judgments of validity.[11] And the pursuit of such consistency is, arguably, a requirement of rationality. The fact that the general statements we operate with are not empirical hypotheses and our particular judgments are not observation statements could mean, as emotivists allege, that moral beliefs cannot be "tested against the world," but it does not follow that there are not other methods of testing them, or that these other methods are any less applications of rationality.[12]

It has been pointed out by many writers, however, that the method of equilibrium cannot be guaranteed to produce just one right answer in any matter under dispute, and even that it is consistent with there being indefinitely many equally good answers. Obviously, if and when this is the case, the pursuit of reflective equilibrium is powerless as a method of rationally resolving disputes. But equally obviously, whether this is true or not is a matter that will vary according to the particular case and context. There is no reason to believe a priori that the method will never produce good resolutions. Moreover, there is no requirement on those who employ it to employ it alone. Indeed, it is hard to see how it could be used anywhere to any effect entirely on its own.

Consider, for instance, the examination of a historical hypothesis. The proposition that the Holocaust never took place requires criticism and refutation by reference to all the existing evidence, the significance of which is a matter of judgment. To begin with, there can be disagreement about what is to be regarded as "all the evidence," and in the second place, because every piece of evidence *can* be declared the result of misidentification, faulty memory, or deliberate falsification, the pursuit of consistency on its own cannot result in refutation. Nor can the true claim that observational evidence is in play be made to rescue it, for notoriously in history every piece of evidence requires interpretation. But in this particular case, consistency can be preserved only by more and more improbable "explainings away." Past a certain point, such improbabilities and the concerted effort to make them fit together will be declared as "unreasonable" not because they introduce inconsistencies or involve false observations but because without such declarations, reasoning can accomplish nothing.

If this is correct, Harman's claims about the role of observation in science and in ethics are not entirely to the point. Unless there is some other ground, we must conclude that reason is no more or less powerful in ethics than in science or history. Of course, it will be claimed by many that the difference is this: the fundamental principles of ethics are culture-relative or subjective. But such a claim can hardly be brought to the defence of Mackie or Harman, because this was the conclusion their arguments were supposed to show.

IV

So far we have seen no good reason to accept the contention that moral thinking is radically different from the sort of thinking that goes on in history or science. All thought must operate with standards of reasonableness that cannot be wholly accommodated by standards of accurate observation and valid deduction, so to point to the fact that moral reasoning does not seem to involve the first of these directly is not to locate as radical a difference as might be supposed.

For all that, many people still share Mackie's puzzlement over the "queerness" of moral properties. This puzzlement arises, it will be recalled, from the suggestion that mere perceptible properties can motivate. The puzzlement need not generate a problem for moral objectivism, however, if we first acknowledge, with Mackie, that it is a mistake to construe values in general and moral values in particular as "part of the fabric of the universe." Objectivism can take other forms than Platonic-style ontology, and abandoning the ontology does not prevent us from thinking of evaluative considerations as deriving from objectively defensible principles of practical reason. Indeed, although the relations between metaphysics and epistemology are complex, it does seem possible to give a purely epistemological (as opposed to ontological) reading of all the metaethical positions with which we have been concerned. The heart of at least one dispute in this area is that, at some point or other, the power of reason to decide on questions of right and wrong runs out. Relativists and subjectivists can be construed as disagreeing about where this point is, but both contend, against realists and objectivists, that there is some such point. We might thus characterize the four positions as follows:

1. Subjectivism holds that for no evaluative question is there a right answer, or even a better answer. People might in fact agree on some evaluative matters, but this agreement is at most intersubjective. At any and every point, irresolvable subjective differences can arise.

2. Relativism holds that for some evaluative questions there is no right answer. At the level of particular judgments between people operating within some shared framework, we can apply the notions of correct and incorrect. But when evaluative disputes arise, or seem to arise, between conceptual frameworks, they are rationally irresolvable. These conceptual frameworks, it might be worth noting, need not define distinct cultures. Gallie's well-known claims about essentially contested concepts, such as socialism or Christianity, make him a relativist in my sense, even though

neither socialism nor Christianity can be regarded as a distinct and discrete culture.

3. Realism holds, aside from its ontological claims, that for all evaluative questions there is a right answer. In any particular case, we could fail to find it, but whether we do or not there is in every case a transcendent truth of the matter.

4. Objectivism holds that for any evaluative question there is in principle the possibility of a right answer. There is no class or level of evaluative dispute that the exercise of reason cannot in principle resolve.

These labels—subjectivism, relativism, and so on—are used here for convenience. I do not mean to suggest that the characterizations capture all the variations that have gone by these names or even that they capture those most frequently so called. Indeed, some writers, notably Geoffrey Sayre-McCord, expressly distinguish among these terms in ways that mark out the various positions rather differently.[13] But in my view, nothing much turns on labels, and, defined as I have defined them, they do represent a spectrum on which to place metaethical theories according to the degree to which they extend the scope of reason. Given its place on *this* spectrum, it seems to me, there is scope to defend objectivism in something like the way that Kant defends the postulation of human freedom.

The issue of freedom versus determinism, it will be recalled, is one of Kant's antinomies. Determinism seems the inescapable implication if human beings are regarded as bodies subject to physical laws; regarded as rationally choosing agents, on the other hand, they appear to be free of causal determination. In the final section of *The Groundwork to the Metaphysic of Morals,* Kant allows that he cannot offer a rational resolution of this antinomy. But he also argues that, from the point of view of practical reason, such a resolution is not needed, because the postulation of freedom of the will is an inescapable presupposition of deliberation. That is to say, even if we accept the *metaphysical* thesis of determinism, faced with alternative courses of action, we still have to go through a process of deliberation and choice. The thesis of determinism, we might say, is quite worthless from the point of view of human beings as deliberative choosers.

It seems to me that we can similarly represent the relativist/objectivist dispute as a contest between rival postulations and adjudicate between them in the following way: on which principle can we sensibly engage in the practice of reasoning through dialectic and deliberation? By reasoning here, I mean something rather general, not the application of formalizable systems of induction and deduction but merely the taking of thought with a view to arriving at a better view or opinion. Clearly, subjectivism as characterized renders such reasoning about matters of value otiose; if we can say at the outset that there are no better or worse answers in this case, we cannot sensibly deliberate about finding them. Of course, as the emotivists observed, this does not mean that there is nothing to *say;* expression and propagation of opinion is still a possibility. But it does mean that what we say to each other is not part of a reflective discovery but of a moral shouting match. In the terminology Kant uses in the *Critique of Judgement,* quarreling is possible but disputing is not. On the subjectivist view, then, any attempt at deliberation is misguided. But as communicating agents, we still have to decide what to say, and this in turn raises the question of what it would be best to say. From the point of view of the deliberator, therefore, the a priori claim that there are never any right answers is of as little interest or use as a belief in metaphysical determinism is to someone faced with a dinner menu.

On the relativist view, by contrast, there are some right answers to be found by reflection. What relativism does not tell us, however, except in abstract terms ("at the boundaries of conceptual schemes," say), is just where the power of reason runs out. Once we actually engage in deliberative reflection, therefore, relativism, even if true, never actually gives us reason to stop. If we can go on to deliberate fruitfully, the relevant boundaries have not been reached, and if we cannot, as yet, relativism gives us no reason to suppose that we never will. Once more, whether relativism is true or false it cannot figure in the practical postulates of the deliberating agent.

Neither can realism. Even if there are indeed transcendentally true answers to all evaluative questions, this, too, is an a priori assertion of no interest from the deliberative point whose concern is not to know whether there is an answer or not, but whether it can be found.

To all three, the response of the deliberative reasoner must be the same: None gives any good reason to engage in reasoning other than open-mindedly, without assuming that there is, or is not, an answer that deliberative reasoning can bring us to. This just is the presupposition of objectivism as I characterized it, the belief that for any evaluative question there could be a right answer and that we always have reason to try and find it.

V

I have been arguing that the practice of practical deliberation and social dialectic gives us reason, as reasoners, to accept objectivism, understood as an epistemological rather than an ontological account of evaluation, in preference to other metaethics. Objectivism as I have characterized it can alone adequately account for practical reason from the point of view of practical reason itself. However, even if this is accepted, the connection with toleration might remain obscure. As I noted earlier, there are two possibilities here: it might be claimed that a belief in objectivism implies a belief in toleration, or that a belief in the virtue of toleration requires subscription to objectivism. The first of these, it seems to me, is too strong, so let us consider the second.

Brink remarks, "There is no special affinity between realism and intolerance or antirealism and intolerance. If anything, the appropriate sort of commitment to tolerance seems to presuppose the truth of moral realism."[14] His use of the term "realism" differs from mine, but the thought is largely the same, so the task here is to dispel, or at least abate, the uncertainty implied in the "if anything." Why should I tolerate, still less *believe* in tolerating, the opinions of others when I hold their opinions to be false or erroneous? One obvious answer, the answer that historically lies at the heart of the belief in religious toleration, is voluntarism, the claim that a large measure of the value that attaches to religious and moral belief arises from individuals coming to believe and accept moral and religious truths *for themselves*. Belief that is induced or coerced is not worth having, on one's own part or on the part of fellow believers. This is an argument that Luther uses and, more famously after him, Locke.[15] But rather obviously, the intelligibility of this defence arises from there *being* religious truth and error and from there actually being different ways of the mind's arriving at it. If all such beliefs are subjective or in the end relative to time and place, all that can matter is convergence and conformity for some other end—social cohesion or the maintenance of public order. It does not matter whether this is brought about by coercion or propaganda; no value attaches to voluntarism. If so, it is in this way that the connection between objectivism and toleration is to be made; the justification of toleration lies in voluntarism, and voluntarism is intelligible only on the presumption of objectivism.

What about the other way around? Cannot a belief in objectivism be consistent with an attitude of intolerance? The short answer is "yes," clearly, because there is no logical incompatibility between the belief that one's own beliefs are true and intolerance of those that conflict with them. Yet there is still something to be said, along the lines that Mill follows in *On Liberty.* If we think that the emergence of truth requires a process of conjecture and refutation and further think, as Mill does, that the validity of moral, religious, and philosophical doctrines requires the constant challenge presented by false competitors, we will have to allow social space for *some* false conjectures. Only by doing so will our grasp of the truth and that of others remain "lively," Mill thinks; more important, only by allowing the possibility of tolerated false conjectures can we reasonably look for the avoidance of error and the emergence of new truths, because "The fatal tendency of mankind to leave off thinking about a thing when it is no longer doubtful, is the cause of half their errors."[16]

Mill's argument has often been vilified but does have some force, in my view. However, we should note in the first place that the necessity of tolerated error for the emergence of new knowledge is an empirical claim about the consequences of certain contingent conditions; it has long been held that God can reveal truths to us independently of any of our inquiries and if so, there is no logical necessity that knowledge of the truth be the outcome of inquiry. Whether this renders Mill's argument less compelling in the world as we know it, of course, is another matter. More important, even where we can show that toleration is a necessary concomitant of the emergence of truth and understanding, just what degree of toleration concern with the truth requires is uncertain.

First, even if true, the contention that acquiring knowledge requires tolerating error does not imply that all beliefs must be tolerated. Consistent with it is the view that beliefs that are so easily shown to be false or foolish that they never count as serious conjectures need not be tolerated. Thus, the attitude of the Christian believers in toleration to the "conjectures" of Nazism about financial conspiracy among the Jews, or the incoherencies of modern-day American witchcraft ("wickism"), can be quite different from their attitudes to the "conjectures" of Islam or Judaism consistent with Mill's argument and with a belief in objectivism. Here there is an easy parallel with other spheres, one alluded to by Railton in the passage quoted above: though medical progress requires the toleration of false conjectures, many "folk" remedies need be given no hearing, though which these are is a different and more difficult question.

Second, if the defence of toleration for the sake of truth rests on a consequentialist argument about contingent conditions, it admits of trade-offs. That is to say, the emergence of truth and its perpetual validation are not the only social values we might hold. Others, such as protecting public order or social cohesion, could on occasion figure more prominently. Locke recognizes this in the *Letter on Toleration,* for, in the interest of public order, he thinks that toleration should stop short of atheism, just as a modern-day state might reasonably hold that certain varieties of Islamic fundamentalism ought not to be accorded the freedom and respect of other religious views. Whether this is a weakness in the argument for toleration, however, is uncertain, for it is hard to see that any social principles can be maintained that do not admit of any trade-offs.

There remains a final objection to be considered. It is parallel to one that has frequently been brought against Kant's defence of freedom, namely, that the argument presupposes what it is supposed to show. Kant's defence of freedom assumes that we are, in one respect at least, rational agents. But the "fact" of our rational agency is dependent on the falsehood of metaphysical determinism. If determinism is true, then rational agency is an illusion and there is no point of view from which Kant's transcendental argument can be made. Similarly, the argument I have mounted in favor of objectivism appeals to the "fact" that there is a practice of deliberative reason. But if radical subjectivism is true, this is false and any appearance to the contrary an illusion. How is this objection to be countered?

Commentators have found Kant's argument plausible to varying degrees, but in my view there is an incontestable truth in the claim that the point of view of action is inescapable for us as human beings. Even if it is an illusion, it is one we have no choice but to indulge, and, given the undecidability of the metaphysical question, given, that is to say, that it really is an antinomy, this gives us reason to make our own behavior intelligible by the presupposition of freedom. In a similar fashion, the possibility of deliberation is an ever-present one for us. Deliberation arises from a socially sustained pressure to produce reasons for our beliefs and desires. Given this fact, whether or not it is based on some grand delusion, there is pressure to give reasons for the reason giving. It is this that generates the argument I have deployed. Certainly, the argument as I have set it out amounts to less than an a priori proof, but given the general absence of such proofs in this area, it might nonetheless be the best that we can hope for.

VI

I have been arguing, contrary to common opinion, that we can forge more satisfactory connections between toleration and objectivism than with any of its rival metaethics. The connection that takes us from a belief in the value of toleration to a subscription to objectivism as I have construed it is traceable and substantial; the connection from the plausibility of objectivism to the merits of toleration is less so. But sufficient has been said, I hope, to throw doubt on associations and dichotomies whose apparent strength lies in their being largely unquestioned.[17]

NOTES

1. This view is expressly endorsed by David Wong in *Moral Relativity* (Berkeley: University of California Press, 1984), chap. 12.

2. David O. Brink, *Moral Realism and the Foundations of Ethics* (Cambridge and New York: Cambridge University Press, 1989), chap. 8.

3. For an alternative definition, see Gilbert Harman "What Is Moral Relativism?" in *Values and Morals,* ed. A. I. Goldman and Jaegwon Kim (Dordrecht: D. Reidel, 1978), pp. 143–61.

4. Thomas Hurka, *Perfectionism* (Oxford and New York: Oxford University Press, 1993), chap. 6.

5. Brink, p. 93

6. J. L. Mackie, *Ethics: Inventing Right and Wrong* (Harmondsworth: Penguin Books, 1977), pp. 36–37.

7. Peter Railton, "What the Non-Cognitivist Helps Us to See, the Naturalist Must Help Us to Explain," in *Reality, Representation and Projection,* ed. Haldane and Wright (New York: Oxford University Press, 1993), pp. 281–82.

8. Gilbert Harman, *The Nature of Morality* (New York: Oxford University Press, 1977), pp. 6–7.

9. Ibid., p. 10.

10. See especially Gilbert Harman, "Moral Explanations of Natural Facts—Can Moral Claims Be Tested against Moral Reality?" and the reply by Nicholas L. Sturgeon in *Spindel Conference 1986: Moral Realism, The Southern Journal of Philosophy,* ed. Norman Gillespie, vol. 24, supplement.

11. Nelson Goodman, *Fact, Fiction and Forecast,* 3d ed. Indianapolis, Ind.: Hackett, 1979).

12. It should be noted here that Harman, somewhat oddly perhaps, regards theories of practical reason as reductionist in his sense (see note 10 above). But even if this is so, they might still satisfactorily illustrate the possibility of objective rationality.

13. See Sayre-McCord, "The Many Moral Realisms," in *Spindel Conference 1986,* pp. 1–23. On Sayre-McCord's account, for example, subjectivism can attribute truth values to moral judgments, which my version of subjectivism cannot do.

14. Brink, p. 94.

15. See, for instance, "Secular Authority," in *Martin Luther: Selections from His Writings,* ed. John Dillenberger (New York: Anchor Books, 1961), pp. 363–402.

16. J. S. Mill, *On Liberty,* in *Three Essays* (Oxford and New York: Oxford University Press, 1975), p. 54.

17. I am grateful to my colleague Dr. Berys Gaut for many helpful comments on this essay.

16 *Ethics*

THOMAS NAGEL

I

Let me now turn to the question of whether moral reasoning is also fundamental and inescapable. Unlike logical or arithmetical reasoning, it often fails
to produce certainty, justified or unjustified. It is easily subject to distortion
by morally irrelevant factors, social and personal, as well as outright error. It
resembles empirical reason in not being reducible to a series of self-evident
steps.

I take it for granted that the objectivity of moral reasoning does not
depend on its having an external reference. There is no moral analogue of the
external world—a universe of moral facts that impinge on us causally. Even
if such a supposition made sense, it would not support the objectivity of
moral reasoning. Science, which this kind of reifying realism takes as its
model, doesn't derive its objective validity from the fact that it starts from
perception and other causal relations between us and the physical world. The
real work comes after that, in the form of active scientific reasoning, without
which no amount of causal impact on us by the external world would generate a belief in Newton's or Maxwell's or Einstein's theories, or the chemical
theory of elements and compounds, or molecular biology.

If we had rested content with the causal impact of the external world on
us, we'd still be at the level of sense perception. We can regard our scientific
beliefs as objectively true not because the external world causes us to have
them but because we are able to *arrive at* those beliefs by methods that have a
good claim to be reliable, by virtue of their success in selecting among rival
hypotheses that survive the best criticisms and questions we can throw at
them. Empirical confirmation plays a vital role in this process, but it cannot
do so without theory.

Moral thought is concerned not with the description and explanation of
what happens but with decisions and their justification. It is mainly because
we have no comparably uncontroversial and well-developed methods for
thinking about morality that a subjectivist position here is more credible than

Reprinted, by permission of the publisher and copyright holder, from Thomas Nagel, "Ethics,"
in Nagel, *The Last Word*, pp. 101–125. New York: Oxford University Press, 1997.

it is with regard to science. But just as there was no guarantee at the beginnings of cosmological and scientific speculation that we humans had the capacity to arrive at objective truth beyond the deliverances of sense-perception—that in pursuing it we were doing anything more than spinning collective fantasies— so there can be no decision in advance as to whether we are or are not talking about a real subject when we reflect and argue about morality. The answer must come from the results themselves. Only the effort to reason about moral- ity can show us whether it is possible—whether, in thinking about what to do and how to live, we can find methods, reasons, and principles whose validity does not have to be subjectively or relativistically qualified.

Since moral reasoning is a species of practical reasoning, its conclusions are desires, intentions, and actions, or feelings and convictions that can moti- vate desire, intention, and action. We want to know how to live, and why, and we want the answer in general terms, if possible. Hume famously believed that because a "passion" immune to rational assessment must underly every motive, there can be no such thing as specifically practical reason, nor specif- ically moral reason either. That is false, because while "passions" are the source of some reasons, other passions or desires are themselves motivated and/or justified by reasons that do not depend on still more basic desires. And I would contend that either the question whether one should have a cer- tain desire or the question whether, given that one has that desire, one should act on it, is always open to rational consideration.

The issue is whether the procedures of justification and criticism we employ in such reasoning, moral or merely practical, can be regarded finally as just something we do—a cultural or societal or even more broadly human collective practice, within which reasons come to an end. I believe that if we ask ourselves seriously how to respond to proposals for contextualization and relativistic detachment, they usually fail to convince. Although it is less clear than in some of the other areas we've discussed, attempts to get entirely outside of the object language of practical reasons, good and bad, right and wrong, and to see all such judgments as expressions of a contingent, nonob- jective perspective will eventually collapse before the independent force of the first-order judgments themselves.

II

Suppose someone says, for example, "You only believe in equal opportunity because you are a product of Western liberal society. If you had been brought up in a caste society or one in which the possibilities for men and women were radically unequal, you wouldn't have the moral convictions you have or accept as persuasive the moral arguments you now accept." The second, hypothetical sentence is probably true, but what about the first—specifically the "only"? In general, the fact that I wouldn't believe something if I hadn't learned it proves nothing about the status of the belief or its grounds. It may be impossible to explain the learning without invoking the content of the belief itself, and the reasons for its truth; and it may be clear that what I have learned is such that even if I hadn't learned it, it would still be true. The reason the genetic fallacy is a fallacy is that the explanation of a belief can sometimes confirm it.

To have any content, a subjectivist position must say more than that my moral convictions are my moral convictions. That, after all, is something we can all agree on. A meaningful subjectivism must say that they are *just* my moral convictions—or those of my moral community. It must *qualify* ordinary moral judgments in some way, must give them a self-consciously first-person (singular or plural) reading. That is the only type of antiobjectivist view that is worth arguing against or that it is even possible to disagree with.

But I believe it is impossible to come to rest with the observation that a belief in equality of opportunity, and a wish to diminish inherited inequalities, are merely expressions of our cultural tradition. True or false, those beliefs are essentially objective in intent. Perhaps they are wrong, but that too would be a nonrelative judgment. Faced with the fact that such values have gained currency only recently and not universally, one still has to try to decide whether they are right—whether one ought to continue to hold them. That question is not displaced by the information of contingency: The question remains, at the level of moral content, whether I would have been in error if I had accepted as natural, and therefore justified, the inequalities of a caste society, or a fairly rigid class system, or the orthodox subordination of women. It can take in additional facts as material for reflection, but the question of the relevance of those facts is inevitably a moral question: Do these cultural and historical variations and their causes tend to show that I and others have less reason than we had supposed to favor equality of opportunity? Presentation of an array of historically and culturally conditioned attitudes, including my own, does not disarm first-order moral judgment but simply gives it something more to work on—including information about influences on the formation of my convictions that may lead me to change them. But the relevance of such information is itself a matter for moral reasoning—about what are and are not good grounds for moral belief.

When one is faced with these real variations in practice and conviction, the requirement to put oneself in everyone's shoes when assessing social institutions—some version of universalizability—does not lose any of its persuasive force just because it is not universally recognized. It dominates the historical and anthropological data: Presented with the description of a traditional caste society, I have to ask myself whether its hereditary inequalities are justified, and there is no plausible alternative to considering the interests of all in trying to answer the question. If others feel differently, they must say why they find these cultural facts relevant—why they require some qualification to the objective moral claim. On both sides, it is a moral issue, and the only way to defend universalizability or equal opportunity against subjectivist qualification is by continuing the moral argument. It is a matter of understanding exactly what the subjectivist wants us to give up, and then asking whether the grounds for those judgments disappear in light of his observations.

In my opinion, someone who abandons or qualifies his basic methods of moral reasoning on historical or anthropological grounds alone is nearly as irrational as someone who abandons a mathematical belief on other than mathematical grounds. Even with all their uncertainties and liability to controversy and distortion, moral considerations occupy a position in the system of human thought that makes it illegitimate to subordinate them completely to anything else. Particular moral claims are constantly being discredited for all kinds of reasons, but moral considerations per se keep rising again to challenge in their own right any blanket attempt to displace, defuse, or subjectivize them.

This is an instance of the more general truth that the normative cannot be transcended by the descriptive. The question "What should I do?" like the question "What should I believe?" is always in order. It is always possible to think about the question in normative terms, and the process is not rendered pointless by any fact of a different kind—any desire or emotion or feeling, any habit or practice or convention, any contingent cultural or social background. Such things may in fact guide our actions, but it is always possible to take their relation to action as an object of further normative reflection and ask, "How should I act, given that these things are true of me or of my situation?"

The type of thought that generates answers to this question is practical reason. But, further, it is always possible for the question to take a specifically moral form, since one of the successor questions to which it leads is, "What should anyone in my situation do?"—and consideration of that question leads in turn to questions about what everyone should do, not only in this situation but more generally.

Such universal questions don't always have to be raised, and there is good reason in general to develop a way of living that makes it usually unnecessary to raise them. But if they are raised, as they always can be, they require an answer of the appropriate kind—even though the answer may be that in a case like this one may do as one likes. They cannot be ruled out of order by pointing to something more fundamental—psychological, cultural, or biological—that brings the request for justification to an end. Only a justification can bring the request for justifications to an end. Normative questions in general are not undercut or rendered idle by anything, even though particular normative answers may be. (Even when some putative justification is exposed as a rationalization, that implies that something else could be said about the justifiability or nonjustifiability of what was done.)

III

The point of view to defeat, in a defense of the reality of practical and moral reason, is in essence the Humean one. Although Hume was wrong to say that reason was fit only to serve as the slave of the passions, it is nevertheless true that there are desires and sentiments prior to reason that it is not appropriate for reason to evaluate—that it must simply treat as part of the raw material on which its judgments operate. The question then arises how pervasive such brute motivational data are, and whether some of them cannot perhaps be identified as the true sources of those grounds of action which are usually described as reasons. Hume's theory of the "calm" passions was designed to make this extension, and resisting it is not a simple matter—even if it is set in the context of a minimal framework of practical rationality stronger than Hume would have admitted.

If there is such a thing as practical reason, it does not simply dictate particular actions but, rather, governs the *relations* among actions, desires, and beliefs—just as theoretical reason governs the relations among beliefs and requires some specific material to work on. Prudential rationality, requiring uniformity in the weight accorded to desires and interests situated at different times in one's life, is an example—and the example about which Hume's skepticism is most implausible, when he says it is not contrary to reason "to prefer even my own acknowledged lesser good to my greater, and have a more ardent affection for the former than the latter."[1] Yet Hume's position always seems a possibility, because whenever such a consistency requirement or similar pattern has an influence on our decisions, it seems possible to represent this influence as the manifestation of a systematic second-order desire or calm passion, which has such consistency as its object and without which we would not be susceptible to this type of "rational" motivation. Hume need then only claim that while such a desire (for the satisfaction of one's future interests) is quite common, to lack it is not contrary to reason, any more than to lack sexual desire is contrary to reason. The problem is to show how this misrepresents the facts.

The fundamental issue is about the order of explanation, for there is no point in denying that people have such second-order desires: the question is whether they are sources of motivation or simply the manifestation in our motives of the recognition of certain rational requirements. A parallel point could be made about theoretical reason. It is clear that the belief in modus ponens, for example, is not a rationally ungrounded *assumption* underlying our acceptance of deductive arguments that depend on modus ponens: Rather, it is simply a recognition of the validity of that form of argument.[2]

The question is whether something similar can be said of the "desire" for prudential consistency in the treatment of desires and interests located at different times. I think it can be and that if one tries instead to regard prudence as simply a desire among others, a desire one happens to have, the question of its appropriateness inevitably reappears as a normative question, and the answer can only be given in terms of the principle itself. The normative can't be displaced by the psychological.

If I think, for example, "What if I didn't care about what would happen to me in the future?" the appropriate reaction is not like what it would be to the supposition that I might not care about movies. True, I'd be missing something if I didn't care about movies, but there are many forms of art and entertainment, and we don't have to consume them all. Note that even this is a judgment of the *rational acceptability* of such variation—of there being no reason to regret it. The supposition that I might not care about my own future cannot be regarded with similar tolerance: It is the supposition of a real fail-ure—the paradigm of something to be regretted—and my recognition of that failure does not reflect merely the antecedent presence in me of a contingent second-order desire. Rather, it reflects a judgment about what is and what is not relevant to the justification of action against a certain factual background.

Relevance and consistency both get a foothold when we adopt the stand-point of decision, based on the total circumstances, including our own condi-tion. This standpoint introduces a subtle but profound gap between desire and action, into which the free exercise of reason enters. It forces us to the idea of the difference between doing the right thing and doing the wrong thing (here, without any specifically ethical meaning as yet)—given our total situation, *including* our desires. Once I see myself as the subject of certain desires, as well as the occupant of an objective situation, I still have to decide what to do, and that will include deciding what justificatory weight to give to those desires.

This step back, this opening of a slight space between inclination and decision, is the condition that permits the operation of reason with respect to belief as well as with respect to action, and that poses the demand for gener-alizable justification. The two kinds of reasoning are in this way parallel. It is only when, instead of simply being pushed along by impressions, memories, impulses, desires, or whatever, one stops to ask "What should I do?" or "What should I believe?" that reasoning becomes possible—and, having become possible, becomes necessary. Having stopped the direct operation of impulse by interposing the possibility of decision, one can get one's beliefs and actions into motion again only by thinking about what, in light of the cir-cumstances, one should do.

The controversial but crucial point, here as everywhere in the discussion of this subject, is that the standpoint from which one assesses one's choices after this step back is not just first-personal. One is suddenly in the position of judging what one ought to do, against the background of all one's desires and beliefs, in a way that does not merely flow from those desires and beliefs but *operates* on them—by an assessment that should enable anyone else also to see what is the right thing for you to do against that background.

It is not enough to find some higher order desires that one happens to have, to settle the matter: such desires would have to be placed among the background conditions of decision along with everything else. Rather, even in the case of a purely self-interested choice, one is seeking the right answer. One is trying to decide what, given the inner and outer circumstances, *one should do*—and that means not just what *I* should do but what *this person* should do. The same answer should be given to that question by anyone to whom the data are presented, whether or not he is in your circumstances and shares your desires. That is what gives practical reason its generality.

The objection that has to be answered, here as elsewhere, is that this sense of unconditioned, nonrelative judgment is an illusion—that we cannot, merely by stepping back and taking ourselves as objects of contemplation, find a secure platform from which such judgment is possible. On this view whatever we do, after engaging in such an intellectual ritual, will still inevitably be a manifestation of our individual or social nature, not the deliverance of impersonal reason—for there is no such thing.

But I do not believe that such a conclusion can be established a priori, and there is little reason to believe it could be established empirically. The subjectivist would have to show that all purportedly rational judgments about what people have reason to do are really expressions of rationally unmotivated desires or dispositions of the person making the judgment—desires or dispositions to which normative assessment has no application. The motivational explanation would have to have the effect of *displacing* the normative one—showing it to be superficial and deceptive. It would be necessary to make out the case about many actual judgments of this kind and to offer reasons to believe that something similar was true in all cases. Subjectivism involves a positive claim of empirical psychology.

Is it conceivable that such an argument could succeed? In a sense, it would have to be shown that all our supposed practical reasoning is, at the limit, a form of rationalization. But the defender of practical reason has a general response to all psychological claims of this type. Even when some of his actual reasonings are convincingly analyzed away as the expression of merely parochial or personal inclinations, it will in general be reasonable for him to add this new information to the body of his beliefs about himself and then step back once more and ask, "What, in light of all this, do I have reason to do?" It is logically conceivable that the subjectivist's strategy might succeed by exhaustion; the rationalist might become so discouraged at the prospect of being once again undermined in his rational pretensions that he would give up trying to answer the recurrent normative question. But it is far more likely that the question will always be there, continuing to appear significant and to demand an answer. To give up would be nothing but moral laziness.

More important, as a matter of substance I do not think the subjectivist's project can be plausibly carried out. It is not possible to give a debunking psychological explanation of prudential rationality, at any rate. For suppose it is said, plausibly enough, that the disposition to provide for the future has survival value and that its implantation in us is the product of natural selection. As with any other instinct, we still have to decide whether acting on it is a good idea. With some biologically natural dispositions, both motivational and intellectual, there are good reasons to resist or limit their influence. That this does not seem the right reaction to prudential motives (except insofar as we limit them for moral reasons) shows that they cannot be regarded simply as desires that there is no reason to have. If they were, they wouldn't give us the kind of reasons for action that they clearly do.[3] It will never be reasonable for the rationalist to concede that prudence is just a type of consistency in action that he happens, groundlessly, to care about, and that he would have no reason to care about if he didn't already.

The null hypothesis—that in this unconditional sense there are no reasons—is acceptable only if from the point of view of detached self-observation it is superior to the alternatives; and as elsewhere, I believe it fails that test.

IV

Bernard Williams is a prominent contemporary representative of the opposite view. In chapter 4 of *Ethics and the Limits of Philosophy*,[4] he argues that reflective practical reason, unlike reflective theoretical reason, always remains first-personal: One is always trying to answer the question "What shall (or should) *I* do?" and the answer must derive from something internal to what he calls one's "motivational set." Williams says that in theoretical reasoning, by contrast, while it is true that one is trying to decide what to believe, the question "What should I believe?" is in general replaceable by a substantive question which need make no first-person reference: a question like "Did Wagner ever meet Verdi?" or "Is strontium a metal?" This means that the pursuit of freedom through the rational, reflective assessment of the influences on one's beliefs leads, in the theoretical case, to the employment of objective, non-first-personal standards. To decide what to believe, I have to decide, in light of the evidence available to me, and by standards that it would be valid for anyone to use in drawing a conclusion from that evidence, what is probably true.

But Williams holds that in deciding what to do, even if I try to free myself from the blind pressures of my desires and instincts by reflecting on those influences and evaluating their suitability as reasons for action, such reflection will never take me outside of the domain of first-personal thought. Even at my most reflective, it will still be a decision about what *I* should do and will have to be based on *my* reflective assessment of my motives and reasons. To believe that at some point I will reach a level of reflection where I can consider truly objective reasons, valid for anyone, that reveal what *should be done* by this person in these circumstances, is to deceive myself. In the practical domain, there is no such standpoint of assessment.[5]

It has to be admitted that phenomenologically, the subjectivist view is more plausible in ethics than in regard to theoretical reason. When I step back from my practical reasonings and ask whether I can endorse them as correct, it is possible to experience this as a move to a deeper region of myself rather than to a higher universal standpoint. Yet at the same time there seems to be no limit to the possibility of asking whether the first-personal reasoning I rely on in deciding what to do is also objectively acceptable. It always seems appropriate to ask, setting aside that the person in question is oneself, "What ought to happen? What is the right thing to do in this case?"

That the question can take this form does not follow merely from the fact that it is always possible to step back from one's present intentions and motives and consider whether one wishes to change them. The fact that the question "What should I do?" is always open, or reopenable, is logically consistent with the answer's always being a first-personal answer. It might be, as Williams believes, that the highest freedom I can hope for is to ascend to higher order desires or values that are still irreducibly my own—values that determine what kind of person I as an individual wish to be—and that all apparently objective answers to the question are really just the first person masquerading as the third. But do values really disappear into thin air when we adopt the external point of view? Since we can reach a *descriptive* standpoint from which the first person has vanished and from which one regards oneself impersonally, the issue is whether at that point description outruns evaluation. If it does not, if evaluation of some sort keeps pace with it, then we will finally have to evaluate our conduct from a non-first-person standpoint.

Clearly, description can outrun some evaluations. If I don't like shrimp, there simply is no higher order evaluation to be made of this preference. All I can do is to observe that I have it; and no higher order value seems to be involved when it leads me to refrain from ordering a dish containing shrimp or to decline an offer of shrimp when the hors d'oeuvres are passed at a cocktail party. However external a view I may take of the preference, I am not called on either to defend it or to endorse it: I can just accept it. But there are other evaluations, by contrast, that seem at least potentially to be called into question by an external, descriptive view, and the issue is whether those questions always lead us finally to a first-person answer.

Suppose I reflect on my political preferences—my hope that candidate X will not win the next presidential election, for example. What external description of this preference, considered as a psychological state, is consistent with its stability? Can I regard my reasons for holding it simply as facts about myself, as my dislike of shrimp is a fact about myself? Or will any purely descriptive observation of such facts give rise to a further evaluative question—one that cannot be answered simply by a reaffirmation that this is the kind of person I am?

Here, as elsewhere, I don't think we can hope for a decisive proof that we are asking objective questions and pursuing objective answers. The possibility that we are deceiving ourselves is genuine. But the only way to deal with that possibility is to think about it, and one must think about it by weighing the plausibility of the debunking explanation against the plausibility of the ethical reasoning at which it is aimed. The claim that, at the most objective level, the question of what we should do becomes meaningless has to compete head-to-head with specific claims about what in fact we should do, and their grounds. So in the end, the contest is between the credibility of substantive ethics and the credibility of an external psychological reduction of that activity.

V

There is a deep philosophical problem about the capacity to step back and evaluate either one's actions or one's beliefs; it is the problem of free will.

Suppose you became convinced that *all* your choices, decisions, and conclusions were determined by rationally arbitrary features of your psychological makeup or by external manipulation, and then tried to ask yourself what, in the light of this information, you should do or believe. There would really be no way to answer the question, because the arbitrary causal control of which you had become convinced would apply to whatever you said or decided.[6] You could not simultaneously believe this about yourself and try to make a free, rational choice. Not only that, but if the very belief in the causal system of control was itself a product of what you thought to be reasoning, then it too would lose its status as a belief freely arrived at, and your attitude toward it would have to change. (Though even *that* is a rational argument, whose conclusion you are no longer in a position to draw!)

Doubt about your own rationality is unstable; it leaves you really with nothing to think. So although the hypothesis of nonrational control seems a contingent possibility, it is no more possible to entertain it with regard to yourself than it is to consider the possibility that you are not thinking. I have never known how to respond to this conundrum.

However, a more specialized version of the problem can be raised about practical reason alone. The hypothesis that practical reason does not exist is not self-contradictory. In spite of everything I have said, one might intelligibly suppose, without having to abandon *all* one's reasoning, that decisions to act are all ultimately due to arbitrary desires and dispositions—perhaps higher order and partly unconscious—that lie beyond the possibility of rational assessment. Consider the hypothesis that this is true in particular whenever we take ourselves to be engaged in practical reasoning. If someone actually believed this, he could not ask, "In light of all that, what should I do?" To ask that, hoping for a genuinely rational evaluation of the alternatives, would contradict the supposition of nonrational determination, which is supposed to apply to all choices, including this one. So if one really accepted the hypothesis, one would have to abandon the practice of rational assessment, all things considered, as an illusion, and limit the practical employment of reason to an instrumental role.

But is that possible? I don't think so; rather, I think the illusion is on the other side, in trying to see oneself as nonrationally determined. What we have here is a face-off between two attitudes—not, as in the case of subjectivism about theoretical reason, between two theories about how things are. The opposition here is between a theory about how things are and a practice that would be impossible if this was how things were. If we go on trying to make up our minds about what to do on the basis of the best reasons, we implicitly reject the hypothesis of an ultimately nonrational determination of what we do. (I leave open the possibility that there is a form of causal determination that is compatible with rationality; if so, we could simultaneously engage in practical and theoretical reasoning and believe that we were so determined—including being so determined to believe that we were.)

The unquenchable persistence of the conviction that it is up to me to decide, all things considered, what I should do, is what Kant called the *fact of reason*.[7] It reveals itself in decision, not in contemplation—in the permanent capacity we have to contemplate all the personal, contingent features of our motivational circumstances and ask, once again, "What should I do?"—and in our persistent attempts to answer the question, even if it is very difficult. The sense of freedom depends on the decision's not being merely from *my* point of view. It is not just a working out of the implications of my own perspective, but the demand that my actions conform to universally applicable standards that make them potentially part of a harmonious collective system. Thus I find within myself the universal standards that enable me to get outside of myself. (In Kant's example, I am directly aware of the fact of reason when the tyrant threatens to kill me unless I bear false witness against an innocent man: I know that I *can* refuse—whether or not I will be brave enough to do so—because I know that I *ought* to refuse.)[8]

There is a direct analogy here with the operation of theoretical reason, which employs universal principles of belief formation to bring my thoughts into harmony with a consistent system of objective beliefs in which others can also hold a share—more commonly known as *the truth*. Reason is an attempt to turn myself into a local representative of the truth, and in action of the right. Freedom requires holding oneself in one's hands and choosing a direction in thought or action for the highly contingent and particular individual that one is, from a point of view outside oneself, that one can nevertheless reach from inside oneself.

This picture is opposed to the Humean alternative which limits reason to thought and gives it no direct application to conduct. According to that view, we may transcend ourselves to develop a truer and more objective conception of how the world is, but this transcendence influences our conduct only instrumentally—by revealing how we may most effectively act on our motives, which remain entirely perspectival. Even where an objective view of the facts leads us to pursue practical harmony with others, the motives remain personal.

But I believe that alternative is untenable. Even a moral system like that of Hobbes, based on the rational construction of collective self-interest, affirms the rationality of the self-interest on which it depends. And that puts it in competition with other conceptions of what is rational.

We cannot evade our freedom. Once we have developed the capacity to recognize our own desires and motives, we are faced with the choice of whether to act as they incline us to act, and in facing that choice we are inevitably faced with an evaluative question. Even if we refuse to think about it, that refusal can itself be evaluated. In this sense I believe Kant was right: The applicability to us of moral concepts is the consequence of our freedom—freedom that comes from the ability to see ourselves objectively, through the new choices which that ability forces on us.[9]

VI

Even a "subjective"-seeming solution to this problem—like the answer that there are no universal standards for determining what we should do, and that each person may follow his own inclinations—is itself an objective, universal claim and therefore a limiting case of a moral position. But that position obviously has competitors, and one or another of the moralities that require some kind of impartial consideration for everyone is much more plausible. Let me now sketch out in a series of rough steps the familiar kinds of substantive practical reasoning that lead to this conclusion and that resist a Humean reduction.

The first step on the path to ethics is the admission of *generality* in practical judgments. That is actually equivalent to the admission of the existence of reasons, for a reason is something one person can have only if others would also have it if they were in the same circumstances (internal as well as external). In taking an objective view of myself, the first question to answer is whether I have, in this generalizable sense, any reason to do anything, and a negative answer is nearly as implausible as a negative answer to the analogous question of whether I have any reason to believe anything. Neither of those questions—though they are, to begin with, about me—is essentially first-personal, since they are supposed not to depend for their answers on the fact that I am asking them.

It is perhaps less impossible to answer the question about practical reasons in the negative than the question about theoretical reasons. (And by a negative answer, remember, we mean the position that there *are* no reasons, not merely that I have no reason to believe, or do, anything rather than anything else—the skeptical position, which is also universal in its grounds and implications.) If one ceased to recognize theoretical reasons, having reached a reflective standpoint, it would make no sense to go on having beliefs, though one might be unable to stop. But perhaps action wouldn't likewise become senseless if one denied the existence of practical reasons: One could still be moved by impulse and habit, without thinking that what one did was justified in any sense—even by one's inclinations—in a way that admitted generalization.

However, this seems a very implausible option. It implies, for example, that none of your desires and aversions, pleasures and sufferings, or your survival or death, give you any generalizable reason to do anything—that all we can do from an objective standpoint is to observe, and perhaps try to predict, what you *will* do. The application of this view to my own case is outlandish: I can't seriously believe that I have *no reason* to get out of the way of a truck that is bearing down on me in the street—that my motive is a purely psychological reaction not subject to rational endorsement. Clearly I have a reason, and clearly it is generalizable.

The second step on the path to familiar moral territory is the big one: the choice between agent-relative, essentially egoistic (but still general) reasons and some alternative that admits agent-neutral reasons[10] or in some other way acknowledges that each person has a noninstrumental reason to consider the interests of others. It is possible to understand this choice partly as a choice of the way in which one is going to value oneself and one's own interests. It has strong implications in that regard.

Morality is possible only for beings capable of seeing themselves as one individual among others more or less similar in general respects—capable, in other words, of seeing themselves as others see them. When we recognize that although we occupy only our own point of view and not that of anyone else, there is nothing cosmically unique about it, we are faced with a choice. This choice has to do with the relation between the value we naturally accord to ourselves and our fates from our own point of view, and the attitude we take toward these same things when viewed from the impersonal standpoint that assigns to us no unique status apart from anyone else.

One alternative would be not to "transfer" to the impersonal standpoint in any form those values which concern us from the personal standpoint. That would mean that the impersonal standpoint would remain purely descriptive and our lives and what matters to us as we live them (including the lives of other people we care about) would not be regarded as mattering at all if considered apart from the fact that they are ours, or personally related to us. Each of us, then, would have a system of values centering on his own perspective and would recognize that others were in exactly the same situation.

The other alternative would be to assign to one's life and what goes on in it some form of impersonal as well as purely perspectival value, not dependent on its being one's own. This would then imply that everyone else was also the subject of impersonal value of a similar kind.

The agent-relative position that all of a person's reasons derive from his own interests, desires, and attachments means that I have no reason to care about what happens to other people unless what happens to them matters to me, either directly or instrumentally. This is compatible with the existence of strong derivative reasons for consideration of others—reasons for accepting systems of general rights, and so forth—but it does not include those reasons at the ground level. It also means, of course, that others have no reason to care about what happens to me—again, unless it matters to them in some way, emotionally or instrumentally. All the practical reasons that any of us have, on this theory, depend on what is valuable *to us.*

It follows that we each have value only to ourselves and to those who care about us. Considered impersonally, we are valueless and provide no intrinsic reasons for concern to anyone. So the egoistic answer to the question of what kinds of reasons there are amounts to an assessment of oneself, along with everyone else, as *objectively worthless.* In a sense, it doesn't matter (except to ourselves) what happens to us: Each person has value only *for himself,* not *in himself.*

Now this judgment, while it satisfies the generality condition for reasons, and while perfectly consistent, is in my opinion highly unreasonable and difficult to honestly accept. Can you really believe that objectively, it doesn't matter whether you die of thirst or not—and that your inclination to believe that it does is just the false objectification of your self-love? One could really ask the same question about anybody else's dying of thirst, but concentrating on your own case stimulates the imagination, which is why the fundamental moral argument takes the form, "How would you like it if someone did that to you?" The concept of reasons for action faces us with a question about their content that it is very difficult to answer in a consistently egoistic or agent-relative style.

VII

This step takes us to the basic platform of other-regarding moral thought, but at that point the path forward becomes more difficult to discern. We may admit that a system of reasons should accord to persons and their interests some kind of objective, as well as subjective, worth, but there is more than one way to do this, and none of them is clearly the right one; no doubt there are other ways, not yet invented, which are superior to those that have been. As a final illustration of the attempt to discover objective practical reasons, let me discuss the familiar contrast between two broad approaches to the interpretation of objective worth, represented by utilitarian and contractualist (or rights-based) moral theories, respectively. This is also, I must admit, the type of case where skepticism about the objectivity of reasons is most plausible, precisely because the substantive arguments are not decisive.

The problem is to give more specific content to the idea that persons have value not just *for* themselves but *in* themselves—and therefore for everyone. That means we all have some kind of reason to consider one another, but what kind is it? What is the right way to think from an objective standpoint about the nonegoistic system of reasons generated by multiple individual lives?

Each of the two approaches answers the question in a way that attempts to give equal value to everyone; the difference between them lies in the kind of equality they endorse. Utilitarianism assigns equal value to people's actual experiences, positive and negative: Everyone's personal good *counts* the same, as something to be advanced. The equal moral value that utilitarianism assigns to everyone is equality as a *component* of the totality of value. This leads to the characteristic aggregative and maximizing properties of utilitarian moral reasoning. Everyone is treated equally as a source of inputs to the calculation of value, but once that is done, it is total value rather than equality that takes over as the goal. Utilitarianism may have problems supplying a usable common measure of well-being for combinatorial purposes, but it is certainly a viable method of moral reasoning. If it is taken as the whole truth about morality, then rights, obligations, equality, and other deontological elements have to be explained derivatively, on the ground of their instrumental value in promoting the greatest overall good for people in the long run. The rule-utilitarian treatment of those topics is well developed and familiar.

The other approach is associated with the social contract tradition and Kant's categorical imperative. It accords to everyone not equality of input into the totality of value, but equality of status and treatment in certain respects. The way it acknowledges everyone's objective value is to offer certain universal substantive guarantees—protections against violation and provision of basic needs. Equality in moral status is therefore much closer to the surface of contractualist than of utilitarian moral recognition. Contractualism uses a system of priorities rather than maximization of total well-being as the method of settling conflicts between interests. It also allows the admission of rights, obligations, and distributive equality as fundamental features of the system of moral reasons rather than as derivative features justified only by their instrumental value. The resulting system will include certain guaranteed protections to everyone, in the form of individual rights against interference, as well as priority in the provision of benefits to serve the most urgent needs, which are in general to be met before less urgent interests, even of larger numbers of persons, are addressed.

The dispute between a priority or rights-based theory and a maximizing, aggregative theory is really a disagreement over the best way to interpret the extremely general requirement of impartial interpersonal concern.[11] The issue is at the moment highly salient and controversial, and I do not propose to take it further here. I introduce it only as an example of a large substantive question of moral theory, one that firmly resists subjectivist or relativist interpretation: The question demands that we look for the right answer rather than relying on our feelings or the consensus of our community.

Once we admit the existence of some form of other-regarding reasons that are general in application, we have to look for a way of specifying their content and principles of combination. That is not a first-person enterprise. We are trying to decide what reasons there are, having already decided that there must be *some*, in a certain broad category—a generally applicable way of answering the question "What is the right thing to do in these circumstances?" That is simply a continuation of the original task of objective judgment that faced us when we took the first reflective step, by asking whether, from an impersonal point of view, we have any reasons to do anything at all. To answer the question it is not enough to consult my own inclinations; I have to try to arrive at a judgment. Such judgments often take the form of moral intuitions, but those are not just subjective reactions, at least in intention: They are beliefs about what is right.

The situation here is like that in any other basic domain. First-order thoughts about its content—thoughts expressed in the object language—rise up again as the decisive factor in response to all second-order thoughts about their psychological character. They look back at the observer, so to speak. And those first-order thoughts aim to be valid without qualification, however much pluralism or even relativism may appear as part of their (objective) content. It is in that sense that ethics is one of the provinces of reason, if it is. That is why we can defend moral reason only by abandoning metatheory for substantive ethics. Only the intrinsic weight of first-order moral thinking can counter the doubts of subjectivism. (And the less its weight, the more plausible subjectivism becomes.)[12]

NOTES

1. *A Treatise of Human Nature,* book 2, part 3, sec. 3 (L. A. Selby-Bigge, ed., Oxford University Press, 1888), p. 416. I'm afraid it's unavoidable to revisit the subject of prudence in a discussion of practical reason, overworked as it is.

2. See Barry Stroud, "Inference, Belief, and Understanding," *Mind* 88 (1979), p. 187: "For every proposition or set of propositions the belief or acceptance of which is

involved in someone's believing one proposition on the basis of another there must be something else, not simply a further proposition accepted, that is responsible for the one belief's being based on the other."

3. For a very persuasive argument that brute desires or preferences in themselves *never* provide reasons for action, see Warren Quinn, "Putting Rationality in Its Place," in his *Morality and Action* (Cambridge University Press, 1993).

4. Harvard University Press, 1985.

5. Actually, there is a bit of obscurity in Williams's view on this point, since he may believe there is an objective answer, discoverable by anyone, to the question of what a particular person should do, given the contents of his "motivational set." See the essay "Internal and External Reasons" in his collection *Moral Luck* (Cambridge University Press, 1981), pp. 103–5.

6. Recall the scrambled-brain hypothesis in chapter 4 of Nagel, *The Last Word* (New York: Oxford University Press, 1997).

7. *Critique of Practical Reason* (trans. Lewis White Beck, Bobbs-Merrill, 1956), original in vol. 5 of the Prussian Academy edition of Kant's works, pp. 31, 42.

8. *Critique of Practical Reason,* pp. 30, 155–9.

9. For an illuminating treatment of this subject, see Christine Korsgaard, *The Sources of Normativity* (Cambridge University Press, 1996).

10. For this terminology, see *The View from Nowhere* (Oxford University Press, 1986), pp. 152–3.

11. For an alternative position see Christine Korsgaard's essay "The Reasons We Can Share: An Attack on the Distinction between Agent-relative and Agent-neutral Values," *Social Philosophy and Policy* 10, no. 1 (1993).

12. For Ronald Dworkin's closely related treatment of these issues, see his essay "Objectivity and Truth: You'd Better Believe It," *Philosophy & Public Affairs* 25, no. 2 (1996).

PART FIVE

RELATIVISM, REALISM, AND RATIONALITY

17 The Subjectivity of Values

J. L. MACKIE

1. MORAL SCEPTICISM

There are no objective values. This is a bald statement of the thesis of this chapter, but before arguing for it I shall try to clarify and restrict it in ways that may meet some objections and prevent some misunderstanding.

The statement of this thesis is liable to provoke one of three very different reactions. Some will think it not merely false but pernicious; they will see it as a threat to morality and to everything else that is worthwhile, and they will find the presenting of such a thesis in what purports to be a book on ethics, paradoxical or even outrageous. Others will regard it as a trivial truth, almost too obvious to be worth mentioning, and certainly too plain to be worth much argument. Others again will say that it is meaningless or empty, that no real issue is raised by the question whether values are or are not part of the fabric of the world. But, precisely because there can be these three different reactions, much more needs to be said.

The claim that values are not objective, are not part of the fabric of the world, is meant to include not only moral goodness, which might be most naturally equated with moral value, but also other things that could be more loosely called moral values or disvalues—rightness and wrongness, duty, obligation, an action's being rotten and contemptible, and so on. It also includes non-moral values, notably aesthetic ones, beauty and various kinds of artistic merit. I shall not discuss these explicitly, but clearly much the same considerations apply to aesthetic and to moral values, and there would be at least some initial implausibility in a view that gave the one a different status from the other. . . .

The main tradition of European moral philosophy from Plato onwards has combined the view that moral values are objective with the recognition that moral judgements are partly prescriptive or directive or action-guiding. Values themselves have been seen as at once prescriptive and objective. In Plato's theory the Forms, and in particular the Form of the Good, are eternal, extra-mental, realities. They are a very central structural element in the fabric

Reprinted, by permission of the publisher and copyright holder, from J. L. Mackie, "The Subjectivity of Values," in Mackie, *Ethics: Inventing Right and Wrong*, pp. 15, 23–25, 27–48. London: Penguin, 1977.

of the world. But it is held also that just knowing them or "seeing" them will not merely tell men what to do but will ensure that they do it, overruling any contrary inclinations. The philosopher-kings in the *Republic* can, Plato thinks, be trusted with unchecked power because their education will have given them knowledge of the Forms. Being acquainted with the Forms of the Good and Justice and Beauty and the rest they will, by this knowledge alone, without any further motivation, be impelled to pursue and promote these ideals. Similarly, Kant believes that pure reason can by itself be practical, though he does not pretend to be able to explain how it can be so. Again, Sidgwick argues that if there is to be a science of ethics—and he assumes that there can be, indeed he defines ethics as "the science of conduct"—what ought to be "must in another sense have objective existence: it must be an object of knowledge and as such the same for all minds"; but he says that the affirmations of this science "are also precepts," and he speaks of happiness as "an end *absolutely* prescribed by reason." Since many philosophers have thus held that values are objectively prescriptive, it is clear that the ontological doctrine of objectivism must be distinguished from descriptivism, a theory about meaning.

But perhaps when Hare says that he does not understand what is meant by "the objectivity of values" he means that he cannot understand how values could be objective, he cannot frame for himself any clear, detailed, picture of what it would be like for values to be part of the fabric of the world. This would be a much more plausible claim; as we have seen, even Kant hints at a similar difficulty. Indeed, even Plato warns us that it is only through difficult studies spread over many years that one can approach the knowledge of the Forms. The difficulty of seeing how values could be objective is a fairly strong reason for thinking that they are not so; this point will be taken up in Section 9, but it is not a good reason for saying that this is not a real issue.

I believe that as well as being a real issue it is an important one. It clearly matters for general philosophy. It would make a radical difference to our metaphysics if we had to find room for objective values—perhaps something like Plato's Forms—somewhere in our picture of the world. It would similarly make a difference to our epistemology if it had to explain how such objective values are or can be known, and to our philosophical psychology if we had to allow such knowledge, or Kant's pure practical reason, to direct choices and actions. Less obviously, how this issue is settled will affect the possibility of certain kinds of moral argument. For example, Sidgwick considers a discussion between an egoist and a utilitarian, and points out that if the egoist claims that his happiness or pleasure is objectively desirable or good, the utilitarian can argue that the egoist's happiness "cannot be more objectively desirable or more a good than the similar happiness of any other person: the mere fact . . . that *he is he* can have nothing to do with its objective desirability or goodness." In other words, if ethics is built on the concept of objective goodness, then egoism as a first order system or method of ethics can be refuted, whereas if it is assumed that goodness is only subjective it cannot. But Sidgwick correctly stresses what a number of other philosophers have missed, that this argument against egoism would require the objectivity specifically of goodness: the objectivity of what ought to be or of what it is rational to do would not be enough. If the egoist claimed that it was objectively rational, or obligatory upon him, to seek his own happiness, a similar argument about the irrelevance of the fact that *he is he* would lead only to the conclusion that it was objectively rational or obligatory for each other person to seek *his* own happiness, that is, to a universalized form of egoism, not to the refutation of egoism. And of course insisting on the universalizability of moral judgements, as opposed to the objectivity of goodness, would yield only the same result. . . .

6. HYPOTHETICAL AND CATEGORICAL IMPERATIVES

We may make this issue clearer by referring to Kant's distinction between hypothetical and categorical imperatives, though what he called imperatives are more naturally expressed as "ought"-statements than in the imperative mood. "If you want X, do Y" (or "You ought to do Y") will be a hypothetical imperative if it is based on the supposed fact that Y is, in the circumstances, the only (or the best) available means to X, that is, on a causal relation between Y and X. The reason for doing Y lies in its causal connection with the desired end, X; the oughtness is contingent upon the desire. But "You ought to do Y" will be a categorical imperative if you ought to do Y irrespective of any such desire for any end to which Y would contribute, if the oughtness is not thus contingent upon any desire. But this distinction needs to be handled with some care. An "ought"-statement is not in this sense hypothetical merely because it incorporates a conditional clause. "If you promised to do Y, you ought to do Y" is not a hypothetical imperative merely on account of the stated if-clause; what is meant may be either a hypothetical or a categorical imperative, depending upon the implied reason for keeping the supposed promise. If this rests upon some such further unstated conditional as "If you want to be trusted another time," then it is a hypothetical imperative; if not, it is categorical. Even a desire of the agent's can figure in the antecedent of what, though conditional in grammatical form, is still in Kant's sense of a categorical imperative. "If you are strongly attracted sexually to young children you ought not to go in for school teaching" is not, in virtue of what it explicitly says, a hypothetical imperative: the avoidance of school teaching is not being offered as a means to the satisfaction of the desires in question. Of course, it could still be a hypothetical imperative, if the implied reason were a prudential one; but it could also be a categorical imperative, a moral requirement where the reason for the recommended action (strictly, avoidance) does not rest upon that action's being a means to the satisfaction of any desire that the agent is supposed to have. Not every conditional ought-statement or command, then, is a hypothetical imperative; equally, not every non-conditional one is a categorical imperative. An appropriate if-clause may be left unstated. Indeed, a simple command in the imperative mood, say a parade-ground order, which might seem most literally to qualify for the title of a categorical imperative, will hardly ever be one in the sense we need here. The implied reason for complying with such an order will almost always be some desire of himself, the law that he thus makes is determinate and necessary. Aristotle begins the *Nicomachean Ethics* by saying that the good is that at which all things aim, and that ethics is part of a science which he calls "politics," whose goal is not knowledge but practice; yet he does not doubt that there can be *knowledge* of what is the good for man, nor, once he has identified this as well-being or happiness, *eudaimonia*, that it can be known, rationally determined, in what happiness consists; and it is plain that he thinks that this happiness is intrinsically desirable, not good simply because it is desired. The rationalist Samuel Clarke holds that

> these eternal and necessary differences of things make it *fit and reasonable* for creatures so to act ... even separate from the consideration of these rules being the *positive will* or *command of God;* and also antecedent to any respect or regard, expectation or apprehension, of any *particular private and personal advantage or disadvantage, reward or punishment,* either present or future ...

Even the sentimentalist Hutcheson defines moral goodness as "some quality apprehended in actions, which procures approbation ... ," while saying that the moral sense by which we perceive virtue and vice has been given to us (by the Author of nature) to direct our actions. Hume indeed was on the other side, but he is still a witness to the dominance of the objectivist tradition, since he claims that when we "see that the distinction of vice and virtue is not founded merely on the relations of objects, nor is perceiv'd by reason," this "wou'd subvert all the vulgar systems of morality." And Richard Price insists that right and wrong are "real characters of actions," not "qualities of our minds," and are perceived by the understanding; he criticizes the notion of moral sense on the ground that it would make virtue an affair of taste, and moral right and wrong "nothing in the objects themselves"; he rejects Hutcheson's view because (perhaps mistakenly) he sees it as collapsing into Hume's.

But this objectivism about values is not only a feature of the philosophical tradition. It has also a firm basis in ordinary thought, and even in the meanings of moral terms. No doubt it was an extravagance for Moore to say that "good" is the name of a non-natural quality, but it would not be so far wrong to say that in moral contexts it is used as if it were the name of a supposed non-natural quality, where the description "non-natural" leaves room for the peculiar evaluative, prescriptive, intrinsically action-guiding aspects of this supposed quality. This point can be illustrated by reflection on the conflicts and swings of opinion in recent years between non-cognitivist and naturalist views about the central, basic, meanings of ethical terms. If we reject the view that it is the function of such terms to introduce objective values into discourse about conduct and choices of action, there seem to be two main alternative types of account. One (which has importantly different subdivisions) is that they conventionally express either attitudes which the speaker purports to adopt towards whatever it is that he characterizes morally, or prescriptions or recommendations, subject perhaps to the logical constraint of universalizability. Different views of this type share the central thesis that ethical terms have, at least partly and primarily, some sort of non-cognitive, non-descriptive, meaning. Views of the other type hold that they are descriptive in meaning, but descriptive of natural features, partly of such features as everyone, even the non-cognitivist, would recognize as distinguishing kind actions from cruel ones, courage from cowardice, politeness from rudeness, and so on, and partly (though these two overlap) of relations between the actions and some human wants, satisfactions, and the like. I believe that views of both these types capture part of the truth. Each approach can account for the fact that moral judgements are action-guiding or practical. Yet each gains much of its plausibility from the felt inadequacy of the other. It is a very natural reaction to any non-cognitive analysis of ethical terms to protest that there is more to ethics than this, something more external to the maker of moral judgements, more authoritative over both him and those of or to whom he speaks, and this reaction is likely to persist even when full allowance has been made for the logical, formal, constraints of full-blooded prescriptivity and universalizability. Ethics, we are inclined to believe, is more a matter of knowledge and less a matter of decision than any non-cognitive analysis allows. And of course naturalism satisfies this demand. It will not be a matter of choice or decision whether an action is cruel or unjust or imprudent or whether it is likely to produce more distress than pleasure. But in satisfying this demand, it introduces a converse deficiency. On a naturalist analysis, moral judgements can be practical, but their practicality is wholly relative to desires or possible satisfactions of the person or persons whose actions are to be guided; but moral judgements seem to say more than this. This view leaves out the categorical quality of moral requirements. In fact both naturalist and non-cognitive analyses leave out the apparent authority of ethics, the one by excluding the categorically imperative aspect, the other the claim to objective validity or truth. The ordinary user of moral language means to say something about whatever it is that he characterizes morally, for example a possible action, as it is in itself, or would be if it were realized, and not about, or even simply expressive of, his, or anyone else's, attitude or relation to it. But the something he wants to say is not purely descriptive, certainly not inert, but something that involves a call for action or for the refraining from action, and one that is absolute, not contingent upon any desire or preference or policy or choice, his own or anyone else's. Someone in a state of moral perplexity, wondering whether it would be wrong for him to engage, say, in research related to bacteriological warfare, wants to arrive at some judgement about this concrete case, his doing this work at this time in these actual circumstances; his relevant characteristics will be part of the subject of the judgement, but no relation between him and the proposed action will be part of the predicate. The question is not, for example, whether he really wants to do this work, whether it will satisfy or dissatisfy him, whether he will in the long run have a proattitude towards it, or even whether this is an action of a sort that he can happily and sincerely recommend in all relevantly similar cases. Nor is he even wondering just whether to recommend such action in all relevantly similar cases. He wants to the person addressed, perhaps simply the desire to keep out of trouble. If so, such an apparently categorical order will be in our sense a hypothetical imperative. Again, an imperative remains hypothetical even if we change the "if" to "since": the fact that the desire for X is actually present does not alter the fact that the reason for doing Y is contingent upon the desire for X by way of Y's being a means to X. In Kant's own treatment, while imperatives of skill relate to desires which an agent may or may not have, imperatives of prudence relate to the desire for happiness which, Kant assumes, everyone has. So construed, imperatives of prudence are no less hypothetical than imperatives of skill, no less contingent upon desires that the agent has at the time the imperatives are addressed to him. But if we think rather of a counsel of prudence as being related to the agent's future welfare, to the satisfaction of desires that he does not yet have—not even to a present desire that his future desires should be satisfied—then a counsel of prudence is a categorical imperative, different indeed from a moral one, but analogous to it.

A categorical imperative, then, would express a reason for acting which was unconditional in the sense of not being contingent upon any present desire of the agent to whose satisfaction the recommended action would contribute as a means—or more directly: "You ought to dance," if the implied reason is just that you want to dance or like dancing, is still a hypothetical imperative. Now Kant himself held that moral judgements are categorical imperatives, or perhaps are all applications of one categorical imperative, and it can plausibly be maintained at least that many moral judgements contain a categorically imperative element. So far as ethics is concerned, my thesis that there are no objective values is specifically the denial that any such categorically imperative element is objectively valid. The objective values which I am denying would be action-directing absolutely, not contingently (in the way indicated) upon the agent's desires and inclinations.

Another way of trying to clarify this issue is to refer to moral reasoning or moral arguments. In practice, of course, such reasoning is seldom fully explicit: but let us suppose that we could make explicit the reasoning that supports some evaluative conclusion, where this conclusion has some action-guiding force that is not contingent upon desires or purposes or chosen ends. Then what I am saying is that somewhere in the input to this argument—perhaps in one or more of the premises, perhaps in some part of the form of the argument—there will be something which cannot be objectively validated—some premiss which is not capable of being simply true, or some form of argument which is not valid as a matter of general logic, whose authority or cogency is not objective, but is constituted by our choosing or deciding to think in a certain way.

7. THE CLAIM TO OBJECTIVITY

If I have succeeded in specifying precisely enough the moral values whose objectivity I am denying, my thesis may now seem to be trivially true. Of course, some will say, valuing, preferring, choosing, recommending, rejecting, condemning, and so on, are human activities, and there is no need to look for values that are prior to and logically independent of all such activities. There may be widespread agreement in valuing, and particular value-judgements are not in general arbitrary or isolated: they typically cohere with others, or can be criticized if they do not, reasons can be given for them, and so on: but if all that the subjectivist is maintaining is that desires, ends, purposes, and the like figure somewhere in the system of reasons, and that no ends or purposes are objective as opposed to being merely inter-subjective, then this may be conceded without much fuss.

But I do not think that this should be conceded so easily. As I have said, the main tradition of European moral philosophy includes the contrary claim, that there are objective values of just the sort I have denied. I have referred already to Plato, Kant, and Sidgwick. Kant in particular holds that the categorical imperative is not only categorical and imperative but objectively so: though a rational being gives the moral law to know whether this course of action would be wrong in itself. Something like this is the everyday objectivist concept of which talk about non-natural qualities is a philosopher's reconstruction.

The prevalence of this tendency to objectify values—and not only moral ones—is confirmed by a pattern of thinking that we find in existentialists and those influenced by them. The denial of objective values can carry with it an extreme emotional reaction, a feeling that nothing matters at all, that life has lost its purpose. Of course this does not follow; the lack of objective values is not a good reason for abandoning subjective concern or for ceasing to want anything. But the abandonment of a belief in objective values can cause, at least temporarily, a decay of subjective concern and sense of purpose. That it does so is evidence that the people in whom this reaction occurs have been tending to objectify their concerns and purposes, have been giving them a fictitious external authority. A claim to objectivity has been so strongly associated with their subjective concerns and purposes that the collapse of the former seems to undermine the latter as well.

This view, that conceptual analysis would reveal a claim to objectivity, is sometimes dramatically confirmed by philosophers who are officially on the other side. Bertrand Russell, for example, says that "ethical propositions should be expressed in the optative mood, not in the indicative"; he defends himself effectively against the charge of inconsistency in both holding ultimate ethical valuations to be subjective and expressing emphatic opinions on ethical questions. Yet at the end he admits:

> Certainly there *seems* to be something more. Suppose, for example, that some one were to advocate the introduction of bull-fighting in this country. In

opposing the proposal, I should *feel*, not only that I was expressing my desires, but that my desires in the matter are *right*, whatever that may mean. As a matter of argument, I can, I think, show that I am not guilty of any logical inconsistency in holding to the above interpretation of ethics and at the same time expressing strong ethical preferences. But in feeling I am not satisfied.

But he concludes, reasonably enough, with the remark: "I can only say that, while my own opinions as to ethics do not satisfy me, other people's satisfy me still less."

I conclude, then, that ordinary moral judgements include a claim to objectivity, an assumption that there are objective values in just the sense in which I am concerned to deny this. And I do not think it is going too far to say that this assumption has been incorporated in the basic, conventional, meanings of moral terms. Any analysis of the meanings of moral terms which omits this claim to objective, intrinsic, prescriptivity is to that extent incomplete; and this is true of any non-cognitive analysis, any naturalist one, and any combination of the two.

If second order ethics were confined, then, to linguistic and conceptual analysis, it ought to conclude that moral values at least are objective: that they are so is part of what our ordinary moral statements mean: the traditional moral concepts of the ordinary man as well as of the main line of western philosophers are concepts of objective value. But it is precisely for this reason that linguistic and conceptual analysis is not enough. The claim to objectivity, however ingrained in our language and thought, is not self-validating. It can and should be questioned. But the denial of objective values will have to be put forward not as the result of an analytic approach, but as an "error theory," a theory that although most people in making moral judgements implicitly claim, among other things, to be pointing to something objectively prescriptive, these claims are all false. It is this that makes the name "moral scepticism" appropriate.

But since this is an error theory, since it goes against assumptions ingrained in our thought and built into some of the ways in which language is used, since it conflicts with what is sometimes called common sense, it needs very solid support. It is not something we can accept lightly or casually and then quietly pass on. If we are to adopt this view, we must argue explicitly for it. Traditionally it has been supported by arguments of two main kinds, which I shall call the argument from relativity and the argument from queerness, but these can, as I shall show, be supplemented in several ways.

8. THE ARGUMENT FROM RELATIVITY

The argument from relativity has as its premiss the well-known variation in moral codes from one society to another and from one period to another, and also the differences in moral beliefs between different groups and classes within a complex community. Such variation is in itself merely a truth of descriptive morality, a fact of anthropology which entails neither first order nor second order ethical views. Yet it may indirectly support second order subjectivism: radical differences between first order moral judgements make it difficult to treat those judgements as apprehensions of objective truths. But it is not the mere occurrence of disagreements that tells against the objectivity of values. Disagreement on questions in history or biology or cosmology does not show that there are no objective issues in these fields for investigators to disagree about. But such scientific disagreement results from speculative inferences or explanatory hypotheses based on inadequate evidence, and it is hardly plausible to interpret moral disagreement in the same way. Disagreement about moral codes seems to reflect people's adherence to and participation in different ways of life. The causal connection seems to be mainly that way round: it is that people approve of monogamy because they participate in a monogamous way of life rather than that they participate in a monogamous way of life because they approve of monogamy. Of course, the standards may be an idealization of the way of life from which they arise: the monogamy in which people participate may be less complete, less rigid, than that of which it leads them to approve. This is not to say that moral judgements are purely conventional. Of course there have been and are moral heretics and moral reformers, people who have turned against the established rules and practices of their own communities for moral reasons, and often for moral reasons that we would endorse. But this can usually be understood as the extension, in ways which, though new and unconventional, seemed to them to be required for consistency, of rules to which they already adhered as arising out of an existing way of life. In short, the argument from relativity has some force simply because the actual variations in the moral codes are more readily explained by the hypothesis that they reflect ways of life than by the hypothesis that they express perceptions, most of them seriously inadequate and badly distorted, of objective values.

But there is a well-known counter to this argument from relativity, namely to say that the items for which objective validity is in the first place to be claimed are not specific moral rules or codes but very general basic principles which are recognized at least implicitly to some extent in all society— such principles as provide the foundations of what Sidgwick has called different methods of ethics: the principle of universalizability, perhaps, or the rule that one ought to conform to the specific rules of any way of life in which one takes part, from which one profits, and on which one relies, or some utilitarian principle of doing what tends, or seems likely, to promote the general happiness. It is easy to show that such general principles, married with differing concrete circumstances, different existing social patterns or different preferences, will beget different specific moral rules; and there is some plausibility in the claim that the specific rules thus generated will vary from community to community or from group to group in close agreement with the actual variations in accepted codes.

The argument from relativity can be only partly countered in this way. To take this line the moral objectivist has to say that it is only in these principles that the objective moral character attaches immediately to its descriptively specified ground or subject: other moral judgements are objectively valid or true, but only derivatively and contingently—if things had been otherwise, quite different sorts of actions would have been right. And despite the prominence in recent philosophical ethics of universalization, utilitarian principles, and the like, these are very far from constituting the whole of what is actually affirmed as basic in ordinary moral thought. Much of this is concerned rather with what Hare calls "ideals" or, less kindly, "fanaticism." That is, people judge that some things are good or right, and others are bad or wrong, not because—or at any rate not only because they exemplify some general principle for which widespread implicit acceptance could be claimed, but because something about those things arouses certain responses immediately in them, though they would arouse radically and irresolvably different responses in others. "Moral sense" or "intuition" is an initially more plausible description of what supplies many of our basic moral judgements than "reason." With regard to all these starting points of moral thinking the argument from relativity remains in full force.

9. THE ARGUMENT FROM QUEERNESS

Even more important, however, and certainly more generally applicable, is the argument from queerness. This has two parts, one metaphysical, the other epistemological. If there were objective values, then they would be entities or qualities or relations of a very strange sort, utterly different from anything else in the universe. Correspondingly, if we were aware of them, it would have to be by some special faculty of moral perception or intuition, utterly different from our ordinary ways of knowing everything else. These points were recognized by Moore when he spoke of non-natural qualities, and by the intuitionists in their talk about a "faculty of moral intuition." Intuitionism has long been out of favour, and it is indeed easy to point out its implausibilities. What is not so often stressed, but is more important, is that the central thesis of intuitionism is one to which any objectivist view of values is in the end committed: intuitionism merely makes unpalatably plain what other forms of objectivism wrap up. Of course the suggestion that moral judgements are made or moral problems solved by just sitting down and having an ethical intuition is a travesty of actual moral thinking. But, however complex the real process, it will require (if it is to yield authoritatively prescriptive conclusions) some input of this distinctive sort, either premisses or forms of argument or both. When we ask the awkward question, how we can be aware of this authoritative prescriptivity, of the truth of these distinctively ethical premisses or of the cogency of this distinctively ethical pattern of reasoning, none of our ordinary accounts of sensory perception or introspection or the framing and confirming of explanatory hypotheses or inference or logical construction or conceptual analysis, or any combination of these, will provide a satisfactory answer; "a special sort of intuition" is a lame answer, but it is the one to which the clearheaded objectivist is compelled to resort.

Indeed, the best move for the moral objectivist is not to evade this issue, but to look for companions in guilt. For example, Richard Price argues that it is not moral knowledge alone that such an empiricism as those of Locke and Hume is unable to account for, but also our knowledge and even our ideas of essence, number, identity, diversity, solidity, inertia, substance, the necessary existence and infinite extension of time and space, necessity and possibility in general, power, and causation. If the understanding, which Price defines as the faculty within us that discerns truth, is also a source of new simple ideas of so many other sorts, may it not also be a power of immediately perceiving right and wrong, which yet are real characters of actions?

This is an important counter to the argument from queerness. The only adequate reply to it would be to show how, on empiricist foundations, we can construct an account of the ideas and beliefs and knowledge that we have of all these matters. I cannot even begin to do that here, though I have undertaken some parts of the task elsewhere. I can only state my belief that satisfactory accounts of most of these can be given in empirical terms. If some supposed metaphysical necessities or essences resist such treatment, then they too should be included, along with objective values, among the targets of the argument from queerness.

This queerness does not consist simply in the fact that ethical statements are "unverifiable." Although logical positivism with its verifiability theory of descriptive meaning gave an impetus to non-cognitive accounts of ethics, it is not only logical positivists but also empiricists of a much more liberal sort who should find objective values hard to accommodate. Indeed, I would not only reject the verifiability principle but also deny the conclusion commonly drawn from it, that moral judgements lack descriptive meaning. The assertion that there are objective values or intrinsically prescriptive entities or features of some kind, which ordinary moral judgements presuppose, is, I hold, not meaningless but false.

Plato's Forms give a dramatic picture of what objective values would have to be. The Form of the Good is such that knowledge of it provides the knower with both a direction and an overriding motive; something's being good both tells the person who knows this to pursue it and makes him pursue it. An objective good would be sought by anyone who was acquainted with it, not because of any contingent fact that this person, or every person, is so constituted that he desires this end, but just because the end has to-be-pursuedness somehow built into it. Similarly, if there were objective principles of right and wrong, any wrong (possible) course of action would have not-to-be-doneness somehow built into it. Or we should have something like Clarke's necessary relations of fitness between situations and actions, so that a situation would have a demand for such-and-such an action somehow built into it.

The need for an argument of this sort can be brought out by reflection on

Hume's argument that "reason"—in which at this stage he includes all sorts of knowing as well as reasoning—can never be an "influencing motive of the will." Someone might object that Hume has argued unfairly from the lack of influencing power (not contingent upon desires) in ordinary objects of knowledge and ordinary reasoning, and might maintain that values differ from natural objects precisely in their power, when known, automatically to influence the will. To this Hume could, and would need to, reply that this objection involves the postulating of value-entities or value-features of quite a different order from anything else with which we are acquainted, and of a corresponding faculty with which to detect them. That is, he would have to supplement his explicit argument with what I have called the argument from queerness.

Another way of bringing out this queerness is to ask, about anything that is supposed to have some objective moral quality, how this is linked with its natural features. What is the connection between the natural fact that an action is a piece of deliberate cruelty—say, causing pain just for fun—and the moral fact that it is wrong? It cannot be an entailment, a logical or semantic necessity. Yet it is not merely that the two features occur together. The wrongness must somehow be "consequential" or "supervenient"; it is wrong because it is a piece of deliberate cruelty. But just what *in the world* is signified by this "because"? And how do we know the relation that it signifies, if this is something more than such actions being socially condemned, and condemned by us too, perhaps through our having absorbed attitudes from our social environment? It is not even sufficient to postulate a faculty which "sees" the wrongness: something must be postulated which can see at once the natural features that constitute the cruelty, and the wrongness, and the mysterious consequential link between the two. Alternatively, the intuition required might be the perception that wrongness is a higher order property belonging to certain natural properties; but what is this belonging of properties to other properties, and how can we discern it? How much simpler and more comprehensible the situation would be if we could replace the moral quality with some sort of subjective response which could be causally related to the detection of the natural features on which the supposed quality is said to be consequential.

It may be thought that the argument from queerness is given an unfair start if we thus relate it to what are admittedly among the wilder products of philosophical fancy—Platonic Forms, non-natural qualities, self-evident relations of fitness, faculties of intuition, and the like. Is it equally forceful if applied to the terms in which everyday moral judgements are more likely to be expressed—though still, as has been argued in Section 7, with a claim to objectivity—"you must do this," "you can't do that," "obligation," "unjust," "rotten," "disgraceful," "mean," or talk about good reasons for or against possible actions? Admittedly not; but that is because the objective prescriptivity, the element a claim for whose authoritativeness is embedded in ordinary moral thought and language, is not yet isolated in these forms of speech, but is presented along with relations to desires and feelings, reasoning about the means to desired ends, interpersonal demands, the injustice which consists in the violation of what are in the context the accepted standards of merit, the psychological constituents of meanness, and so on. There is nothing queer about any of these, and under cover of them the claim for moral authority may pass unnoticed. But if I am right in arguing that it is ordinarily there, and is therefore very likely to be incorporated almost automatically in philosophical accounts of ethics which systematize our ordinary thought even in such apparently innocent terms as these, it needs to be examined, and for this purpose it needs to be isolated and exposed as it is by the less cautious philosophical reconstructions.

10. PATTERNS OF OBJECTIFICATION

Considerations of these kinds suggest that it is in the end less paradoxical to reject than to retain the common-sense belief in the objectivity of moral values, provided that we can explain how this belief, if it is false, has become established and is so resistant to criticisms. This proviso is not difficult to satisfy.

On a subjectivist view, the supposedly objective values will be based in fact upon attitudes which the person has who takes himself to be recognizing and responding to those values. If we admit what Hume calls the mind's"propensity to spread itself on external objects," we can understand the supposed objectivity of moral qualities as arising from what we can call the projection or objectification of moral attitudes. This would be analogous to what is called the "pathetic fallacy," the tendency to read our feelings into their objects. If a fungus, say, fills us with disgust, we may be inclined to ascribe to the fungus itself a non-natural quality of foulness. But in moral contexts there is more than this propensity at work. Moral attitudes themselves are at least partly social in origin: socially established—and socially necessary—patterns of behavior put pressure on individuals, and each individual tends to internalize these pressures and to join in requiring these patterns of behaviour of himself and of others. The attitudes that are objectified into moral values have indeed an external source, though not the one assigned to them by the belief in their absolute authority. Moreover, there are motives that would support objectification. We need morality to regulate interpersonal relations, to control some of the ways in which people behave towards one another, often in opposition to contrary inclinations. We therefore want our moral judgements to be authoritative for other agents as well as for ourselves: objective validity would give them the authority required. Aesthetic values are logically in the same position as moral ones; much the same metaphysical and epistemological considerations apply to them. But aesthetic values are less strongly objectified than moral ones; their subjective status, and an "error theory" with regard to such claims to objectivity as are incorporated in aesthetic judgements, will be more readily accepted, just because the motives for their objectification are less compelling.

But it would be misleading to think of the objectification of moral values as primarily the projection of feelings, as in the pathetic fallacy. More important are wants and demands. As Hobbes says, "whatsoever is the object of any man's Appetite or Desire, that is it, which he for his part calleth *Good*"; and certainly both the adjective "good" and the noun "goods" are used in non-moral contexts of things because they are such as to satisfy desires. We get the notion of something's being objectively good, or having intrinsic value, by reversing the direction of dependence here, by making the desire depend upon the goodness, instead of the goodness on the desire. And this is aided by the fact that the desired thing will indeed have features that make it desired, that enable it to arouse a desire or that make it such as to satisfy some desire that is already there. It is fairly easy to confuse the way in which a thing's desirability is indeed objective with its having in our sense objective value. The fact that the word "good" serves as one of our main moral terms is a trace of this pattern of objectification.

Similarly related uses of words are covered by the distinction between hypothetical and categorical imperatives. The statement that someone "ought to" or, more strongly, "must" do such-and-such may be backed up explicitly or implicitly by reference to what he wants or to what his purposes and objects are. Again, there may be a reference to the purposes of someone else, perhaps the speaker: "You must do this"—"Why?"—"Because I want such-and-such." The moral categorical imperative which could be expressed in the same words can be seen as resulting from the suppression of the conditional clause in a hypothetical imperative without its being replaced by any such reference to the speaker's wants. The action in question is still required in something like the way in which it would be if it were appropriately related to a want, but it is no longer admitted that there is any contingent want upon which its being required depends. Again this move can be understood when we remember that at least our central and basic moral judgements represent social demands, where the source of the demand is indeterminate and diffuse. Whose demands or wants are in question, the agent's, or the speaker's, or those of an indefinite multitude of other people? All of these in a way, but there are advantages in not specifying them precisely. The speaker is expressing demands which he makes as a member of a community, which he has developed in and by participation in a joint way of life; also, what is required of this particular agent would be required of any other in a relevantly similar situation; but the agent too is expected to have internalized the relevant demands, to act as if the ends for which the action is required were his own. By suppressing any explicit reference to demands and making the imperatives categorical we facilitate conceptual moves from one such demand relation to another. The moral uses of such words as "must" and "ought" and "should," all of which are used also to express hypothetical imperatives, are traces of this pattern of objectification.

It may be objected that this explanation links normative ethics too closely with descriptive morality, with the mores or socially enforced patterns of behavior that anthropologists record. But it can hardly be denied that moral thinking starts from the enforcement of social codes. Of course it is not confined to that. But even when moral judgments are detached from the mores of any actual society they are liable to be framed with reference to an ideal community of moral agents, such as Kant's kingdom of ends, which but for the need to give God a special place in it would have been better called a commonwealth of ends.

Another way of explaining the objectification of moral values is to say that ethics is a system of law from which the legislator has been removed. This might have been derived either from the positive law of a state or from a supposed system of divine law. There can be no doubt that some features of modern European moral concepts are traceable to the theological ethics of Christianity. The stress on quasi-imperative notions, on what ought to be done or on what is wrong in a sense that is close to that of "forbidden," are surely relics of divine commands. Admittedly, the central ethical concepts for Plato and Aristotle also are in a broad sense prescriptive or intrinsically action-guiding, but in concentrating rather on "good" than on "ought" they show that their moral thought is an objectification of the desired and the satisfying rather than of the commanded. Elizabeth Anscombe has argued that modern, non-Aristotelian, concepts of *moral* obligation, *moral* duty, of what is *morally* right and wrong, and of the *moral* sense of "ought" are survivals outside the framework of thought that made them really intelligible, namely the belief in divine law. She infers that "ought" has "become a word of mere mesmeric force," with only a "delusive appearance of content," and that we would do better to discard such terms and concepts altogether, and go back to Aristotelian ones.

There is much to be said for this view. But while we can explain some distinctive features of modern moral philosophy in this way, it would be a mistake to see the whole problem of the claim to objective prescriptivity as merely local and unnecessary, as a post-operative complication of a society from which a dominant system of theistic belief has recently been rather hastily excised. As Cudworth and Clarke and Price, for example, show, even those who still admit divine commands, or the positive law of God, may believe moral values to have an independent objective but still action-guiding authority. Responding to Plato's *Euthyphro* dilemma, they believe that God commands what he commands because it is in itself good or right, not that it is good or right merely because and in that he commands it. Otherwise God himself could not be called good. Price asks, "What can be more preposterous, than to make the Deity nothing but will; and to exalt this on the ruins of all his attributes?" The apparent objectivity of moral value is a widespread phenomenon which has more than one source: the persistence of a belief in something like divine law when the belief in the divine legislator has faded out is only one factor among others. There are several different patterns of objectification, all of which have left characteristic traces in our actual moral concepts and moral language.

11. THE GENERAL GOAL OF HUMAN LIFE

The argument of the preceding sections is meant to apply quite generally to moral thought, but the terms in which it has been stated are largely those of the Kantian and post-Kantian tradition of English moral philosophy. To those who are more familiar with another tradition, which runs through Aristotle and Aquinas, it may seem wide of the mark. For them, the fundamental notion is that of the good for man, or the general end or goal of human life, or perhaps of a set of basic goods or primary human purposes. Moral reasoning consists partly in achieving a more adequate understanding of this basic goal (or set of goals), partly in working out the best way of pursuing and realizing it. But this approach is open to two radically different interpretations. According to one, to say that something is the good for man or the general goal of human life is just to say that this is what men in fact pursue or will find ultimately satisfying, or perhaps that it is something which, if postulated as an implicit goal, enables us to make sense of actual human strivings and to detect a coherent pattern in what would otherwise seem to be a chaotic jumble of conflicting purposes. According to the other interpretation, to say that something is the good for man or the general goal of human life is to say that this is man's proper end, that this is what he ought to be striving after, whether he in fact is or not. On the first interpretation we have a descriptive statement, on the second a normative or evaluative or prescriptive one. But this approach tends to combine the two interpretations, or to slide from one to the other, and to borrow support for what are in effect claims of the second sort from the plausibility of statements of the first sort.

I have no quarrel with this notion interpreted in the first way. I would only insert a warning that there may well be more diversity even of fundamental purposes, more variation in what different human beings will find ultimately satisfying, than the terminology of "*the* good for man" would suggest. Nor indeed, have I any quarrel with the second, prescriptive, interpretation, provided that it is recognized as subjectively prescriptive, that the speaker is here putting forward his own demands or proposals, or those of some movement that he represents, though no doubt linking these demands or proposals with what he takes to be already in the first, descriptive, sense fundamental human goals. But if it is claimed that something is objectively the right or proper goal of human life, then this is tantamount to the assertion of something that is objectively categorically imperative, and comes fairly within the scope of our previous arguments. Indeed, the running together of what I have here called the two interpretations is yet another pattern of objectification: a claim to objective prescriptivity is constructed by combining the normative element in the second interpretation with the objectivity allowed by the first, by the statement that such and such are fundamentally pursued or ultimately satisfying human goals. The argument from relativity still applies: the radical diversity of the goals that men actually pursue and find satisfying makes it implausible to construe such pursuits as resulting from an imperfect grasp of a unitary true good. So too does the argument from queerness; we can still ask what this objectively prescriptive rightness of the true goal can be, and how this is linked on the one hand with the descriptive features of this goal and on the other with the fact that it is *to some extent* an actual goal of human striving.

To meet these difficulties, the objectivist may have recourse to the purpose of God: the true purpose of human life is fixed by what God intended (or, intends) men to do and to be. Actual human strivings and satisfactions have some relation to this true end because God made men for this end and made them such as to pursue it—but only *some* relation, because of the inevitable imperfection of created beings.

I concede that if the requisite theological doctrine could be defended, a kind of objective ethical prescriptivity could be thus introduced. Since I think that theism cannot be defended, I do not regard this as any threat to my argument. Those who wish to keep theism as a live option can read my arguments hypothetically, as a discussion of what we can make of morality without recourse to God, and hence of what we can say about morality if, in the end, we dispense with religious belief.

12. CONCLUSION

I have maintained that there is a real issue about the status of values, including moral values. Moral scepticism, the denial of objective moral values, is not to be confused with any one of several first order normative views, or with any linguistic or conceptual analysis. Indeed, ordinary moral judgements involve a claim to objectivity which both non-cognitive and naturalist analyses fail to capture. Moral scepticism must, therefore, take the form of an error theory, admitting that a belief in objective values is built into ordinary moral thought and language, but holding that this ingrained belief is false. As such, it needs arguments to support it against "common sense." But solid arguments can be found. The considerations that favour moral scepticism are: first, the relativity or variability of some important starting points of moral thinking and their apparent dependence on actual ways of life; secondly, the metaphysical peculiarity of the supposed objective values, in that they would have to be intrinsically action-guiding and motivating; thirdly, the problem of how such values could be consequential or supervenient upon natural features; fourthly, the corresponding epistemological difficulty of accounting for our knowledge of value entities or features and of their links with the features on which they would be consequential; fifthly, the possibility of explaining, in terms of several different patterns of objectification, traces of which remain in moral language and moral concepts, how even if there were no such objective values people not only might have come to suppose that there are but also might persist firmly in that belief. These five points sum up the case for moral scepticism; but of almost equal importance are the preliminary removal of misunderstandings that often prevent this thesis from being considered fairly and explicitly, and the isolation of those items about which the moral sceptic is sceptical from many associated qualities and relations whose objective status is not in dispute.

BIBLIOGRAPHY

My views on the subject of this chapter were first put forward in "A Refutation of Morals," published in the *Australasian Journal of Psychology and Philosophy* 24 (1946), but substantially written in 1941. Discussions current at about that time which helped to determine the main outlines of my position are recorded in, for example, Charles L. Stevenson's *Ethics and Language* (New Haven, 1941) and A. J. Ayer's *Language, Truth, and Logic* (London, 1936). An unjustly neglected work which anticipates my stress on objectification is E. Westermarck's *Ethical Relativity* (London, 1932). But the best illustration and support for the arguments of this chapter, and for much else in the book, are provided by the works of such earlier writers as Hobbes, Locke, Samuel Clarke, Hutcheson, Butler, Balguy, Hume, and Richard Price, of which substantial selections are edited by D. D. Raphael in *British Moralists 1650–1800* (Oxford, 1969): for example, Balguy brings out very clearly what I call the "claim to objectivity."

There is a full survey of recent controversy between critics and defenders of naturalism in "Recent Work on Ethical Naturalism" by R. L. Franklin in *Studies in Ethics, American Philosophical Quarterly Monograph No. 7* (1973). Concentration on questions of meaning is criticized by P. Singer in "The Triviality of the Debate over "Is-ought" and the Definition of " 'Moral' " in the *American Philosophical Quarterly* 10 (1973).

The quotations from R. M. Hare are from "Nothing Matters," in his *Applications of Moral Philosophy* (London, 1972). This article was written in 1957. Hare's present view is given in "Some Confusions about Subjectivity" in *Freedom and Morality*, edited by J. Bricke (University of Kansas Lindley Lectures, 1976). References to Sidgwick throughout this book are to *Methods of Ethics* (London, 1874), and those to Kant are to *Groundwork of the Metaphysic of Morals*, translated (for example) by H. J. Paton in *The Moral Law* (London, 1948). The quotation from Russell is from his "Reply to Criticisms" in *The Philosophy of Bertrand Russell*, edited by P. A. Schlipp (Evanston, 1944). G. E. M. Anscombe's view is quoted from"Modern Moral Philosophy," in *Philosophy* 33 (1958), reprinted in *The Definition of Morality*, edited by G. Wallace and A. D. M. Walker (London, 1970). The argument of Section 11 owes much to private discussion with J. M. Finnis.

18   *Relativism Refuted?*

RICHARD BRANDT

Many social scientists and philosophers have counted themselves moral relativists in some sense or other. We cannot deal with all the various views which are properly called forms of "moral relativism"; so I propose to explain a form of moral relativism which seems to me an interesting, and somewhat plausible theory. This theory comprises the following three affirmations: (1) The *basic* moral principles (standards) of different individuals *or* groups sometimes are, or *can be,* in some important sense conflicting. (Anthropologists tend to be more interested in group differences, but since individuals at least appear to disagree even in primitive societies, it seems wise to expand the theory to include individual differences.) (2) When there is such fundamental conflict of basic principles or standards, there is either always, or at least sometimes, no way to show that one view is better justified even in the presence of ideally complete factual information; in that sense the principles are equally justified or "valid." (3) But there is a sense in which a particular moral belief may be mistaken or unjustified, if it is a *misapplication* of the basic principles of the individual or group, e.g., if the basic principles plus statements of known or knowable facts entail a moral proposition incompatible with it. As stated, moral relativism could be true even though in fact, accidentally, all individuals agree in their basic moral principles.

When is a moral principle said to be *basic?* Suppose we had before us all the moral judgments an individual would make, if called upon to appraise any situation, and we require of him that he identify the general principles to which he would appeal in explanation of these judgments. Then we inquire whether there is some more general principle to which he would appeal in justification of the first-level general principles. We proceed further in the same way until we have reached a minimal set of principles sufficient to yield his particular appraisals, when taken with factual beliefs of his. We then have a set of principles of the form, "All acts of the kind K are morally wrong (or *prima facie* wrong, or reprehensible, or morally excused, as the case may be)," where the "kind K" is spelled out sufficiently so that the person is willing to call *all* actions of that kind wrong (etc.). (It is convenient to absorb any neces-

Reprinted, by permission of the publisher and copyright holder, from Richard Brandt, "Relativism Refuted?," in *The Monist* 67 (1984): 297–307.

sary qualifications about the circumstances into the description of the action-type K.) If one party thinks that all acts of the kind K are morally wrong, and the other party thinks that at least some acts of the kind K are morally permissible (and the same, *mutatis mutandis,* for other moral concepts), their principles are fundamentally in conflict, at least on what we might call the "common-sense" level.

We should notice, however, that a person who tried to identify his basic principles in this way might find that the principles to which he has been appealing are not consistent among themselves; or he might find that they imply appraisals of particular situations he is unwilling to accept. As a result of such a finding, he might make some adjustments in his principles or particular evaluations, finding himself with a somewhat modified but more coherent system of moral views. (Much moral discussion takes the form of identifying implications of a person's principles which he can't stomach, or particular evaluations which would require appeal to principles which the person cannot accept.) We should notice that if a person changes his moral evaluations or principles in this way, it is not that it has been *proved* to him that some evaluation or principle was mistaken; it has only been shown that his earlier set of beliefs was incoherent, and he has moved to a coherent system, among several open to him, which he finds more convincing. We could say, following some terminology of Rawls, that the person has moved to a state of "reflective equilibrium in the narrow sense." It could be that the principles of two persons (groups) still differ at this reflective level. One kind of relativism will say that they will. Let us call this kind of theory "moral relativism for moral principles (standards) in narrow reflective equilibrium."

We might, however, set a stricter standard for what counts as a person's (society's) basic moral principles. We might say that a person's really basic principles are those he *would* subscribe to after a process of education: after reading available (or perhaps ideally possible?) literature in philosophy, psychology, and anthropology. For example, he might examine Harsanyi's or Hare's arguments for utilitarianism, or Rawls's argument for certain principles of natural duty. Or he might read psychologists on how we come by our moral predilections, and it might become clear that he would take a more utilitarian view about the force of promises if he had not been irrationally influenced by his father. (Of course, if some of the philosophical arguments turn out to be cogent, e.g., Hare's argument for utilitarianism, there will no longer be any room for disagreement except about matters of fact.) It is possible that after persons had gone through this ideally complete education they would still have conflicting moral principles (just as Rawls and Nozick seem to do, about tax and welfare policies). A relativist might say there is, or could be, a clash of principles of this sort, between persons whose moral views Rawls would say are in "wide reflective equilibrium." If he does, we might say he is a relativist about moral principles "at the philosophical level."

I believe the most interesting question about relativism is whether relativism about moral principles at the philosophical level is a correct theory.

Social scientists have not, I believe, been much interested in this somewhat speculative issue, although the second thesis of relativism, in the vague form in which I have stated it ("no way to show that one view is better justified even in the presence of ideally complete factual information"), might be construed so as, in effect, to make relativism a theory about moral principles on the philosophical level.

How shall we decide whether relativism in this sense is a correct theory? I believe that, if we are to do this, we have to place ourselves, as best we can, in the position of a person who has read the more important relevant work of philosophers, psychologists, anthropologists, and perhaps others, and then to make up our minds, in view of our knowledge of moral language, morality, the place of moral language in morality, the place of morality in society, and so on, about the central questions of metaethics, in particular what moral statements do mean in ordinary speech, or about what they would mean if they were used in an optimally clear and helpful fashion. The present paper, however, is obviously not the place to review various possible proposals, and to argue on behalf of one or more of them. I shall simply set forth a view which is currently convincing to me and which I have defended in recent writing.[1] This view is that, although we may reasonably describe a performatory function which a moral statement has in particular contexts (say, condemning, advising, expressing an attitude, etc.), we cannot identify a cognitive content of such statements beyond perhaps a claim that the performatory impact of the utterance is *justified*, in some appropriate sense. The view also is that *there are reasons for using and understanding and teaching* "A is morally wrong" both as expressing a condemning attitude and making a claim that this attitude has *a specific kind* of justification. The specific kind of justification that it is useful (etc.) to claim is that the condemnation of the agent of A is called for by the moral system which all rational (fully informed, etc.) persons would tend to support, in preference to any other, if they expected to live in the society of the agent of A. (What I mean by a "moral system" is roughly adults having aversions to performing acts of certain types, e.g., injuring another person, feeling guilty if they act in one of these forbidden ways except when there is justification or excuse, and disapproving of other persons if they behave in a forbidden way, except when there is justification or excuse. Thus a "moral system" is defined in terms of motivational concepts. Obviously "justification" and "excuse" must be spelled out, in a fuller account.) There is, however, an alternative view that is simpler: that the justificatory claim is the primary thing, so that "A was morally wrong" should be construed as "A would be prohibited by the moral system which all rational persons would tend to support . . ." and so on as before. In this case the utterance would be condemnatory in virtue of what is asserted. The reasons for using moral language in this general way obviously cannot be rehearsed in this paper. But we have to notice that there is an important possibility which may call for some revision of the above proposed definitions. For is it not possible that *not all* rational persons would tend to support either condemning A or one and the same moral system for the society of the agent of *A?* In order to provide for this contingency, we have to consider an alternate reading: "*A* was morally wrong" is to be used as expressing condemnation of *A* (or the agent of *A*), and making the claim "My condemning *A* is called for by the moral code which I, *if I were fully rational* (etc.), would tend to support, in preference to any other, if I expected to live in the society of the agent of *A*." Or, to take the simpler form, "*A* would be prohibited by that moral code which I, *if I were fully rational* (etc.), would support for the society of the agent of *A*, if I expected to live there." This statement would express condemnation because of what is affirmed. These last two construals of "*A* is wrong" are *relativist,* in the sense that the truth of the statement made is *relative* to something about the speaker—what he would prefer under specified ideal conditions. One can adopt either of them, and consistently also defend the theses of relativism on the philosophical level. The former two construals are not consistent with the theses of relativism. Since I am not *sure* whether or not all fully informed rational (etc.) persons would support the same moral system, I don't know whether we *need* the complicating relativist definition of "morally wrong," as contrasted with the absolutist reading. Both of my definitions are far from implying that an action is right if and only if it conforms with the moral code actually prevalent in the society of the agent (or speaker), or if it conforms with the actual moral code of the agent or speaker as an individual.

So far, then, it appears that relativism can be developed as a coherent theory. Nevertheless, I—and I suspect most other philosophers—have an antirelativist predilection, at least when we come to moral issues which are important. Therefore I would welcome a showing that something or other is seriously amiss with relativism, either with the relativist construal of moral language, or elsewhere. I should particularly welcome a showing that something is logically amiss somewhere, or that there is a cogent philosophical argument against one of the central features of the relativist theory. I should also welcome a showing that conflicting attitudes toward conceptually the same actions, or moral systems, when these attitudes are properly qualified (by full knowledge, etc.) are causally impossible, on the basis of well-supported psychological theory. And I should welcome a showing that commonsense observations of the attitudes of people with whom we interact, and the observations of anthropologists, provide no serious support for the view that fully informed (etc.) persons do or can have clashing preferences among moral systems. Unfortunately, I think psychology goes the other way, even if one were to grant that sociobiological reasoning supports a degree of native altruism in everyone, or even some principles of justice,[2] since the role of conditioning and models in the acquisition of moral attitudes and preferences in general points toward probable variation. The same for anthropology. Consider the Hopi, who do not (at least did not) condemn cruelty to small animals, but condemn strongly anyone getting drunk as well as mild forms of violence (fist-fighting). It is hard to believe that such data do not establish a presumption that there is conflict of attitudes among people who agree in their conceptions of what they are appraising, and that they might well continue to disagree if they approach an ideally qualified state of mind. Or, doubtless better, we might compare the views of Henry Sidgwick with those of W. D. Ross, or those of John Rawls with those of Robert Nozick. Of course, there is no easy proof here, from such types of comparison. What a philosopher with antirelativist predilections will hope for most is a showing of a logical fault somewhere in relativism, either in the proposed construals of moral language or elsewhere; or, if there is no logical incoherence one would like to find some conclusive philosophical objection. One would like to find such a showing somewhere in the literature.

For these reasons I wish to look at recent important contributions by Professor David Lyons and Professor Philippa Foot.

First Professor Lyons.[3] Lyons would first point out that the above relativistic definition of "wrong" has the implication that it is *possible* for A to say correctly that it is right for Claudia to have an abortion, and for B to say, equally correctly, that it is wrong, provided they have the respective attitudes of tolerance and condemnation, and also are fully informed, rational, and want different sets of moral principles for Claudia's society. This result Lyons finds objectionable, because it conflicts with "the conviction shared by laymen and philosophers that only one of these judgments could possibly be right, and also our ways of discussing such cases, which include advancing reasons that are held to warrant drawing or refusing one judgment or the other."[4] This reason seems of doubtful force. Convictions shared by laymen and philosophers need not be all that sound. There is even doubt whether laymen do take this view, considering how widespread relativism is today, and there are surely many philosophers who think that if A and B are fully informed (etc.) and still disagree, there is no more to be said. Of course, a relativist has good reasons for advancing *arguments* for his moral views, and for thinking they should have impact (if they carry weight with him); Claudia's husband might well wish to reach agreement with her and put forward reasons which he thinks or hopes will modify her views about the morality of abortion, or about the desirability of a certain moral stance about it.

Lyons would feel slightly better if my above definition were amended, replacing "which I if I were fully rational (etc.) would" by "which *the agent*, if she were fully rational (etc.) would . . ." Then, at least, conflicting ethical judgments would not be said to be correct.[5] But, as he agrees for other reasons, this strategy does not meet the difficulty. For surely I might still think it morally right, or even obligatory, for Claudia to have an abortion, even if she thinks it wrong or would support a moral system condemning abortion if she were fully informed. (I might think Claudia's attitudes have been deeply molded by a conservative Catholic upbringing.)

Lyons does not discuss precisely the status of the relativistic analysis of moral judgments explained above, but we can infer what he would say from what he says about a very similar view.[6] Take my suggestion that "A was morally wrong" is to be used and understood as "A would be prohibited by that moral code which I, if I were fully rational (etc.), would tend to support . . . ," a statement which in context would express condemnation. Suppose now X says it is right (in this sense) for Claudia to have an abortion, whereas Y says it is wrong. Lyons says that on the surface it appears that X and Y are saying incompatible things about the proposed abortion. "But, according to this sort of theory, they are confused if they believe their judgments to be incompatible. In fact, the theory says, they are actually talking at cross purposes." But *are* they talking at cross-purposes? It is true that the two statements do not contradict one another, but, in context, the one expresses condemnation and the other withholds it. So there is practical disagreement—quite enough reason for each to explore whether he may not bring reasons to make the other change his mind. Lyons, in fact, is prepared to admit this.[7]

Lyons accuses relativists of offering relativist analyses of moral statements for no better reason than to save their general relativistic position.[8] There *could*, however, be another reason—the difficulties faced by other analyses. Lyons does not tell us positively where he tends to stand; for all he says, he may be a nonnaturalist about moral statements, or some kind of naturalist. He says, criticizing Hare, that Hare "fails to consider seriously the possibility of logically sound nondeductive arguments from factual premises to moral conclusions."[9] But he does not explain what he has in mind. Until some plausible alternative account is forthcoming, the relativist need not feel very uncomfortable.

Let me now turn to Professor Foot. She is somewhat sympathetic toward a limited form of relativism, but she thinks that some moral statements are *logically* guaranteed. She says, for instance, that "it is clearly an objective moral fact that the Nazi treatment of the Jews was morally indefensible, given the facts and their knowledge of the facts. . . . It was impossible, logically speaking, for them to argue that the killing of millions of innocent people did not need any moral justification, or that the extension of the German Reich was in itself a morally desirable end."[10] In her 1970 British Academy Lecture she says: "A moral system seems necessarily to be one aimed at removing particular dangers and securing certain benefits, and it would follow that some things do and some do not count as objections to a line of conduct from a moral point of view. There may be strict proof of some moral propositions, such as that Hitler's treatment of the Jews was morally indefensible. . . . There are . . . starting-points fixed by the concept of morality. We might call them 'definitional criteria' of moral good and evil, so long as it is clear that they belong to the concept of morality. . . . What we say about such definitional criteria will be objectively true or false."[11] So, she says, relativism "as a theory of *all* moral judgment . . . is, of course, false if the thesis of definitional criteria is correct.[12] Professor Foot does not, however, claim that these objectively true moral statements *provide reasons for action* for everybody; if a man does not care about justice or the good of other people, telling him what he objectively ought to do need not move him, even if he is rational.[13]

What are we to make of the claim that there is "strict proof" of some moral propositions? Let me first state two possible views of how this might be. I have above described what is the form of the "moral system" which appears to be instanced by all societies: aversions to tokens of some act-types for no further reason, tendencies to feel guilt if one acts in one of these ways with no excuse, disapproval of others if their conduct manifests a below-standard level of these aversions. Now this conception of a moral code permits that there be different, and conflicting, demands made by different codes. But this need not leave us no possibility of adjudicating between them; we may have good reason to think one code is better than another (as indeed W. G. Sumner did). What I have argued in a recent book is that we can ask whether all rational (informed, etc.) persons would prefer one moral code, for a society in which they expected to live, to all others. And I claimed that it is true that all (or virtually all) rational persons would prefer a moral code which had certain central features to a code otherwise the same which lacked them. Even perfectly selfish persons would want a moral system which provided protection against unprovoked assault on person or reputation. And I argued that rational persons will want a system fostering self-restraints, mutual trust, openness, the absence of need to be on one's guard against malicious attacks.[14] In that sense one moral system can be said to be preferable to another. Certain features which are not necessarily part of a moral system as such can be present in one which rational persons would prefer, for a society in which they expected to live. Is this a "strict proof" that unprovoked assault on another person is immoral? Well, it depends on a psychological fact: that rational persons would not *want* a moral code without such a prohibition.

Professor Foot's account seems to be at least somewhat different. She says that a "moral system seems necessarily to be aimed" at certain things, and there are "starting-points fixed by the concept of morality." But the functional or teleological language about the necessary aim of moral codes is surely not, defensible by appeal to any scientific theories or facts—sociobiology or anything else. It looks as if she can only say that a moral system *necessarily* aims at certain things in the sense that, if it didn't, we wouldn't call it a "moral" system. So it turns out that it is a fact about our use of "moral" that the Nazi treatment of the Jews was morally indefensible. As she said in an earlier paper,[15] "Anyone who uses moral terms at all . . . must abide by the rules for their use, including the rules about which shall count as evidence for or against the moral judgment concerned. . . . It is open to us to inquire whether moral terms do lose their meaning when divorced from the pleasure principle, or from some other set of criteria. . . . To me it seems that this is clearly the case; I do not know what could be meant by saying that it was someone's duty to do something unless there was an attempt to show why it mattered if this sort of thing was not done."[16] These lines were first printed in 1958, and appear to represent a theory of meaning which was popular in Oxford then, and possibly now, but has never received a convincing defense; it is reminiscent of an earlier positivism. Why should we think that some consideration which most, or even all, people would regard as a pro-point for holding a certain statement to be true should be somehow incorporated into the *meaning* of that statement? A certain pattern of temperature changes is a strong sign of typhoid fever, but no one would say that such a pattern is part of what it *means* to have typhoid fever. Or take Bohr's conception of the hydrogen atom. Bohr's concept, taken with principles taken as established, explained the spectral lines of hydrogen. But no one would take the fact of the spectral lines as part of Bohr's *concept* of the hydrogen atom. Suppose I say that a certain action taken by a public official was morally right both because it fostered the general welfare, and because it promoted economic equality, and because it conformed with the will of the electorate. Are we really supposed to say that these concepts are all somehow comprised in the meaning of "right"? And just how would the explanation go? Professor Foot appears to hold that "wrong" means one thing, different from the evidence which supports it, but nevertheless it would be *meaningless* to say something is wrong while affirming that it doesn't *matter* whether it was done.[17] One can wonder about this: an action might not make society better off, but promote equality, and fulfill a promise. Is the concept of "matters" so nebulous that in this situation one can say the action *matters*? Just what is added to the description of the "evidence," by the affirmation that the act is wrong? Professor Foot herself anticipates that critics will say she has taken principles of her own preferred morality, elevated their status to that of rules of inference special to moral thinking and partially definitive of "moral" so that it is self-contradictory to deny them, but still holds that something important is being said, if one says these principles are "moral principles." What is it that is important that is being said, and why should one be especially interested in whether one's principle is "moral" in this sense?

Professor Foot recognizes the possibility of a conception of morality, or a moral code or moral system, or "having moral principles," somewhat like that defended by me above. But she asks "Why should it be supposed that the concept of morality is to be caught in this particular kind of net? The consequences of such an assumption are very hard to stomach; for it follows that a rule which was admitted by those who obeyed it to be completely pointless could yet be recognized as a moral rule."[18] True: but is this impossible to stomach? Would W. D. Ross find it hard to stomach saying that the obligation to keep a promise, when so doing serves no utility, is a "pointless" moral rule? The Hopi did not feel unhappy in their condemnation of incest, although they had no explanation of its benefits, beyond saying that "only dogs do that."

According to my alternative proposal, "moral codes" refers to a psychological structure at least virtually universal among peoples, but with variable content.[19] If one does not like to call such phenomena "moral codes," one may drop that term and call them something else. But one can still ask an important question about them: whether rational persons, given their human nature and the principles of psychology and the world they live in, would support, or prefer, one set of such rules for their society compared with all other possible rules. I believe that, at least for the central core of moral codes, the answer is that all informed rational persons would want them in the social moral code; perhaps on some there would not be agreement. But this is not just a matter of logic, or of "rules of evidence" for moral terminology. Even the distorted views of Nazis about genocide are not ruled out by sheer logic.

In her more recent Lindley Lecture, Professor Foot has a paragraph independent of her other view (also expressed in the same lecture) about the sheer logical certification of certain moral statements. She writes: "There is a great deal that all men have in common. All need affection, the cooperation of others, a place in a community, help in trouble. It isn't true to suppose that human beings can flourish without these things—being isolated, despised or embattled, or without courage or hope. We are not, therefore, simply expressing values that we happen to have if we think of some moral systems as good moral systems and others as bad."[20] That is true, as long as it is understood that the values that are necessary are so in the sense of causal, not logical necessity. Rational people will necessarily, in that sense, want certain features in the moral code of their society. Professor Foot goes on to say something else with which one can agree: whereas some people think that such "objective evaluation of moral systems can go only a little way, . . . one wonders . . . why people who say this kind of thing are so sure that they know where discussions will lead and therefore where they will end."[21] I agree; and it is for this reason that I think it *may* well turn out that on important but complex issues such as abortion, termination of defective newborns, euthanasia, and civil disobedience there is one and only one right answer.

NOTES

1. R. B. Brandt, *A Theory of the Good and the Right,* 1979, Clarendon Press, Oxford, p. 194; "The Explanation of Moral Language," in *Morality, Reason, and Truth,* ed. David Copp (Totowa, N.J.: Rowman & Allanheld, 1984), pp. 104–19.

2. See R. L. Trivers, "The Evolution of Reciprocal Altruism," *Quarterly Review of Biology* 53 (1971), 35–57, and Allan Gibbard, "Human Evolution and the Sense of Justice," *Midwest Studies in Philosophy* 7 (1982), 31–46.

3. David Lyons, "Ethical Relativism and the Problem of Incoherence." *Ethics* 86 (1976), 107–21; reprinted in Michael Krausz and J. W. Meiland (eds.), *Relativism: Cognitive and Moral,* 1982, Notre Dame: University of Notre Dame, pp. 152–68. Page references are to the reprint.

4. Ibid., p. 210.

5. Ibid., p. 212.

6. Ibid., p. 222.

7. Ibid.

8. See my "The Explanation of Moral Language," for a statement of reasons which may be advanced for a certain type of "reforming" definition. It is evident that no predilection for a relativist analysis has anything to do with it. Lyons writes as if he thinks a satisfactory explanation of moral language as it is actually used by ordinary people can be provided, but he gives no hint what this would be or how the analysis could be defended.

9. Lyons, p. 219.

10. P. Foot, "Moral Relativism," The Lindley Lecture at the University of Kansas, 1978; reprinted in Krausz and Meiland, op. cit. References to this reprint, here p. 163.

11. P. Foot, "Morality and Art," *Proceedings of the British Academy* 56 (1970), 131–44. The citation is from pp. 132–33.

12. "Morality and Art," p. 136.

13. Ibid., p. 142.

14. *A Theory of the Good and the Right*, Ch. 11.

15. "Moral Arguments," *Mind* 67 (1958); reprinted in her *Virtues and Vices*, 1978, University of California Press, Berkeley. The references are to this reprint, here p. 105. For an interesting defense of this view on the basis of a kind of Davidsonian theory of meaning, see David Cooper, "Moral Relativism," in *Midwest Studies in Philosophy, III*, 1978, Minneapolis, MN: University of Minnesota Press, pp. 105–06.

16. Ibid., p. 105. This view may be shared by Lyons; see the passage quoted from him supra, op. cit., p. 219. A very similar view is suggested by Steven Lukes, "Relativism: Cognitive and Moral," *Supplementary Volume, The Aristotelian Society*, 48 (1974), p. 188.

17. See her *Virtues and Vices*, p. 105, also 107–08.

18. *Virtues and Vices*, p. 107. She seems to have Professor Hare in mind.

19. Professor David Cooper (see n15) has raised some possible objections to this view, aimed to show that most *moral* judgments must agree.

20. In Krausz and Meiland, p. 164.

21. Ibid.

19

Relativism and Normative Nonrealism: Basing Morality on Rationality

THOMAS L. CARSON
PAUL K. MOSER

1. PROBLEMS AND PROJECTS

Realist moral theories often countenance certain moral facts as preconditions for facts about rationality, thus presuming those moral facts to be logically prior to facts about what is rational or irrational. Moral realism implies that some things are good or bad or right or wrong independently of facts about the attitudes (for example, the beliefs and desires) of moral agents—even under ideal conditions. Attitude-independent moral facts, according to certain realist moral theories, determine—at least partly and defeasibly—what is rational and what is irrational. On these realist moral theories, standards of rationality include such principles as the following: It is prima facie irrational to prefer the bad to the good; it is prima facie irrational to prefer a lesser good to a greater good; it is prima facie irrational to prefer a greater bad to a lesser bad.[1]

Moral nonrealism, in contrast, denies, first, that some things are good or bad or right or wrong independently of facts about the attitudes of moral agents, and, second, that attitude-independent moral facts determine what is rational. Many important nonrealist moral theories, including the theories of Rawls, Firth, Gauthier, Brandt, and Hare, are based squarely on theories of rationality.[2] These theories take facts about what is rational or irrational to be logically prior to what is moral; they assume that things are right or good because it is rational to choose them or at least to have a certain attitude of approval toward them. Such theories assume three things: (a) that moral realism is false or at least unjustifiable, (b) that there is a conceptual connection between morality and rationality, and (c) that the theory of rationality

Reprinted, by permission of the publisher and copyright holder, from Thomas Carson and Paul Moser, "Relativism and Normative Nonrealism: Basing Morality on Rationality," in *Metaphilosophy* 27 (1996): 277–295.

endorsed by the theory is the correct account of rationality. Rawls, Firth, Gauthier, Brandt, and Hare are all committed to (c). Because their moral theories have theories of rationality at their foundations, each of these theorists must defend a particular account of rationality. Otherwise we may reasonably prefer an alternative moral theory based on a different account of rationality. The arguments of these nonrealist theories for their first-order moral judgments are no stronger, in the end, than the arguments for their theories of rationality. Rawls's argument, for example, that parties to the original position would prefer his two principles of justice to the principle of average utility depends on his assumption that it is rational for those in the original position to adopt a maximin strategy—rather than some other strategy, such as the policy of maximizing expected utility.[3]

Assuming that (a) and (b) are true (if only for the sake of argument), we find that assumption (c) poses a serious problem for nonrealist normative theories that oppose relativism about morality and rationality. In accepting (a) and (b) while rejecting (c), one will be open to a troublesome kind of relativism about morality and rationality. We may briefly illustrate this point in connection with a straightforward nonrealist moral theory based on a theory of rationality: Roderick Firth's ideal-observer theory. Firth takes his ideal-observer theory to offer both a standard of correctness and a theory of meaning for moral judgments. Let's grant, if only for the sake of argument, Firth's assumption that a moral judgment (say, that an action is right) is true if and only if an ideal observer would have a certain attitude of approval (in this case, toward the action is question). A particular definition of "ideal observer," given Firth's theory, presupposes a certain understanding of rationality, as the features characteristic of an ideal observer are essential, at least by Firth's lights, to a *rational* moral judge. Suppose that Firth were to reject assumption (c), adding that there is no reason to choose between three contrary theories of rationality, R1, R2, and R3. In that case, Firth must also grant that there is no reason to prefer any one of the following contrary theories of morality over the others: (i) the ideal-observer theory wherein an ideal observer is characterized by R1; (ii) the ideal-observer theory wherein an ideal observer is characterized by R2; and (iii) the ideal-observer theory wherein an ideal observer is characterized by R3. We shall show that (c) is dubious, especially when understood as implying that there is a single theory of rationality most suitable as a basis for nonrealist normative theories. Our argument may fall short of showing that (c) is false, but it will show that a heavy burden of proof rests with proponents of (c). We shall argue that normative nonrealism based on a theory of rationality cannot oppose relativism in a non-question-begging manner, in a manner that does not beg certain important questions against critics of the normative theory proposed. In begging the questions to be identified, nonrealists will simply assume contested, inadequately defended answers to those questions.[4]

We shall argue that a theory of rationality (such as that underlying familiar versions of normative nonrealism) cannot be defended against relativism, in a non-question-begging manner, on *semantic* grounds, by appeal to "the meaning" of "rational." Two considerations will arise. First, it is highly doubtful that the word "rational" has a single, univocal meaning in either ordinary language or philosophical discourse. Second, even if there were a single, univocal meaning of "rational," one might sensibly ask, "Why should I care about being rational in that sense?" We shall also consider pragmatic arguments for adopting a particular approach to rationality. Although there are pragmatic arguments favoring a full-information theory of rationality, these arguments, we shall see, appeal to contingent features of humans that are not shared by every human. These arguments, we shall contend, cannot establish the correctness of a full-information theory of rationality in a non-question-begging manner, given certain unanswered "Why care?" questions that motivate relativism. We shall focus on a full-information approach to rationality, such as that recently proposed by Richard Brandt, but our conclusions will bear on various kinds of normative nonrealism that depend on a theory of rationality but oppose relativism.

2. RATIONALITY AND MEANING

No particular theory of rationality can find unqualified support just in semantic considerations: for example, in "the" meaning of the word "rationality." We do not have a single specific concept of rationality that accommodates all familiar uses of the term "rational." Here we may think of one's concept of rationality as one's semantic standards constitutive of correctness in one's use of "rational" or some synonymous term (perhaps even a term in German or French, for example). Such standards determine for one the *category* of correctness—what it is to be correct—regarding the use of certain terms. We shall construe "concept" broadly, allowing any of one's conceptual truths about rationality to contribute to one's concept of rationality. (Talk of "one's" conceptual truths is not equivalent to talk of what one believes to be conceptually true; it rather signifies what is true given just one's conceptual, or semantic, commitments). We shall also allow that even if two people share a general, nonspecific concept of rationality, they can still have divergent concepts of rationality at a level of specificity.[5] One common area of divergence concerns whether a notion of impartiality figures in one's specific concept of rationality; egoistic approaches to rationality, often found in treatments of individual decision theory, exclude basic requirements of impartiality from rationality.[6]

Even if there were just one widely shared specific notion of rationality in circulation, a troublesome question could still remain open: Why care about being rational in *that* widely shared sense of "rational"? Motivation for this question might run as follows: Even if the sense in question captures what most English speakers mean when they use the word "rational," I do not care to be rational in *that* sense. I simply do not care whether my attitudes and actions satisfy the proposed conditions for being rational. If right and wrong and good and bad are determined by what is rational in that sense of "rational," then I care not at all about what is right or wrong or good or bad. Nothing about my purposes, including my intrinsic desires, recommends that I care about being rational in the sense in question. The demand that I be rational in that sense has no motivational force for me—no supporting motivational reason for me. It thus is not relevantly different from the infinity of other possible demands lacking motivational significance for me. That demand would therefore not be accompanied by a motivationally cogent answer, for me, to the aforementioned question, "Why care?" Such considerations, arising from the open question "Why care?," can confront any attempt to justify a particular theory of rationality solely on semantic grounds for all conceivable rational agents.

Given a variety of specific notions of rationality, we evidently cannot use semantic considerations by themselves to justify, in a non-question-begging manner, adoption of a particular notion of rationality as a basis for morality for all concerned. Can we give some other sort of justification for adopting a particular nonrelativist approach to rationality that underlies normative non-realism? Let us turn to some considerations that might seem to favor a non-relativist full-information account of rationality.

3. RATIONALITY AND FULL INFORMATION

An attitude or action of yours is rational, on a full-information account, if and only if you would endorse that attitude or action were you "fully informed."[7] Perhaps this principle is more relevant to an account of objective rightness or optimality than to an account of rationality. We sometimes speak of people acting rationally on the basis of *in*complete information. This indicates that at least one ordinary use of the term "rational" is apparently at odds with a full-information account. Considerations of ordinary use, however, are not decisive against a full-information account of rationality as a basis for a normative theory.

In *A Theory of the Good and the Right*, Richard Brandt writes:

> I shall pre-empt the term "rational" to refer to actions, desires, or moral systems which survive maximal criticism and correction by facts and logic. We could of course use some other term, like "fully informed," but the choice of "rational" seems as good as any.[8]

Brandt holds that statements of the form "It would be rational to perform act A" serve to guide action by recommending action and evaluating available action in terms of a standard.

More recently, Brandt has characterized the prospective use of "would be rational for X to do A" as follows:

> I hereby recommend that X do A, while [a] taking as my objective maximizing satisfaction of the transitive mood-independent ultimate desires of X, as

they would be if they had been subjected to repeated vivid reflection on relevant facts, and [b] having as my beliefs about options for actions and consequences those which are justified on X's evidence—a recommendation made because A is that one among the options justifiably believed to be open, choice of which exemplifies a strategy for decision-making which we know will in the long run satisfy the (as above) corrected desires of X as effectively as any other strategy can be known to do.[9]

A constraint on rational action, according to Brandt's account, comes from ultimate desires that are *corrected* in that they can withstand "cognitive psychotherapy": that is, suitable reflection on all relevant facts, or on full relevant information.

Cognitive psychotherapy raises special problems in Brandt's theory.[10] It seems possible that cognitive psychotherapy will fail to extinguish irrational desires in certain cases, but Brandt's view implies that this is *logically impossible*. Suppose that a desire of yours was caused by obviously false beliefs arising from just wishful thinking, and that this desire would not be extinguished in cognitive psychotherapy when those false beliefs are corrected. Such a desire could nonetheless be irrational given its basis only in irrational beliefs. According to Brandt, however, the fact that a desire persists in the light of cognitive psychotherapy *guarantees* that it is rational. Brandt thus seems unduly optimistic about the causal efficacy of cognitive psychotherapy. A full-information account need not, however, incorporate Brandt's specific approach to cognitive psychotherapy, but can invoke a different approach.[11] For current purposes, we need not digress to the latter topic.

4. ARGUMENTS FOR A
FULL-INFORMATION APPROACH

Certain considerations might seem to recommend a full-information account of rationality. First, most psychologically normal adults evidently would be willing, on suitable reflection, to endorse a policy of regulating their attitudes and actions in the light of full information. On suitable reflection, they would regard the standpoint of full information as ideal for assessing attitudes and actions. Consider the preferences to purchase an ante-bellum mansion, marry the person next door, and pursue a lucrative dental career. Most people having such preferences will be open to criticizing them in light of new or corrected information: for example, learning that the mansion has termites, knowing vividly what it would be like to be married to the person next door, or learning that the dental career is ultimately tedious. Most psychologically normal people would, on suitable reflection, regard full information as an ideal standpoint for deciding these issues.

Appeal to the preferences of "most psychologically normal people" does not yield a decisive argument for a nonrelativist full-information approach to rationality. Even if it is a fact about most psychologically normal people that on suitable reflection they would regard full information as an ideal stand-point for decision-making, we can still ask about the significance of that fact for an account of rationality. Are questions about the relevance of an approach to rationality for everyone to be settled by majority rule: that is, by what most (normal) people would hold on suitable reflection? In particular, is everyone subject to the requirements of a full-information approach to rationality because on suitable reflection *most* (normal) people would regard full information as an ideal decision-making standpoint? An affirmative answer promotes what will seem arbitrariness, if not mere dogmatism, from the standpoint of those outside the majority.

Decision-makers outside the majority will press the following open ques-tion: Why care about being rational in the sense endorsed by most (normal) people on reflection? This question calls for an answer that is not readily forth-coming. An answer resting just on semantic grounds will face an open "Why care?" question of the sort noted previously, in Section 2. A full-information theorist might contend, in reply, that people *should* care, that people are guilty of an important mistake in not caring. Such a contention must itself, however, withstand "Why care?" questions of the sort under scrutiny: in this case, why care about avoiding "mistakes" of the kind in question (as if they would be serious, genuine mistakes)? The latter task, we shall see, is a tall order.

The second consideration seemingly favoring a full-information account is that virtually every person has conflicting preferences all of which cannot be satisfied. In light of such conflicting preferences, we typically have the metapreference that our preferences be satisfied efficiently, with minimal loss—especially relative to the preferences we deem important. Full informa-tion is arguably the ideal standpoint for satisfying our preferences efficiently. If you act on incomplete or incorrect information, you may be acting in igno-rance of relevant consequences of your preferences or actions. Such acting is ordinarily conducive to inefficient satisfaction of one's overall preferences.

A likely reply is that we are typically interested in having only *adequately reliable* information, not necessarily full information. Many people think that they often have adequate information on which to act rationally, even though they lack full information. People rarely take the effort to acquire full infor-mation—or even all available information—about a decision. Even so, our taking full information as the ideal standpoint for decision-making is consis-tent with our rarely desiring full information enough to pay the cost of acquiring it. We seldom, if ever, can acquire all information relevant to assess-ing our attitudes and actions. You are now incapable, for example, of acquir-ing all the information relevant to the purchase of a certain Toyota you like. Full information includes not only all facts relevant to the performance of that Toyota, but also all facts about every other available Toyota for sale within your price range. Given the availability of thousands of Toyotas for sale, you could devote an indefinite amount of time, effort, and expense to gathering information about the purchase of a Toyota. Most people would agree that it is rational for you in such a case to act on information less com-plete than all relevant information. The price, in monetary terms alone, of obtaining all relevant information far exceeds the value of any Toyota. It would seemingly be irrational, in such a case, for anyone to take the effort to obtain all relevant information. This fits, however, with the claim that full information is the ideal standpoint for making decisions. Saying that full information is the ideal standpoint for making decisions permits that it is often not worth the effort to obtain all relevant information. We shall clarify why this is so.

The claim that full information is the ideal standpoint for decision-making entails that in choosing between the following two options, we should prefer the second option:

1. Making the decision in accord with our preferences given our present incomplete information,

and

2. Making the decision in accord with what we would prefer given full information.

Regarding a decision between choosing a car in accord with our preferences given our present incomplete information and choosing a car in accord with what we would prefer given full information, most psychologically normal people would probably prefer the latter. The costs and difficulty of obtaining information do not count against the claim that it is preferable to choose 2 to 1.

We typically regard full information as a better standard for decision-making than all *available* information. Consider the choice between:

3. Making the decision in accord with what we would prefer given all information available to us,

and

2. Making the decision in accord with what we would prefer given full information.

Since it is possible that some important information is now unavailable to us, most psychologically normal people would prefer 2 to 3. Full-information accounts entail that we should do so.

5. OBJECTIONS TO A
FULL-INFORMATION APPROACH

Some people prefer not to have certain information, even when obtaining it involves no real cost. You may not want to know, for example, the details of torture because having such knowledge would be severely distressing for you. A similar problem arises from cases where one's having full information produces a psychological breakdown from cognitive overload or otherwise renders one incapable of effective choice. In a different case, you may not want to know what certain people really think about you, owing to fear that it might upset you or otherwise negatively affect you. In particular, you might be in a situation where impartiality is required but is jeopardized by full information. Your knowing what your students think about you as a teacher, for instance, could affect your decision about what grades to assign; and you might recognize that such knowing would affect your decision. In such a case, full information would not be the ideal standpoint for your deciding on grades. These are just a few of many cases where one may, it seems, rationally not prefer to have full information.

The cases involving severe distress and psychological breakdown illustrate that one's *having* full information can have unwelcome consequences. In saying that full information is the ideal standpoint for decision-making, one is not committed to having full information or even to preferring that one have full information. One is committed only to preferring that one's decision fit with *what one would prefer given full information.* Our decision about a certain Toyota, for instance, can fit with what we would prefer given full information even if we neither have nor prefer to have full information. This consideration removes the threat from the case involving severe distress. That case would be troublesome if a full-information account of rationality required that one prefer to have full information; but this is not required.

A serious problem comes from the case of psychological breakdown from cognitive overload. Suppose that if you were vividly aware, in excruciating detail, of all the suffering caused by such a large-scale catastrophe as World War II, you would lose your sanity. In that case, what you would prefer given full information is what you would prefer given a psychological breakdown from cognitive overload. You might, of course, have some bizarre preferences after a psychological breakdown. It is thus doubtful that you would now endorse what you would prefer given a psychological breakdown, or given the full information that will produce such a breakdown. This case requires that a full-information theorist suitably restrict the counterfactual conditions under which one has full information.

One might specify what it is rational for *you* to prefer by appeal to what *someone else*—someone impervious to psychological breakdown—would prefer given full information. One might appeal, in this vein, to what an omnipotent being would prefer given full information. (One thus might seek a parallel between a divine-command theory of moral rightness and a divine-command theory of rationality.) This move can avoid the problem of psychological breakdown only at the expense of inviting an unanswered "Why care?" question: Why care about what *someone else* would prefer given full information? It is not obvious that what someone else would prefer given full information bears on what is rational *for you.* If we try to settle this matter by semantic considerations, we shall face the "Why care?" question from Section

2. The problem from psychological breakdown thus leads to a serious problem for a full-information account of rationality. We see no cogent way to resolve that problem in favor of a full-information account.

What about the previous case involving a requirement of impartiality? In that case, fair grading requires that you not factor into the grading what your students think of you. If you knew what your students think of you, you would (by hypothesis) prefer a vindictive grading policy lacking impartiality. You now, however, prefer impartiality in your grading, and thus prefer not to have full information about your students. The problem here, therefore, does not arise from a preference for full information. It arises rather from what preferences about grading you *would have given full information.* Regardless of whether you now prefer full information, we can imagine that given full information, you would lose impartiality in grading. This, we can suppose, is just a fact about your vindictive character. Given that you now prefer impartiality in grading, you thus do not prefer to grade in accord with what you would prefer given full information. Since we cannot plausibly regard your preference for impartiality in grading as necessarily irrational, the present case raises a problem for full-information accounts.

One might reply that the appropriate standpoint for making decisions is all *relevant* information, instead of full information. The key constraint on rationality, on this reply, comes from what one would prefer given all relevant information. Regarding the problem at hand, the reply assumes that your knowing what your students think of you is irrelevant to what grades you should assign. This seems plausible enough, but we now face a difficult problem of specifying the exact conditions for *relevant* information. Clearly, we cannot say simply that relevant information is information that would "make a difference." Information about what your students think of you would, by hypothesis, make a big difference to your grading policy. Such is your vindictive nature, regardless of your commitment to impartiality given your current incomplete information. Let us not digress, however, to the difficult task of supplying a suitable notion of relevant information.[12] Even given such a notion, a serious problem remains. We turn now to this problem.

6. REASONS AND MOTIVES: INTERNALISM AND EXTERNALISM

What is the perceived value of deciding in accord with what we would prefer given full information or at least full relevant information? Perhaps the value consists in removing the risk of forgoing expected desirable consequences and of causing unexpected unwelcome consequences given preferences on incomplete information. What we would prefer given full information could omit certain current preferences that, on incomplete information, will lead to unexpected unwelcome consequences. Given incomplete information, we may have preferences whose satisfaction will have unexpected undesirable consequences. Your current preference to own your neighbor's used Toyota could leave you with a car whose motor is, unexpectedly, defective beyond repair. Your preference on full information would definitely not be for your neighbor's Toyota. Preferences on incomplete information thus risk unexpected unwelcome consequences, whereas preferences on full information avoid such risk. This, coupled with the risk of forgoing expected desirable consequences, explains why most normal people prefer making decisions (at least typically) in accord with what they would prefer given full information.

Full-information accounts assume that rational preferences match what one would prefer on full information—where one has no risk of unexpected unwelcome consequences. Suppose, however, that you actually prefer the risk of unexpected unwelcome consequences, and do not prefer what you would prefer on full information in the absence of risk of unexpected unwelcome consequences. You actually prefer not the unexpected undesirable consequences themselves, but only the risk thereof. Such risk is pleasurable, indeed invigorating, for you. You thus prefer decision-making in the presence of such risk.

Full-information theorists can allow for your preference for decision-making in the presence of risk, and can acknowledge the unavoidability of risk for us humans. Your preferences are rational, according to such theorists, only if they agree with what you would prefer given full information. Even so, your current preferences may (rationally) rest on incomplete information and thus face the risk of unexpected unwelcome consequences. Full-information theorists can thus accommodate your preference for risk of unexpected unwelcome consequences. A preference for such risk is quite compatible with the view that rational preferences fit with what one would prefer given full information.

Even though full-information theories can accommodate a preference for risk, those who prefer to take risks may have no reason whatever to care about what they would prefer given full information. Suppose that you do not care at all to avoid the risk, given preferences on incomplete information, of forgoing expected desirable consequences and having unexpected unwelcome consequences. You might care, or have reason to care, only about your *actual* preferences, while neither preferring nor having reason to prefer what you would prefer given full information. You thus lack an answer to this question: Why care about satisfying preferences you do not actually have but only *would have* given full information?

We can coherently suppose that your purposes, including your intrinsic purposes, support no preference for what you would prefer given full information. The demand that you prefer what you would prefer given full information would then have no motivational force for you—no supporting motivational reason for you. That demand would not then be relevantly different from the infinity of other possible demands lacking motivational significance for you. In short, that demand would not be accompanied by a motivationally cogent answer to the aforementioned question, "Why care?" Such a demand would stem, relative to your standpoint of motivational reasons, from a kind of arbitrariness or mere dogmatism inappropriate to what is motivationally cogent for you. If a full-information account of rationality is proposed as binding on every conceivable rational agent, it will condone such alleged arbitrariness or dogmatism. The unacceptability of such arbitrariness and dogmatism, many theorists will argue, recommends that we consider alternatives to a full-information account.

The motivations of some people provide them with no reason whatever to care about what they would do if fully informed. Full-information theorists have the burden of showing that such motivational sets (consisting at least of one's preferences, desires, and intentions) are somehow mistaken or defective. It is not sufficient for full-information theorists simply to claim that people *ought* to care about what they would want if they had full information. Such a claim must itself resist "Why care?" questions of the sort at hand: for example, why care about satisfying the proposed requirement?

Full-information theorists might appeal to the difference between the following:

4. The preferences you would have if you had full information, allowing that your having full information alters at least some of your current intrinsic preferences,

and

5. The preferences you would have if you had full information, disallowing that your having full information alters any of your current intrinsic preferences.

The contention of a full-information theorist would be that, to the extent that one's actual preferences differ from those one would have given full information, one's actual preferences are mistaken owing to their reliance on ignorance or false beliefs.

The option allowing alteration of current intrinsic preferences (namely, 4) needs support to be cogent. An attempt to support that option merely on semantic grounds will fail, as Section 2 suggests. Such an attempt will face "Why care?" questions that will not be left open by a motivationally cogent account of rationality—an account that is nonarbitrary and nondogmatic from the motivational standpoint of agents raising such questions. Aside from semantic considerations, option 4 must face this open question: Why care about satisfying ideal preferences that one does not actually have? A cogent answer to this question must identify a relevant difference between (a) the demand that we care about satisfying ideal preferences and (b) the infinity of other possible demands that lack supporting reasons for us. This is a big task if one aims to make rationality a function of 4 for every conceivable, or even every actual, rational agent.

An alternative strategy for full-information theorists claims that rationality is a function of the preferences one would have if one had full information while all one's current intrinsic preferences remained unchanged (namely, 5 rather than 4). This option ties rationality more closely to our actual motivations than does 4, and thus seems better able to handle "Why care?" questions. Someone might object as follows: "Why should I care about what I would prefer if I were fully informed and my current preferences remained unaltered? I suspect that my current preferences are largely mistaken owing to their reliance on false beliefs." In reply, we should note that someone sincerely objecting thus will typically have the metapreference that her ideal preferences override her actual preferences in cases of conflict. Given that metapreference, the satisfaction of one's actual preferences (which include the former metapreference) will not contradict one's ideal preferences. Still, one's actual preferences could be mistaken, in some sense, and this prompts the foregoing question.

Let us call certain standards of rationality *motivationally cogent* for you if and only if those standards have the power, on the basis of your actual evidential and motivational set, to regulate—to compel or to constrain—attitudes or actions for you. In addition, let us understand *internalism* as the view that the standards of rationality binding on a person must be motivationally cogent for that person; *externalism,* in contrast, denies that standards of rationality must be thus cogent. Motivationally cogent standards of rationality depend on perspectival reasons—reasons that have a basis in one's actual motivational perspective, including one's preferences, desires, and intentions. Standards of rationality lacking corresponding perspectival reasons for one thus lack motivational cogency for one, according to internalism. Such standards are at best arbitrary from the standpoint of one's perspectival reasons. The arbitrariness is illustrated by the absence of a relevant difference, from one's motivational standpoint, between such standards and the infinity of other possible standards lacking motivational significance for one. Standards of rationality that rely *just* on preferences one simply *would have* under ideal conditions will thus be arbitrary at best for one from the standpoint of one's motivational reasons.

Nonarbitrary standards for the regulation of attitudes and actions cannot, according to internalism, rest just on evidential reasons—reasons indicating that such-and-such is the case. Even if certain evidential standards indicate that you rationally should perform action *A,* you can plausibly ask: Why care about satisfying *those* evidential standards? This question will remain open if you have no reason whatever in your motivational set for doing *A.* The claim that doing *A* is rationally required for you will then be arbitrary at best from your motivational perspective; and an approach to rationality entailing this arbitrary claim will itself lack motivational cogency for you. Given internalism, nonarbitrary standards for rational regulation must be sensitive to one's motivational set.[13]

A decisive test for an internalist approach to rationality comes from this question: Why care about the satisfaction of one's own evidential and motivational set? If this question remains open for any conceivable agent, internalists face a problem of the sort raised previously for full-information accounts. This question will not remain open so long as all pertinent "Why care?" questions seek perspectival reasons based in the questioner's own evidential and motivational set. An internalist approach to rationality will specify what is rationally required, optimal, and satisfactory for one relative to one's own evidential and motivational set. It will thus construe those categories of what is rational in terms of one's own perspectival reasons. So long as "Why care?" questions seek perspectival reasons, an internalist approach to rationality will face no threat from such questions.

What about "Why care?" questions that do not seek perspectival motivational reasons? This question forces us to face externalist alternatives to internalism about reasons. Why care about the "Why care?" questions that motivate an internalist approach to rationality? An externalist might begin an objection with that question. An internalist might reply as follows: Since "Why care?" questions seek reasons in one's actual evidential and motivational set, and since one desires to achieve the satisfaction of one's evidential and motivational set, one *does* care about satisfying that set. One does care, then, about satisfying the evidential and motivational set yielding the perspectival reasons that can answer "Why care?" questions.

An externalist will object to an internalist approach on the ground that it neglects certain normatively important "Why care?" questions. In particular, an externalist will reply that internalists have failed to answer why one *should* care about satisfying one's actual evidential and motivational set. An externalist will deny that internalists can answer the latter question simply by claiming that one *does* care to satisfy one's evidential and motivational set. An externalist here uses "should" in a way irreducible to something explicable in terms of what one actually desires; for to the extent that what one actually desires rests on faulty beliefs, one's desires may be faulty as well. Internalism implies that there is a prima facie reason for you to (prefer to) do A if and only if your motivational (and evidential) set recommends, explicitly or by implication, that you (prefer to) do A. Externalism, in contrast, implies that you can have a prima facie reason to (prefer to) do A even if your motivational set does not recommend that you (prefer to) do A. One species of externalism comes from full-information accounts that tie reasons for actions to the motivational set one *would have* if fully informed.

Both internalists and externalists can construe the question "Why care?" as "Why *should* I care?" The difference is that internalists, unlike externalists, hold that one's reasons and rational requirements must have a basis in one's actual motivational set, including one's actual preferences, desires, and intentions. Internalists will treat externalist "Why care?" questions as follows: "I do not care about so-called 'rationality' of an externalist sort and, furthermore, I am not guilty of any kind of error in not caring; so I do not see why I *should* care."

Consider externalist "Why care?" questions seeking reasons not in one's actual evidential and motivational set, but rather in some ideal evidential and motivational set. Suppose that someone knowingly prefers reasons based in an ideal evidential and motivational set, and thus seeks such reasons in asking "Why care?" questions. Would not such a person be concerned with

"Why care?" questions different from those underlying a perspectival, internalist approach to rationality? No. The case at issue includes someone who "knowingly prefers reasons based in an ideal evidential and motivational set." That preference is itself part of the person's actual evidential and motivational set. It thus provides a perspectival reason of the sort underlying internalism. We do not have here, then, a problem for internalism. Externalists need a different formulation of the objection at hand.

An externalist does not demand that requirements of rationality have a basis in the motivational set of the person for whom they are rational requirements. An externalist might claim, for example, that I am rationally required to help my poor neighbors even though nothing in my motivational set inclines me to do so. An externalist could hold that it is irrational for me not to help my poor neighbors, and that I should care about helping them— regardless of my actual inclinations. An internalist must face such an externalist approach to what we should care about.

An internalist will counter that the main problem with externalism about rationality surfaced previously in this section. According to internalism, an externalist requirement of rationality will be arbitrary, if not simply dogmatic, from the standpoint of agents lacking a supporting reason in their motivational (and evidential) sets. Externalism, in short, does not guarantee motivationally cogent, perspectival reasons. An internalist will thus charge that externalism itself lacks motivational cogency as an approach to rationality. The internalist's perspectival approach to rationality does guarantee motivationally cogent reasons, and thus arguably avoids the dogmatism and motivational irrelevance threatening alternative accounts of rationality. So long as we shun arbitrariness and dogmatism in standards of rationality, according to the internalist, we shall have good reason to endorse a perspectival, internalist approach to rationality. An externalist will, however, be unmoved; for externalism rests on an approach to a regulative normative reason that does not require actual motivational efficacy.

We now face two conflicting approaches to a regulative reason for attitudes and actions. An internalist approach assumes a necessary connection between a regulative normative reason and a motivational reason. An externalist approach disclaims any such connection. We can highlight the difference by asking whether ultimate consistent desires can be mistaken from a rational point of view. Externalists think so, and internalists disagree. Externalists hold that certain considerations can determine normative reasons and rational requirements even for a person altogether disinclined to conform to those reasons and requirements (and anything entailing those reasons and requirements).

Put broadly, the key issue is this: Is something, X, rationally preferable for you because you prefer X (or at least prefer something requiring X)? Or, alternatively, does the rationality of your preferring X depend on things independent of your actual desires?[14] Internalists answer "yes" to the former question and "no" to the latter, while externalists give opposite answers. Even if internalists and externalists can agree on some very general, rather vague thesis about rationality, their approaches to rationality diverge at a level of specificity.

How shall we decide between an internalist and an externalist approach to rationality? Some philosophers will appeal to our "intuitive," pre-theoretic judgments to decide the matter; some others will look for an answer in our "ordinary use" of the terms "rational" and "reason." It is doubtful, however, that either intuitive judgments or ordinary use will settle the matter without variability. Intuitive judgments about rationality and reasons vary significantly among philosophers. Philosophical disputes about rationality illustrate this, if they illustrate anything. Similarly, common use of the terms "rational" and "reason" offers no unmixed standard for recommending either internalism or externalism. Common use seems sometimes to favor internalism, and sometimes, externalism. Given nonrealism, one will lack the resources to exclude, in a non-question-begging manner, internalist approaches to reasons. Accordingly, one will lack non-question-begging answers to "Why care?" questions arising from an internalist perspective. It follows that a nonrealist who endorses externalism about reasons will not be able to offer a non-question-begging defense against relativism; for such a nonrealist, in the presence of internalist "Why care?" questions, cannot give a non-question-begging argument in favor of any particular account of rationality. This threat of normative relativism seems inescapable by the nonrealist. Obviously analogous points apply to the internalist who is a nonrealist. Both the externalist and the internalist, then, will be hard put to resist relativism in a non-question-begging manner.

We cannot avoid the problem by claiming that a particular concept of rationality is required to undergird everything qualifying as a *moral* system. One might argue otherwise on semantic grounds, claiming that it is part of "the concept of morality" that morality requires rationality of a certain sort: for example, impartiality or "impartial reason." This claim would appeal straightforwardly to "the" concept of morality, and thus would invite an open "Why care?" question analogous to that noted previously, in Section 2. Given a claim that morality requires us to be rational, in a certain sense of "rational," one can plausibly ask why we should care about being moral in *that* sense of "morality."[15] Here we confront direct analogues, concerning morality, of the previous points about rationality. The "Why care?" questions that trouble appeals to rationality thus have close cousins that are equally troublesome for appeals to reason-based morality.

7. CONCLUSION

"Why care?" questions wreak havoc for nonrelativist nonrealist approaches to rationality and reason-based morality. Such nonrealist approaches must now explain how we can handle the troublesome "Why care?" questions just raised. Nonrealists might offer a normative theory independent of a theory of rationality, but no such nonrelativist normative theory is now prominent. The prominent nonrelativist versions of nonrealism in circulation, such as those cited previously, must face the argument of this paper. *Perhaps* moral realism of some sort can support a non-question-begging rejection of relativism about rationality, but, in doing so, it must likewise handle the aforementioned "Why care" questions. Whether moral realism can actually do so remains as an issue worthy of separate investigation.[16]

NOTES

1. Recent proponents of normative realism include David Wiggins, "Truth, Invention, and the Meaning of Life," in Geoffrey Sayre McCord, ed., *Essays on Moral Realism* (Ithaca: Cornell University Press, 1988), pp. 127–65; E. J. Bond, *Reason and Value* (Cambridge: Cambridge University Press, 1983); and Panayot Butchvarov, *Skepticism in Ethics* (Bloomington: Indiana University Press, 1989).

2. See Rawls, *A Theory of Justice* (Cambridge, Mass.: Harvard University Press, 1970), pp. 143, 401; Firth, "Ethical Absolutism and the Ideal Observer," *Philosophy and Phenomenological Research* 12 (1952), 317–45; Gauthier, *Morals by Agreement* (Oxford: Clarendon Press, 1986), chap. 1; Brandt, *A Theory of the Good and the Right* (Oxford: Clarendon Press, 1979), p. 112; Hare, *Moral Thinking* (Oxford: Clarendon Press, 1981), pp. 214–17. Our characterization of Rawls applies to his views in *A Theory of Justice*, not to his most recent views. Even if it is conceivable that a version of normative nonrealism is independent of a theory of rationality, the prominent nonrelativist versions are not so; and the latter provide the focus of this paper. Brandt has some relativistic tendencies, but they are not motivated by the considerations central to this paper.

3. See Rawls, *A Theory of Justice*, pp. 155–57. Unless they follow a maximin strategy, people in the original position will have no reason to choose a principle of distribution designed to make the position of the least well-off group as good as possible, instead of an alternative distribution principle that (from the perspective of the original position) might afford them greater expected utility. Rawls's argument for thinking that people in the original position would be rational to adopt a maximin strategy have been widely criticized; see, for example, Brian Barry, *The Liberal Theory of Justice* (Oxford: Oxford University Press, 1973), chap. 9; Thomas Nagel, "Rawls on Justice," in Norman Daniels, ed., *Reading Rawls* (New York: Basic Books, 1976), pp. 11–12; and R. M. Hare, "Rawls' Theory of Justice," in *Reading Rawls*, pp. 102–107.

4. For doubts about any purely formal criterion of begging questions, see Roy Sorensen, "'*P*, Therefore, *P*' without Circularity," *The Journal of Philosophy* 88 (1991), 245–66.

5. On the distinction between general and specific concepts, with special attention to notions of correctness and rightness, see Paul Moser, *Philosophy After Objectivity* (New York/Oxford: Oxford University Press, 1993), chap. 4. Common general moral concepts may arise from common general moral ends, such as simply "getting to believe and getting to act." On the latter ends, see Neil Cooper, *The Diversity of Moral Thinking* (Oxford: Clarendon Press, 1981), chap. 12.

6. On egoistic approaches to rationality, see William Frankena, "Concepts of Rational Action in the History of Ethics," *Social Theory and Practice* 9 (1983), 165–97.

7. We shall not pursue a detailed account of full information itself, but shall allow for a range of accounts. For one technical difficulty that may bear on such an account, see Patrick Grim, "There Is No Set of All Truths," *Analysis* 44 (1984), 206–208.

8. Brandt, *A Theory of the Good and the Right*, p. 10. Brandt does not propose his theory as an analysis of the meaning of "rational," he rather suggests that we can "replace" talk of rationality with his talk of desires and actions that withstand suitable reflection on full information. Our comments in the previous section were thus not directed at Brandt. Our concern now is with the familiar view that a full-information approach provides the best *general policy* for action and preference.

9. Brandt, "The Concept of Rational Action," *Social Theory and Practice* 9 (1983), 161.

10. See, on some of the problems, Allan Gibbard, "A Noncognitivistic Analysis of Rationality in Action," *Social Theory and Practice* 9 (1983), 204–205; and Robert Audi, "Rationality and Valuation," in Paul Moser, ed., *Rationality in Action* (Cambridge: Cambridge University Press, 1990), pp. 429–30.

11. For some alternative accounts, see Stephen Darwall, *Impartial Reason* (Ithaca: Cornell University Press, 1983), chap. 8; Thomas Carson, *The Status of Morality* (Dordrecht: Reidel, 1984), pp. 178–79; and Richard Foley, *The Theory of Epistemic Rationality* (Cambridge, Mass.: Harvard University Press, 1987), chap. 1.

12. On some of the difficulties, see Thomas Carson, *The Status of Morality*, pp. 57–58.

13. An internalist must face this question: Is one's motivational set sufficient for generating the perspectival reasons essential to the rational regulation of attitudes and actions? If it is, your preferring to do *A* while having no contravening preference suffices for your having a reason to do *A*. Suppose, however, that you prefer to do *A* but have no indication whatever that you prefer this. You might even have every indication—say, from salient behavioral and memorial evidence—that you do not prefer to do *A*. If you have no evidence whatever that you prefer to do *A*, the claim that you have a reason to do *A* will be arbitrary at best relative to your evidential perspective on your own motivational set. Your indications regarding what constitutes your own motivational set will not then support your doing *A*, and thus will not then provide a reason for your doing *A*. An internalist might hold, therefore, that perspectival reasons for regulating attitudes and actions must arise from one's evidential set as well as one's motivational set. Cases involving conflicting—jointly unsatisfiable—motivational components require that an internalist approach be complicated somewhat. An internalist can let an individual's own preferences about the relative significance of her conflicting preferences determine priority. On the latter approach, one can steer clear of the sort of arbitrariness and dogmatism that arguably threatens full-information accounts.

14. In *General Theory of Value* (Cambridge, Mass.: Harvard University Press, 1926), p. 4. R. B. Perry raises an analogous question: "Is a thing valuable because it is valued? Is England valuable because Englishmen love it; and, in a negative sense, because Germans hate it? Or is a thing valued because it is valuable?" Perry identifies this issue in Spinoza (cf. *Ethics*, Pt. III, Prop. 9, note). Wiggins, op. cit., p. 141, identifies a related issue in Aristotle (*Metaphysics* 1072a29). Of course, a normative realist will typically be an externalist in the relevant sense, but the concern of this paper is nonrealism.

15. For an elaboration on this line of response, see Thomas Carson, "Could Ideal Observers Disagree?," *Philosophy and Phenomenological Research* 50 (1989), 123.

16. We thank Robert Audi, Richard Brandt, John Heil, Dwayne Mulder, David Schmidtz, and Mark Timmons for comments. We presented an earlier version of this paper at an APA Eastern Division Symposium.

PART SIX

CASE STUDY
ON RELATIVISM

20

Female Circumcision/ Genital Mutilation and Ethical Relativism

LORETTA M. KOPELMAN

In Northern Africa and Southern Arabia many girls undergo ritual surgery involving removal of parts of their external genitalia; the surgery is often accompanied by ceremonies intended to honor and welcome the girls into their communities. About 80 million living women have had this surgery, and an additional 4 or 5 million girls undergo it each year (Kouba and Muasher 1985; Ntiri 1993). Usually performed between infancy and puberty, these ancient practices are supposed to promote chastity, religion, group identity, cleanliness, health, family values, and marriage goals. This tradition is prevalent and deeply embedded in many countries, including Ethiopia, the Sudan, Somalia, Sierra Leone, Kenya, Tanzania, Central African Republic, Chad, Gambia, Liberia, Mali, Senegal, Eritrea, Ivory Coast, Upper Volta, Mauritania, Nigeria, Mozambique, Botswana, Lesotho, and Egypt (Abdalla 1982; Ntiri 1993; Calder et al. 1993; Rushwan 1990; El Dareer 1982; Koso-Thomas 1987). Modified versions of the surgeries are also performed in Southern Yemen and Musqat-Oman (Abdalla 1982). Tragically, the usual ways of performing these surgeries deny women sexual orgasms, cause significant morbidity or mortality among women and children, and strain the overburdened health care systems in these developing countries. Some refer to these practices as *female circumcision,* but those wishing to stop them increasingly use the description *female genital mutilation.*

Impassioned cultural clashes erupt when people from societies practicing female circumcision/genital mutilation settle in other parts of the world and bring these rites with them. It is practiced, for example, by Muslim groups in the Philippines, Malaysia, Pakistan, Indonesia, Europe, and North America (Kluge 1993; Thompson 1989; Abdalla 1982; Koso-Thomas 1987). Parents may use traditional practitioners or seek medical facilities to reduce the morbidity or mortality of this genital surgery. Some doctors and nurses

Reprinted with permission from Kopelman, Loretta M. 1994. "Female Circumcision/Genital Mutilation and Ethical Relativism." *Second Opinion* 20, no. 2 (October): 55–71.

perform the procedures for large fees or because they are concerned about the
unhygienic techniques that traditional practitioners may use. In the United
Kingdom, where about 2,000 girls undergo the surgery annually, it is classified as child abuse (Thompson 1989). Other countries have also classified it as
child abuse, including Canada and France (Kluge 1993).

Many international agencies like UNICEF, the International Federation
of Gynecology and Obstetrics, and the World Health Organization (WHO)
openly condemn and try to stop the practices of female genital mutilation
(WHO 1992; Rushwan 1990). Such national groups as the American Medical
Association (AMA 1991) have also denounced these rituals. Women's groups
from around the world protest these practices and the lack of notice they
receive. (A common reaction to the attention given to the Bobbitt case, where
an abused wife cut off her husband's penis, was, "Why was there a media cir-
cus over one man's penis while the excision of the genitalia of millions of girls
annually receives almost no attention?")

Most women in cultures practicing female circumcision/genital mutilation, when interviewed by investigators from their culture, state that they do
not believe that such practices deprive them of anything important (Koso-
Thomas 1987). They do not think that women can have orgasms or that sex
can be directly pleasing to women but assume that their pleasure comes only
from knowing they contribute to their husbands' enjoyment (El Dareer 1982;
Abdalla 1982). Some critics argue that women who hold such beliefs cannot
be understood to be making an informed choice; they thus condemn this custom as a form of oppression (Sherwin 1992; Walker 1992).

International discussion, criticisms, and condemnation of female circum-
cision/genital mutilation help activists who struggle to change these rites
that are thoroughly entrenched in their own cultures (El Dareer 1982; Ntiri
1993; Kouba and Muasher 1985; Koso-Thomas 1987; Abdalla 1982). Not surprisingly, people who want to continue these practices resent such criticisms,
seeing them as assaults upon their deeply embedded and popular cultural
traditions.

Underlying intercultural disputes is often a basic moral controversy:
Does praise or criticism from outside a culture or society have any moral
authority within it? That is, do the moral judgments from one culture have
any relevance to judgments about what is right or wrong within another culture? According to some versions of ethical relativism, to say that something
is right means that it is approved of in the speaker's culture; to say that something is wrong means that it is disapproved. If this is correct, there is no
rational basis for establishing across cultures that one set of culturally established moral values is right and the other wrong. The right action is one that
is approved by the person's society or culture, and the wrong action is one
that is disapproved by the person's society or culture; there are moral truths,
but they are determined by the norms of the society. On this view, then, the
cultural approval of female circumcision/genital mutilation means that the
practice is right; disapproval means that it is wrong.

In contrast to such versions of ethical relativism, other traditions hold that to say something is morally right means that the claim can be defended with reasons in a certain way. Saying that something is approved (such as slavery) does not settle whether it is right, because something can be wrong even when it is approved by most people in a culture. Moral judgments do not describe what is approved but prescribe what ought to be approved; if worthy of being called moral or ethical judgments, they must be defensible with reasons that are consistent and empirically defensible. As we shall find, advocates of the practice of female circumcision/genital mutilation do not say, "We approve of these rituals, and that is the end of the matter." Rather, they try to defend the practice as useful in promoting many important goals. In fact, however, the practice is inconsistent with important goals and values of the cultures in which it is practiced. We find that we can evaluate some of the reasons given for performing these rituals and that despite our cultural differences about what to value and how to act, we share many methods of discovery, evaluation, and explanation. These enable us sometimes correctly to judge other cultures, and they us. Moral judgments can be evaluated at least in terms of their consistency and their relation to stable evidence, like medical or scientific findings. By this means certain moral claims can be challenged, even where we have different cultural values, and the practice of female circumcision/genital mutilation shown to be wrong. Thus, both intercultural and intracultural discussions, criticisms, and condemnation of female genital mutilation as well as support for activists seeking to stop the practice can have moral authority, or so I argue.

After considering some of the health hazards of female circumcision/genital mutilation, I review the version of ethical relativism that denies moral authority to cross-cultural moral judgments. By examining the cultural reasons used to justify female circumcision/genital mutilation. I want to show that many aspects of this discussion are open to cross-cultural evaluation and understanding and hence that this version of ethical relativism fails. After discussing some anticipated objections, I conclude that these relativists have a heavy burden of proof to show why we cannot make intercultural judgments that have moral force concerning female genital mutilation, just as we do concerning such things as oppression, intolerance, exploitation, waste, aggression, and torture or imprisonment of dissidents.

TYPES OF SURGERY AND THEIR
HEALTH CONSEQUENCES

Female circumcision/genital mutilation takes three forms. Type 1 circumcision involves pricking or removing the clitoral hood, or prepuce. This is the least mutilating type and should not preclude sexual orgasms in later life, unlike other forms. When this surgery is performed on infants and small children, however, it may be difficult to avoid removal of additional tissue, because infants genitalia are small, and the tools commonly used are pins, scissors, razors, and knives. In the southern Arabian countries of Southern

Yemen and Musqat-Oman, Type 1 circumcision is commonly practiced.[1] In African countries, however, Type 1 circumcision is often not regarded as a genuine circumcision (Koso-Thomas 1987; Abdalla 1982). Only about 3 percent of the women in one east African survey had this type of circumcision (El Dareer 1982), and none in another (Ntiri 1993) where all the women surveyed had been circumcised.

Type 2, or intermediary, circumcision involves removal of the clitoris and most or all of the labia minora. In Type 3 circumcision, or infibulation, the clitoris, labia minora, and parts of the labia majora are removed. The gaping wound to the vulva is stitched tightly closed, leaving a tiny opening so that the woman can pass urine and menstrual flow. (Type 3 is also known as Pharaonic circumcision, suggesting that it has been done since the time of the pharaohs [Abdalla 1982].) In some African countries most young girls between infancy and 10 years of age have Type 3 circumcision (Abdalla 1982; Ntiri 1993; Calder et al. 1993). Traditional practitioners often use sharpened or hot stones, razors, or knives, frequently without anesthesia or antibiotics (Rushwan 1990; Abdalla 1982; El Dareer 1982). In many communities thorns are used to stitch the wound closed, and a twig is inserted to keep an opening. The girl's legs may be bound for a month or more while the scar heals (Abdalla 1982; El Dareer 1982).[2]

Types 2 and 3, both of which preclude orgasms, are the most popular forms. More than three-quarters of the girls in the Sudan, Somalia, Ethiopia, and other north African and southern Arabian countries undergo Type 2 or Type 3 circumcision, with many of the others circumcised by Type 1 (El Dareer 1982; Ntiri 1993; Calder et al. 1993; Koso-Thomas 1987; Ogiamien 1988). One survey by Sudanese physician Asma El Dareer (1982) shows that over 98 percent of Sudanese women have had this ritual surgery, 12 percent with Type 2 and 83 percent with Type 3. A 1993 study of 859 Somali women finds that all were circumcised, 98 percent with Type 3 and 2 percent with Type 2; on 70 percent of them, the surgery was done with a machete (Ntiri 1993).

Medical science is divided over whether the practice of male circumcision has any benefits (see American Academy of Pediatrics 1989 and Alibhai 1993 for discussion of the pros and cons). In contrast, female circumcision/genital mutilation has no benefits and is harmful in many ways, with both short- and long-term complications documented in a series of studies from Nigeria (Ozumba 1992), the Sudan (El Dareer 1982), Sierra Leone (Koso-Thomas 1987), and Somalia (Abdalla 1982; Ntiri 1993; Dirie and Lindmark 1992).

Almost all girls experience immediate pain following the surgery (Rushwan 1990; El Dareer 1982). El Dareer found other immediate consequences, including bleeding, infection, and shock correlating with the type of circumcision: Type 1, 8.1 percent; Type 2, 24.1 percent; and Type 3, 25.6 percent. Bleeding occurred in all forms of circumcision, accounting for 21.3 percent of the immediate medical problems in El Dareer's survey. She writes, "Hemorrhage can be either primary, from injuries to arteries or veins, or secondary, as a result of infection" (1982:33). Infections are frequent because the surgical conditions are often unhygienic (Rushwan 1990; El Dareer 1982). The inability to pass urine was common, constituting 21.65 percent of the immediate complications (El Dareer 1982). El Dareer found 32.2 percent of the women surveyed had long-term problems, with 24.54 percent suffering urinary tract infections and 23.8 percent suffering chronic pelvic infection. The published studies by investigators from the regions where these rituals are practiced uniformly find that women expressed similar complaints and had similar complications from female circumcision/genital mutilation: at the site of the surgery, scarring can make penetration difficult and intercourse painful; cysts may form, requiring surgical repairs; a variety of menstrual problems arise if the opening left is too small to allow adequate drainage; fistulas or tears in the bowel or urinary tract are common, causing incontinence, which in turn leads to social as well as medical problems; maternal-fetal complications and prolonged and obstructed labor are also well-established consequences (Kouba and Muasher 1985; Rushwan 1990; El Dareer 1982; Koso-Thomas 1987; Abdalla 1982; Ozumba 1992; Ntiri 1993; Dirie and Lindmark 1992; Ogiamien 1988; Thompson 1989). El Dareer (1982:iii–iv) writes, "The result almost invariably causes immediate and long-term medical complications, especially at childbirth. Consummation of marriage is always a difficult experience for both partners, and marital problems often result. Psychological disturbances in girls due to circumcision are not uncommon." The operation can also be fatal because of shock, tetanus, and septicemia (Rushwan 1990).

As high as the rates of these reported complications are, investigator El Dareer (1982) believes that the actual rates are probably even higher for several reasons. First, female circumcision/genital mutilation, although widely practiced, is technically illegal, and people are reluctant to discuss illegal activities.[3] Second, people may be ashamed to admit that they have had complications, fearing they are to blame for them. Third, some women believe that female circumcision/genital mutilation is necessary for their health and well-being and so may not fully associate these problems with the surgery but assume that their problems would have been worse if they had been uncircumcised. Many women, as these studies show, are well aware of the complications from this ritual surgery. Nonetheless they strongly support continuing these practices. One study (Ntiri 1993) reports that 92 percent of the Somali women surveyed favor continuing Type 3 (76 percent) or Type 2 (24 percent) for their daughters.

ETHICAL RELATIVISM

Female circumcision/genital mutilation serves as a test case for some versions of ethical relativism because the practice has widespread approval within the cultures where it is practiced and widespread disapproval outside those cultures. *Relativism,* however, means different things to different "academic cultures." Indeed one of the most striking things about the term *relativism* is that it is used in so many different ways, spanning the banal to the highly controversial. In the *Encyclopedia of Philosophy,* Richard D. Brandt (1967:75) writes, "Contemporary philosophers generally apply the term [ethical relativism] to some position they disagree with or consider absurd, seldom to their own views; social scientists, however, often classify themselves as relativists." Philosophers and those in religious studies often distinguish two ways to understand relativism: one is controversial, and the other is not (Brandt 1967; Sober 1991). The noncontroversial, descriptive version, often called *descriptive relativism,* is the view that people from different cultures *do* act differently and have distinct norms. Social scientists often work as descriptive relativists: they try to understand cultural differences and look for any underlying similarities. Those studying or criticizing female circumcision/genital mutilation, of course, recognize that we do act differently and have different values. But descriptions about how or in what way we *are* different do not entail statements about how we *ought* to act.

The controversial position, called *ethical relativism,* is that an action is right if it is approved in a person's culture and wrong if it is disapproved. Another version of this controversial view is that to say something is right means it has cultural approval; to say something is wrong means it has cultural disapproval. According to this view, which some call *cultural relativism* (Holmes 1993), there is no way to evaluate moral claims across cultures; positions taken by international groups like the World Health Organization merely express a cluster of particular societal opinions and have no moral standing in other cultures. On this view it is incoherent to claim that something is wrong in a culture yet approved, or right yet disapproved; people can express moral judgments about things done in their own or other cultures, but they are expressing only their cultural point of view, not one that has moral authority in another culture.

Many social scientists and (despite what Brandt says) some philosophers defend ethical relativism. For example, philosopher Bernard Williams (1985) argues that moral knowledge is inherited by people within particular cultural traditions and has objectivity only within those cultures. Anthropologists Faye Ginsberg (1991) and Nancy Scheper-Hughes (1991) point out that ethical relativism has held an important place in anthropology despite the uncomfortable consequence that acceptance of that position means that practices like female circumcision are right within the cultures where they are approved. Anthropologists by their own admission, however, do not use the terms *cultural relativism* or *ethical relativism* consistently (Shweder 1990). Often relativism is presented as the only alternative to clearly implausible views such as absolutism or cultural imperialism; sometimes it is used to stress the obvious points that different rankings and interpretations of moral values or rules by different groups may be justifiable, or employed to highlight the indisputable influence of culture on moral development, reasoning, norms, and decisions. It may also be used to show that decisions about what we ought to do depend on the situation—for example, that it may not be wrong to lie in some cases. These points are not in dispute herein or even controversial, so my comments do not apply to these versions of relativism.

Nor do the criticisms offered herein necessarily challenge relativists who agree that cross-cultural moral judgments sometimes have moral force. Generally they wish to accent the role of culture in shaping our moral judgments, showing why it is dangerous to impose external cultural judgments hastily or stressing that there is often a link between established moral systems and oppression. For example, moral philosopher Susan Sherwin maintains that "normative conclusions reached by traditional theorists generally support the mechanism of oppression; for example, by promoting subservience among women" and concludes, "Feminist moral relativism remains absolutist on the question of the moral wrong of oppression but is relativist on other moral matters" (1992:58, 75). She uses this form of relativism to argue that female circumcision is wrong.

In contrast, the distinctive feature of the version of ethical relativism criticized herein is its defense of the skeptical position that one can *never* make a sound cross-cultural moral judgment, that is, one that has moral force outside one's culture.[4] This version of ethical relativism is false if people from one culture can *sometimes* make judgments that have moral authority about actions in another society. Its defenders regard their view to be the consequence of a proper understanding of the limits of knowledge (Williams 1985; Ginsberg 1991; Shweder 1990). Many attacks, however, have been made on the skepticism underlying such ethical relativism (Bambrough 1979; Hampshire 1989), and my remarks are in this tradition.

I would begin by observing that we seem to share methods of discovery, evaluation, negotiation, and explanation that can be used to help assess moral judgments. For example, we agree how to evaluate methods and research in science, engineering, and medicine, and on how to translate, debate, deliberate, criticize, negotiate, and use technology. To do these things, however, we must first have agreed to some extent on how to distinguish good and bad methods and research in science, engineering, and medicine, and what constitutes a good or bad translation, debate, deliberation, criticism, negotiation, or use of technology. These shared methods can be used to help evaluate moral judgments from one culture to another in a way that sometimes has moral authority. An example of a belief that could be evaluated by stable medical evidence is the assertion by people in some regions that the infant's "death could result if, during delivery, the baby's head touches the clitoris" (Koso-Thomas 1987:10). In addition, some moral claims can be evaluated in terms of their coherence. It seems incompatible to promote maternal-fetal health as a good and also to advocate avoidable practices known to cause serious perinatal and neonatal infections.

We need not rank values similarly with people in another culture, or our own, to have coherent discussions about their consistency, consequences, or factual presuppositions. That is, even if some moral or ethical (I use these terms interchangeably) judgments express unique cultural norms, they may still be morally evaluated by another culture on the basis of their logical consistency and their coherence with stable and cross-culturally accepted empirical information. In addition, we seem to share some moral values, goals, and judgments such as those about the evils of unnecessary suffering and lost opportunities, the need for food and shelter, the duty to help children, and the goods of promoting public health and personal well-being (Hampshire 1989). Let us consider, therefore, the reasons given by men and women who practice female circumcision/genital mutilation in their communities. The information presented herein is based upon studies done by investigators who come from these cultures, some of whom had this ritual surgery as children (El Dareer is one such investigator). We can examine whether these reasons allow people from other cultures any way of entering the debate based upon such considerations as consistency or stable medical findings.

REASONS GIVEN FOR FEMALE CIRCUMCISION/GENITAL MUTILATION

According to four independent series of studies conducted by investigators from countries where female circumcision is widely practiced (El Dareer 1982; Ntiri 1993; Koso-Thomas 1987; Abdalla 1982), the primary reasons given for performing this ritual surgery are that it (1) meets a religious requirement, (2) preserves group identity, (3) helps to maintain cleanliness and health, (4) preserves virginity and family honor and prevents immorality, and (5) furthers marriage goals including greater sexual pleasure for men.

El Dareer conducted her studies in the Sudan, Dr. Olayinka Koso-Thomas in and around Sierra Leone, and Raquiya Haji Dualeh Abdalla and Daphne Williams Ntiri in Somalia. They argue that the reasons for continuing this practice in their respective countries float on a sea of false beliefs, beliefs that thrive because of a lack of education and open discussion about reproduction and sexuality. Insofar as intercultural methods for evaluating factual and logical statements exist, people from other cultures should at least be able to understand these inconsistencies or mistaken factual beliefs and use them as a basis for making some judgments having intercultural *moral* authority.

First, according to these studies the main reason given for performing female circumcision/genital mutilation is that it is regarded as a religious requirement. Most of the people practicing this ritual are Muslims, but it is not a practice required by the Koran (El Dareer 1982; Ntiri 1993). El Dareer writes:

> Circumcision of women is not explicitly enjoined in the Koran, but there are two implicit sayings of the Prophet Mohammed: "Circumcision is an ordinance in men and an embellishment in women" and, reportedly Mohammed said to Om Attiya, a woman who circumcised girls in El Medina, "Do not go deep. It is more illuminating to the face and more enjoyable to the husband." Another version says, "Reduce but do not destroy. This is enjoyable to the woman and preferable to the man." But there is nothing in the Koran to sug-

gest that the Prophet commanded that women be circumcised. He advised that it was important to both sexes that very little should be taken. (1992:72)

Female circumcision/genital mutilation, moreover, is not practiced in the spiritual center of Islam, Saudi Arabia (Calder et al. 1993). Another reason for questioning this as a Muslim practice is that clitoridectomy and infibulation predate Islam, going back to the time of the pharaohs (Abdalla 1982; El Dareer 1992).

Second, many argue that the practice helps to preserve group identity. When Christian colonialists in Kenya introduced laws opposing the practice of female circumcision in the 1930s, African leader Kenyatta expressed a view still popular today:

> This operation is still regarded as the very essence of an institution which has enormous educational, social, moral and religious implications, quite apart from the operation itself. For the present, it is impossible for a member of the [Kikuyu] tribe to imagine an initiation without clitoridectomy . . . the abolition of IRUA [the ritual operation] will destroy the tribal symbol which identifies the age group and prevent the Kikuyu from perpetuating that spirit of collectivism and national solidarity which they have been able to maintain from time immemorial. (Scheper-Hughes 1991:27)

In addition, the practice is of social and economic importance to older women who are paid for performing the rituals (El Dareer 1982; Koso-Thomas 1987; Abdalla 1982; Ginsberg 1991).

Drs. Koso-Thomas, El Dareer, and Abdalla agree that people in these countries support female circumcision as a good practice, but only because they do not understand that it is a leading cause of sickness or even death for girls, mothers, and infants, and a major cause of infertility, infection, and maternal-fetal and marital complications. They conclude that these facts are not confronted because these societies do not speak openly of such matters. Abdalla writes, "There is no longer any reason, given the present state of progress in science, to tolerate confusion and ignorance about reproduction and women's sexuality" (1982:2). Female circumcision/genital mutilation is intended to honor women as male circumcision honors men, and members of cultures where the surgery is practiced are shocked by the analogy of clitoridectomy to removal of the penis (El Dareer 1982).

Third, the belief that the practice advances health and hygiene is incompatible with stable data from surveys done in these cultures, where female circumcision/genital mutilation has been linked to mortality or morbidity such as shock, infertility, infections, incontinence, maternal-fetal complications, and protracted labor. The tiny hole generally left for blood and urine to pass is a constant source of infection (El Dareer 1982; Koso-Thomas 1987; Abdalla 1982; Calder et al. 1993; Ntiri 1993). Koso-Thomas writes,

> As for cleanliness, the presence of these scars prevents urine and menstrual flow escaping by the normal channels. This may lead to acute retention of

urine and menstrual flow, and to a condition known as *hematocolpos,* which is highly detrimental to the health of the girl or woman concerned and causes odors more offensive than any that can occur through the natural secretions. (Koso-Thomas 1987:10).

Investigators completing a recent study wrote:

> The risk of medical complications after female circumcision is very high as revealed by the present study [of 290 Somali women, conducted in the capital of Mogadishu]. Complications which cause the death of the young girls must be a common occurrence especially in the rural areas. . . . Dribbling urine incontinence, painful menstruations, haematocolpos and painful intercourse are facts that Somali women have to live with—facts that strongly motivate attempts to change the practice of female circumcision. (Dirie and Lindmark 1992:482)

Fourth, investigators found that circumcision is thought necessary in these cultures to preserve virginity and family honor and to prevent immorality. Type 3 circumcision is used to keep women from having sexual intercourse before marriage and conceiving illegitimate children. In addition, many believe that Types 2 and 3 circumcision must be done because uncircumcised women have excessive and uncontrollable sexual drives. El Dareer, however, believes that this view is not consistently held—that women in the Sudan are respected and that Sudanese men would be shocked to apply this sometimes-held cultural view to members of their own families. This reason also seems incompatible with the general view, which investigators found was held by both men and women in these cultures, that sex cannot be pleasant for women (El Dareer 1982; Koso-Thomas 1987; Abdalla 1982). In addition, female circumcision/genital mutilation offers no foolproof way to promote chastity and can even lead to promiscuity because it does not diminish desire or libido even where it makes orgasms impossible (El Dareer 1982). Some women continually seek experiences with new sexual partners because they are left unsatisfied in their sexual encounters (Koso-Thomas 1987). Moreover, some pretend to be virgins by getting stitched up tightly again (El Dareer 1982).

Fifth, interviewers found that people practicing female circumcision/genital mutilation believe that it furthers marriage goals, including greater sexual pleasure for men. To survive economically, women in these cultures must marry, and they will not be acceptable marriage partners unless they have undergone this ritual surgery (Abdalla 1982; Ntiri 1993). It is a curse, for example, to say that someone is the child of an uncircumcised woman (Koso-Thomas 1987). The widely held belief that infibulation enhances women's beauty and men's sexual pleasure makes it difficult for women who wish to marry to resist this practice (Koso-Thomas 1987; El Dareer 1992). Some men from these cultures, however, report that they enjoy sex more with uncircumcised women (Koso-Thomas 1987). Furthermore, female circumcision/genital mutilation is inconsistent with the established goals of some of these cultures because it is a leading cause of disability and contributes to the high mortality rate among mothers, fetuses, and children. Far from promoting the goals of marriage, it causes difficulty in consummating marriage, infertility, prolonged and obstructed labor, and morbidity and mortality.

CRITICISMS OF ETHICAL RELATIVISM

Examination of the debate concerning female circumcision suggests several conclusions about the extent to which people from outside a culture can understand or contribute to moral debates within it in a way that has moral force. First, the fact that a culture's moral and religious views are often inter-twined with beliefs that are open to rational and empirical evaluation can be a basis of cross-cultural examination and intercultural moral criticism (Bam-brough 1979). Defenders of female circumcision/genital mutilation do not claim that this practice is a moral or religious requirement and end the dis-cussion; they are willing to give and defend reasons for their views. For example, advocates of female circumcision/genital mutilation claim that it benefits women's health and well-being. Such claims are open to cross-cul-tural examination because information is available to determine whether the practice promotes health or causes morbidity or mortality. Beliefs that the practice enhances fertility and promotes health, that women cannot have orgasms, and that allowing the baby's head to touch the clitoris during deliv-ery causes death to the baby are incompatible with stable medical data (Koso-Thomas 1987). Thus an opening is allowed for genuine cross-cultural discus-sion or criticism of the practice.

Some claims about female circumcision/genital mutilation, however, are not as easily open to cross-cultural understanding. For example, cultures practicing the Type 3 surgery, infibulation, believe that it makes women more beautiful. For those who are not from these cultures, this belief is difficult to understand, especially when surveys show that many women in these cul-tures, when interviewed, attribute to infibulation their keloid scars, urine retention, pelvic infections, puerperal sepsis, and obstetrical problems (Ntiri 1993; Abdalla 1982). Koso-Thomas writes:

> None of the reasons put forward in favor of circumcision have any real sci-entific or logical basis. It is surprising that aesthetics and the maintenance of cleanliness are advanced as grounds for female circumcision. The scars could hardly be thought of as contributing to beauty. The hardened scar and stump usually seen where the clitoris should be, or in the case of the infibu-lated vulva, taut skin with an ugly long scar down the middle, present a hor-rifying picture. (Koso-Thomas 1987:10)

Thus not everyone in these cultures believes that these rituals enhance beauty; some find such claims difficult to understand.

Second, the debate over female circumcision/genital mutilation illus-trates another difficulty for defenders of this version of ethical relativism con-

cerning the problem of differentiating cultures. People who brought the practice of female circumcision/genital mutilation with them when they moved
to another nation still claim to be a distinct cultural group. Some who moved
to Britain, for example, resent the interference in their culture represented by
laws that condemn the practice as child abuse (Thompson 1989). If ethical relativists are to appeal to cultural approval in making the final determination
of what is good or bad, right or wrong, they must tell us how to distinguish
one culture from another.

How exactly do we count or separate cultures? A society is not a nation-
state, because some social groups have distinctive identities within nations. If
we do not define societies as nations, however, how do we distinguish among
cultural groups, for example, well enough to say that an action is child abuse
in one culture but not in another? Subcultures in nations typically overlap
and have many variations. Even if we could count cultural groups well
enough to say exactly how to distinguish one culture from another, how and
when would this be relevant? How big or old or vital must a culture, subcul-
ture, group, or cult be in order to be recognized as a society whose moral distinctions are self-contained and self-justifying?

A related problem is that there can be passionate disagreement, ambiva-
lence, or rapid changes within a culture or groups over what is approved or
disapproved. According to ethical relativism, where there is significant disagreement within a culture there is no way to determine what is right or
wrong. But what disagreement is significant? As we saw, some people in
these cultures, often those with higher education, strongly disapprove of
female circumcision/genital mutilation and work to stop it (El Dareer 1982;
Koso-Thomas 1987; Ntiri 1993; Dirie and Lindmark 1992; Abdalla 1982). Are
they in the same culture as their friends and relatives who approve of these
rituals? It seems more accurate to say that people may belong to various
groups that overlap and have many variations. This description, however,
makes it difficult for ethical relativism to be regarded as a helpful theory for
determining what is right or wrong. To say that something is right when it
has cultural approval is useless if we cannot identify the relevant culture.
Moreover, even where people agree about the rightness of certain practices,
such as these rituals, they can sometimes be inconsistent. For example, in
reviewing reasons given within cultures where female circumcision/genital
mutilation is practiced, we saw that there was some inconsistency concerning
whether women needed this surgery to control their sexual appetites, to
make them more beautiful, or to prevent morbidity or mortality. Ethical relativists thus have extraordinary problems offering a useful account of what
counts as a culture and establishes cultural approval or disapproval.

Third, despite some clear disagreement such as that over the rightness of
female circumcision/genital mutilation, people from different parts of the
world share common goals like the desirability of promoting people's health,
happiness, opportunities, and cooperation, and the wisdom of stopping war,
pollution, oppression, torture, and exploitation. These common goals make
us a world community, and using shared methods of reasoning and evalua-

tion, we can discuss how they are understood or how well they are implemented in different parts of our world community. We can use these shared goals to assess whether female circumcision/genital mutilation is more like respect or oppression, more like enhancement or diminishment of opportunities, or more like pleasure or torture. While there are, of course, genuine differences between citizens of the world, it is difficult to comprehend how they could be identified unless we could pick them out against a background of our similarities. Highlighting our differences, however useful for some purposes, should not eclipse the truth that we share many goals and values and are similar enough that we can assess each other's views as rational beings in a way that has moral force. Another way to express this is to say that we should recognize universal human rights or be respectful of each other as persons capable of reasoned discourse.

Fourth, this version of ethical relativism, if consistently held, leads to the abhorrent conclusion that we cannot make intercultural judgments with moral force about societies that start wars, practice torture, or exploit and oppress other groups; as long as these activities are approved in the society that does them, they are allegedly right. Yet the world community believed that it was making a cross-cultural judgment with moral force when it criticized the Communist Chinese government for crushing a pro-democracy student protest rally, the South Africans for upholding apartheid, the Soviets for using psychiatry to suppress dissent, and the Bosnian Serbs for carrying out the siege of Sarajevo. And the judgment was expressed without anyone's ascertaining whether the respective actions had widespread approval in those countries. In each case, representatives from the criticized society usually said something like, "You don't understand why this is morally justified in our culture even if it would not be in your society." If ethical relativism were convincing, these responses ought to be as well.

Relativists who want to defend sound social cross-cultural and moral judgments about the value of freedom and human rights in other cultures seem to have two choices. On the one hand, if they agree that some cross-cultural norms have moral authority, they should also agree that some intercultural judgments about female circumcision/genital mutilation may have moral authority. Some relativists take this route (see, for example, Sherwin 1992), thereby abandoning the version of ethical relativism being criticized herein. On the other hand, if they defend this version of ethical relativism yet make cross-cultural moral judgments about the importance of values like tolerance, group benefit, and the survival of cultures, they will have to admit to an inconsistency in their arguments. For example, anthropologist Scheper-Hughes (1991) advocates tolerance of other cultural value systems; she fails to see that she is saying that tolerance between cultures is *right* and that this is a cross-cultural moral judgment using a moral norm (tolerance). Similarly, relativists who say it is wrong to eliminate rituals that give meaning to other cultures are also inconsistent in making a judgment that presumes to have genuine cross-cultural moral authority. Even the sayings sometimes used by defenders of ethical relativism—such as "When in Rome do as the Romans"

(Scheper-Hughes 1991)—mean it is *morally permissible* to adopt all the cultural norms in operation wherever one finds oneself. Thus it is not consistent
for defenders of this version of ethical relativism to make intercultural moral
judgments about tolerance, group benefit, intersocietal respect, or cultural
diversity.

The burden of proof, then, is upon defenders of this version of ethical relativism to show why we cannot do something we think we sometimes do
very well, namely, engage in intercultural moral discussion, cooperation, or
criticism and give support to people whose welfare or rights are in jeopardy
in other cultures. In addition, defenders of ethical relativism need to explain
how we can justify the actions of international professional societies that take
moral stands in adopting policy. For example, international groups may take
moral stands that advocate fighting pandemics, stopping wars, halting
oppression, promoting health education, or eliminating poverty, and they
seem to have moral authority in some cases. Some might respond that our
professional groups are themselves cultures of a sort. But this response raises
the already discussed problem of how to individuate a culture or society.

OBJECTIONS

Some standard rejoinders are made to criticism of relativism, but they leave
untouched the arguments against the particular version of ethical relativism
discussed herein. First, some defenders argue that cross-cultural moral judgments perpetuate the evils of absolutism, cultural dogmatism, or cultural
imperialism. People rarely admit to such transgressions, often enlisting medicine, religion, science, or the "pure light of reason" to arrive at an allegedly
impartial, disinterested, and justified conclusion that they should "en-
lighten" and "educate" the "natives," "savages," or "infidels." Anthropologist Scheper-Hughes writes, "I don't 'like' the idea of clitoridectomy any better than any other woman I know. But I like even less the western 'voices of
reason' [imposing their views]" (1991:27). Scheper-Hughes and others suggest that, in arguing that we can make moral judgments across cultures, we
are thereby claiming a particular culture knows best and has the right to
impose its allegedly superior knowledge on other cultures.

Claiming that we can sometimes judge another culture in a way that has
moral force, however, does not entail that one culture is always right, that
absolutism is legitimate, or that we can impose our beliefs on others. Relativists sometimes respond that even if this is not a strict logical consequence,
it is a practical result. Sherwin writes, "Many social scientists have endorsed
versions of relativism precisely out of their sense that the alternative promotes cultural dominance. They may be making a philosophical error in
drawing that conclusion, but I do not think that they are making an empirical
one" (1992:63–64).

The version of ethical relativism we have been considering, however, does
not avoid cultural imperialism. To say that an act is right, on this view, means

that it has cultural approval, including acts of war, oppression, enslavement, aggression, exploitation, racism, or torture. On this view, the disapproval of other cultures is irrelevant in determining whether these acts are right or wrong; accordingly, the disapproval of people in other cultures, even victims of war, oppression, enslavement, aggression, exploitation, racism, or torture, does not count in deciding what is right or wrong except in their own culture. This view thus leads to abhorrent conclusions. It entails not only the affirmation that female circumcision/genital mutilation is right in cultures where it is approved but the affirmation that anything with wide social approval is right, including slavery, war, discrimination, oppression, racism, and torture. If defenders of the version of ethical relativism criticized herein are consistent, they will dismiss any objections by people in other cultures as merely an expression of their own cultural preferences, having no moral standing whatsoever in the society that is engaging in the acts in question.

Defenders of ethical relativism must explain why we should adopt a view leading to such abhorrent conclusions. They may respond that cultures sometimes overlap and hence that the victims' protests within or between cultures ought to count. But this response raises two further difficulties for defenders of ethical relativism. First, it is inconsistent if it means that the views of people in other cultures have moral standing and oppressors ought to consider the views of victims. Such judgments are inconsistent with this version of ethical relativism because they are cross-cultural judgments with moral authority. The second difficulty with this defense, also discussed above, is that it raises the problem of how we differentiate a culture or society.

Second, some defenders of ethical relativism argue that we cannot know enough about another culture to make any cross-cultural moral judgments. We cannot *really* understand another society well enough to criticize it, they claim, because our feelings, concepts, or ways of reasoning are too different; our so-called ordinary moral views about what is permissible are determined by our upbringing and environments to such a degree that they cannot be transferred to other cultures. There are two ways to understand this objection (Sober 1991). The first is that nothing counts as understanding another culture except being raised in it. If that is what is meant, then the objection is valid in a trivial way. But it does not address the important issue of whether we can comprehend well enough to make relevant moral distinctions or engage in critical ethical discussions about the universal human right to be free of oppression.

The second, and nontrivial, way to understand this objection is that we cannot understand another society well enough to justify claiming to know what is right or wrong in that society or even to raise moral questions about what enhances or diminishes life, promotes opportunities, and so on. Overwhelming data, however, suggest that we think we can do this very well. Travelers to other countries often quickly understand that approved practices in their own country are widely condemned elsewhere, sometimes for good reasons. For example, they learn that the U.S. population consumes a disproportionate amount of the world's resources, a fact readily noticed and condemned by citizens in other cultures. We ordinarily view international criticism and international responses concerning human rights violations, aggression, torture, and exploitation as important ways to show that we care about the rights and welfare of other people, and in some cases these responses have moral authority.

People who deny the possibility of genuine cross-cultural moral judgments must account for why we think we can and should make them, or why we sometimes agree more with people from other cultures than with our own relatives and neighbors about the moral assessments of aggression, oppression, capital punishment, abortion, euthanasia, rights to health care, and so on. International meetings, moreover, seem to employ genuinely cross-cultural moral judgments when they seek to distinguish good from bad uses of technology, promote better environmental or health policies, and so on.

Third, some defenders of ethical relativism object that eliminating important rituals from a culture risks destroying the society. They insist that these cultures cannot survive if they change such a central practice as female circumcision (Scheper-Hughes 1991). This counterargument, however, is not decisive. Slavery, oppression, and exploitation are also necessary to some ways of life, yet few would defend these actions in order to preserve a society. Others reply to this objection by questioning the assumption that these cultures can survive only by continuing clitoridectomy or infibulation (El Dareer 1982). These cultures, they argue, are more likely to be transformed by war, famine, disease, urbanization, and industrialization than by the cessation of this ancient ritual surgery. A further argument is that if slavery, oppression, and exploitation are wrong whether or not there are group benefits, then a decision to eliminate female circumcision/genital mutilation should not depend on a process of weighing its benefits to the group. It is also incoherent or inconsistent to hold that group benefit is so important that other cultures should not interfere with local practices. For this view elevates group benefit as an overriding cross-cultural value, something that these ethical relativists claim cannot be justified. If there are no cross-cultural values about what is wrong or right, a defender of ethical relativism cannot consistently say such things as "One culture ought not interfere with others," "We ought to be tolerant," "Every culture is equally valuable," or "It is wrong to interfere with another culture."

COMMENT

We have sufficient reason, therefore, to conclude that these rituals of female circumcision/genital mutilation are wrong. For me to say they are wrong does not mean that they are disapproved by most people in my culture but wrong for reasons similar to those given by activists within these cultures who are working to stop these practices. They are wrong because the usual forms of the surgery deny women orgasms and because they cause medical complications and even death. It is one thing to say that these practices are wrong and that activists should be supported in their efforts to stop them; it is another matter to determine how to do this effectively. All agree that education may be the most important means to stop these practices. Some activists in these cultures want an immediate ban (Abdalla 1982). Other activists in these cultures encourage Type 1 circumcision (pricking or removing the clitoral hood) in order to "wean" people away from Types 2 and 3 by substitution. Type 1 has the least association with morbidity or mortality and, if there are no complications, does not preclude sexual orgasms in later life. The chance of success through this tactic is more promising and realistic, they hold, than what an outright ban would achieve; and people could continue many of their traditions and rituals of welcome without causing so much harm (El Dareer 1982). Other activists in these countries, such as Raquiya Abdalla, object to equating Type 1 circumcision in the female with male circumcision: "To me and to many others, the aim and results of any form of circumcision of women are quite different from those applying to the circumcision of men" (1982:8). Because of the hazards of even Type 1 circumcision, especially for infants, I agree with the World Health Organization and the American Medical Association that it would be best to stop all forms of ritual genital surgery on women. Bans have proven ineffective: this still-popular practice has been illegal in most countries for many years (Rushwan 1990; Ntiri 1993; El Dareer 1982). Other proposals by activists focus on education, fines, and carefully crafted legislation (El Dareer 1982; Abdalla 1982; Ozumba 1992; Dirie and Lindmark 1992; WHO 1992).

The critique of the reasons given to support female circumcision/genital mutilation in cultures where it is practiced shows us how to enter discussions, disputes, or assessments in ways that can have moral authority. We share common needs, goals, and methods of reasoning and evaluation. Together they enable us to evaluate many claims across cultures and sometimes to regard ourselves as part of a world community with interests in promoting people's health, happiness, empathy, and opportunities as well as desires to stop war, torture, pandemics, pollution, oppression, and injustice. Thus, ethical relativism—the view that to say something is right means it has cultural approval and to say it is wrong means it has cultural disapproval—is implausible as a useful theory, definition, or account of the meaning of moral judgments. The burden of proof therefore falls upon upholders of this version of ethical relativism to show why criticisms of other cultures always lack moral authority. Although many values are culturally determined and we should not impose moral judgments across cultures hastily, we sometimes know enough to condemn practices approved in other cultures. For example, we can understand enough of the debate about female circumcision/genital mutilation to draw some conclusions: it is wrong, oppressive, and not a voluntary practice in the sense that the people doing it comprehend information relevant to their decision. Moreover, it is a ritual, however well-meant, that violates justifiable and universal human rights or values supported in the human community, and we should promote international moral support for advocates working to stop the practice wherever it is carried out.

NOTES

The author wishes to thank Robert Holmes, Suzanne Poirier, Sandy Pittman, Barbara Hofmaier, Richard McCarty, and Holly Mathews for their help in reviewing this manuscript, Juan Garcia for providing the drawings, and Jean Fourcroy for reviewing the drawings for accuracy. [Editors' note: This reprinting omits the drawings in the original.]

1. According to Abdalla (1982:16), in these regions the unusual practice is followed of putting "salt into the vagina after childbirth . . . [because this] induces the narrowing of the vagina . . . to restore the vagina to its former shape and size and make intercourse more pleasurable for the husband."

2. Some authors cite incidences of a very rare operation they call Type 4, or introcision, where the vaginal opening is enlarged by tearing it downward, cutting the perineum (see, for example, Rushwan 1990). It is practiced in Mali and sometimes in Senegal and northern Nigeria (Kouba and Muasher 1985).

3. These laws are often the unenforced remnants of colonial days or governments do not care to apply them. For a fuller discussion of the history of these rituals see Abdalla 1982; El Dareer 1982; Fourcroy 1983; Ntiri 1993; and Ruminjo 1992.

4. In contrast to normative ethical relativism, opponents may take one of several general positions about the meaning of right and wrong. They may hold that rightness and wrongness are the same in some ways but not in others for different cultures; that they depend upon something in human nature, the natural order of things, or the human condition; or that they are absolute and unchanging, either in form or substance, for all people (Holmes 1993).

REFERENCES

Abdalla, Raquiya H. D. 1982. *Sisters in Affliction: Circumcision and Infibulation of Women in Africa.* London: Zed Press.

Alibhai, Shabbir M. H. 1993. "Male and Female Circumcision in Canada" (letter to the editor). *Canadian Medical Association Journal* 149, no. 1 (1 July): 16–17.

American Academy of Pediatrics. 1989. "Report of the Task Force on Circumcision." *Pediatrics* 84, no. 2 (August): 388–91. (Published erratum appears in *Pediatrics* 84, no. 5 [November 1989]: 761.)

American Medical Association. 1991. "Surgical Modification of Female Genitalia." House of Delegates Amended Resolution 13 (June).

Bambrough, Renford. 1979. *Moral Scepticism and Moral Knowledge.* London: Routledge and Kegan Paul.

Brandt, Richard D. 1967. *Encyclopedia of Philosophy,* s.v. "ethical relativism."

Calder, Barbara L., Yvonne M. Brown, and Donna I. Rac. 1993. "Female Circumcision/Genital Mutilation: Culturally Sensitive Care." *Health Care for Women International* 14, no. 3 (May–June): 227–38.

Dirie, M. A., and G. Lindmark. 1992. "The Risk of Medical Complication after Female Circumcision." *East African Medical Journal* 69, no. 9 (September): 479–82.

El Dareer, Asma. 1982. *Woman, Why Do You Weep? Circumcision and Its Consequences.* London: Zed Press.

Fourcroy, Jean L. 1983. "L'Eternal Couteau: Review of Female Circumcision." *Urology* 22, no. 4 (October): 458–61.

Ginsberg, Faye. 1991. "What Do Women Want?: Feminist Anthropology Confronts Clitoridectomy." *Medical Anthropology Quarterly* 5, no. 1 (March): 17–19.

Hampshire, Stuart. 1989. *Innocence and Experience.* Cambridge, Mass.: Harvard University Press.

Holmes, Robert L. 1993. *Basic Moral Philosophy.* Belmont, Calif.: Wadsworth Publishing.

Kluge, Eike-Henner. 1993. "Female Circumcision: When Medical Ethics Confronts Cultural Values" (editorial). *Canadian Medical Association Journal* 148, no. 2 (15 January): 288–89.

Koso-Thomas, Olayinka. 1987. *The Circumcision of Women.* London: Zed Press.

Kouba, Leonard J., and Judith Muasher. 1985. "Female Circumcision in Africa: An Overview." *African Studies Review* 28, no. 1 (March): 95–109.

Ntiri, Daphne Williams. 1993. "Circumcision and Health among Rural Women of Southern Somalia as Part of a Family Life Survey." *Health Care for Women International* 14, no. 3 (May–June): 215–16.

Ogiamien, T. B. E. 1998. "A Legal Framework to Eradicate Female Circumcision." *Medicine, Science and the Law* 28, no. 2 (April): 115–19.

Ozumba, B. C. 1992. "Acquired Gynetresia in Eastern Nigeria." *International Journal of Gynaecology and Obstetrics* 37, no. 2: 105–9.

Ruminjo, J. 1992. "Circumcision in Women." *East African Medical Journal* 69, no. 2 (September): 477–78.

Rushwan, Hamid. 1990. "Female Circumcision." *World Health.* April–May, 24–25.

Scheper-Hughes, Nancy. 1991. "Virgin Territory: The Male Discovery of the Clitoris." *Medical Anthropology Quarterly* 5, no. 1 (March): 25–28.

Sherwin, Susan. 1992. *No Longer Patient: Feminist Ethics and Health Care.* Philadelphia: Temple University Press.

Shweder, Richard. 1990. "Ethical Relativism: Is There a Defensible Version?" *Ethos* 18:205–18.

Sober, Elliott. 1991. *Core Questions in Philosophy.* New York: Macmillan.

Thompson, June. 1989. "Torture by Tradition." *Nursing Times* 85, no. 15: 17–18.

Walker, Alice. 1992. *Possessing the Secret of Joy.* New York: Harcourt Brace Jovanovich.

Williams, Bernard. 1985. *Ethics and the Limits of Philosophy.* Cambridge, Mass.: Harvard University Press.

World Health Organization. 1992. *International Journal of Gynaecology and Obstetrics* 37, no. 2: 149.

Bibliography

Thomas L. Carson and Paul K. Moser

1. GENERAL ISSUES

Arrington, Robert. *Rationalism, Realism, and Relativism.* Ithaca, N.Y.: Cornell University Press, 1989.

Bambrough, Renford. *Moral Scepticism and Moral Knowledge.* London: Routledge, 1979.

Brandt, Richard. *Ethical Theory.* Englewood Cliffs, N.J.: Prentice-Hall, 1959.

———. "Ethical Relativism." In *The Encyclopedia of Philosophy,* Vol. 3, edited by Paul Edwards, 75–78. New York: Macmillan, 1967.

Carson, Thomas. *The Status of Morality.* (Dordrecht, the Netherlands: Reidel, 1984).

———. "An Approach to Relativism." *Teaching Philosophy* 22 (1999): 161–184.

Chang, Ruth, ed. *Incommensurability, Incomparability, and Practical Reason.* Cambridge: Harvard University Press, 1997.

Copp, David. *Morality, Normativity, and Society.* Oxford: Oxford University Press, 1995.

Davidson, Donald. "On the Very Idea of a Conceptual Scheme." *Proceedings and Addresses of the American Philosophical Association* 47 (1973–74): 5–20.

Frankena, William K. *Ethics,* 2nd ed. Englewood Cliffs, N.J.: Prentice-Hall, 1973.

———. "The Principles of Morality." In *Skepticism and Moral Principles,* edited by C. Carter, 43–76. Evanston, Ill.: New University Press, 1973.

———. *Perspectives on Morality.* Edited by K. E. Goodpaster. Notre Dame, Ind.: University of Notre Dame Press, 1976.

Haack, Susan. "Reflections on Relativism: From Momentous Tautology to Seductive Contradiction." *Manifesto of a Passionate Moderate,* 149–166. Chicago: University of Chicago Press, 1998.

Hales, Steven. "A Consistent Relativism." *Mind* 106 (1997): 33–52.

Hare, R. M. "How to Decide Moral Questions Rationally." *Essays in Ethical Theory,* 99–112. Oxford: Oxford University Press, 1989.

———. *Sorting Out Ethics.* Oxford: Oxford University Press, 1997.

Harman, Gilbert. "What Is Moral Relativism?" In *Values and Morals,* edited by A. I. Goldman and J. Kim, 143–162. Dordrecht, the Netherlands: Reidel, 1978.

Harman, Gilbert, and Judith Thomson. *Moral Relativism and Moral Objectivity.* Oxford: Blackwell, 1996. (There is a symposium on this book in *Philosophy and Phenomenological Research* 58 (1998): 161–222.)

Harre, Rom, and Michael Krausz. *Varieties of Relativism.* Oxford: Blackwell, 1996.

Hollis, Martin, and Steven Lukes, eds. *Rationality and Relativism.* Oxford: Blackwell, 1982.

Hospers, John, and Wilfrid Sellars, eds. *Readings in Ethical Theory,* 2nd ed. Englewood Cliffs, N.J.: Prentice-Hall, 1970.

Krausz, Michael, ed. *Relativism: Interpretation and Confrontation.* Notre Dame, Ind.: University of Notre Dame Press, 1989.

Krausz, Michael, and Jack Meiland, eds. *Relativism: Cognitive and Moral.* Notre Dame, Ind.: University of Notre Dame Press, 1982.

Ladd, John, ed. *Ethical Relativism.* Belmont, Calif.: Wadsworth, 1973.

Lewis, Clarence I. *An Analysis of Knowledge and Valuation.* LaSalle, Ill.: Open Court, 1946.

———. "The Objectivity of Value Judgments." In *The Collected Papers of Clarence Irving Lewis,* edited by John Goheen and John Mothershead, 162–174. Stanford: Stanford University Press, 1970.

MacIntyre, Alasdair. "Relativism, Power, and Philosophy" *Proceedings and Addresses of the American Philosophical Association* 59 (1985): 5–22.

———. *Whose Justice? Which Rationality?* Notre Dame, Ind.: University of Notre Dame Press, 1989.

Mackie, J. L. *Ethics.* Middlesex, England: Penguin, 1978.

Miller, Richard. *Moral Differences.* Princeton: Princeton University Press, 1992.

Moser, Paul K. "A Dilemma for Normative Moral Relativism." *Southern Journal of Philosophy* 26 (1988): 207–216.

Nagel, Thomas. "Subjective and Objective." *Mortal Questions,* 196–213. Cambridge: Cambridge University Press, 1979.

———. *The View from Nowhere.* New York: Oxford University Press, 1986.

Nussbaum, Martha. "Judging Other Cultures: The Case of Female Genital Mutilation." *Sex and Social Justice,* 118–129. Oxford: Oxford University Press, 1999.

Rachels, James. "The Challenge of Cultural Relativism." *The Elements of Moral Philosophy,* 3rd ed., pp. 20–36. New York: Random House, 1999.

Scanlon, T. M. *What We Owe to Each Other.* Cambridge.: Harvard University Press, 1998.

Singer, M. "Moral Skepticism." In *Skepticism and Moral Principles,* edited by C. Carter, 77–108. Evanston, Ill.: New University Press, 1973.

Stace, Walter. *The Concept of Morals.* New York: Macmillan, 1937.

Swoyer, Chris. "True For." In *Relativism: Cognitive and Moral,* edited by Michael Krausz and Jack Meiland, 84–108. Notre Dame, Ind.: University of Notre Dame Press, 1982.

Throop, William. "Relativism and Error: Putnam's Lessons for the Relativist." *Philosophy and Phenomenological Research* 49 (1989): 675–686.

Timmons, Mark. *Morality without Foundations.* New York: Oxford University Press, 1999.

Trigg, Roger. *Reason and Commitment.* Cambridge: Cambridge University Press, 1973.

Westermarck, Edward. *Ethical Relativity.* Westport, Conn.: Greenwood, 1970.

Williams, Bernard. *Ethics and the Limits of Philosophy.* Cambridge: Harvard University Press, 1985.

Wilson, Bryan, ed. *Rationality.* Oxford: Blackwell, 1970.

Winch, Peter. *The Idea of a Social Science.* London: Routledge and Kegan Paul, 1958.

Wong, David. *Moral Relativity.* Berkeley: University of California Press, 1984.

———. "Relativism." In *A Companion to Ethics,* edited by Peter Singer, 442–450. Oxford: Blackwell, 1991.

2. RELATIVISM AND MORAL DIVERSITY

Asch, Solomon. *Social Psychology.* Englewood Cliffs, N.J.: Prentice Hall, 1952.

Benedict, Ruth. "Anthropology and the Abnormal." *The Journal of General Psychology* 10 (1934): 59–80.

————. *Patterns of Culture.* New York: Pelican Books, 1946.

Brandt, Richard. *Hopi Ethics.* Chicago: University of Chicago Press, 1954.

Cook, John. *Morality and Cultural Differences.* Oxford: Oxford University Press, 1998.

Cooper, Neil. *The Diversity of Moral Thinking.* Oxford: Oxford University Press, 1981.

Düncker, Karl. "Ethical Relativity." *Mind* 48 (1939): 39–57.

Evans-Pritchard, E. E. *Witchcraft, Oracles and Magic among the Zande.* London: Oxford University Press, 1937.

————. *Social Anthropology and Other Essays.* New York: The Free Press, 1962.

Geertz, Clifford. *The Interpretation of Cultures.* New York: Basic Books, 1973.

Ginsberg, Morris. *The Diversity of Morals.* New York: Macmillan, 1956.

Herskovits, Melville. *Man and His Works.* New York: Knopf, 1948.

Kluckhohn, Clyde. "Ethical Relativity: Sic et Non." *Journal of Philosophy* 52 (1955): 663–677.

Ladd, John. *The Structure of a Moral Code.* Cambridge: Harvard University Press, 1957.

McClintock, Thomas. "The Argument for Ethical Relativism from the Diversity of Morals." *The Monist* 47 (1963): 528–544.

Midgley, Mary. *Heart and Mind: The Varieties of Moral Experience.* New York: St. Martin's Press, 1981.

Moody-Adams, Michele. *Fieldwork in Familiar Places.* Cambridge: Harvard University Press, 1997.

Nielsen, Kai. "Anthropology and Ethics." *Journal of Value Inquiry* 5 (1971): 253–266.

————. "Ethical Relativism and the Facts of Cultural Relativity." In *Understanding Moral Philosophy,* edited by James Rachels, 14–26. Encino, Calif.: Dickenson, 1976.

Paul, Ellen, Fred Miller, and Jeffrey Paul. *Cultural Pluralism and Moral Knowledge.* Cambridge: Cambridge University Press, 1994.

Sumner, William G. *Folkways.* Boston: Ginn, 1906.

Taylor, Paul W. "Social Science and Ethical Relativism." *Journal of Philosophy* 55 (1958): 32–44.

Wellman, Carl. "The Ethical Implications of Cultural Relativity." *Journal of Philosophy* 55 (1963): 169–185.

Westermarck, Edward A. *Origin and Development of the Moral Ideas.* London: Macmillan, 1906.

Winch, Peter. "Understanding a Primitive Society." *Ethics and Action,* 8–49. London: Routledge and Kegan Paul, 1972.

Wong, David. "Three Kinds of Incommensurability." In *Relativism: Interpretation and Confrontation,* edited by M. Krausz, 140–158. Notre Dame, Ind.: University of Notre Dame Press, 1989.

[See also Westermarck, Wong 1984, and Wong 1991 in section 1 of the Bibliography.]

3. ON THE COHERENCE OF MORAL RELATIVISM

Carson, Thomas. "Relativism and Nihilism." *Philosophia* 15 (1985): 1–23.

Coburn, Robert. "Morality, Truth and Relativism." *Ethics* 92 (1982): 661–669.

Lyons, David. "Ethical Relativism and the Problem of Incoherence." *Ethics* 86 (1976): 107–121.

Olafson, Frederick. "Meta-Ethics and the Moral Life." *Philosophical Review* 65 (1956): 159–178.

Postow, B. C. "Dishonest Relativism." *Analysis* 39 (1979): 45–48.

Scanlon, T. M. "Fear of Relativism." In *Virtues and Reasons,* edited by Rosalind Hursthouse, Gavin Lawrence, and Warren Quinn, 219–245. New York: Oxford University Press, 1995.

Williams, Bernard. "Vulgar Relativism." *Morality,* 20–26. New York: Harper, 1972.

[See also Hales in section 1 of the Bibliography and Foot, Graham, and Nagel in section 4.]

4. DEFENSE AND CRITICISM

Dreier, James. "Internalism and Speaker Relativism." *Ethics* 101 (1990): 6–25.

Düncker, K. "Ethical Relativity." *Mind* 48 (1939): 39–53.

Foot, Philippa. "Moral Relativism." The Lindley Lecture, University of Kansas, 1978.

Geertz, C. "Anti Anti-Relativism." In *Relativism: Interpretation and Confrontation,* edited by M. Krausz, 12–34. Notre Dame, Ind.: University of Notre Dame Press, 1989.

Graham, Gordon. "Tolerance, Pluralism, and Relativism." In *Toleration: An Elusive Virture,* edited by David Heyd, pp. 44–59. Princeton: Princeton University Press, 1996.

Harman, Gilbert. "Moral Relativism Defended." *Philosophical Review* 84 (1975): 3–22.

——— . "Is There a Single True Morality?" In *Morality, Reason, and Truth,* edited by David Copp and David Zimmerman, 27–48. Totowa, N.J.: Rowman & Allanheld, 1984.

Thomas Nagel. "Ethics." *The Last Word,* 101–125. New York: Oxford University Press, 1997.

Norris, Christopher. *Against Relativism.* Oxford: Blackwell, 1997.

Nussbaum, Martha. "Non-Relative Virtues." In *The Quality of Life,* edited by Martha Nussbaum and Amartya Sen, 242–269. Oxford: Oxford University Press, 1993.

Postow, B. C. "Moral Relativism Avoided." *The Personalist* 39 (1979): 95–100.

Williams, Bernard. "The Truth in Relativism." *Moral Luck,* 132–143. Cambridge: Cambridge University Press, 1981.

[See also Bambrough, Brandt 1959, Harman, Harman and Thomson, Westermarck, Wong 1984, and Wong 1991 in section 1 of the Bibliography.]

5. RELATIVISM, REALISM, AND RATIONALITY

Benn, S. I., and G. W. Mortimore. *Rationality and the Social Sciences.* London: Routledge and Kegan Paul, 1976.

Blackburn, Simon. "Moral Relativism." In *Morality and Moral Reasoning,* edited by John Casey, 101–124. London: Methuen, 1971.

——— . "Rule-Following and Moral Realisms." In *Wittgenstein: To Follow a Rule,* edited by Steven Holtzman and Christopher M. Leich, 163–187. London: Routledge & Kegan Paul, 1981.

——— . *Spreading the Word.* Oxford: Oxford University Press, 1984.

——— . "Errors and the Phenomenology of Value." In *Morality and Objectivity,* edited by Ted Honderich, 1–22. London: Routledge and Kegan Paul, 1985.

——— . *Essays in Quasi-Realism.* Oxford: Oxford University Press, 1993.

Brandt, Richard. "The Definition of an 'Ideal Observer' in Ethics." *Philosophy and Phenomenological Research* 15 (1954): 407–413.

———. "Some Comments on Professor Firth's Reply." *Philosophy and Phenomenological Research* 15 (1954): 422–423.

———. *A Theory of the Good and the Right.* Oxford: Oxford University Press, 1979.

———. "The Concept of Rational Action." *Social Theory and Practice* 9 (1983): 143–165.

———. "Relativism Refuted?" *The Monist* 67 (1984): 297–307.

Brink, David O. "Moral Realism and the Sceptical Arguments from Disagreement and Queerness." *Australasian Journal of Philosophy* 62 (1984): 111–125.

———. *Moral Realism and the Foundations of Ethics.* Cambridge: Cambridge University Press, 1989.

Carson, Thomas. "Could Ideal Observers Disagree?: A Reply to Taliaferro." *Philosophy and Phenomenological Research* 50 (1989): 115–124.

———. *Value and the Good Life.* Notre Dame, Ind.: University Notre Dame Press, 2000.

Carson, Thomas, and Paul Moser. "Relativism and Normative Nonrealism: Basing Morality on Rationality." *Metaphilosophy* 27 (1996): 277–295.

Firth, Roderick. "Ethical Absolutism and the Ideal Observer." *Philosophy and Phenomenological Research* 12 (1952): 317–345.

———. "A Reply to Professor Brandt." *Philosophy and Phenomenological Research* 15 (1954): 414–421.

Frankena, William. "Concepts of Rational Action in the History of Ethics." *Social Theory and Practice* 9 (1983): 165–197.

Gauthier, David. *Morals by Agreement.* Oxford: Oxford University Press, 1986.

Gert, Bernard. "Rationality and Lists." *Ethics* 100 (1990): 279–300.

Gibbard, Alan. "A Noncognitivistic Analysis of Rationality in Action." *Social Theory and Practice* 9 (1983): 199–222.

———. *Wise Choices and Apt Feelings.* Cambridge: Harvard University Press, 1990.

Harman, Gilbert. *The Nature of Morality.* Oxford: Oxford University Press, 1977.

Hare, R. M. "Ethics and Ontology." *Essays in Ethical Theory,* 82–98. Oxford: Oxford University Press, 1989.

Horgan, Terrance and Timmons, Mark. "Troubles on Moral Twin Earth: Moral Queerness Revived." *Synthese* 92 (1992): 221–260.

———. "Troubles for New Wave Moral Semantics: 'The Open Question Argument' Revived." *Philosophical Papers* 3 (1992): 153–175.

———. "From Moral Realism to Moral Relativism in One Easy Step." *Critica* 28 (1996): 3–39.

Lovibond, Sabina. *Realism and Imagination in Ethics.* Minneapolis: University of Minnesota Press, 1983.

Moser, Paul. *Philosophy after Objectivity.* New York: Oxford University Press, 1993.

———, ed. *Rationality in Action.* Cambridge: Cambridge University Press, 1990.

Platts, Mark. *Ways of Meaning.* London: Routledge and Kegan Paul, 1979.

———. "Moral Reality and the End of Desire." *Reference, Truth, and Reality,* 69–82. London: Routledge & Kegan Paul, 1981.

———. *Moral Realities.* London: Routledge & Kegan Paul, 1991.

Putnam, Hilary. *Mind, Language, and Reality.* Vol. 2 of *Philosophical Papers.* Cambridge: Cambridge University Press, 1975.

———. *Reason, Truth, and History.* New York: Cambridge University Press, 1981.

———. *Realism with a Human Face.* Cambridge: Harvard University Press, 1990.

———. *Renewing Philosophy.* Cambridge: Harvard University Press, 1992.

Rorty, Richard. *Objectivity and Relativism.* Vol. 1 of *Philosophical Papers.* Cambridge: Cambridge University Press, 1998.

———— . *Truth and Progress.* Vol. 3 of *Philosophical Papers.* Cambridge: Cambridge University Press, 1998.

Sayre-McCord, Geoffrey, ed. *Essays on Moral Realism.* Ithaca, N.Y.: Cornell University Press, 1988.

———— . "Being a Realist about Relativism (in Ethics)." *Philosophical Studies* 88 (1991): 155–176.

Taliaferro, Charles. "Relativising the Ideal Observer Theory," *Philosophy and Phenomenological Research* 49 (1988): 123–138.

Timmons, Mark, "Putnam's Moral Objectivism." *Erkenntnis* 42 (1991): 371–399.

———— . "Irrealism and Error in Ethics," *Philosophia* 22 (1992): 373–406.

Williams, Bernard. "Internal and External Reasons." *Moral Luck,* 101–113. Cambridge: Cambridge University Press, 1981.

Wren, Thomas. *Caring about Morality.* Cambridge: MIT Press, 1991.

Wright, Crispin. *Truth and Objectivity.* Cambridge: Harvard University Press, 1992.

———— . *Realism, Meaning and Truth,* 2nd ed. Oxford: Blackwell, 1993.

[See also Arrington, Copp, and Mackie in section 1 of the Bibliography.]

Index